A Special Issue of
The Quarterly Journal of Experimental Psychology

Human Contingency Learning: Recent Trends in Research and Theory

Edited by

Tom Beckers
University of Leuven, Leuven, Belgium

Jan De Houwer
Ghent University, Ghent, Belgium

and

Helena Matute
Deusto University, Bilbao, Spain

Psychology Press
Taylor & Francis Group
HOVE AND NEW YORK

First published 2007 by Psychology Press
27 Church Road, Hove, East Sussex BN3 2FA

Simultaneously published in the USA and Canada
by Psychology Press
711 Third Avenue, New York, NY 10017

First issued in paperback 2015

*Psychology Press is an imprint of the Taylor & Francis Group,
an informa business*

British Library Cataloguing in Publication Data
A catalogue record for this book is available from the British Library

ISBN 13: 978-1-138-87771-9 (pbk)
ISBN 13: 978-1-84169-824-3 (hbk)
ISSN: 1747–0218

Cover design by Anú Design, Tara, Co. Meath, Ireland.
Typeset in the UK by Techset Composition Ltd, Salisbury, Wiltshire.

CONTENTS*

---

*This book is also a special issue of the *Quarterly Journal of Experimental Psychology*, and forms issue 3 of Volume 60 (2007). The page numbers are taken from the journal and so begin with p. 289.

THE QUARTERLY JOURNAL OF EXPERIMENTAL PSYCHOLOGY
2007, 60 (3), 289–290

Editorial: Human contingency learning

Tom Beckers
University of Leuven, Leuven, Belgium

Jan De Houwer
Ghent University, Ghent, Belgium

Helena Matute
Deusto University, Bilbao, Spain

The present special issue presents an overview of recent developments and controversies in research on human contingency learning. The aim of this research is to understand the way in which humans learn about causal and noncausal relations between events. It seems quite appropriate that an issue on human contingency learning is the first special issue to feature in the newly remerged *Quarterly Journal of Experimental Psychology*. In few areas of research has the interplay between human and animal experimental research been so intense and fruitful, with findings and theories mutually influencing each other. Whereas initially, research on human contingency learning was greatly stimulated by the suggestion that models derived from animal conditioning research could be applied to human contingency learning (e.g., Dickinson, Shanks, & Evenden, 1984; Shanks, 1985), in subsequent decades findings and theoretical developments in human learning research have also begun to stimulate developments in animal conditioning (e.g., Beckers, Miller, De Houwer, & Urushihara, 2006; Miller & Matute, 1996). As such, research on human contingency learning spans both former sections of the *Quarterly Journal of Experimental Psychology*. Indeed, many papers on contingency learning that have over the years appeared in either section could just as well have been published in the other section. The reunited journal will undoubtedly represent an enduring forum for the exchange of ideas and cross-fertilization between animal and human learning research.

We are very pleased that David Shanks has kindly agreed to provide an introductory address for the special issue (Shanks, 2007). It was his seminal work with Anthony Dickinson (e.g., Dickinson et al., 1984; Shanks, 1985, 1986, 1987) that has provided much of the impetus for the renewed interest in human contingency learning since the 1980s, and his sustained and important input to the field has been part of what has kept the field thriving ever since. His address not only identifies a number of questions that should inspire future research, but also provides a (sometimes provocative) framework for the contributions that make up this issue. These contributions range from purely fundamental, theoretical analyses (see the paper by Pineño & Miller, 2007), over empirically oriented reports (see Booth & Buehner, 2007; Cobos, López, & Luque, 2007; De Houwer, Vandorpe, & Beckers, 2007; Hagmayer & Waldmann, 2007; Karazinov & Boakes, 2007; Mitchell, Livesey, & Lovibond,

Correspondence should be addressed to Tom Beckers, Department of Psychology, University of Leuven, Tiensestraat 102, 3000 Leuven, Belgium. E-mail: tom.beckers@psy.kuleuven.be

Tom Beckers is a postdoctoral fellow of the Research Foundation–Flanders (FWO–Vlaanderen, Belgium).

DOI:10.1080/17470210601000532

2007; Vadillo & Matute, 2007; and Vandorpe, De Houwer, & Beckers, 2007), to more applied contributions (see Allan, Siegel, & Hannah, 2007, and Msetfi, Murphy, & Simpson, 2007), again reflecting the breadth of contemporary research on human contingency learning. In compound, these papers attest to the richness and diversity of current research on human contingency learning and indicate key issues that will need to be addressed in future research.

This special issue originated from an expert meeting on human contingency learning that the three of us organized in May 2004 in Lignely, Belgium. We gratefully acknowledge the support of the Research Foundation–Flanders (FWO–Vlaanderen, Belgium) and the FWO Scientific Research Network on the Acquisition, Representation, and Activation of Evaluative Judgements and Emotion in the organization of this meeting and the compilation of the present special issue.

REFERENCES

Allan, L. G., Siegel, S., & Hannah, S. (2007). The sad truth about depressive realism. *Quarterly Journal of Experimental Psychology*, 60, 482–495.

Beckers, T., Miller, R. R., De Houwer, J., & Urushihara, K. (in press). Reasoning rats: Forward blocking in Pavlovian animal conditioning is sensitive to constraints of causal inference. *Journal of Experimental Psychology: General*.

Booth, S. L., & Buehner, M. J. (2007). Asymmetries in cue competition in forward and backward blocking designs: Further evidence for causal model theory. *Quarterly Journal of Experimental Psychology*, 60, 387–399.

Cobos, P. L., López, F. J., & Luque, D. (2007). Interference between cues of the same outcome depends on the causal interpretation of the events. *Quarterly Journal of Experimental Psychology*, 60, 369–386.

De Houwer, J., Vandorpe, S., & Beckers, T. (2007). Statistical contingency has a different impact on preparation judgments than on causal judgments. *Quarterly Journal of Experimental Psychology*, 60, 418–432.

Dickinson, A., Shanks, D. R., & Evenden, J. L. (1984). Judgement of act–outcome contingency: The role of

selective attribution. *Quarterly Journal of Experimental Psychology*, 36A, 29–50.

Hagmayer, Y., & Waldmann, M. R. (2007). Inferences about unobserved causes in human contingency learning. *Quarterly Journal of Experimental Psychology*, 60, 330–355.

Karazinov, D. M., & Boakes, R. A. (2007). Second order conditioning in human predictive judgements when there is little time to think. *Quarterly Journal of Experimental Psychology*, 60, 448–460.

Miller, R. R., & Matute, H. (1996). Biological significance in forward and backward blocking: Resolution of a discrepancy between animal conditioning and human causal judgment. *Journal of Experimental Psychology: General*, 125, 370–386.

Mitchell, C. J., Livesey, E., & Lovibond, P. F. (2007). A dissociation between causal judgement and the ease with which a cause is categorised with its effect. *Quarterly Journal of Experimental Psychology*, 60, 400–417.

Msetfi, R. M., Murphy, R. A., & Simpson, J. (2007). Depressive realism and the effect of inter-trial-interval on judgements of zero, positive and negative contingencies. *Quarterly Journal of Experimental Psychology*, 60, 461–481.

Pineño, O., & Miller, R. R. (2007). Comparing associative, statistical, and inferential reasoning accounts of human contingency learning. *Quarterly Journal of Experimental Psychology*, 60, 310–329.

Shanks, D. R. (1985). Continuous monitoring of human contingency judgment across trials. *Memory & Cognition*, 13, 158–167.

Shanks, D. R. (1986). Selective attribution and the judgment of causality. *Learning and Motivation*, 17, 311–334.

Shanks, D. R. (1987). Acquisition functions in contingency judgment. *Learning and Motivation*, 18, 147–166.

Shanks, D. R. (2007). Associationism and cognition: Human contingency learning at 25. *Quarterly Journal of Experimental Psychology*, 60, 291–309.

Vadillo, M. A., & Matute, H. (2007). Predictions and causal estimations are not supported by the same associative structure. *Quarterly Journal of Experimental Psychology*, 60, 433–447.

Vandorpe, S., De Houwer, J., & Beckers, T. (2007). Outcome maximality and additivity training also influence cue competition in causal learning when learning involves many cues and events. *Quarterly Journal of Experimental Psychology*, 60, 356–368.

THE QUARTERLY JOURNAL OF EXPERIMENTAL PSYCHOLOGY
2007, 60 (3), 291–309

Associationism and cognition: Human contingency learning at 25

David R. Shanks

University College London, London, UK

A major topic within human learning, the field of contingency judgement, began to emerge about 25 years ago following publication of an article on depressive realism by Alloy and Abramson (1979). Subsequently, associationism has been the dominant theoretical framework for understanding contingency learning but this has been challenged in recent years by an alternative cognitive or inferential approach. This article outlines the key conceptual differences between these approaches and summarizes some of the main methods that have been employed to distinguish between them.

In the preface to his 1952 revision of McGeoch's classic textbook *The Psychology of Human Learning*, Irion wrote that "many of the concepts now employed in the explanation and understanding of human learning have been borrowed from the field of conditioning" (McGeoch & Irion, 1952, p. x), and the book continued a tradition, going back at least to Thorndike's (1931) essays on human learning, of assuming an associationist explanatory framework. Yet only a few years later a student taught from McGeoch's book would have found the field of human learning almost unrecognizable. Between about 1960 and 1980 attention moved away from issues that had previously dominated research, such as reinforcement and the principles of conditioning, as researchers were swept along in the cognitive revolution and focused instead on topics much more closely related to stimulus meaning such as the role of organization in learning (e.g., Tulving & Donaldson, 1972). At the same time, the close relationship between human and animal learning research, which was very explicit for McGeoch and Irion in terms of both data and concepts, became much weaker during the cognitive period. When Crowder (1976) wrote his text on learning and memory about 20 years later, the range of topics that he included bore remarkably little resemblance to those of McGeoch and Irion, and no findings from animal learning were mentioned, including conditioning. It is hard to believe that the two books are on the same subject. Put differently, the classic associationist mainstay of learning—the idea that one idea can carry the mind automatically to another—was displaced by a cognitive one. In writing that

---

Correspondence should be addressed to David R. Shanks, Department of Psychology, University College London, Gower St., London WC1E 6BT, UK. E-mail: d.shanks@ucl.ac.uk

I am very grateful to the United Kingdom Economic and Social Research Council and Biotechnology and Biological Sciences Research Council for their longstanding financial support. I thank Tom Beckers, Jan De Houwer, and Helena Matute for very helpful comments on this article. It is a particular pleasure to acknowledge colleagues with whom I have collaborated over many years, especially Tony Dickinson, Francisco López, Klaus Melchers, and José Perales.

---

http://www.psypress.com/qjep

DOI:10.1080/17470210601000581

"conditioning in human subjects is produced through the operation of higher mental processes, rather than vice versa", Brewer (1974, p. 1) articulated what was, perhaps, the most extreme manifestation of this emerging cognitive imperialism.

This special issue of the *Quarterly Journal of Experimental Psychology* directs attention to some of the major changes that have taken place since around 1980 in the study of human learning, which can be characterized, no doubt oversimplistically, as (a) the rehabilitation of the associationist perspective, the resumption by researchers of animal and human learning of overlapping research agendas, and a growing concern once more with basic issues in learning such as reinforcement, in tandem (b) with a much more sophisticated challenge or set of challenges to associationism in the guise of cognitive or inferential theories of elementary human learning. The present article attempts to put developments in the past 25 or so years—particularly those emerging from research in human contingency learning—into perspective with a view to using historical context as a means of casting fresh light on some of the current major points of debate, and it also tries to clarify the key differences between associationism and cognitivism.

After embracing cognitivism, the field was ripe for an associationist reorientation in the late 1970s and early 1980s. In the animal learning world, the Rescorla–Wagner theory had come to dominate the research agenda. This theory offered a formal model that allowed researchers to explain a much broader range of phenomena than had previously been possible and that also made numerous striking predictions, which researchers were busy testing. Alternative models had emerged (Mackintosh, 1975; Pearce & Hall, 1980), which added still more impetus to the research agenda. Yet this major theoretical advance had had very little impact on students of human learning. The two fields had moved apart, were concerned with different issues, and did not publish in the same journals. Then in 1979 Alloy and Abramson published their famous article on contingency learning in depression, speculating that depressed and nondepressed individuals differ in their ability to learn contingencies between events and drawing the counterintuitive inference, which they backed up empirically, that depressives might actually be better than nondepressed people at avoiding the judgemental bias of seeing relationships between unrelated events (see the articles by Allan, Siegel, & Hannah, 2007, and Msetfi, Murphy, & Simpson, 2007-this issue). Significantly, Alloy and Abramson approached contingency learning and the effects of depression on performance from the perspective of contemporary animal learning theory[1] and speculated (p. 476) that "these striking parallels between animals and humans in contingency learning situations suggest that there may be certain fundamental processes underlying contingency learning across species. If there are such basic processes common to animals and humans, then other variables shown to affect the magnitude and duration of preasymptotic conditioning ... in animals may be predicted similarly to affect illusions of control in humans."

Although Alloy and Abramson (1979) discussed Rescorla–Wagner and learning theory at length, they did not explicitly consider the theory as a mechanism for human contingency learning. However, their intriguing speculations were sufficient to encourage Anthony Dickinson, John Evenden, and myself (Dickinson, Shanks, & Evenden, 1984) to set up an experimental task suited to contingency learning and to apply the Rescorla–Wagner theory to the results. To investigate the possibility that Alloy and Abramson had raised—that experimental variables should have similar effects—we tested what we thought at the time (wrongly, as it turned out) was a unique prediction of associative theories—namely, that selective learning effects should be observable in human contingency judgement. Specifically, we sought evidence of blocking, a phenomenon

---

[1] There had been some prior work on human contingency learning (Jenkins & Ward, 1965; Smedslund, 1963) but it was the connection with associative theory that made Alloy and Abramson's (1979) paper so significant (and hence the reference to 25 years in the title of this article).

known in animal learning research since 1968, whereby learning about a predictive relationship between Cue A and an outcome attenuates or blocks later learning about a relationship between Cue B and the outcome when A and B are paired together. Our studies found evidence of this effect and provided formal simulations of the Rescorla–Wagner and Pearce–Hall theories, which reproduced the data well.

As I have suggested, interest in human contingency learning accelerated during the 1980s in part because it fostered closer links with animal learning research,[2] and this rapprochement was of course strongly encouraged by the growth of connectionism. McClelland and Rumelhart (1981) and the contributors to Hinton and Anderson (1989), amongst many others, were beginning to show how extraordinarily complex functions could emerge from networks of simple associative computing elements. These researchers were not strongly driven by classic learning theory, however, but more by computational neurophysiology (Hebb, 1949; Rosenblatt, 1962).

Another—and in a way more interesting—reason why attention to human contingency learning increased is that it suggested that a "high-level" human cognitive capacity for predictive or causal judgement could be explained in what many took to be a rather reductionist way—namely, in terms of associative learning. This notion was challenged by Waldmann and Holyoak (1990) and a number of subsequent researchers who—taking a similar stance to Brewer (1974) with respect to conditioning—sought to provide evidence that contingency learning and, in particular, causal judgement depend on much richer cognitive processes. In part, what stimulated this countermovement was a seemingly trivial aspect of the tasks used by Alloy and Abramson (1979), Dickinson, Shanks, and Evenden (1984), and others—namely, the use of a verbal judgement as the dependent measure. Although the use of

such measures made good sense in the context of research seeking to understand how learning depended on event contingencies, very little work up to that time had measured human learning with verbal responses, and for many people verbalization is the signature of cognition. For reasons elaborated below, I profoundly disagree with the claim that associative learning, of which Pavlovian conditioning is one type, falls in the realm of unconscious or implicit processes and that verbal judgements depend on conscious, explicit processes (Lovibond & Shanks, 2002; Shanks & St. John, 1994), but for many researchers the use of verbal reports as our dependent measure was a step too far. If we had used traditional nonverbal behavioural responses such as outcome predictions (i.e., button presses to indicate which of several events is anticipated) much of the subsequent debate might never have taken place. It is important, I would argue, for research in contingency learning to continue to use verbal judgements as its primary dependent measure precisely in order to ensure that theoretical debate remains concentrated on explicit processes. If we move more towards more conventional behavioural measures then many cognitive researchers will simply claim that we are studying implicit processes and that they have no problem with interpreting such processes in associative language. The opportunity for associative and cognitive accounts to confront each other head-on will be lost.

The alternative cognitive or inferential approach to contingency learning is discussed in several of the papers in this issue, and grappling with the contrasting nature and implications of the associative and cognitive frameworks has been a major preoccupation for researchers (Shanks, Holyoak, & Medin, 1996). This same basic reason also explains why the closely related work by McClelland and Rumelhart (1985) and Gluck and Bower (1988) has been so influential. Although the area of application is slightly different

---

[2] Many of the advocates of the associative approach to human contingency learning have been well known as animal learning researchers. Their concern to generalize their animal work to humans has been supplemented, perhaps, by an understandable desire to widen their research in a climate in which funding for purely behavioural work with animals has become harder and harder to obtain.

in those studies (human concept and category learning), the issue has been similar—namely, the extent to which a seemingly high-level cognitive capacity can be explained in noncognitive terms or, conversely, the extent to which an apparently low-level capacity such as conditioning requires a high-level cognitive explanation.

Associative and cognitive theories

My main aim in this article is to try to provide a perspective on the associative/cognitive debate and to characterize as clearly as possible what the key differences are (and are not) between the alternative approaches. In order to do this, it is first necessary to show that this contrast is not the same as the well-known one between procedural and declarative knowledge. I therefore begin by contrasting procedural and declarative representations on the one hand alongside associative and cognitive representations on the other.

The essence of the procedural/declarative distinction is that some forms of representation directly include an instruction for action whereas others do not. The statement "when it's raining, take an umbrella" gives a condition (rain) and an action to take (carry an umbrella) when that condition is triggered. Procedural representations such as this have the virtue of motivating behaviour in an almost trivial way—one could readily build a robot programmed with such a piece of knowledge and wired up so that when its sensors detected rain, its robot arm would reach out to pick up the umbrella. This is automatic and not open to other external influences. In contrast, knowledge can be coded in a more flexible way but one less readily connected to behaviour: "When it's raining, an umbrella will keep you dry." Such declarative representations are facts about the world rather than instructions and can be combined with other facts to draw new inferences. Note also that declarative representations are behaviourally inert. Thinking

that "when it's raining, an umbrella will keep you dry" is just that, a *thought*. It does not translate into or cause any behaviour such as the picking up of the umbrella. "Umbrella" in this example is a symbol that stands for an umbrella, in the same way that rain on a weather map in a newspaper stands for rain and does not make you wet. Such a map can no more produce rain than the concept "umbrella" can cause one to pick up an umbrella. To do so, some further knowledge structure would have to exist to connect the symbol with something that can have behavioural potency, such as the image of reaching out one's arm. As is well known, the procedural/declarative distinction is often framed in terms of awareness (Squire, 1994). On this view, declarative knowledge can be consciously brought to mind and reported while procedural knowledge cannot. I discuss issues of awareness shortly.

Orthogonal to the procedural/declarative distinction, which focuses on the directness with which behaviour is triggered, is the distinction between associative and cognitive representations. This contrast is between knowledge representations that influence thought and behaviour via structured inference and those that deploy simple connections. The essence of cognitive representations is that they have internal semantic or propositional structure in the same way that language does. The English sentences "John chased Mary" and "Mary chased John" have the same elements but do not mean the same thing as they are internally structured in different ways. The alternative to such propositional or cognitive representations is an association that simply connects the mental images of a pair of events in such a way that activation of one image causes activation (or inhibition) of the other.[3] And, as Thorndike (1931, p. 103) noted, "a connection is no less a connection when the things connected are the subtlest relations known by man and the most elusive intellectual adjustments he can make".

---

[3] Of course, in casual language we might refer to a symbolic proposition such as "the light predicts shock" as an association, but I am explicitly avoiding such usage. In common with the Humean tradition, I am assuming that associations have the defining properties of automatically carrying the mind from one idea to another and of being semantically transparent or contentless (Fodor, 2003). Neither of these is true of propositions.

It is perhaps worth briefly reminding ourselves why associationism is the dominant framework for understanding many basic learning processes (for a much fuller treatment, see Mackintosh, 1983).[4] Consider a trivial act such as approaching a food source, which we would intuitively interpret as a goal-directed behaviour controlled in humans, and perhaps many other species, by some form of inference or thought. In fact, such behaviours are often generated very differently. Hershberger (1986) created a Lewis Carroll runway in which as chicks moved towards a food cup, it receded twice as fast as they approached it. In order to get to the food in the cup, the chicks had to move backwards. Despite many opportunities to learn a different response tendency, the chicks persistently chased the cup and failed to obtain the food. Plainly, there is a link between the sight of a food source and the energizing of approach behaviour that seems to be triggered automatically. This is precisely how a mental association is assumed to operate. Another classic example is autoshaping, the tendency of pigeons to peck at a keylight that predicts food (Brown & Jenkins, 1968). There is no instrumental reason for the pigeons to do this, as food is delivered whether they peck or not. Indeed pecking is often to their disadvantage as it means they have to run from the key to the food, and if this distance is great they miss out on food that would otherwise be available. Again, there seems to be a link between a stimulus and a response.

It is not only procedural stimulus–response (S–R) associations that can drive behaviour, however: Declarative links between stimuli (S–S) can also be formed. An elegant example comes from a study by Holland (1990), in which rats observed two tones A and B each paired with a distinct food. Tone A was then repeatedly paired with injection of the toxin lithium chloride, and finally the animals' consumption of the two foods was measured. Holland found that an aversion had developed to the food paired with Tone A and

concluded that the only explanation of this was that this tone evoked, via an S–S association, a mental image of its paired food on the trials in which it preceded illness. It is far from obvious how this behaviour could be "rationalized" by any form of inferential thinking as no causal structure in which food causes illness is implied by the events. Instead, the tone is a common cause of both the food and illness. A virus can be a common cause of runny nose and headache but we would not infer that the former causes the latter.

Although these studies all relate to animal behaviour, examples from human behaviour are also easy to find. In an evaluative conditioning procedure, for instance, initially neutral stimuli such as pictures are paired repeatedly with affectively positive or negative stimuli (Field, 2005). As a result, the neutral stimuli tend themselves to become affectively valenced, and the properties of the learning process seem to be entirely consistent with associative theory. Moreover, once again it is hard to see why a set of cognitive operations would yield such an outcome: There is nothing rational about such transfer of affect (preferences need no inferences, as Zajonc, 1980, famously said).

A final reason for taking associationism seriously in the context of human learning is that it offers a simple and elegant account of a fundamental property of behaviour—namely, generalization. Not only do we respond appropriately to objects we have encountered before, but we also generalize in intelligent ways to novel objects. Having formed an aversion to prawns, we might avoid other forms of shellfish. Associative accounts assume that generalization comes about as a by-product of shared elements between any pair of objects (Hall, 1991). When we learn an association involving Stimulus A, associative strength is distributed across the numerous elements making up A. Another object, B, will share some of those elements but possess some unique elements too, so that the degree to which B inherits A's associative strength depends on the number of

---

[4] Associative processes, of course, play a substantial role even in information-processing theories of higher cognitive functions such as memory. To describe something as a "retrieval cue" for a "memory representation", for instance, is to refer to an associative mechanism, and this is quite explicit in many theories of retrieval.

common elements. Cognitive theories, in contrast, have rarely considered in any formal way how generalization might occur.

In response to this weight of evidence for associative processes, the standard way of interpreting Pavlovian conditioning is in terms of associative stimulus substitution: The conditioned stimulus (CS) becomes associated with, and hence able to activate, a representation of the unconditioned stimulus (US) and comes to evoke a response in much the same way that the US itself does. This was Pavlov's view (Dickinson, 1980) and has been discussed frequently in the context of human learning too (Shanks, 1990).

Table 1 illustrates the four knowledge types formed by crossing the procedural/declarative and associative/cognitive contrasts in the context of a simple conditioning procedure in which a tone CS predicts a puff of air to the eye (the US). Several pairings of the tone and airpuff will be sufficient to trigger eyeblinks to the tone prior to the delivery of the airpuff. Procedural representations formed in such a scenario directly code for behaviour (blinking) and do so via either a proposition or a simple excitatory connection. Declarative representations do not include direct behavioural terms but rather express a relationship, again either propositionally or via connections.

In several studies with my colleagues, I have developed a framework for learning and memory that denies the psychological significance or reality of the procedural/declarative distinction and its relevance to the causation of human behaviour (Kinder & Shanks, 2001, 2003; Lovibond &

Shanks, 2002; Shanks, 2005b; Shanks & Lovibond, 2002). The primary reason for this strong position is that, in my view, there are no compelling examples of behaviour being procedurally triggered without accompanying declarative knowledge. It is clear from the procedural/declarative dichotomy that people should often behave without knowing the reasons for their behaviour: They should carry umbrellas when it's raining or blink in the presence of the tone *without knowing why they are doing so*. If behaviour is driven by activation of a procedural representation, whether it be a cognitive one or an association, the person should not have the means to justify his or her behaviour. To be able to say "because when it's raining, an umbrella will keep you dry" is to have access to a declarative, not a procedural, representation. Likewise, justifying one's blinking by reference to the relationship between the tone and airpuff requires access to a declarative representation. Our procedural robot, even if programmed with language, would have not any basis for translating the procedural knowledge into an explanation of it behaviour—it just acts.

Although much of the evidence against the procedural/declarative distinction comes from other domains (Perruchet & Amorim, 1992; Ryan & Cohen, 2003; Zaki, 2005), studies of simple learning point to the same conclusion: Learning is accompanied by awareness in standard human conditioning (Lovibond & Shanks, 2002; but see Smith, Clark, Manns, & Squire, 2005), in evaluative conditioning (Field, 2005; Shanks & Dickinson, 1990), and in contingency learning (Shanks & Dickinson, 1991). Of course one could assume that procedural and declarative representations are always created in parallel. Indeed this is the essence of classic two-process theories of learning (Rescorla & Solomon, 1967), which assume that a conditioning procedure links the tone CS simultaneously with the airpuff and the eyeblink. Such theories did not fare particularly well in learning theory during the 1980s and, moreover, lack the parsimony that comes from only allowing a singular form of representation.

How, though, does one generate behaviour? I argue that behaviour emerges not from

Table 1. *Types of representation inferred from pairings of a tone with a puff of air to the eye*

	Cognitive	Associative
Procedural	"when the tone is detected, blink"	tone → blink
Declarative	"the tone predicts an airpuff"	tone → airpuff

Note: Pairings reliably cause a preparatory eyeblink before delivery of the airpuff. Terms in quotes refer to propositions; terms connected by an arrow (→) are constituents of an excitatory link.

representations that connect an antecedent condition with a response but rather from mental representations that are themselves acts or behaviours. On this view, the representation of an airpuff is not distinct from the behaviour of blinking one's eye, but instead these two things are inextricably bound together into a single mental representation. Part of what it is to think about an airpuff is to think about blinking. I believe that the literature on priming leads inevitably towards the view that concepts and behaviour are intrinsically linked and doubt that many representations are purely symbolic (declarative) or purely behavioural (procedural).

An experiment by Bargh, Chen, and Burrows (1996) illustrates this vividly. In that study, participants were asked to unscramble sets of words into meaningful sentences. For some participants, the sentences included many words associated with old age whereas for others the words did not have such associations. Bargh et al. then measured the speed with which the participants walked down the corridor to leave the building and found that age-primed participants took longer. One does not have a concept of age, such results imply, that floats free from behaviour. Instead, behaviour is part of the concept itself, and thinking about old age makes us behave as if we're old. Barsalou has written extensively about this "situated" view of concepts (e.g., Barsalou, Simmons, Barbey, & Wilson, 2003) and has shown, for example, that looking at pictures of appetizing foods activates parts of the brain involved in gustation. Based on research on perception and action planning, Hommel and his colleagues (e.g., Hommel, Müsseler, Aschersleben, & Prinz, 2001) have likewise proposed integrated representations for events and behaviour.

Hence the major distinction of relevance to human learning and behaviour is between cognitive and associative representations. In the context of causal reasoning and contingency judgement, this translates into the idea that behaviour is sometimes based on rational, cognitive, symbolic thought and sometimes is driven associatively. As Gallistel and Gibbon (2001) have noted, the strength of an association depends on many

factors such as contiguity, contingency, number of pairings, and so on and hence "does not represent any objective fact about the world, and the associative bond does not participate in information processing (computational) operations. Associations, unlike symbols, are not added, subtracted, multiplied, and divided in order to generate new associations" (p. 146). In contrast, cognitive accounts assume that the brain calculates such things as the intervals and contingencies between events and "records the results in memory for later use in the computations that mediate decisions" (p. 147) on whether or not to behave in a particular way.

Casting the key distinction as that between associative and *statistical* models (e.g., Pineño & Miller, 2007) does not, in my view, correctly capture the fundamental contrast. Statistical models refer to simple algebraic rules for combining the frequencies or probabilities of different event types (e.g., the probability of an effect given a cue), the well-known ΔP rule being an example. But even an associative model such as the Rescorla–Wagner theory is rule based and statistical in the sense of giving an algebraic rule for deriving judgements (the model in fact generates associative strengths that at asymptote and under certain assumptions are equivalent to ΔP: Danks, 2003). Rather, what distinguishes associative and statistical models is that in the latter the terms refer to conceptually analysed entities such as cause and effect (Cheng, 1997) whereas in the former they refer to "raw" unanalysed events. This emphasizes that the central feature of statistical models is that they assume the involvement of cognitive processes in transforming a perceptual event stream into a series of concepts, not that they embody a statistical rule.

It is important to realise that when arguing for a contribution of associative processes, supporters of this approach have never denied that rational causal thinking takes place. Of course, this would be absurd, and students of learning have been grappling with the relationship between association and "higher" mental processes for almost a century, at least since Tilton (1926). Much of science is concerned precisely with developing the tools to allow rational thinking. Rather, the question is whether all causal thought is of this form, or whether instead there might be a separate type of thinking (associative) when people make intuitive judgements under conditions of less reflection.[5] This is the question that has been at the heart of work on causal learning for the past 20 or so years.[6] Thus the contrast is essentially the same as that drawn by Kahneman (2003) between rational and intuitive thought. Just as Kahneman studied intuitive judgement and choice and never denied that there exists a separate realm of rational thought, so the focus of work on human contingency learning has been on intuitive covariation or causal judgements.

Particularly compelling will be evidence that when people reflect on their own intuitive judgements, they acknowledge them to be misguided. Indeed, in the absence of any better alternatives, this might serve as our definition of what the term means. If a participant agrees, on reflection, that a judgement was nonnormative or irrational, we can regard it as driven by intuition.

Research illustrates the deliberative/intuitive contrast directly in contingency judgement and associative learning (e.g., Winman, Wennerholm, Juslin, & Shanks, 2005). For example, Shanks and Darby (1998) have suggested that humans may be able to respond to a stimulus in a discrimination experiment not only on the basis of associative knowledge, mediated by surface similarity, but also on the basis of rule-based knowledge, mediated by deeper and more abstract properties. The key idea is that humans may, in appropriate circumstances, induce rules that describe the deep structure of a stimulus domain. In one experiment, participants received intermixed AB +, A−, and B− trials together with CD−, C +, and D + trials in the training stage where A−D are cues, + is the outcome, and − is no outcome. According to associative theories, these trial types should have led to the formation of a set of associations, with the AB, C, and D representations being associated with the outcome, and the A, B, and CD representations being associated with no outcome. However, another possibility is that participants may have learned a patterning rule of the form *A compound and its elements predict opposite outcomes*. One important difference between these accounts concerns the generalizations that they support, and these can be contrasted by considering the results of a test phase. In addition to the above trial types, participants also saw E +, F +, and GH− trials during the training phase and were then tested on the novel stimuli EF, G, and H. According to associative theories, E and F will be associated with the outcome, and the EF compound will therefore elicit a degree of generalized associative strength from E and F. At the same time, G and H should elicit very low levels of responses. In contrast, if participants have learned the patterning rule, then they should predict the outcome on G and H trials but not on EF trials. Of course, we assumed that mastery of the outcomes of the various training trials is necessary before the patterning rule can be induced.

Consistent with the idea that these two processes are distinct, Shanks and Darby (1998) found that participants whose accuracy in the training stage was fairly low showed the pattern of test responses predicted by associative learning theories whereas participants performing more accurately in the training stage responded in the way predicted by rule induction theories. It seems that humans are capable of learning about

---

[5] This dual-process view of the mind has gained many influential followers in recent years (e.g., Kahneman, 2003). The evidence for two systems is indeed very persuasive (Osman, 2004; Shanks & St. John, 1994). Where the evidence is, in my view, much weaker is in the claim that one of these systems is procedural, implicit, or unconscious.

[6] There may appear to be a contradiction here. Earlier I argued that the use of verbal measures is important to ensure that we remain within the realm of explicit processes, whereas I am now arguing that we should focus on intuitive judgement as associative theory will not be able to challenge cognitive approaches in the domain of "rational" or "reflective" judgements. But intuitive judgements are invariably explicit rather than implicit (Tunney & Shanks, 2003). Intuitive judgements may be made without inference but they are still conscious and can usually be justified.

the deep structure of stimulus domains in ways that go beyond the scope of associative learning models. Thus the question is not about whether there are circumstances in which cognitive processes become involved in contingency learning, but about the extent to which associative processes do. Even supporters of inferential theories acknowledge an essential role for associations. As Mitchell, Livesey, and Lovibond (2007) point out, "the alternative inferential view allows that associations, in some sense of the term, will form between mental representations such that the one can bring to mind the other. However, according to this view, although contiguous pairings of a cue and an outcome will allow the observer to recall that the cue 'went with' the outcome, the causal attribution (that the cue causes the outcome) requires a further inferential step."

Adequacy of empirical tests

How should we proceed if our goal is to distinguish between cognitive and associative theories? This is the crux of the problem. It is perhaps easier to say something about ways that will not be adequate. For example, showing that causal or contingency judgements tend to conform to the predictions of an associative theory such as the Rescorla–Wagner model cannot possibly suffice as one could always generate a cognitive theory in which the weight or confidence with which a causal proposition such as "the tone causes the airpuff" is held is determined by the very same rules. These theories are mathematical formalisms mapping objective properties of a sequence of events onto some measure of response strength: For every interpretation of such a theory in terms of association formation, there is a behaviourally equivalent one in which responses are generated by an inferential process with beliefs carrying varying strengths. Rescorla and Wagner themselves were silent on the issue of the representational structures that they thought underlie conditioning—their model is equally applicable to excitatory links as it is to structured representations. To exemplify this, Shanks and Pearson (1987) described an

implementation of the Rescorla–Wagner model in the propositional language PROLOG. What can be ruled out, of course, by demonstrations of the conformity of causal judgements to the Rescorla–Wagner model are alternative models (whether couched in associative or cognitive terms), which employ different mathematical rules. For instance, Perales and Shanks (2003) compared the asymptotic predictions of a variety of associative and other models and were able to reject many of them on the grounds of deviation from observed behaviour.

Also inadequate will be studies that are more likely to probe reasoned than intuitive judgements. In studies that employ only one or two cues it seems very likely that cognitive processes will intrude. Lovibond's (2003) evidence that verbal instructions are sometimes interchangeable with actual learning trials suggests exactly this point.

Top-down influences

So how can associative and cognitive theories be contrasted? The key point is that associative theories are severely limited because of the automaticity of transfer of activation of excitation from one representation to another and because of the transparency of the link between representations. Thus associative theories predict that the activation of one idea or representation by another should be impervious to knowledge and beliefs (i.e., cognitively impenetrable). A much-tested instantiation of this logic (see the articles in this issue by Booth & Buehner, 2007; Cobos, López, & Luque, 2007) is the prediction that it should make no difference in a learning context whether the antecedent event is described as the cause and the subsequent event as the effect or vice versa. In both cases, the law of contiguity implies that a unidirectional association will be formed, which will carry the mind from the antecedent to the subsequent event. To elaborate, consider a situation in which two cues (A and B) signal another event (Z). If no causal interpretation of the events is provided, or if A and B are described as causes and Z as an effect, then the expected outcome on both types of theory will be that judgements of the predictive or causal role of A will be overshadowed by the presence of B and hence reduced from the level that would be observed if B was not paired with A. This prediction has been confirmed in causal judgement situations by López, Cobos, and Caño (2005), Waldmann (2001), and Cobos et al. (2002), amongst others.

Now consider what would happen if participants are informed in the instructions that, in fact, Z is the cause, and A and B are effects of Z. In López et al.'s study, Z was a switch on a box, and A and B were lights. However, the temporal structure was such that participants first learned about A and B and then had to infer (or diagnose) from this the state of Z. Now associative and cognitive theories make divergent predictions. If participants are reasoning intuitively, then associative theory predicts that overshadowing will continue to occur as directional associations are formed competitively between A and B and Z. This overshadowing will then be evident when participants are asked to judge the extent to which A and B predict or diagnose Z. No such overshadowing will be anticipated by cognitive theories as they will incorporate the important causal constraint that multiple independent causes of a single effect are possible but not multiple independent effects of a single cause. One can have a runny nose because of a virus or because of an allergy, and these latter events need not be correlated; hence evidence that the virus is correlated with the runny nose should lead one to discount the allergy as a cause, and vice versa. But if a virus causes both a runny nose and a temperature, then these two events must be correlated, and evidence that the virus causes the runny nose should not affect one's belief about whether or not it also causes the temperature.

I expect that supporters of both the associative and cognitive approaches will now agree that there are compelling demonstrations of symmetry between different described causal orders (Arcediano, Matute, Escobar, & Miller, 2005; Cobos et al., 2002; López et al., 2005; Tangen, Allan, & Sadeghi, 2005). Hence there are situations in which people make causal judgements in line with associative theory, unaffected by an important cognitive constraint on the nature of

causation. Of course, there are also situations in which asymmetry is observed (e.g., Cobos et al., 2007). López et al. (2005) provide a particularly compelling illustration of how symmetry can be turned into asymmetry by the mere addition of a single sentence in the task instructions emphasizing the causal structure of the task. From a theoretical point of view, what such results suggest is that people can reason normatively, but that there is also a mechanism for making causal judgements that is nonnormative and that operates in the way anticipated by associative theory. To focus (as many researchers do, including Booth & Buehner, 2007) on the fact that there is a pattern of judgements (asymmetry) that is inconsistent with associative theory is to miss the point: To repeat, it is not a matter of debate that people can reason normatively or logically under certain circumstances. As is frequently done in the judgement and decision-making field, it is instructive to ask how people would evaluate their own behaviour if allowed to reflect on it. I think there is little doubt that participants who showed symmetry in López et al.'s experiment would, given time to consider, realize that their judgements were normatively inappropriate. This is a key feature of intuitive judgements.

Analysis of blocking

Inferential accounts (see Beckers, De Houwer, Pineño, & Miller, 2005; De Houwer, Vandorpe, & Beckers, 2005b; Lovibond, Been, Mitchell, Bouton, & Frohardt, 2003; Mitchell & Lovibond, 2002) assuming effortful controlled reasoning have received considerable support in recent years from a range of further findings, including the influences of additivity pretraining and maximality information on cue competition effects such as blocking (Vandorpe, De Houwer, & Beckers, 2007). These accounts argue that the explanation for why a blocked cue (i.e., Cue B after A+, AB+ training) receives low ratings of contingency is that participants engage in reasoning about the roles of the cues. For example, they might reason that if B were an independent predictor of the outcome, then the scale or magnitude of the outcome should be greater after AB than after A alone, but since this is not the case, B cannot be a predictor. If such reasoning does indeed contribute to blocking, then it is clear that it should depend on what the participants believe about the magnitude of the outcome. If they believe the outcome to be occurring at its maximal level, then blocking should be weak because participants would know that even if B were a predictor, it could not increase the magnitude of the outcome. On the other hand blocking should be particularly strong if participants believe that the outcome is not at its maximal level.

Additivity pretraining refers to presenting participants, prior to the main blocking treatment, with a problem that encourages them to believe that the outcome (+) is not maximal. For example, this pretraining might comprise X+, Y+, and YZ++ trials, which provide information about the possibility of an outcome of greater magnitude (++) such as a strong allergic reaction versus a weak one. Consistent with the prediction of inferential accounts, additivity pretraining does indeed enhance blocking (Beckers et al., 2005; Lovibond et al., 2003). Maximality information provides a simpler test of inferential accounts by explicitly indicating during a blocking procedure whether the outcome is at a maximal or submaximal level. For instance, De Houwer, Beckers, and Glautier (2002) found that blocking was much greater when the outcome was described as occurring at a submaximal level ("10/20") than when it was described as maximal.

Because blocking has been a touchstone of associative theory for several decades, these findings are particularly striking as they suggest a completely different explanation. Whereas blocking is normally thought of as arising from a process of reinforcement driven by prediction error, the studies of additivity and maximality point to a very different, and cognitive, process in which participants try to figure out an underlying rational explanation of predictive roles. There have been some attempts (e.g., Livesey & Boakes, 2004) to reconcile additivity pretraining effects with associative theory by considering the balance induced by the pretraining between elemental and configural

processing. It is well known, and entirely consistent with associative theory (Brandon, Vogel, & Wagner, 2000; Pearce, 1994), that stimuli can sometimes be treated as composed of independent elements and sometimes as configural "wholes". Indeed, it is even well established that people can be induced to code the same stimulus either elementally or configurally (Shanks, 2005a; Williams, Sagness, & McPhee, 1994). Thus the possibility arises that additivity pretraining has its effect via switching the balance between elemental and configural training. Specifically, if it tended to induce a more elemental approach (which, of course, would be expected after X+, Y+, and YZ++ trials) then an enhancement of blocking would be expected as blocking requires treating the two cues as separate elements. Indeed, Livesey and Boakes (2004) showed that additivity instructions are rendered inadequate to generate blocking if the cues are presented in a way that strongly encourages configural processing. The fact, however, that additivity training can enhance blocking even when it is given *after* the blocking trials (Beckers et al., 2005) is a particularly powerful piece of evidence for the inferential account as it would seem to rule out an explanation solely in terms of elemental/configural processing, although there may be some contribution from this shift.

On the other hand, experiments almost invariably obtain reliable blocking even when participants are given no reason to believe that the outcome in the blocking trials is submaximal. This is problematic for the inferential approach. Suppose a participant is asked to rate Cue B after A+, AB+ training and believes the outcome to be maximal. Although he or she may reason that there is insufficient evidence on which to base a judgement, the same applies to the control case (e.g., CD+) in which neither element is pretrained. Hence the observation of blocking under such circumstances is unexpected on the cognitive approach. Blocking is also observed when the learning task is combined with a secondary task designed to engage working memory (De Houwer & Beckers, 2003). A hallmark of inferential processes is that they are disrupted by load on working memory. Hence both of these findings fit more comfortably with associative accounts, as does the finding that recall of the relationship between Cue B and the outcome after A+, AB+ training is much weaker than that in the control group (Mitchell, Lovibond, Minard, & Lavis, in press). Exactly as anticipated on the associative analysis of blocking, a competing cue seems to impair the formation of a memory unit featuring the blocked cue. Le Pelley, Oakeshott, and McLaren (2005) have recently demonstrated an unblocking effect in intuitive causal ratings, which was abolished when it was made easier for participants to engage in controlled reasoning. As noted earlier, it is particularly compelling that a judgement is based on some noncognitive process if participants, under less stressful conditions, behave differently. Finally, Karazinov and Boakes' (2007) demonstration of second-order conditioning in a cue competition design is hard to reconcile with the reasoning approach.

Different types of judgement
Another general way in which associative and cognitive approaches may be contrasted is by comparing different types of judgement elicited after identical learning experiences. Once again, associative models are very tightly constrained as they assume that knowledge of a cue–outcome relationship is coded simply by an associative bond, and this bond should therefore function similarly regardless of the precise semantics of the test question. Many examples have now been reported of different patterns of judgements under, for example, causal versus predictive questions, and this provides evidence for the cognitive approach, which can utilize a much richer set of representations. For instance, causal judgements might be based on contingency while predictive judgements are based on the conditional probability of the effect. Vadillo and Matute (2007) present convincing evidence for this hypothesis. However, they also offer an ingenious argument about how an influence of test question might be partially accommodated by associative theories. The basic idea is that causal estimates are a function of the associative weight of the cue

alone whereas predictive judgements or probability estimates depend on the combined weight of the cue and the context. Such an account would seem to be applicable also to the dissociation between causal and "preparation" judgements described by De Houwer, Vandorpe, and Beckers (2007).

We ourselves (Collins & Shanks, 2006) have found different patterns of judgements made in response to causal ("to what extent does A cause B") and counterfactual ("in a situation in which B would not occur if A was absent, how likely would B be if A were introduced?") questions. In general, these influences of test question on qualitative patterns of judgement are not easily reconciled with associative theories. Some current work points to the possibility that contingency judgements might be decomposable into distinct parts, some of which are generated according to associative principles and some of which are not (Allan, Siegel, & Tangen, 2005; Perales, Catena, Shanks, & González, 2005).

Retrospective revaluation
Associative theories have been challenged by a range of other phenomena, some of which are genuinely problematic for the entire approach. Others, in contrast, call for revisions to the theories themselves. Retrospective revaluation is a good example of the latter. Theories such as Rescorla–Wagner propose that the outcome of a learning episode is highly dependent upon the order in which events are presented. Whereas blocking of a target cue, B, is expected when it is paired with a treatment cue, A, that has previously been paired with the outcome (Stage 1: A+; Stage 2: AB+), this is not expected when the two stages are reversed. The reason is that in classical learning theories a cue can only undergo a change in its associative strength on trials in which it is present. In the reversed design (Stage 1: AB+; Stage 2: A+), B acquires associative strength during Stage 1 and retains it during Stage 2. Thus the motivation for the earliest experiments on backward blocking (Shanks, 1985) was the expectation that it would not occur, that forward and backward blocking would be of different magnitude, and that such a

result would strongly support the associative approach.

Although the surprising occurrence of backward blocking and other examples of retrospective revaluation (De Houwer & Beckers, 2002; Larkin, Aitken, & Dickinson, 1998; Melchers, Lachnit, & Shanks, 2004; Williams, 1996) certainly adds weight to alternative cognitive approaches (and these effects occur in situations in which participants learn many concurrent contingencies and therefore unquestionably probe intuitive rather than reasoned judgements), another way to react to such findings is to ask whether they can be observed in animal learning and, if so, whether a better response might not be to revise the associative theories. Research has now documented fairly convincingly the occurrence of retrospective revaluation in animal conditioning (Balleine, Espinet, & González, 2005; Denniston, Savastano, Blaisdell, & Miller, 2003; Shevill & Hall, 2004), and this has been followed by modifications of associative theories, some of them fairly straightforward (Dickinson & Burke, 1996; Ghirlanda, 2005), which allow them to generate retrospective changes in response strength.

There are other features of retrospective revaluation whose reconciliation with associative theory seems more challenging. For instance, some studies (De Houwer & Beckers, 2002; Melchers et al., 2004) have found higher order retrospective revaluation in which revaluation occurs across a chain of event pairings. In those experiments, Cue A was, for example, presented in compound with another cue, B, and Cue B was separately presented in compound with Cue C. Both of these compounds were reinforced (AB+, BC+). Cue C was then presented alone and was either reinforced in one condition or nonreinforced in another condition. Second order retrospective revaluation of Cue A was found with larger responses for A in the group where C was reinforced and smaller responses when C was nonreinforced. This implies a chain of inference along the lines of "if C is individually a cause, then B must not be a cause; if B is not a cause, then A must be". Although this seems hard to reconcile with associative learning, Melchers et al. (2004)

have speculated (and presented some evidence) that the effect may come about through normal associative processes supplemented by rehearsal, during the final stage of C+ or C− trials, of the earlier trial types. Such rehearsed trials might act vicariously like actual training trials in which case the higher order effects would be anticipated by associative theories.

Inferential accounts assume that forward and backward blocking result from essentially identical chains of reasoning and hence predict that they should generally be very similar. Although this often appears to be the case, there is nevertheless some evidence that they differ in information-processing terms. For instance, Melchers et al. (2004; in press) found that knowledge of within-compound associations formed between the elements of a compound correlated with backward but not forward blocking.

Finally, there are other issues such as inferring the nature of unobserved causes, which bear some resemblance to inferences in retrospective revaluation, where associative accounts have been strongly challenged (e.g., Hagmayer & Waldmann, 2007).

Neuroscientific evidence

In this fast-developing cognitive neuroscience age, another general approach to comparing cognitive and associative accounts is via brain imaging data. Put very simplistically, if the brain networks engaged in a contingency learning task overlap more closely with those associated with conditioning tasks than with those activated in other cognitive or inferential tasks (or vice versa), that could of course form the basis for a neurally based argument about underlying psychological processes. Interpreting brain activation patterns is, as we all know, wrought with difficulty, and as yet very little research has studied contingency judgements. However, some of our research (Corlett et al., 2004; Fletcher et al., 2001; Turner et al., 2004) has shown that a brain network associated with reward and error (Schultz & Dickinson, 2000) is consistently activated in human contingency learning in a way that is highly consistent with the form of error-correcting learning proposed in the Rescorla–Wagner model and other associative theories. Clearly, however, research taking this approach is in its infancy, and much more needs to be done. It will be of considerable interest, for instance, to determine whether common brain networks are activated in rule-based inference tasks (such as the Wisconsin card-sorting task) and in contingency judgement tasks employing additivity instructions.

CONCLUSIONS

I have argued that associative links between stimuli play a significant role in human learning and judgement. Such links should not be considered as either procedural (S–R) or declarative (S–S) but as inextricably combining both kinds of representation. This explains how it is that verbal and associative knowledge can interact with one another: verbally and associatively activated concepts are simply the same thing. A more interesting distinction is between associative and cognitive theories where the former invoke the transmission of activation or inhibition between representations, and the latter assume some calculus for combining and manipulating semantically interpretable symbols to yield rational inferences.

After a considerable body of research pointed to the involvement of associative mechanisms in human contingency learning, attention has shifted recently to a range of cognitive or inferential processes. These inferential accounts are supported by a number of phenomena such as the influence of outcome additivity training and maximality information on cue competition. However, these theories need, and will doubtless receive, much more development in coming years. At present, they tend only to make predictions for deterministic relationships such as those employed in typical blocking designs. The approaches of De Houwer, Lovibond, and their colleagues have little to say about what is perhaps the key question in contingency judgement research—namely, the function that determines the strength of a contingency belief as a function of variations in the probability of the outcome given the cue, $P(O|C)$, and the probability of the outcome in the absence of the cue, $P(O|-C)$. Put differently, current cognitive/inferential theories are theories of performance rather than theories of learning. Associative theories have a great deal to say about learning processes but face many difficulties in dealing with performance phenomena. Similarly, inferential theories can provide an explanation of the strength of contingency or causal judgements but fare less well with other behavioural outcomes such as evaluative ratings. It is hard to see how transfer of affect in an evaluative conditioning procedure, for instance, can be explained by an inference process.

There is no doubt that cognitive approaches can explain many of the phenomena of contingency judgement and that discriminating between the different classes of theory often calls for very subtle experimental tests. Indeed, De Houwer, Beckers, and Vandorpe (2005a), in an excellent review of the strength of reasoning accounts, stated that they did "not know of any evidence that uniquely supports the hypothesis that cue competition in human learning can be due to competitive associative learning" (p. 246). In response to this challenge I would offer the following as the most compelling illustration that I am aware of. Recall that the essence of associative approaches is that they assume that presentation of a cue automatically calls to mind the outcome with which it was associated such that the cue in some sense stands for or takes on properties of or at the very least evokes an image of the outcome. Now consider a situation in which cue competition occurs, for example between a pair of conditions in which the probability of the outcome given the cue, $P(O|C)$, is identical but the probability of the outcome in the absence of the cue, $P(O|-C)$, differs. For example, in one condition $P(O|C) = .75$ and $P(O|-C) = 0$ and in the other $P(O|C) = .75$ and $P(O|-C) = .75$. We know that judgements of contingency will differ between these conditions, manifesting cue competition (between the cue and the context in this case). But we also know that judgements of the probability of the outcome given the cue will differ between these conditions, despite being identical (e.g., De Houwer et al., 2007; Lagnado

& Shanks, 2002; López, Cobos, Caño, & Shanks, 1998; Price & Yates, 1993). Associative theories have been used to explain (and indeed to predict) this effect by proposing that the associative weight, which differs between the two conditions, is part of the evidence that we use to make our probability judgement. Even though the probabilities are the same in the two conditions, the cue much more strongly makes us think of the outcome in the contingent than in the noncontingent condition, and this mental activation unavoidably biases our probability judgement. Although this effect focuses on probability rather than contingency judgements, no other explanation apart from the associative one has to date been offered, and it provides, I suggest, direct evidence of an associatively mediated influence on judgement. (Of course, this is an intuitive judgement as participants would certainly, on reflection, acknowledge their error.)

Both associative and cognitive theories have achieved considerable success in explaining aspects of human contingency learning but equally face many problems. Addressing these problems will be a prominent feature in the next 25 years of research on contingency learning.

REFERENCES

Allan, L. G., Siegel, S., & Hannah, S. (2007). The sad truth about depressive realism. *Quarterly Journal of Experimental Psychology, 60*, 482–495.

Allan, L. G., Siegel, S., & Tangen, J. M. (2005). A signal detection analysis of contingency data. *Learning & Behavior, 33*, 250–263.

Alloy, L. B., & Abramson, L. Y. (1979). Judgment of contingency in depressed and nondepressed students: Sadder but wiser? *Journal of Experimental Psychology: General, 108*, 441–485.

Arcediano, F., Matute, H., Escobar, M., & Miller, R. R. (2005). Competition between antecedent and between subsequent stimuli in causal judgments. *Journal of Experimental Psychology: Learning, Memory, and Cognition, 31*, 228–237.

Balleine, B. W., Espinet, A., & González, F. (2005). Perceptual learning enhances retrospective revaluation of conditioned flavor preferences in rats. *Journal of Experimental Psychology: Animal Behavior Processes, 31*, 341–350.

Bargh, J. A., Chen, M., & Burrows, L. (1996). Automaticity of social behavior: Direct effects of trait construct and stereotype activation on action. *Journal of Personality and Social Psychology, 71*, 230–244.

Barsalou, L. W., Simmons, W. K., Barbey, A. K., & Wilson, C. D. (2003). Grounding conceptual knowledge in modality-specific systems. *Trends in Cognitive Sciences, 7*, 84–91.

Beckers, T., De Houwer, J., Pineño, O., & Miller, R. R. (2005). Outcome additivity and outcome maximality influence cue competition in human causal learning. *Journal of Experimental Psychology: Learning, Memory, and Cognition, 31*, 238–249.

Booth, S. L., & Buehner, M. J. (2007). Asymmetries in cue competition in forward and backward blocking designs: Further evidence for causal model theory. *Quarterly Journal of Experimental Psychology, 60*, 387–399.

Brandon, S. E., Vogel, E. H., & Wagner, A. R. (2000). A componential view of configural cues in generalization and discrimination in Pavlovian conditioning. *Behavioural Brain Research, 110*, 67–72.

Brewer, W. F. (1974). There is no convincing evidence for operant or classical conditioning in adult humans. In W. B. Weimer & D. S. Palermo (Eds.), *Cognition and the symbolic processes* (pp. 1–42). Hillsdale, NJ: Lawrence Erlbaum Associates, Inc.

Brown, P. L., & Jenkins, H. M. (1968). Auto-shaping of the pigeon's key peck. *Journal of the Experimental Analysis of Behavior, 11*, 1–8.

Cheng, P. W. (1997). From covariation to causation: A causal power theory. *Psychological Review, 104*, 367–405.

Cobos, P. L., López, F. J., Caño, A., Almaraz, J., & Shanks, D. R. (2002). Mechanisms of predictive and diagnostic causal induction. *Journal of Experimental Psychology: Animal Behavior Processes, 28*, 331–346.

Cobos, P. L., López, F. J., & Luque, J. L. (2007). Interference between cues of the same outcome depends on the causal interpretation of the events. *Quarterly Journal of Experimental Psychology, 60*, 369–386.

Collins, D. J., & Shanks, D. R. (2006). Conformity to the power PC theory of causal induction depends on the type of probe question. *Quarterly Journal of Experimental Psychology, 59*, 225–232.

Corlett, P. R., Aitken, M. R. F., Dickinson, A., Shanks, D. R., Honey, G. D., Honey, R. A. E., et al. (2004).

Prediction error during retrospective revaluation of causal associations in humans: fMRI evidence in favor of an associative model of learning. *Neuron*, *44*, 877–888.

Crowder, R. G. (1976). *Principles of learning and memory*. Hillsdale, NJ: Lawrence Erlbaum Associates, Inc.

Danks, D. (2003). Equilibria of the Rescorla–Wagner model. *Journal of Mathematical Psychology*, *47*, 109–121.

De Houwer, J., & Beckers, T. (2002). Higher-order retrospective revaluation in human causal learning. *Quarterly Journal of Experimental Psychology*, *55B*, 137–151.

De Houwer, J., & Beckers, T. (2003). Secondary task difficulty modulates forward blocking in human contingency learning. *Quarterly Journal of Experimental Psychology*, *56B*, 345–357.

De Houwer, J., Beckers, T., & Glautier, S. (2002). Outcome and cue properties modulate blocking. *Quarterly Journal of Experimental Psychology*, *55A*, 965–985.

De Houwer, J., Beckers, T., & Vandorpe, S. (2005a). Evidence for the role of higher order reasoning processes in cue competition and other learning phenomena. *Learning & Behavior*, *33*, 239–249.

De Houwer, J., Vandorpe, S., & Beckers, T. (2005b). On the role of controlled cognitive processes in human associative learning. In A. J. Wills (Ed.), *New directions in human associative learning* (pp. 41–63). Mahwah, NJ: Lawrence Erlbaum Associates, Inc.

De Houwer, J., Vandorpe, S., & Beckers, T. (2007). Statistical contingency has a different impact on preparation judgements than on causal judgements. *Quarterly Journal of Experimental Psychology*, *60*, 418–432.

Denniston, J. C., Savastano, H. I., Blaisdell, A. P., & Miller, R. R. (2003). Cue competition as a retrieval deficit. *Learning and Motivation*, *34*, 1–31.

Dickinson, A. (1980). *Contemporary animal learning theory*. Cambridge, UK: Cambridge University Press.

Dickinson, A., & Burke, J. (1996). Within-compound associations mediate the retrospective revaluation of causality judgements. *Quarterly Journal of Experimental Psychology*, *49B*, 60–80.

Dickinson, A., Shanks, D. R., & Evenden, J. L. (1984). Judgement of act–outcome contingency: The role of selective attribution. *Quarterly Journal of Experimental Psychology*, *36A*, 29–50.

Field, A. P. (2005). Learning to like (or dislike): Associative learning of preferences. In A. J. Wills (Ed.), *New directions in human associative learning* (pp. 221–252). Mahwah, NJ: Lawrence Erlbaum Associates, Inc.

Fletcher, P. C., Anderson, J. M., Shanks, D. R., Honey, R., Carpenter, T. A., Donovan, T., et al. (2001). Responses of human frontal cortex to surprising events are predicted by formal associative learning theory. *Nature Neuroscience*, *4*, 1043–1048.

Fodor, J. A. (2003). *Hume variations*. Oxford, UK: Clarendon Press.

Gallistel, C. R., & Gibbon, J. (2001). Computational versus associative models of simple conditioning. *Current Directions in Psychological Science*, *10*, 146–150.

Ghirlanda, S. (2005). Retrospective revaluation as simple associative learning. *Journal of Experimental Psychology: Animal Behavior Processes*, *31*, 107–111.

Gluck, M. A., & Bower, G. H. (1988). From conditioning to category learning: An adaptive network model. *Journal of Experimental Psychology: General*, *117*, 227–247.

Hagmayer, Y., & Waldmann, M. R. (2007). Inferences about unobserved causes in human contingency learning. *Quarterly Journal of Experimental Psychology*, *60*, 330–355.

Hall, G. (1991). *Perceptual and associative learning*. Oxford, UK: Clarendon Press.

Hebb, D. O. (1949). *Organization of behavior*. New York: Wiley.

Hershberger, W. A. (1986). An approach through the looking-glass. *Animal Learning & Behavior*, *14*, 443–451.

Hinton, G. E., & Anderson, J. A. (Eds.). (1989). *Parallel models of associative memory*. Hillsdale, NJ: Lawrence Erlbaum Associates, Inc.

Holland, P. C. (1990). Event representation in Pavlovian conditioning: Image and action. *Cognition*, *37*, 105–131.

Hommel, B., Müsseler, J., Aschersleben, G., & Prinz, W. (2001). The theory of event coding (TEC): A framework for perception and action planning. *Behavioral and Brain Sciences*, *24*, 849–937.

Jenkins, H. M., & Ward, W. C. (1965). Judgment of contingency between responses and outcomes. *Psychological Monographs*, *79*(Whole Number 594).

Kahneman, D. (2003). A perspective on judgment and choice: Mapping bounded rationality. *American Psychologist*, *58*, 697–720.

Karazinov, D. M., & Boakes, R. A. (2007). Second order conditioning in human predictive judgments when there is little time to think. *Quarterly Journal of Experimental Psychology*, *60*, 448–460.

Kinder, A., & Shanks, D. R. (2001). Amnesia and the declarative/nondeclarative distinction: A recurrent network model of classification, recognition, and repetition priming. *Journal of Cognitive Neuroscience*, *13*, 648–669.

Kinder, A., & Shanks, D. R. (2003). Neuropsychological dissociations between priming and recognition: A single-system connectionist account. *Psychological Review*, *110*, 728–744.

Lagnado, D. A., & Shanks, D. R. (2002). Probability judgment in hierarchical learning: A conflict between predictiveness and coherence. *Cognition*, *83*, 81–112.

Larkin, M. J. W., Aitken, M. R. F., & Dickinson, A. (1998). Retrospective revaluation of causal judgments under positive and negative contingencies. *Journal of Experimental Psychology: Learning, Memory, and Cognition*, *24*, 1331–1352.

Le Pelley, M. E., Oakeshott, S. M., & McLaren, I. P. L. (2005). Blocking and unblocking in human causal learning. *Journal of Experimental Psychology: Animal Behavior Processes*, *31*, 56–70.

Livesey, E. J., & Boakes, R. A. (2004). Outcome additivity, elemental processing and blocking in human causality judgements. *Quarterly Journal of Experimental Psychology*, *57B*, 361–379.

López, F. J., Cobos, P. L., & Caño, A. (2005). Associative and causal reasoning accounts of causal induction: Symmetries and asymmetries in predictive and diagnostic inferences. *Memory & Cognition*, *33*, 1388–1398.

López, F. J., Cobos, P. L., Caño, A., & Shanks, D. R. (1998). The rational analysis of human causal and probability judgment. In M. Oaksford & N. Chater (Eds.), *Rational models of cognition* (pp. 314–352). Oxford, UK: Oxford University Press.

Lovibond, P. F. (2003). Causal beliefs and conditioned responses: Retrospective revaluation induced by experience and by instruction. *Journal of Experimental Psychology: Learning, Memory, and Cognition*, *29*, 97–106.

Lovibond, P. F., Been, S.-L., Mitchell, C. J., Bouton, M. E., & Frohardt, R. (2003). Forward and backward blocking of causal judgment is enhanced by additivity of effect magnitude. *Memory & Cognition*, *31*, 133–142.

Lovibond, P. F., & Shanks, D. R. (2002). The role of awareness in Pavlovian conditioning: Empirical evidence and theoretical implications. *Journal of Experimental Psychology: Animal Behavior Processes*, *28*, 3–26.

Mackintosh, N. J. (1975). A theory of attention: Variations in the associability of stimuli with reinforcement. *Psychological Review*, *82*, 276–298.

Mackintosh, N. J. (1983). *Conditioning and associative learning*. Oxford, UK: Clarendon Press.

McClelland, J. L., & Rumelhart, D. E. (1981). An interactive activation model of context effects in letter perception: Part 1. An account of basic findings. *Psychological Review*, *88*, 375–407.

McClelland, J. L., & Rumelhart, D. E. (1985). Distributed memory and the representation of general and specific information. *Journal of Experimental Psychology: General*, *114*, 159–188.

McGeoch, J. A., & Irion, A. L. (1952). *The psychology of human learning* (2nd ed.). New York: Longmans, Green & Co.

Melchers, K. G., Lachnit, H., & Shanks, D. R. (2004). Within-compound associations in retrospective revaluation and in direct learning: A challenge for comparator theory. *Quarterly Journal of Experimental Psychology*, *57B*, 25–53.

Melchers, K. G., Lachnit, H., & Shanks, D. R. (2006). The comparator theory fails to account for the selective role of within-compound associations in cue selection effects. *Experimental Psychology*, *53*, 316–320.

Mitchell, C. J., Livesey, E., & Lovibond, P. F. (2007). A dissociation between causal judgement and the ease with which a cause is categorised with its effect. *Quarterly Journal of Experimental Psychology*, *60*, 400–417.

Mitchell, C. J., & Lovibond, P. F. (2002). Backward and forward blocking in human electrodermal conditioning: Blocking requires an assumption of outcome additivity. *Quarterly Journal of Experimental Psychology*, *55B*, 311–329.

Mitchell, C. J., Lovibond, P. F., Minard, E., & Lavis, Y. (2006). Forward blocking in human learning sometimes reflects the failure to encode a cue–outcome relationship. *Quarterly Journal of Experimental Psychology*, *59*, 830–844.

Msetfi, R. M., Murphy, R. A., & Simpson, J. (2007). Depressive realism and the effect of intertrial interval on judgements of zero, positive and negative contingencies. *Quarterly Journal of Experimental Psychology*, *60*, 461–481.

Osman, M. (2004). An evaluation of dual-process theories of reasoning. *Psychonomic Bulletin & Review*, *11*, 988–1010.

Pearce, J. M. (1994). Similarity and discrimination: A selective review and a connectionist model. *Psychological Review, 101*, 587–607.

Pearce, J. M., & Hall, G. (1980). A model for Pavlovian conditioning: Variations in the effectiveness of conditioned but not of unconditioned stimuli. *Psychological Review, 87*, 532–552.

Perales, J. C., Catena, A., Shanks, D. R., & González, J. A. (2005). Dissociation between judgments and outcome-expectancy measures in covariation learning: A signal detection theory approach. *Journal of Experimental Psychology: Learning, Memory, and Cognition, 31*, 1105–1120.

Perales, J. C., & Shanks, D. R. (2003). Normative and descriptive accounts of the influence of power and contingency on causal judgment. *Quarterly Journal of Experimental Psychology, 56A*, 977–1007.

Perruchet, P., & Amorim, M.-A. (1992). Conscious knowledge and changes in performance in sequence learning: Evidence against dissociation. *Journal of Experimental Psychology: Learning, Memory, and Cognition, 18*, 785–800.

Pineño, O., & Miller, R. R. (2007). Comparing associative, statistical, and inferential reasoning accounts of human contingency learning. *Quarterly Journal of Experimental Psychology, 60*, 310–329.

Price, P. C., & Yates, J. F. (1993). Judgmental overshadowing: Further evidence of cue interaction in contingency judgment. *Memory & Cognition, 21*, 561–572.

Rescorla, R. A., & Solomon, R. L. (1967). Two-process learning theory: Relationships between Pavlovian and instrumental learning. *Psychological Review, 74*, 151–182.

Rosenblatt, F. (1962). *Principles of neurodynamics*. New York: Spartan.

Ryan, J. D., & Cohen, N. J. (2003). Evaluating the neuropsychological dissociation evidence for multiple memory systems. *Cognitive, Affective, & Behavioral Neuroscience, 3*, 168–185.

Schultz, W., & Dickinson, A. (2000). Neuronal coding of prediction errors. *Annual Review of Neuroscience, 23*, 473–500.

Shanks, D. R. (1985). Forward and backward blocking in human contingency judgement. *Quarterly Journal of Experimental Psychology, 37B*, 1–21.

Shanks, D. R. (1990). On the cognitive theory of conditioning. *Biological Psychology, 30*, 171–179.

Shanks, D. R. (2005a). Connectionist models of basic human learning processes. In G. Houghton (Ed.), *Connectionist models in cognitive psychology* (pp. 45–82). Hove, UK: Psychology Press.

Shanks, D. R. (2005b). Implicit learning. In K. Lamberts & R. L. Goldstone (Eds.), *Handbook of cognition* (pp. 202–220). London: Sage.

Shanks, D. R., & Darby, R. J. (1998). Feature- and rule-based generalization in human associative learning. *Journal of Experimental Psychology: Animal Behavior Processes, 24*, 405–415.

Shanks, D. R., & Dickinson, A. (1990). Contingency awareness in evaluative conditioning: A comment on Baeyens, Eelen, and van den Bergh. *Cognition & Emotion, 4*, 19–30.

Shanks, D. R., & Dickinson, A. (1991). Instrumental judgment and performance under variations in action–outcome contingency and contiguity. *Memory & Cognition, 19*, 353–360.

Shanks, D. R., Holyoak, K. J., & Medin, D. L. (Eds.). (1996). *The psychology of learning and motivation: Vol. 34. Causal learning*. San Diego, CA: Academic Press.

Shanks, D. R., & Lovibond, P. F. (2002). Autonomic and eyeblink conditioning are closely related to contingency awareness: Reply to Wiens and Öhman (2002) and Manns et al. (2002). *Journal of Experimental Psychology: Animal Behavior Processes, 28*, 38–42.

Shanks, D. R., & Pearson, S. M. (1987). A production system model of causality judgment. *Proceedings of the Ninth Annual Conference of the Cognitive Science Society* (pp. 210–220). Hillsdale, NJ: Lawrence Erlbaum Associates, Inc.

Shanks, D. R., & St. John, M. F. (1994). Characteristics of dissociable human learning systems. *Behavioral and Brain Sciences, 17*, 367–447.

Shevill, I., & Hall, G. (2004). Retrospective revaluation effects in the conditioned suppression procedure. *Quarterly Journal of Experimental Psychology, 57B*, 331–347.

Smedslund, J. (1963). The concept of correlation in adults. *Scandinavian Journal of Psychology, 4*, 165–173.

Smith, C. N., Clark, R. E., Manns, J. R., & Squire, L. R. (2005). Acquisition of differential delay eyeblink classical conditioning is independent of awareness. *Behavioral Neuroscience, 119*, 78–86.

Squire, L. R. (1994). Declarative and nondeclarative memory: Multiple brain systems supporting learning and memory. In D. L. Schacter & E. Tulving (Eds.), *Memory systems* (pp. 203–231). Cambridge, MA: MIT Press.

Tangen, J. M., Allan, L. G., & Sadeghi, H. (2005). Assessing (in)sensitivity to causal asymmetry: A matter of degree. In A. J. Wills (Ed.), *New directions in human associative learning* (pp. 65–93). Mahwah, NJ: Lawrence Erlbaum Associates, Inc.

Thorndike, E. L. (1931). *Human learning.* New York: Century.

Tilton, J. W. (1926). *The relation between association and the higher mental processes.* New York: Teachers College.

Tulving, E., & Donaldson, W. (1972). *Organization and memory.* New York: Academic Press.

Tunney, R. J., & Shanks, D. R. (2003). Subjective measures of awareness and implicit cognition. *Memory & Cognition, 31,* 1060–1071.

Turner, D. C., Aitken, M. R. F., Shanks, D. R., Sahakian, B. J., Robbins, T. W., Schwarzbauer, C., et al. (2004). The role of the lateral frontal cortex in causal associative learning: Exploring preventative and super-learning. *Cerebral Cortex, 14,* 872–880.

Vadillo, M. A., & Matute, H. (2007). Predictions and causal estimations are not supported by the same associative structure. *Quarterly Journal of Experimental Psychology, 60,* 433–447.

Vandorpe, S., De Houwer, J., & Beckers, T. (2007). Outcome maximality and additivity training also influence cue competition in causal learning when learning involves many cues and events. *Quarterly Journal of Experimental Psychology, 60,* 356–368.

Waldmann, M. R. (2001). Predictive versus diagnostic causal learning: Evidence from an overshadowing paradigm. *Psychonomic Bulletin & Review, 8,* 600–608.

Waldmann, M. R., & Holyoak, K. J. (1990). Can causal induction be reduced to associative learning? *Proceedings of the Twelfth Annual Conference of the Cognitive Science Society* (pp. 190–197). Hillsdale, NJ: Lawrence Erlbaum Associates, Inc.

Williams, D. A. (1996). A comparative analysis of negative contingency learning in humans and nonhumans. In D. R. Shanks, K. J. Holyoak, & D. L. Medin (Eds.), *The psychology of learning and motivation: Vol. 34. Causal learning* (pp. 89–131). San Diego, CA: Academic Press.

Williams, D. A., Sagness, K. E., & McPhee, J. E. (1994). Configural and elemental strategies in predictive learning. *Journal of Experimental Psychology: Learning, Memory, and Cognition, 20,* 694–709.

Winman, A., Wennerholm, P., Juslin, P., & Shanks, D. R. (2005). Evidence for rule-based processes in the inverse base-rate effect. *Quarterly Journal of Experimental Psychology, 58A,* 789–815.

Zajonc, R. B. (1980). Feeling and thinking: Preferences need no inferences. *American Psychologist, 35,* 151–175.

Zaki, S. R. (2005). Is categorization performance really intact in amnesia? A meta-analysis. *Psychonomic Bulletin & Review, 11,* 1048–1054.

THE QUARTERLY JOURNAL OF EXPERIMENTAL PSYCHOLOGY
2007, 60 (3), 310–329

Comparing associative, statistical, and inferential reasoning accounts of human contingency learning

Oskar Pineño
University of Seville, Seville, Spain

Ralph R. Miller
State University of New York at Binghamton, Binghamton, NY, USA

For more than two decades, researchers have contrasted the relative merits of associative and statistical theories as accounts of human contingency learning. This debate, still far from resolution, has led to further refinement of models within each family of theories. More recently, a third theoretical view has joined the debate: the inferential reasoning account. The explanations of these three accounts differ critically in many aspects, such as level of analysis and their emphasis on different steps within the information-processing sequence. Also, each account has important advantages (as well as critical flaws) and emphasizes experimental evidence that poses problems to the others. Some hybrid models of human contingency learning have attempted to reconcile certain features of these accounts, thereby benefiting from some of the unique advantages of different families of accounts. A comparison of these families of accounts will help us appreciate the challenges that research on human contingency learning will face over the coming years.

"Then you better start swimmin', or you'll sink like a stone, for the times they are a-changin'." With these words of a classic Bob Dylan song, one could describe the feeling left after attending the Human Contingency Learning (HCL) meeting in the Ardennes, Belgium, in May 2004. Why such a feeling? The reason is that a third account of HCL, based on inferential reasoning, joined the debate between statistical and associative theories that has been in progress for the last two decades. Moreover, it became obvious at the HCL meeting that this third account constitutes a challenge to these prior views. Advocates of the inferential reasoning approach claim that both the associative and statistical accounts have ignored the role of higher order, complex cognitive processes and have reported several phenomena that seemingly support this assertion. This challenge will require extending existing associative and statistical theories if they are to survive and will probably bring with it scientific advancement.

Theoretical traditions in HCL

The relevance of the debate among statistical, associative, and inferential reasoning accounts of

Correspondence should be addressed to Ralph R. Miller, Department of Psychology, SUNY-Binghamton, Binghamton, NY 13902-6000, USA. E-mail: rmiller@binghamton.edu

The development of this paper was possible due to support from Department of Universities, Research, and Technology of the Andalucía Government (Junta de Andalucía) and NIMH Grant 33881. We would like to thank Jeffrey C. Amundson, Gonzalo Urcelay, and Daniel Wheeler for their comments on an earlier version of this manuscript.

DOI:10.1080/17470210601000680

HCL can only be understood by considering the issues that demanded the most attention of researchers in HCL over the last 20 years. In fact, each of these theoretical views was developed to account for certain critical findings. In this section we briefly describe these theoretical accounts in relation to the findings that prompted their appearance. It is not our purpose to provide here a detailed discussion on the wide range of different models within each account, but to explain the general ideas underlying these views (for other recent reviews, see Allan & Tangen, 2005; De Houwer & Beckers, 2002a; Wills, 2005). For the sake of simplicity, the statistical, associative, and inferential reasoning families of models are discussed based on the most prominent member of each family.

Early contingency studies: The hegemony of statistical theories

Statistical theories of learning were initially developed as an attempt to explain how human participants learn the contingencies underlying the occurrence of two or more covarying events. The term *contingency* refers to covariation between two or more *binary* variables (i.e., discrete variables with only two possible values; in this sense, the study of contingency learning can be viewed as the study of the simplest instance of correlation learning, since *correlation* implies covariation between two or more *continuous* variables). In a typical contingency learning experiment, participants are given presentations of two or more events, which can be either present or absent on each learning trial (i.e., discrete presentations of a set of responses and/or stimuli). Then, participants are asked to rate the contingent (or sometimes causal) relationship between these events, generally by using a numerical scale in which different values correspond to different degrees of relation. Because of this simple experimental scenario, researchers in HCL were able to collect considerable data, which rapidly opened the door for further and more refined studies.

The first studies of HCL focused on the most basic question—that is, is human learning sensitive to different contingencies? And, if so, how

sensitive is it? Initial studies, such as that of Jenkins and Ward (1965), showed evidence of such a sensitivity in instrumental learning (i.e., between a response and an outcome). This ability of humans to detect response–outcome relations has been extensively documented (e.g., Allan & Jenkins, 1980, 1983; Alloy & Abramson, 1979; Chatlosh, Neunaber, & Wasserman, 1985; Neunaber & Wasserman, 1986; Wasserman, 1990; Wasserman, Chatlosh, & Neunaber, 1983; Wasserman, Elek, Chatlosh, & Baker, 1993; for a review see Wasserman, Kao, Van Hamme, Katagiri, & Young, 1996), as has been the ability of humans to detect cue–outcome relations (e.g., López, Almaraz, Fernández, & Shanks, 1999; Shanks, 1991; for a review see Shanks, López, Darby, & Dickinson, 1996b).

Early evidence demonstrating humans' sensitivity in contingency detection prompted the development of models that explained this kind of learning from a statistical view. Although there are many potential statistical indices of contingency, Allan's (1980; also see Kelley, 1967) ΔP model is the simplest example of this family of models (see Shanks, Holyoak, & Medin, 1996a, for a review of many of these models). Despite being inspired in part by a model originally developed in the animal conditioning literature (i.e., Rescorla, 1968), the impact of the ΔP model was so profound in the HCL literature, that it still has not been totally replaced by recent and more refined statistical models, which now tend to narrow the focus from contingency learning in general, to causal learning in particular (e.g., Cheng, 1997; Cheng & Novick, 1992; Spellman, 1996). Rather, the ΔP measure was implemented, in one way or another, in these new models. Specifically, in the ΔP model information concerning the cue (or response) and outcome is acquired and stored as co-occurrence frequencies in a 2×2 matrix (see Figure 1), which results from the combination of the binary values of the cue (present vs. absent) and the outcome (present vs. absent). In this matrix, Cell *a* records the number (frequency) of trials on which both the cue and the outcome were present (*fa*), Cell *b* records the number of trials on which the cue

	Outcome present	Outcome absent
Cue present	a fa	b fb
Cue absent	c fc	d fd

Figure 1. *2 × 2 contingency matrix. Cells in this matrix store the frequencies of the presence and the absence of the cue and the outcome: Cell a = frequency of cue and outcome present (fa); Cell b = frequency of cue present and outcome absent (fb); Cell c = frequency of cue absent and outcome present (fc); Cell d = frequency of cue and outcome absent (fd).*

was present, and the outcome was absent (*fb*), Cell *c* records the number of trials on which the cue was absent, and the outcome was present (*fc*), and Cell *d* records the number of trials on which both the cue and the outcome were absent (*fd*). These frequencies are used to compute ΔP:

$$\Delta P = \frac{a}{a+b} - \frac{c}{c+d} = P(O|C) - P(O| \sim C) \quad (1)$$

According to Equation 1, ΔP corresponds to the difference between two conditional probabilities: the probability of the outcome given the cue, $P(O|C)$, and the probability of the outcome in the absence of the cue, $P(O|\sim C)$. Therefore, ΔP always adopts a value ranging between $+1$ and -1. When the outcome occurs more frequently in the presence of the cue than in its absence, the cue–outcome contingency is positive (i.e., generative learning in the causal learning tradition and excitatory learning in the animal conditioning tradition). By contrast, when the outcome occurs more frequently in the absence of the cue than in its presence, the cue–outcome contingency is negative (i.e., preventative learning in the causal learning tradition and inhibitory learning in the animal conditioning tradition). Finally, the contingency is 0 when the cue and the outcome occur independently of each other.

Allan's (1980) ΔP model provided a simple account for much observed covariation learning.

As acknowledged even by opponents of statistical models (see Shanks et al., 1996a, for a debate between supporters of statistical and associative accounts), values of ΔP resulting from different frequencies of occurrence of the cue (or response) and the outcome closely resemble the actual ratings or nonverbal responses found in studies assessing sensitivity to different contingencies in humans (for supportive evidence, see, e.g., Wasserman et al., 1996; but for conflicting evidence, see, e.g., Wasserman et al., 1993). However, the hegemony of ΔP in HCL was soon challenged by associative theorists from the animal conditioning tradition, and the difficulty of the basic ΔP model to account for cue competition effects played an important role in this turn of events.

Cue competition effects: The emergence of associative models in HCL

In HCL, cue competition effects refer to phenomena in which ratings of a target cue paired with an outcome are influenced by the presence of a second cue during the pairings. Cue competition was first reported in the classical conditioning literature by Pavlov (1927), who observed the well-known *overshadowing effect*. In overshadowing, two cues, A and X, are presented in compound during their pairings with the outcome (i.e., AX–O trials). As a consequence of the training of X in compound with a typically more salient cue, A, weak responding is observed on test of X, relative to a condition in which X was trained alone (i.e., X–O trials).

Despite the early finding of the overshadowing effect by Pavlov (1927), Kamin's (1968) *blocking effect* is the cue competition effect that has received most attention in the literature. In blocking, as in overshadowing, two cues (A and X) are trained in compound with the outcome, also resulting in weak responding at test of the target cue, X. However, contrary to overshadowing, in blocking A does not compete with X based on its higher salience (i.e., in blocking, A is ordinarily equally or less salient than X), but on its history of additional pairings with the outcome. In a typical forward blocking experiment, A is paired alone with the outcome (i.e., A–O trials) prior to compound conditioning (AX–O trials), and responding to X at test is usually found to be weak, relative to a control condition that received no A–O trials prior to the AX–O trials (instead, this condition usually receives B–O trials).

The blocking effect became a benchmark to be met by accounts of HCL due to the studies of Dickinson, Shanks, and Evenden (1984), who first reported this effect in a HCL task. Their observation of blocking, an effect previously studied in the animal conditioning literature, led researchers to suggest that the same mechanisms may be involved in animal conditioning and HCL. In fact, Dickinson et al. explicitly suggested that associative theories developed to explain classical conditioning in nonhuman animals (e.g., Rescorla & Wagner, 1972) might also be used to account for HCL (see also Gluck & Bower, 1988; Shanks & Dickinson, 1987). Among the many models in the associative tradition (e.g., Dickinson & Burke, 1996; Mackintosh, 1975; Pearce & Hall, 1980; Rescorla & Wagner, 1972; Van Hamme & Wasserman, 1994; Wagner, 1981), the model of Rescorla and Wagner has certainly been the most influential. Despite its having many detractors even in the associative tradition (e.g., Baker, 1974; Bouton, 1993; R. R. Miller, Barnet, & Grahame, 1995), nobody questions its relevance as the focal model that encouraged the development of the associative account of cue competition.

In Rescorla and Wagner's (1972) model, the formation and strengthening of a cue–outcome association proceeds according to Equation 2:

$$\Delta V_{cue}^{n} = \alpha \cdot \beta \cdot (\lambda - V_{Total}^{n-1}) \qquad (2)$$

In this equation, ΔV_{cue}^{n} represents the change in associative strength of the cue on trial n, and α and β are learning-rate parameters representing the associability (sometimes equated with salience) of the cue and the outcome, respectively. These parameters adopt values between 0 and 1, as a function of their corresponding salience. The parenthetical term (i.e., $\lambda - V_{Total}^{n-1}$) represents the discrepancy between the amount of associative strength that can be supported by the outcome

(λ) and the current total associative strength acquired, through trial $n-1$, by all the cues present on trial n (V_{Total}^{n-1}). The value of λ depends on the presence or absence of the outcome on trial n: When the outcome is presented, λ adopts a value of 1; when the outcome is absent, λ adopts a value of 0. Cue–outcome associations are acquired and strengthened based on the discrepancy between the expected and actual occurrence of the outcome (i.e., $\lambda - V_{Total}^{n-1}$). Therefore, in acquisition training (i.e., cue–outcome pairings), the total of the strengths of all of the cue–outcome associations will increase toward unity based on a positive discrepancy (i.e., $1 - V_{Total}^{n-1}$), whereas in extinction and inhibition training (i.e., cue-alone trials), the total of the strengths of all of the cue–outcome association will decrease toward zero based on a negative discrepancy (i.e., $0 - V_{Total}^{n-1}$).

Cue competition effects are explained by Rescorla and Wagner's (1972) model through the discrepancy in the parenthetical term ($\lambda = V_{Total}^{n-1}$), which represents what Kamin (1968) referred to as the surprisingness of the outcome (i.e., the occurrence of the outcome on a given trial is assumed to be more or less surprising based on the associative strength of the cues present on that trial). Specifically, cue competition arises because the discrepancy term for each cue depends on the total associative strength of all the cues present on trial n (V_{Total}^{n-1}). Based on this feature of the model, the associative strength of a cue can have an impact upon the acquisition of associative strength by a second cue with which it was presented. For example, in forward blocking A first gains associative strength during the A–O trials. Then, during the subsequent AX–O trials, the summated associative strength of A and X will be close to the value of λ even on the first AX–O trial, due to A's previously acquired associative strength, thereby resulting in little learning to X. In Kamin's terminology, the outcome is not surprising due to its being already expected based on the presence of A. As a consequence of this small discrepancy, the amount of associative strength available for cue X to acquire will be small, and, hence, a weak X–O association will be formed.

The ΔP model cannot explain the blocking effect. According to this model, the contingency between X and O decreases on trials on which the outcome occurs without X, regardless of whether these trials consist of A–O pairings (i.e., blocking condition) or B–O pairings (control condition). In other words, this model does not address the fact that blocking, and other cue competition effects, are due to outcome presentations, not only in the absence of the target cue, but also in the presence of the target cue's companion stimulus. This inability of the ΔP model to account for cue competition effects in HCL encouraged the development of more sophisticated statistical models, such as Cheng and Novick's (1992) focal-set theory, Cheng's (1997) Power-PC theory, and Spellman's (1996) use of conditional contingencies (see also Spellman, Price, & Logan, 2001). At the same time, new data concerning cue competition in HCL also encouraged the revision of some traditional associative models, such as Van Hamme and Wasserman's (1994) revision of Rescorla and Wagner's (1972) model, and Dickinson and Burke's (1996) revision of Wagner's (1981) SOP model. Specifically, these revisions were prompted by the observation of retrospective revaluation in HCL (e.g., backward blocking, Shanks, 1985), which demonstrated that, contrary to the assumptions of traditional associative models, a cue's associative status could be updated on trials on which this cue was absent, but associatively activated by the presentation of a companion stimulus. Because retrospective revaluation was subsequently also detected in animal conditioning preparations (see, e.g., R. R. Miller & Matute, 1996) the study of HCL, which imported the associative account from the animal learning tradition, soon returned the favour by stimulating the identification of new animal learning phenomena. But the debate between associative and statistical models, despite its being so active during the nineties (e.g., Allan, 1993; Shanks, 1995; Shanks et al., 1996), lost some of its strength over the last few years. Recent exchanges between associative and statistical researchers are no longer aimed at globally comparing the two

families of accounts of HCL, perhaps due to the recognition that whole families of models could not be contrasted due to the open-ended generation of revised models within each family (e.g., R. R. Miller & Escobar, 2001). Instead, HCL studies focused on testing specific models, such as Cheng's Power-PC theory (e.g., Allan, 2003; Buehner, Cheng, & Clifford, 2003; Lober & Shanks, 2000). Moreover, during the last few years a new view of HCL was proposed that introduced a wholly new orientation: the inferential reasoning account.

Effects of outcome additivity and maximality on cue competition: The challenge of the inferential reasoning view

Tracking down the theoretical origins of the inferential reasoning view as applied to HCL is not an easy task. One precursor was probably the propositional logic proposed for higher order information processing in some of the cognitive literature (e.g., Anderson, 1980; Johnson-Laird, 1988; Lindsay & Norman, 1972; G. A. Miller, Galanter, & Pribram, 1960; Wason & Johnson-Laird, 1972), in which propositions are used to solve behavioural tasks. The inferential reasoning view also has roots in the theoretical tradition concerned with causal reasoning, which is represented in the study of HCL by the work of Waldmann (1996, 2000, 2001; see also Waldmann & Holyoak, 1992) and by the philosophically oriented work of Pearl (e.g., Pearl, 1993, 2000). This causal reasoning approach has recently developed into the Bayesian net models (e.g., Glymour, 2003; Waldmann & Hagmayer, 2005; Waldmann & Martignon, 1998).

The inferential reasoning account of HCL has been encouraged by recent studies performed by De Houwer and his collaborators (e.g., Beckers, De Houwer, Pineño, & Miller, 2005; De Houwer, 2002; De Houwer & Beckers, 2003; De Houwer, Beckers, & Glautier, 2002) as well as by Lovibond and his colleagues (e.g., Lovibond, Been, Mitchell, Bouton, & Frohardt, 2003; Mitchell & Lovibond, 2002; Mitchell, Lovibond, & Condoleon, 2005; see also Waldmann & Walker, 2005; Wu & Cheng, 1999, for related proposals). As a whole, these studies have tried to demonstrate that cue competition effects, specifically forward and backward blocking, might arise from inferential processes. Two specific findings can be regarded as the most compelling support for this view: effects of outcome additivity and effects of outcome maximality.

The *outcome additivity effect* (Beckers et al., 2005; Lovibond et al., 2003; Mitchell & Lovibond, 2002; Mitchell et al., 2005) refers to the observation that, prior to target training in cue competition situations, experience with two effective (i.e., reinforced) nontarget cues alone and with an effective compound of the two cues with the same outcome attenuates subsequent cue competition. The inferential account of this phenomenon is based on the notion that, in order for blocking to occur, the participant must assume that multiple effective causes have additive effects on the occurrence (i.e., frequency and/or intensity) of the outcome. This assumption concerning additivity of effective causes upon the outcome, together with the observation in a blocking experiment that the addition of the target cause to the blocking cause does not actually affect the intensity of the outcome, is what, from the inferential reasoning view, produces the blocking effect. More specifically, the blocking effect is postulated to be the result of the following counterfactual reasoning process, akin to a syllogism: (a) if both cues A and X are potential causes of the outcome, then the outcome should be stronger when A and X are presented together than when they are presented alone; (b) the outcome following the AX compound (AX–O trials) is not stronger than that following A alone (A–O trials); (c) thus, A and X are not both effective causes of the outcome; (d) since A alone causes the outcome, and information on the effectiveness of X alone was not provided, it is logical to assume that X is not an effective cause of the outcome. The inferential reasoning account has received support from experiments showing that, if participants are given explicit additivity pretraining with cues different from those involved in the blocking procedure (e.g., C and D separately paired with a moderate outcome; CD compound paired with

an intense outcome, then A–O trials followed by AX–O trials), robust blocking of X is found, whereas explicit nonadditivity pretraining (e.g., C, D, and CD each paired with an outcome of identical intensity, either moderate or intense, then A–O trials followed by AX–O trials), little or no blocking of X is observed (e.g., Beckers et al., 2005; Livesey & Boakes, 2004; Lovibond et al., 2003). This implies that although additivity of causes appears to be the default expectation, experience with nonadditivity of causes can attenuate this expectation.

Related to the outcome additivity effect, the *outcome maximality effect* has also yielded support for the inferential reasoning account. Outcome maximality (Beckers et al., 2005; De Houwer et al., 2002) refers to the notion that, in order for participants to assess outcome additivity, it is critical for them to know that the outcome experienced was not limited by some physical constraint such as a maximum possible frequency or intensity (i.e., a ceiling effect). Additivity is not expected if it requires an outcome that is greater than what the subject believes to be possible. More specifically, in a blocking procedure, participants are only able to determine whether the outcome following an AX compound cue is greater than that produced by A alone or X alone (consistent with the outcome, default, additivity assumption) if the outcome presented on A–O trials is known to be of a submaximal intensity such that more intense outcomes could have been observed. Simply put, if the presentation of A results in a maximal outcome, it is not possible to determine the effectiveness of X as a cause of the outcome based on trials on which the AX compound is also followed by a maximal outcome. By contrast, if A and AX each produce the same submaximal outcome, participants can then logically infer that the presence of cue X does not influence the outcome's intensity because, if it did, a stronger outcome would have occurred following the AX compound.

Other evidence seemingly supportive of the inferential reasoning account includes the observation that increasing the difficulty of a secondary task performed during cue competition treatment attenuates cue competition (De Houwer &

Beckers, 2003; Vandorpe, De Houwer, & Beckers, 2005; Waldmann & Walker, 2005). This suggests that cue competition occurs only when sufficient amounts of limited cognitive faculties can be devoted to inference. It has also been claimed that evidence of inference in cue competition has been provided by studies in which different cover stories were presented in order to provide either a predictive or a causal scenario for the cue–outcome relations. In these studies, competition was obtained only with the causal scenario (De Houwer et al., 2002; for related findings, see Waldmann & Holyoak, 1992). The conclusion here is based on the assumption that outcome additivity is more readily applied to causation than to prediction, an assumption that leaves unexplained other reports of cue competition in clearly predictive situations (e.g., Arcediano, Matute, & Miller, 1997; Chapman, 1991; Chapman & Robbins, 1990; Williams, Sagness, & McPhee, 1994).

Regardless of the specific manipulations used in each study, the message sent by researchers working in the inferential reasoning framework is consistent: Both the associative and statistical accounts of HCL have erred in overlooking the role that higher order cognitive processes may play in cue competition effects. Moreover, the claim that these higher order cognitive processes might be involved in HCL experiments, but not in experiments using nonhuman animals, has been brought into question. As demonstrated by Beckers, Miller, De Houwer, and Urushihara (2006), outcome additivity and maximality effects can be readily found in a Pavlovian conditioning preparation using rats as subjects. Parsimony leads to the tentative conclusion that rats, as well as humans, use inferential processes or, alternatively, that neither do and some noninferential process is actually responsible for these observations.

A comparison of accounts of HCL

Despite differences among the models within each family (statistical, associative, and inferential reasoning), accounts within a family share certain features and assumptions. In the present section we compare these families of accounts

regarding: (a) their levels of explanation of learning phenomena, (b) how information is encoded and treated, (c) their focus on either acquisition or performance processes to explain HCL phenomena, and (d) their ability to explain path-dependence phenomena. As will be seen, each account has certain advantages and disadvantages. However, because these accounts are not totally exclusive, adopting an integrative strategy can solve, at least partially, some of the problems of each account. This integrative strategy has been already followed by some hybrid models.

Explanatory levels in accounts of HCL

Models differ not only in the specific mechanisms they propose to explain phenomena, but also in the level of analysis of their explanations. Although different categories of explanatory levels have been proposed, Marr's (1982) three-level distinction has become commonplace in the study of HCL (e.g., Baker, Murphy, & Vallée-Tourangeau, 1996; López, Cobos, Caño, & Shanks, 1998). According to Marr's distinction, theoretical explanations can be viewed as computational, algorithmic, or implementational. *Computational* models merely describe what the output should be, given an input, remaining silent on the process by which information is transformed going from input to output. With respect to HCL, computational models describe the goals guiding behaviour, speaking of *what* should be expected to occur in a given situation. In this sense, computational models can be viewed as normative models because they describe what is presumably functional—that is, the participant's ideal response under a given set of contingencies. *Algorithmic* models provide a deeper explanatory level than computational models by trying to answer not only what output should be expected in a given situation, but also how this output was arrived at. A model is said to be algorithmic when it provides not only representations for the input and the output, but also an algorithm (i.e., a procedure with a limited number of steps) for transforming the input into the output. Thus, algorithmic models of HCL speak of the mechanisms involved in the acquisition, storage, retrieval, and/or expression of information regarding covarying events. Finally, *implementational* models speak to how the algorithms proposed by algorithmic models can be physically implemented. An implementational model of HCL would attempt to describe the neurobiological basis of contingency learning.

HCL accounts are generally silent on the implementational level[1] and therefore fall in either the computational (normative) or algorithmic categories. Associative models (e.g., Dickinson & Burke, 1996; Mackintosh, 1975; Pearce & Hall, 1980; Rescorla & Wagner, 1972; Van Hamme & Wasserman, 1994; Wagner, 1981) are algorithmic. Thus, associative models provide not only the equations for transforming the input (e.g., the occurrence or absence of the cues and the outcome, together with their saliences) into the output (e.g., response or, at least, associative strength), but also a well-defined set of rules for transforming information step by step. However, this is not the distinctive feature of associative models that makes them algorithmic (i.e., statistical models also provide equations and rules for transforming the input and the output). Rather, associative models are algorithmic because they attempt to describe the psychological mechanisms presumably involved in learning phenomena. Also, as algorithmic models, associative models speak of mental representations of the input (i.e., internal representations of the cues and the outcome) and the outcome (i.e., associative and/or response strengths).

At first glance, statistical models can be considered computational accounts. However, this claim must be qualified, since this assertion is open to controversy. Certainly, statistical models are usually viewed as normative by researchers in the associative tradition (e.g., Baker et al., 1996; López et al., 1998) as well as in the statistical tradition (e.g., Cheng, 1997; Glymour & Cheng, 1998). However, several studies have suggested the possibility that information might be processed through the application of a *statistical mechanism*, which would make them algorithmic. For example, Price and Yates (1995; see also Catena, Maldonado, Megías, & Frese, 2002; Shanks, 1991) suggested that the format in which contingency information is presented (i.e., trial-by-trial vs. summarized presentation in contingency tables) might encourage processing by either an associative mechanism (trial-by-trial) or a statistical mechanism (contingency tables).

Despite occasional proposals that a statistical mechanism could be involved in HCL, however, there is a general agreement on viewing these statistical models as normative accounts. The case of inferential reasoning accounts can be said to be exactly the opposite. Authors working in the inferential reasoning framework (e.g., Beckers et al., 2005; Lovibond et al., 2003) frequently speak of these accounts as a description of cognitive mechanisms actually involved in cue competition phenomena. This is explicit in statements such as "There can be little doubt about the fact that people can make rational inferences about the contingencies or causal relations between events. It is therefore not surprising that contingency judgments *can* depend on causal beliefs or on the retrospective recoding of trials" (De Houwer & Beckers, 2002a, p. 306). In a similar vein, Lovibond et al. (2003, p. 141) stated "According to such an inferential approach, causal judgments may be derived from the same sorts of inferential or deductive processes that participants employ in other complex reasoning tasks". But is the contemporary inferential reasoning account algorithmic? Accounts of cue competition based on inferential processes certainly attempt to explain how higher order cognitive processes influence effects like blocking. Thus, inferential reasoning accounts, like associative accounts, are algorithmic in that they presumably describe the underlying processing of information by the subject. The problem with these accounts is that, at least in their current form, these inferential

---

[1] Although at the implementation level there are models of human learning based on neuroscience, our discussion of HCL models exclusively refers to those within the cognitive tradition.

processes are vaguely defined by a qualitative set of rules. However, we must acknowledge that this account is young and still in an early stage of development. Perhaps, within the next few years the inferential reasoning account of HCL will reach a level of formalization similar to that of associative models.

Information encoding and treatment

HCL accounts differ in the way that contingency-related information is assumed to be encoded. As previously mentioned, statistical models such as ΔP (Allan, 1980) assume that, for a single cue and outcome, subjects behave as if this information is encoded as co-occurrence frequencies for each of the cells of the 2×2 contingency matrix, or perhaps even memories of each trial. In contrast, in associative models (e.g., Rescorla & Wagner, 1972) information is encoded in the form of a few summary statistics, usually a single associative strength. Finally, inferential reasoning models are silent concerning the form of information encoding, although it is implicit that this encoding is detailed. This could be conceptualized as either a 2×2 contingency matrix or a set of rules or propositions based on each cell (e.g., "Cue A produces the outcome"). In this latter case, however, it would not be clear whether information is in fact encoded and stored in these rules or these propositions are mere verbal descriptions of information actually encoded as either frequencies or associations. For example, if information encoding was purely associative, and this information was accessible to conscious awareness, participants could verbalize this information in the form of a rule.

Differences in the way information is encoded foreshadow important advantages and disadvantages of the various HCL accounts. One of the implications of encoding information as co-occurrence frequencies is that it allows for the storage of richer memories than are assumed by associative models, minimally the frequency of each type of trial. This information-encoding strategy, in addition to allowing the computation of the different contingencies among events, allows for the retrieval of specific and detailed information, such as the number of times certain

events were conjointly present or absent (but not necessarily specific memory of each trial). Such nearly veridical memories could not be encoded and stored by associative models, which suffer from a paucity of encoded information. Frequency of co-occurrence information is demanding of memory capacity, more so than simple associative strength but less so than fully veridical memory. However, nearly veridical memories might not be necessary within current models of HCL because they merely attempt to explain the participants' response to a cue based on the cue–outcome relationship, something for which co-occurrence frequencies, associative strengths, and rules or propositions are equally valid. Without further use of co-occurrence frequencies, having encoded them is of no special merit, and one must acknowledge the greater parsimony of associative strength as being uniquely meritorious. Moreover, advocates of the associative account could claim that, although information encoding as frequencies in a contingency matrix allows for the retrieval of information like the number of occasions a specific trial type occurred, not all statistical models make use of this advantage. For example, in the ΔP model, detailed information such as the number of occasions on which different trial types took place only serves the purpose of computing the conditional probabilities of the outcome both in the presence and in the absence of the target cue. These probabilities are then used to compute the expected subject's response or verbal rating (i.e., the value of ΔP). It is therefore fair to say that the co-occurrence frequencies are unused in the framework of the ΔP model after the value of ΔP is computed. Nevertheless, due to its finer grain, information encoded in the form of frequencies in contingency tables can be acquired under more varied circumstances than can associatively encoded information. According to associative models, information can be acquired only through trial-by-trial training, whereas statistical models are open to the acquisition of new information both on a trial-by-trial basis and from frequency lists (e.g., Catena et al., 2002; Price & Yates, 1995; Shanks, 1991). However, the emphasis of associative models on the trial-by-trial encoding of information is not necessarily a disadvantage in all situations. It is precisely this feature that allows associative models to explain some trial-order effects, particularly recency effects (i.e., dominant impact of most recently acquired information on behaviour), which cannot be explained by statistical models without additional assumptions, such as time stamps on memories and weights dependent upon these stamps (for a detailed discussion, see Pineño & Miller, 2005).

Despite the potential advantages of frequency-based encoding relative to associative encoding, it is notable that statistical models make little use of this potential advantage. Moreover, they suffer from problems arising precisely from the way they use these frequencies. Because conditional probabilities are sensitive to relative as opposed to absolute frequencies, statistical models cannot simulate acquisition curves (Baker, Mercier, Vallée-Tourangeau, Frank, & Pan, 1993; Chatlosh et al., 1985; Shanks, 1987; but see Baker, Berbrier, & Vallée-Tourangeau, 1989).[2] For example, these models predict asymptotic responding after only one cue–outcome pairing (i.e., ΔP is 1 after only one acquisition trial provided that it is a Cell a type trial). Inferential models suffer from the same weakness; one reinforced trial (X–O) should establish the proposition that X is followed by O. The prediction of graded acquisition curves is a unique success of associative models.[3]

Acquisition versus performance processes in HCL phenomena

HCL accounts also differ in their emphasizing different stages of information processing to explain HCL phenomena, such as cue competition. In statistical models, as discussed before, subjects behave as if contingency information was directly encoded as co-occurrence frequencies in a contingency matrix. The acquisition of information is assumed to be free from any filter, taking place in a noncompetitive manner. In these models, cue competition arises from the computation of contingency. For example, in Allan's (1980) ΔP, blocking occurs because the A–O trials give rise to a high probability of the occurrence of the outcome in the absence of the target cue, $P(O|{\sim}C)$, which reduces the impact that the probability of the occurrence of the outcome in the presence of the target cue, $P(O|C)$, would otherwise have on the final contingency rating. (Admittedly this is not a compelling account of blocking because blocking is frequently seen, in a group that receives A–O followed by AX–O, relative to a control group that receives B–O followed by AX–O.) Therefore, to the extent that statistical models speak to cue competition, it is due to the impaired expression of the relationship between the target cue and the outcome. Most associative models, by contrast, assume that cue competition arises from processing during the acquisition stage. For example, the Rescorla and Wagner (1972) model assumes that the presence of the competing cue impairs learning of the target cue–outcome association. Finally, the inferential models implicitly hold a performance-focused view because, in order for participants to infer and apply rules, they must be able to process information previously acquired in a noncompetitive manner. In this vein, Beckers et al. (2005) demonstrated that outcome additivity training interpolated between the blocking treatment and test (Experiment 4) enhanced the blocking effect just like it did when it was given prior to the blocking treatment (Experiment 2). Therefore,

---

[2] The problem for statistical models of not predicting acquisition curves might be solved by assuming that the 2×2 contingency table is preexperimentally filled with noise, such that the initial values of the cells are greater than zero—that is, $(fa = fb = fc = fd) > 0$. However, it is not clear how these cells, for a specific cue and a specific outcome, could be available in memory prior to any kind of experience with these stimuli. If this approach were to be adopted, one would have to assume the existence of virtually an infinite number of cells for any possible combination of cues and outcomes.

[3] One might argue that only averaged acquisition curves are gradual because individual curves usually show a step-like function (e.g., Gallistel, Fairhurst, & Balsam, 2004). However, even individual curves do not commonly show an abrupt increase to asymptote after a single cue–outcome pairing, as predicted by statistical and inferential models.

the results of these experiments by Beckers et al. suggest that inferences are compared at the time of test, thereby supporting a view of inferential models as performance focused. However, in another paper De Houwer and Beckers (2003) reported that a distractor task during training (Experiment 1) or during both training and testing (Experiment 2) attenuated blocking, which in the inferential reasoning framework suggests that inferences are initially drawn during training and then compared during testing. Thus, critical information processing appears to occur during both training and testing, which realistically is not surprising. Nevertheless, it would be interesting to examine the consequences of a distractor task only during testing to determine if it too would attenuate blocking.

The stages of information processing in which cue competition is assumed to take place is one of the differentiating features of associative and statistical models of HCL that has received considerable attention (for a review, see R. R. Miller & Escobar, 2001). As part of this debate between acquisition-focused models (most associative models) and performance-focused models (statistical and inferential models), considerable evidence has been marshalled demonstrating that responding elicited at test by a target cue can be strongly affected by treatments performed after training with the target cue that do not directly involve this cue. These effects are referred to as retrospective revaluation (e.g., Dickinson & Burke, 1996), in which following compound training with two cues (e.g., AX−O trials), further training with A influences responding to cue X at test. Specifically, when Cue A is further paired with the outcome (i.e., A−O trials) following AX−O trials, weak responding to X at test is often found—an effect known as backward blocking (e.g., Shanks, 1985; Wasserman & Berglan, 1998). By contrast, when A-alone trials are given following AX−O trials, enhanced responding to X is usually found at test—an effect known as recovery from overshadowing (e.g., Larkin, Aitken, & Dickinson, 1998; Wasserman & Berglan, 1998). Retrospective revaluation cannot be accounted for by traditional associative models

(e.g., Mackintosh, 1975; Pearce & Hall, 1980; Rescorla & Wagner, 1972; Wagner, 1981) because, according to them, the associative strength of a cue can be updated only on trials on which the cue is present. Specifically, according to these models, any change in associative strength undergone by a cue is a direct function (among other factors) of the cue's salience, which adopts a positive value when the cue is present and a zero value when it is absent. Because, in retrospective revaluation effects, the target cue is absent during the revaluation treatment of its companion cue, no change in its associative status is predicted to occur from these models. That is, in this framework any treatment following training with the AX compound that does not include the presence of the target cue, X (e.g., A−O or A-alone trials) is expected to have no impact on X's associative strength. For some years, until the revision of some traditional associative models (e.g., Dickinson & Burke, 1996; Van Hamme & Wasserman, 1994), retrospective revaluation effects and other treatments not directly involving the target cue were considered to be exclusive support for performance-focused models (e.g., statistical models among others). Because, in these models all information is encoded and stored in order to be expressed in a competitive manner at the time of testing, the order in which different trial types take place during training is completely irrelevant. Therefore, A−O or A-alone trials are expected to have the same effect upon responding to X regardless of whether they are given before, during, or after training with the AX compound trials. On the one hand, this readily accounts for retrospective revaluation effects such as backward blocking. On the other hand, that statistical models ignore trial order is a mixed blessing because trial order is not irrelevant despite the occurrence of retrospective revaluation phenomena. For example, forward blocking is most often more robust than backward blocking all other factors being equal (e.g., Melchers, Lachnit, & Shanks, 2004; but see De Houwer et al., 2002).

Retrospective revaluation effects are still a fertile field for research. Recent studies have shown evidence of higher order retrospective reva-luation (e.g., De Houwer & Beckers, 2002b, 2002c; Macho & Burkart, 2002), an effect consist-ing of changes in responding to an absent cue, X, due to training with indirect associates of X. For example, in second order retrospective revaluation, a cue, X, is paired with another cue, A, which in turn is paired with a third cue, B. The effect of further training of Cue B alone is two-fold: (a) a change in responding to Cue A, contrary to the change undergone by B (first order retrospective revaluation) and (b) a change in responding to cue X, in the same direction as the change under-gone by B (second order retrospective revaluation). Findings on higher order retrospective revaluation have posed important difficulties even to models that were able to account for first order retrospec-tive revaluation (e.g., Dickinson & Burke, 1996; Van Hamme & Wasserman, 1994). However, these effects can be readily explained by an exten-sion of the comparator hypothesis (Denniston, Savastano, & Miller, 2001), developed to explain similar phenomena in animal conditioning (Denniston, Savastano, Blaisdell, & Miller, 2003), as well as some statistical models imple-menting recursive probability contrasts (Macho & Burkart, 2002).

Path dependence

Another manner in which statistical models might be viewed as superior to associative models is in their ability to anticipate path dependence. This prediction stems from statistical models' assump-tion of nearly veridical memory, rather than reten-tion of only summary statistics as is assumed by associative models (see earlier section *Information Encoding and Treatment*). Path dependence refers to the influence of a cue's complete training history on its current behavioural control. Path dependence is usually demonstrated by taking two cues that elicit the same responding despite different training histories and showing that radically differ-ent behaviours emerge as a function of a common added treatment. A compelling example of path dependence was provided in a study by Bouton (1984) concerned with reinstatement (i.e., recovery of responding after extinction treatment due to

outcome-alone presentations). In this study (Experiment 5), steps were made to obtain compar-able responding to a cue in conditions receiving different treatments with the cue, either mere acqui-sition training or acquisition training followed by extinction treatment. Despite comparable respond-ing prior to outcome-alone presentations, reinstate-ment was found to occur only in the condition given extinction treatment with the cue.

Evidence of a cue's path dependence poses a problem to associative models because, in these models, the only information that is retained is the current associative strength (and sometimes the current associability) of the cue, regardless of the training conditions that produced the association. The problem of path independence in most associative models (e.g., Rescorla & Wagner, 1972) is profound because, in these models, effects like extinction are due to the destruction of the previously acquired cue–outcome association. In other words, these models hypothesize active erasure of old memories (i.e., catastrophic interference, e.g., McCloskey & Cohen, 1989). Statistical models avoid anticipat-ing catastrophic interference because, according to these models, no memory is assumed to be erased during interference treatments such as extinction. Rather, statistical models explain inter-ference, either between cues (e.g., blocking) or between outcomes (e.g., extinction), as the addition of new information to the contingency matrix, resulting in a weakened contingency esti-mation without any loss of memory of pairings between the target cue and the outcome. For example, extinction training would increase the cue–no-outcome frequency (i.e., Cell *b* in the con-tingency table), thereby directly reducing the probability of the outcome in the presence of the cue, P(O|C). By contrast, cue competition such as blocking would be due to an increase in the no-cue–outcome frequency (i.e., Cell *c* in the con-tingency table). Although this treatment would not directly affect P(O|C), the final contingency rating would be diminished due to the increased probability of the outcome in the absence of the cue, P(O|∼C). Importantly, within the statistical account, no memory is assumed to be erased.

Rather, it is the addition of new memories that results in interference phenomena.

Like statistical models, inferential models are free from the problem of catastrophic interference. According to inferential models, interference (either between cues or between outcomes) is explained as due to the development of new rules that, when successfully applied at the time of testing, result in low ratings of the target cue. For example, extinction training would allow the participants to infer a new rule of the kind "the cue is no longer a predictor or cause of the outcome", without necessarily forgetting the previous cue–outcome pairings. An alternative new inference is "the cue is not consistently a predictor or cause of the outcome". The uncertainty as to which of these alternatives would constitute the new inference illustrates the lack of full specification of inferential theory at this time. Notably, neither inference can readily account for spontaneous recovery as a function of the retention interval.

Hybrid models: The integrative approach

In the previous section we discussed some advantages and problems of the associative, statistical, and inferential reasoning accounts of HCL. It is obvious from this discussion that each family of models has something unique to offer, but that there are flaws intrinsic to each account that cannot be easily overcome without incorporating some assumptions from other families.[4] This is precisely the strategy followed by some researchers: to incorporate some of the notions from different accounts into a single model. This integrative approach, resulting in hybrid models of HCL, has proven able to partially overcome the difficulties of pure models (e.g., strictly associative or statistical models).

Hybrid models in the associative tradition
Some theorists have developed hybrid models that incorporate notions from both statistical and inferential reasoning accounts (e.g., causal Bayes nets, see Glymour, 2003; Waldmann & Hagmayer, 2005; Waldmann & Martignon, 1998). Other types of hybrid model have been developed in the associative tradition in order to account for various types of Pavlovian phenomena. Such is the case of R. R. Miller and Matzel's (1988) comparator hypothesis and Bouton's (1993) retrieval failure model, which are readily applicable to HCL, although each was initially developed to account for specific findings in the Pavlovian paradigm. These two models can be viewed as essentially associative (i.e., they assume that contingency information is encoded and stored as associative strengths); however, they incorporate some mechanisms typical of statistical models. Like statistical theories, in these models interference phenomena are not due to acquisition deficits or unlearning (i.e., catastrophic interference), but to learning of associations that interfere with either retrieval or expression of the target association. In the case of Bouton's model, which was developed to account for interference between outcomes trained apart (e.g., extinction), these effects are due to an inhibitory cue–outcome association that coexists with the excitatory cue–outcome association and interferes with retrieval of the excitatory cue–outcome association at test. By contrast, in R. R. Miller and Matzel's comparator hypothesis, cue competition effects such as blocking are due to the impaired expression of the association between the target cue and the outcome. This expression deficit occurs because the presentation at test of the target cue (X) not only directly activates the outcome (O) representation (i.e., X–O association), but also indirectly activates a second representation of the outcome (i.e., X activates the representation of the competing cue, A, through the X–A within-compound association, and, in turn, this activation of Cue A activates the representation of the outcome through the A–O association).

Through this integrative approach, this hybrid model is able to overcome many of the problems

---

[4] Even a traditional model like ΔP can be viewed as a hybrid model in that it uses an associative structure to represent the cue–outcome pairings chronicled in Cell a.

of each purebred account. For example, the comparator hypothesis proposes a kind of information encoding (i.e., associative) that is economical in comparison to that of statistical models (i.e., frequencies of trial types), but rich enough to allow interactions between different memories at the time of behavioural expression. Therefore, despite this model summarizing information in terms of associative strengths, it bases its explanations of many learning phenomena on specific rules by which associations interact in order to produce responding at test, an approach similar to that of statistical models in their use of frequencies and the corresponding conditional probabilities in computing expected contingency ratings at test. But this integrative approach also involves a trade-off. As occurred with statistical models, because much or all information is acquired and retained as different associations and because associations only interact at the time of testing, this associative–statistical hybrid model is unable, without additional assumptions, to simulate trial-order effects, something that traditional associative models could explain (e.g., Rescorla & Wagner, 1972; for a detailed explanation, see Pineño & Miller, 2005). Notably, Bouton's (1993) model clearly predicts trial-order effects as a result of an additional assumption. Specifically, Bouton suggests that both inhibitory associations and second-learned associations wane with time faster than excitatory associations or first-learned associations. This assumption readily accounts for trial-order phenomena such as spontaneous recovery.

Putting top-down and bottom-up processes together in a single model

Associative accounts of HCL, as previously discussed, assume bottom-up processing of information. Using simple automatic processes, these models explain how humans acquire and transform information on event covariation into adaptative responding. Similarly, statistical accounts of HCL assume that participants behave as if they were doing bottom-up information processing. In contrast, inferential reasoning accounts assume that participants actively contrast hypotheses at

the time of testing, and that behaviour indicative of phenomena such as cue competition arises when these hypotheses are either confirmed or disconfirmed by experience. In these top-down inferential reasoning accounts, higher order cognitive processes control or at least modulate HCL. Moreover, it has been suggested that these processes may even be the basis of classical conditioning phenomena with both humans and nonhumans (Beckers et al., 2006).

However, as we previously mentioned, inferential models are incompletely specified, and their predictions are often vague. Hence, an account that includes both bottom-up processing (either associative or statistical) and top-down processing (inferential reasoning) might provide a more complete picture of HCL. Bottom-up processing is necessary to explain how information concerning covarying events is encoded and stored in the system, something that the inferential reasoning account currently fails to do. Top-down processing would allow covariation learning to be under the influence of more complex cognitive processes. This integrative approach between bottom-up and top-down processes, which has already been followed in the aforementioned Bayes nets, could also be used to account for outcome additivity and maximality effects (e.g., Beckers et al., 2005; Lovibond et al., 2003) in the framework of an associative or statistical model.

Any integration of an associative or statistical model with the inferential reasoning view, however, will face some theoretical difficulties, such as those arising from the mathematical formalization of inferences based on outcome additivity and maximality. However, such a formalization of inferential rules into quantitatively defined algorithms could be achieved by taking advantage of inference's close similarity to Boolean logic, which is already implemented in numerous computer programming languages. Perhaps more challenging, theoretical problems would arise from subtle interactions among the features of each type of model in a single framework. Let us assume that an associative model such as Rescorla and Wagner's (1972) model and an inferential reasoning model were to be the basis for building a hybrid. Some phenomena are explicable within each contributing model, which is unparsimonious, and, more problematic, the relative contributions of each contributing model toward explaining these phenomena would be unclear. For example, it would be necessary to determine what causes cue competition effects in such a hybrid model. That is, are effects like blocking due to an acquisition deficit (Rescorla & Wagner) or to successful acquisition but a failure to observe outcome additivity (inferential process)? If blocking is assumed to be due exclusively to the inferential process, some modifications will have to be made to the Rescorla and Wagner model in order to allow for noncompetitive acquisition of different cue–outcome associations (i.e., akin to the earlier model by Bush & Mosteller, 1951). However, even in this case, it would be necessary to refine the rules for the acquisition of associative strength and rules for drawing inference so that the strength of the associations could somehow be related to the additivity and maximality inferential rules. For example, the maximality rule (i.e., participants can only assess outcome additivity when the outcome is submaximal) applies only in cases in which the associative strength of the blocking cue, A, is already asymptotic. Consider the case in which V_A is 0.5 and V_X is 0.0. Even if a submaximal outcome (e.g., $\lambda = .7$, following Rescorla and Wagner's assumption of 1.0 as the maximal value of λ) were paired with the AX compound, there would still be room for participants to assess if cue X has any impact on the outcome (i.e., because $\lambda - V_{AX} = .2$). In summary, any formalization of a hybrid model that includes inferential reasoning processes will be a difficult task.

Some critical issues will have to be addressed before such a hybrid model can be formalized. For example, although it has been demonstrated that pretraining on outcome additivity enhances the blocking effect (e.g., Beckers et al., 2005), it is well known, since Dickinson et al.'s (1984) original report, that blocking in HCL can be observed with no need of such pretraining. Are we to conclude that humans and other animals presume as a default assumption the additivity of the causal

strengths of different cues presented in compound? The answer to this question is important because such an assumption would open a wide field for new questions such as, are these a priori assumptions innate or are they learned? If so, when and how are they learned? Given that outcome additivity effects have been observed not only in humans but also in rats (Beckers et al., 2006), answering those questions promises to be a difficult but potentially illuminating enterprise.

As an alternative to the possibility of a priori assumptions concerning outcome additivity and maximality, it is possible, although perhaps unparsimonious, that cue competition effects can take place at multiple stages in information processing. For example, such effects could occur due to a low-order process (i.e., acquisition, retrieval, and/or expression failure) as well as inferential reasoning processes. In this case, outcome additivity pretraining could enhance the observed cue competition effect by adding to a low-level process already taking place the impact of higher order reasoning (e.g., outcome additivity). However, the lower level process would have to result in an expression deficit because an acquisition deficit would not provide the knowledge base necessary for the inferential process. In sum, although an integrative approach involving both top-down and bottom-up processes would be able to account for most currently chronicled phenomena in the HCL literature, details are yet to be specified, and the product will suffer the complexities of any hybrid model that tends to thwart unambiguous predictions.

Summary and conclusion

The present paper has offered a brief comparison of the associative, statistical, and inferential reasoning accounts of HCL. Researchers can adopt one or another account of HCL, but it is fair to admit at this time that each account provides different insights on the conditions and processes underlying HCL phenomena. Because of this, we have suggested that, for the short term, future understanding of HCL may depend upon the development of hybrid models that integrate specific notions from different accounts. In fact, some of the already existing hybrid models have proven successful in dealing with those phenomena for which they were developed, relative to the theoretically pure accounts on which they are based. We anticipate that research in HCL during the next few years will prove to be fertile thanks in part to the addition of inferential reasoning accounts to the long-standing debate between associative and statistical accounts.

In the Introduction we mentioned that the field of HCL is rapidly evolving. The inferential reasoning account has sent a message, and we certainly have to take it seriously. Time and research will determine if the inferential reasoning view survives new evidence and further revisions of associative and statistical approaches. Will the inferential account stand on its own or will it symbiotically share assumptions with other accounts (i.e., associative or statistical)? This question will not be answered until the inferential view is more clearly specified. In the meantime, the fresh air brought by the inferential reasoning view to our field will reinvigorate the study of HCL and will encourage revision and development of models of HCL.

REFERENCES

Allan, L. G. (1980). A note on measurement of contingency between two binary variables in judgement tasks. *Bulletin of the Psychonomic Society, 15*, 147–149.

Allan, L. G. (1993). Human contingency judgments: Rule based or associative? *Psychological Bulletin, 114*, 435–448.

Allan, L. G. (2003). Assessing Power PC. *Learning & Behavior, 31*, 192–204.

Allan, L. G., & Jenkins, H. M. (1980). The judgment of contingency and the nature of the response alternatives. *Canadian Journal of Psychology, 34*, 1–11.

Allan, L. G., & Jenkins, H. M. (1983). The effect of representations of binary variables on judgment of influence. *Learning and Motivation, 14*, 381–405.

Allan, L. G., & Tangen, J. M. (2005). Judging relationships between events: How do we do it? *Canadian Journal of Experimental Psychology, 59*, 22–27.

Alloy, L. B., & Abramson, L. Y. (1979). Judgment of contingency in depressed and nondepressed students:

Sadder but wiser? *Journal of Experimental Psychology: General, 108*, 441–485.

Anderson, J. R. (1980). *Cognitive psychology and its implications.* New York: W. H. Freeman and Co.

Arcediano, F., Matute, H., & Miller, R. R. (1997). Blocking of conditioned responding in humans. *Learning and Motivation, 28*, 188–199.

Baker, A. G. (1974). Conditioned inhibition is not the symmetrical opposite of conditioned excitation: A test of the Rescorla–Wagner model. *Learning and Motivation, 5*, 369–379.

Baker, A. G., Berbrier, M. W., & Vallee-Tourangeau, F. (1989). Judgments of a 2 × 2 contingency table: Sequential processing and the learning curve. *Quarterly Journal of Experimental Psychology, 41B*, 65–97.

Baker, A. G., Mercier, P., Vallée-Tourangeau, F., Frank, R., & Pan, M. (1993). Selective associations and causality judgments: Presence of a strong causal factor may reduce judgments of a weaker one. *Journal of Experimental Psychology: Learning, Memory, and Cognition, 19*, 414–432.

Baker, A. G., Murphy, R. A., & Vallee-Tourangeau, F. (1996). Associative and normative models of causal induction: Reacting to versus understanding cause. In D. R. Shanks, K. J. Holyoak, & D. L. Medin (Eds.), *The psychology of learning and motivation* (Vol. 34, pp. 1–45). New York: Academic Press.

Beckers, T., De Houwer, J., Pineño, O., & Miller, R. R. (2005). Outcome additivity and outcome maximality influence cue competition in human causal learning. *Journal of Experimental Psychology: Learning, Memory, and Cognition, 31*, 238–249.

Beckers, T., Miller, R. R., De Houwer, J., & Urushihara, K. (2006). Reasoning rats: Forward blocking in Pavlovian animal conditioning is sensitive to constraints of causal inference. *Journal of Experimental Psychology: General, 135*, 92–102.

Bouton, M. E. (1984). Differential control by context in the inflation and reinstatement paradigms. *Journal of Experimental Psychology: Animal Behavior Processes, 10*, 56–74.

Bouton, M. E. (1993). Context, time, and memory retrieval in the interference paradigms of Pavlovian learning. *Psychological Bulletin, 114*, 80–99.

Buehner, M. J., Cheng, P. W., & Clifford, D. (2003). From covariation to causation: A test of the assumption of causal power. *Journal of Experimental Psychology: Learning, Memory, and Cognition, 29*, 1119–1140.

Bush, R. R., & Mosteller, F. (1951). A mathematical model for simple learning. *Psychological Review, 58,* 313–323.

Catena, A., Maldonado, A., Megias, J. L., & Frese, B. (2002). Judgement frequency, belief revision, and serial processing of causal information. *Quarterly Journal of Experimental Psychology, 55B,* 267–281.

Chapman, G. B. (1991). Trial order affects cue interaction in contingency judgment. *Journal of Experimental Psychology: Learning, Memory, and Cognition, 17,* 837–854.

Chapman, G. B., & Robbins, S. J. (1990). Cue interaction in human contingency judgment. *Memory & Cognition, 18,* 537–545.

Chatlosh, D. L., Neunaber, D. J., & Wasserman, E. A. (1985). Response–outcome contingency: Behavioral and judgmental effects of appetitive and aversive outcomes with college students. *Learning and Motivation, 16,* 1–34.

Cheng, P. W. (1997). From covariation to causation: A causal power theory. *Psychological Review, 104,* 367–405.

Cheng, P. W., & Novick, L. R. (1992). Covariation in natural causal induction. *Psychological Review, 99,* 365–382.

De Houwer, J. (2002). Forward blocking depends on retrospective inferences about the presence of the blocked cue during the elemental phase. *Memory & Cognition, 30,* 24–33.

De Houwer, J., & Beckers, T. (2002a). A review of recent developments in research and theories on human contingency learning. *Quarterly Journal of Experimental Psychology, 55B,* 289–310.

De Houwer, J., & Beckers, T. (2002b). Higher-order retrospective revaluation in human causal learning. *Quarterly Journal of Experimental Psychology, 55B,* 137–151.

De Houwer, J., & Beckers, T. (2002c). Second-order backward blocking and unovershadowing in human causal learning. *Experimental Psychology, 49,* 27–33.

De Houwer, J., & Beckers, T. (2003). Secondary task difficulty modulates forward and backward blocking in human contingency learning. *Quarterly Journal of Experimental Psychology, 56B,* 345–357.

De Houwer, J., Beckers, T., & Glautier, S. (2002). Outcome and cue properties modulate blocking. *Quarterly Journal of Experimental Psychology, 55A,* 965–985.

Denniston, J. C., Savastano, H. I., Blaisdell, A. P., & Miller, R. R. (2003). Cue competition as a retrieval deficit. *Learning and Motivation, 34,* 1–31.

Denniston, J. C., Savastano, H. I., & Miller, R. R. (2001). The extended comparator hypothesis: Learning by contiguity, responding by relative strength. In R. R. Mowrer & S. B. Klein (Eds.), *Handbook of contemporary learning theories.* Hillsdale, NJ: Lawrence Erlbaum Associates, Inc.

Dickinson, A., & Burke, J. (1996). Within-compound associations mediate the retrospective revaluation of causality judgements. *Quarterly Journal of Experimental Psychology, 49B,* 60–80.

Dickinson, A., Shanks, D. R., & Evenden, J. (1984). Judgement of act–outcome contingency: The role of selective attribution. *Quarterly Journal of Experimental Psychology, 36A,* 29–50.

Gallistel, C. R., Fairhurst, S., & Balsam, P. (2004). The learning curve: Implications of a quantitative analysis. *PNAS, 101,* 13124–13131.

Gluck, M., & Bower, G. H. (1988). From conditioning to category learning: An adaptative network model. *Journal of Experimental Psychology: General, 117,* 227–247.

Glymour, C. (2003). Learning, prediction and causal Bayes nets. *Trends in Cognitive Science, 7,* 43–48.

Glymour, C., & Cheng, P. J. (1998). Causal mechanism and probability: A normative approach. In M. Oaksford & N. Chater (Eds.), *Rational models of cognition.* Oxford, UK: Oxford University Press.

Jenkins, H., & Ward, W. (1965). Judgment of contingency between responses and outcomes. *Psychological Monographs, 7,* 1–17.

Johnson-Laird, P. N. (1988). *The computer and the mind: An introduction to cognitive science.* Cambridge, MA: Harvard University Press.

Kamin, L. J. (1968). "Attention-like" processes in classical conditioning. In M. R. Jones (Ed.), *Miami symposium on the prediction of behavior: Aversive stimulation* (pp. 9–31). Miami, FL: University of Miami Press.

Kelley, H. H. (1967). Attribution theory in social psychology. *Nebraska Symposium on Motivation, 15,* 192–238.

Larkin, M. J. W., Aitken, M. R. F., & Dickinson, A. (1998). Retrospective revaluation of causal judgments under positive and negative contingencies. *Journal of Experimental Psychology: Learning, Memory, and Cognition, 24,* 1331–1352.

Lindsay, P. H., & Norman, D. A. (1972). *Human information processing. An introduction to psychology.* New York: Academic Press.

Livesey, E. J., & Boakes, R. A. (2004). Outcome additivity, elemental processing and blocking in human causality judgements. *Quarterly Journal of Experimental Psychology, 57B*, 361–379.

Lober, K., & Shanks, D. R. (2000). Is causal induction based on causal power? Critique of Cheng (1997). *Psychological Review, 107*, 195–212.

López, F. J., Almaraz, J., Fernández, P., & Shanks, D. (1999). Adquisición progresiva del conocimiento sobre relaciones predictivas: Curvas de aprendizaje en juicios de contingencia. *Psicothema, 11*, 337–349.

López, F. J., Cobos, P. L., Caño, A., & Shanks, D. R. (1998). The rational analysis of human causal and probability judgement. In M. Oaksford & N. Chater (Eds.), *Rational models of cognition* (pp. 314–352). Oxford, UK: Oxford University Press.

Lovibond, P. F., Been, S., Mitchell, C. J., Bouton, M. E., & Frohardt, R. (2003). Forward and backward blocking of causal judgment is enhanced by additivity of the effect magnitude. *Memory & Cognition, 31*, 133–142.

Macho, S., & Burkart, J. (2002). Recursive retrospective revaluation of causal judgments. *Journal of Experimental Psychology: Learning, Memory, and Cognition, 28*, 1171–1186.

Mackintosh, N. J. (1975). A theory of attention: Variations in the associability of stimuli with reinforcement. *Psychological Review, 82*, 276–298.

Marr, D. (1982), *Vision: A computational approach*. San Francisco: Freeman & Co.

McCloskey, M., & Cohen, N. (1989). Catastrophic interference in connectionist networks: The sequential learning problem. In G. H. Bower (Ed.), *The psychology of learning and motivation* (Vol. 24, pp. 109–165). San Diego, CA: Academic Press.

Melchers, K. G., Lachnit, H., & Shanks, D. R. (2004). Within-compound associations in retrospective revaluation and in direct learning: A challenge for comparator theory. *Quarterly Journal of Experimental Psychology, 57B*, 25–53.

Miller, G. A., Galanter, E., & Pribram, K. H. (1960). *Plans and the structure of behavior*. New York: Holt, Rinehart & Winston.

Miller, R. R., Barnet, R. C., & Grahame, N. J. (1995). Assessment of the Rescorla–Wagner model. *Psychological Bulletin, 117*, 1–24.

Miller, R. R., & Escobar, M. (2001). Contrasting acquisition-focused and performance-focused models of acquired behavior. *Current Directions in Psychological Science, 10*, 141–145.

Miller, R. R., & Matute, H. (1996). Animal analogues of causal judgment. In D. R. Shanks, K. J.

Holyoak, & D. L. Medin (Ed.), *The psychology of learning and motivation* (Vol. 34, pp. 133–166). San Diego, CA: Academic Press.

Miller, R. R., & Matzel, L. D. (1988). The comparator hypothesis: A response rule for the expression of associations. In G. H. Bower (Ed.), *The psychology of learning and motivation* (Vol. 22, pp. 51–92). San Diego, CA: Academic Press.

Mitchell, C. J., & Lovibond, P. F. (2002). Backward and forward blocking in human electrodermal conditioning: Blocking requires an assumption of outcome additivity. *Quarterly Journal of Experimental Psychology, 55B*, 311–329.

Mitchell, C. J., Lovibond, P. F., & Condoleon, M. (2005). Evidence for deductive reasoning in blocking of causal judgments. *Learning and Motivation, 36*, 77–87.

Neunaber, D. J., & Wasserman, E. A. (1986). The effects of unidirectional versus bidirectional rating procedures on college students' judgments of response–outcome contingency. *Learning and Motivation, 17*, 162–179.

Pavlov, I. P. (1927). *Conditioned reflexes*. London: Clarendon Press.

Pearce, J. M., & Hall, G. (1980). A model for Pavlovian learning: Variations in the effectiveness of conditioned but not of unconditioned stimuli. *Psychological Review, 87*, 532–552.

Pearl, J. (1993). Graphical models, causality, and interventions. *Statistical Science, 8*, 266–269.

Pearl, J. (2000). *Causality: Models, reasoning, and inference*. Cambridge, UK: Cambridge University Press.

Pineño, O., & Miller, R. R. (2005). Primacy and recency effects in extinction and latent inhibition: A selective review with implications for models of learning. *Behavioural Processes, 69*, 223–235.

Price, P. C., & Yates, J. F. (1995). Associative and rule-based accounts of cue interaction in contingency judgement. *Journal of Experimental Psychology: Learning, Memory, and Cognition, 21*, 1639–1655.

Rescorla, R. A. (1968). Probability of shock in the presence and absence of CS in fear conditioning. *Journal of Comparative and Physiological Psychology, 66*, 1–5.

Rescorla, R. A., & Wagner, A. R. (1972). A theory of Pavlovian conditioning: Variations in the effectiveness of reinforcement and nonreinforcement. In A. H. Black & W. F. Prokasy (Eds.), *Classical conditioning II: Current research and theory* (pp. 64–99). New York: Appleton-Century-Crofts.

Shanks, D. R. (1985). Forward and backward blocking in human contingency judgment. *Quarterly Journal of Experimental Psychology, 37B*, 1–21.

Shanks, D. R. (1987). Acquisition functions in contingency judgment. *Learning and Motivation, 18*, 147–166.

Shanks, D. R. (1991). On similarities between causal judgements in experienced and described situations. *Psychological Science, 2*, 341–350.

Shanks, D. R. (1995). Is human learning rational? *Quarterly Journal of Experimental Psychology, 48A*, 29–50.

Shanks, D. R., & Dickinson, A. (1987). Associative accounts of causality judgement. In G. H. Bower (Ed.), *The psychology of learning and motivation* (Vol. 21, pp. 229–261). San Diego, CA: Academic Press.

Shanks, D. R., Holyoak, K. J., & Medin, D. L. (1996a). *Causal learning: The psychology of learning and motivation* (Vol. 34). New York: Academic Press.

Shanks, D. R., López, F. J., Darby, R. J., & Dickinson, A. (1996b). Distinguishing associative and probabilistic contrast theories of human contingency judgment. In D. R. Shanks, K. J. Holyoak, & D. L. Medin (Eds.), *The psychology of learning and motivation: Causal learning* (pp. 265–311). San Diego, CA: Academic Press.

Spellman, B. A. (1996). Acting as intuitive scientists: Contingency judgments are made while controlling for alternative potential causes. *Psychological Science, 7*, 337–342.

Spellman, B. A., Price, C. M., & Logan, J. M. (2001). How two causes are different from one: The use of (un)conditional information in Simpson's paradox. *Memory & Cognition, 29*, 193–208.

Vandorpe, S., De Houwer, J., & Beckers, T. (2005). Further evidence for the role of inferential reasoning in forward blocking. *Memory & Cognition, 33*, 1047–1056.

Van Hamme, L. J., & Wasserman, E. A. (1994). Cue competition in causality judgments: The role of non-presentation of compound stimulus elements. *Learning and Motivation, 25*, 127–151.

Wagner, A. R. (1981). SOP: A model of automatic memory processing in animal behavior. In N. E. Spear & R. R. Miller (Eds.), *Information processing in animals: Memory mechanisms* (pp. 5–47). Hillsdale, NJ: Lawrence Erlbaum Associates, Inc.

Waldmann, M. E. (1996). Knowledge-based causal induction. In D. R. Shanks, K. J. Holyoak, & D. L. Medin (Eds.), *The psychology of learning and motivation*: Vol. 34. *Causal learning* (pp. 47–88). San Diego, CA: Academic Press.

Waldmann, M. R. (2000). Competition among causes but not effects in predictive and diagnostic learning. *Journal of Experimental Psychology: Learning, Memory, and Cognition, 26*, 53–76.

Waldmann, M. R. (2001). Predictive versus diagnostic causal learning: Evidence from an overshadowing paradigm. *Psychonomic Bulletin & Review, 8*, 600–608.

Waldmann, M. R., & Hagmayer, Y. (2005). Seeing versus doing: Two models of accessing causal knowledge. *Journal of Experimental Psychology: Learning, Memory, and Cognition, 31*, 216–227.

Waldmann, M. R., & Holyoak, K. J. (1992). Predictive and diagnostic learning within causal models: Asymmetries in cue competition. *Journal of Experimental Psychology: General, 121*, 222–36.

Waldmann, M. R., & Martignon, L. (1998). A Bayesian network model of causal learning. In M. A. Gernsbacher & S. J. Derry (Eds.), *Proceedings of the Twentieth Annual Conference of the Cognitive Science Society*. Mahwah, NJ: Lawrence Erlbaum Associates, Inc.

Waldmann, M. R., & Walker, J. M. (2005). Competence and performance in causal learning. *Learning & Behavior, 33*, 211–229.

Wason, P. C., & Johnson-Laird, P. N. (1972). *Psychology of reasoning: Structure and content.* Cambridge, MA: Harvard University Press.

Wasserman, E. A. (1990). Detecting response–outcome relations: Toward an understanding of the causal texture of the environment. In G. H. Bower (Ed.), *The psychology of learning and motivation* (Vol. 26, pp. 27–82). San Diego, CA: Academic Press.

Wasserman, E. A., & Berglan, L. R. (1998). Backward blocking and recovery from overshadowing in human causal judgment: The role of within-compound associations. *Quarterly Journal of Experimental Psychology, 51B*, 121–138.

Wasserman, E. A., Chatlosh, D. L., & Neunaber, D. J. (1983). Perception of causal relations in humans: Factors affecting judgments of response–outcome contingencies under free-operant procedures. *Learning and Motivation, 14*, 406–432.

Wasserman, E. A., Elek, S. M., Chatlosh, D. L., & Baker, A. G. (1993). Rating causal relations: Role of probability in judgments of response–outcome contingency. *Journal of Experimental Psychology: Learning, Memory, and Cognition, 19*, 174–188.

Wasserman, E. A., Kao, S.-F., Van Hamme, L. J., Katagiri, M., & Young, M. E. (1996). Causation and association. In D. R. Shanks, K. J. Holyoak, &

D. L. Medin (Eds.), *The psychology of learning and motivation: Causal learning* (pp. 207–264). San Diego, CA: Academic Press.

Williams, D. A., Sagness, K. E., & McPhee, J. E. (1994). Configural and elemental strategies in predictive learning. *Journal of Experimental Psychology: Learning, Memory, and Cognition, 20*, 694–709.

Wills, A. J. (Ed.). (2005). *New directions in human associative learning.* Mahwah, NJ: Lawrence Erlbaum Associates, Inc.

Wu, M., & Cheng, P. W. (1999). Why causation need not follow from statistical association: Boundary conditions for the evaluation of generative and preventive causal powers. *Psychological Science, 10*, 92–97.

THE QUARTERLY JOURNAL OF EXPERIMENTAL PSYCHOLOGY
2007, 60 (3), 330–355

Inferences about unobserved causes in human contingency learning

York Hagmayer and Michael R. Waldmann

University of Göttingen, Göttingen, Germany

Estimates of the causal efficacy of an event need to take into account the possible presence and influence of other unobserved causes that might have contributed to the occurrence of the effect. Current theoretical approaches deal differently with this problem. Associative theories assume that at least one unobserved cause is always present. In contrast, causal Bayes net theories (including Power PC theory) hypothesize that unobserved causes may be present or absent. These theories generally assume independence of different causes of the same event, which greatly simplifies modelling learning and inference. In two experiments participants were requested to learn about the causal relation between a single cause and an effect by observing their co-occurrence (Experiment 1) or by actively intervening in the cause (Experiment 2). Participants' assumptions about the presence of an unobserved cause were assessed either after each learning trial or at the end of the learning phase. The results show an interesting dissociation. Whereas there was a tendency to assume interdependence of the causes in the online judgements during learning, the final judgements tended to be more in the direction of an independence assumption. Possible explanations and implications of these findings are discussed.

Most events have many causes, most of which we do not know or cannot observe. Nevertheless, despite the fact that the observed effects are also influenced by unobserved events, we are capable of learning about the causal efficacy of observed causes. A large body of theoretical and empirical knowledge has been accumulated on how we make causal strength assessments in such situations (Cheng, 1997; Shanks, 1987; Shanks, Holyoak, & Medin, 1996; Waldmann & Hagmayer, 2001; Wasserman, Elek, Chatlosh, & Baker, 1993; White, 2003). However, the question

has largely been neglected in the literature as to what we can learn about the causes that we cannot observe (but see Kushnir, Gopnik, Schulz, & Danks, 2003; Luhmann & Ahn, 2003). For example, in the early days of AIDS nobody knew about the virus and its lethal capacity. The known observable causes included minor infections, which apparently led to serious, live threatening conditions, such as pneumonia. However, the seriousness of the disease in light of the rather harmless causes led to the search for additional unobserved causes. Eventually the

Correspondence should be addressed to Y. Hagmayer or M. Waldmann, Department of Psychology, University of Göttingen, Gosslerstr. 14, 37073 Göttingen, Germany. E-mail: york.hagmayer@bio.uni-goettingen.de or michael.waldmann@bio.uni-goettingen.de

We thank Tom Beckers, Marc Buehner, and an anonymous reviewer for helpful comments on an earlier draft of this paper. We also thank M. Rappe for his help with planning and running Experiment 2. Portions of this research were presented at the Twenty-fifth Annual Conference of the Cognitive Science Society, Chicago, in 2004.

DOI:10.1080/17470210601002470

HIV virus was discovered, and theories were developed that traced the complex causal pathways underlying the disease.

Although most theories of causal learning did not directly address inferences about unobserved causes, most theories took the possibility of such causal factors into account. The question of how to assess causal strength when there are unobserved causes has challenged normative theories of causality and psychological theories of causal reasoning for some time. A number of different accounts have been proposed analysing how the causal strength of an observed factor can be accurately estimated if certain assumptions are made about potential unobserved causes. In this article we study more directly what people infer about unobserved causes during learning. First we give a brief overview of how associative and causal Bayes net theories handle unobserved causes. Based on these theories we derive predictions about the inferences that people should make about the presence and causal influence of unobserved causes. In the second part of the article we present two experiments in which we assessed the assumptions of learners about the strength and probability of unobserved causes. In the final section we discuss potential theoretical implications of these findings.

Theoretical accounts of unobserved causes

Unobserved events can be linked in complex networks and can simultaneously cause several observed events, leading to confoundings (see Pearl, 2000; Spirtes, Glymour, & Scheines, 1993). In the present research we focus on a simple causal situation consisting of a single observable cause C and one possible unobserved cause A, both influencing a joint observable effect E. Figure 1 illustrates the causal model. The two observable events C and E are statistically related. There are three questions one might ask in this kind of situation: How does C influence E? How are C and A related to each other? How does A influence E?

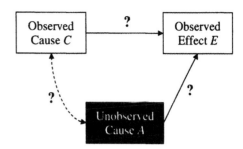

Figure 1. *Causal model of a situation in which an observable cause C and an unobserved cause A both influence an observable effect E. The question marks indicate the relations that participants were requested to assess.*

Associative theories

Associative theories, such as the Rescorla–Wagner theory (Rescorla & Wagner, 1972), would model this task as learning about the association between a cue representing the observed cause and an outcome representing the effect. Along with the observable cause cue a second background (or context) cue would be part of the model. This background cue is assumed to be always present and to represent all other factors that might also generate the outcome. Thus, the background cue would play the role of representing the unobserved cause A in the outlined causal model. According to the Rescorla–Wagner rule, only weights of cues that are present in the learning trial are being updated. Therefore, the permanently present background cue will generally compete with the cause cue in cases in which the cause cue is present. If the outcome is also present, the associative weights of both cues will be raised; if the outcome is absent, the weights will be lowered. However, in cases in which the cause cue is absent, only the weight of the background cue will be altered. At the asymptote of learning the associative weight of the observed cause will equal the contingency of the cause cue and the outcome, which is defined as the numeric difference between the probabilities of the effect in the presence and the absence of the observed cause—that is, $\Delta P = P(e|c) - P(e|\sim c)$; (see Cheng, 1997; Danks, 2003). The associative weight of the background cue will correspond to the probability of the outcome in the absence of the cause cue. Thus, the more often the outcome (= effect) occurs on its own, the higher the associative weight of the background cue will be.

Consequently associative theories would predict that participants assume an unobserved cause to be always present. In addition, these theories predict that at the asymptote the unobserved cause's strength would match the probability of the effect in the observable cause's absence, which corresponds to the associative weight linking the context cue and the effect, and that the estimated causal influence of the observable cause corresponds to the observed contingency.

Causal Bayes nets

Causal Bayes net theories of causal learning offer accounts for a large variety of problems—for example, for hypothesis testing, model generation, and parameter estimation (see Danks, in press; Glymour, 2001; Griffiths & Tenenbaum, 2005; Spirtes et al., 1993; Tenenbaum & Griffiths, 2003). In fact, causal Bayes net theories are a rather heterogeneous group of theories. While all theories agree on the representation of causal structures as acyclic graphs capturing relations of conditional dependence among the events, they assume different processes of learning and inference. Whereas some theories rely on Bayesian inferences involving the application of Bayes' theorem (e.g., Tenenbaum & Griffiths, 2003), other theories do not (e.g., Cheng's, 1997, Power PC theory; see below).

All causal Bayes net theories agree on the assumption that causal learning and reasoning are based on structured causal models (i.e., causal Bayes nets) of a domain. Causal Bayes nets consist of graphs of causal models and parameters representing base rates, causal strength, and causal interactions. The graph depicted in Figure 1 depicts a common-effect structure in which two causes—one observable and one unobserved—affect a single effect. The graphs specify relations of conditional dependence and independence amongst the variables within the model. For example, a common-effect model such as the one depicted in Figure 1 represents the assumption that the observed cause and the unobserved cause

are independent of each other, that the two causes are related to the effect, and that the two causes are negatively related conditional upon the effect—that is, if the effect and one of the causes is observed the presence of the second cause is less likely than its presence (i.e., explaining away). Thus, causal Bayes net theories in general assume that different causes of a common effect are independent of each other, as long as there is no further causal factor that affects the two causes and thereby creates dependence between them.

Power PC theory. Cheng's (1997) Power PC analysis of the causal impact of a single cause can be viewed as a special case of a causal Bayes net in which two causes independently influence a joint common effect (see Glymour, 2001). Based on this theory some predictions for the probability and causal power of an unobserved cause can be inferred. The theory presupposes that the occurrence of the effect E is a consequence of the causal powers of the observed cause C (p_c), of an unobserved cause A (p_a), and of their base rates $P(c)$ and $P(a)$. Formally the probability of the effect equals the sum of the base rates of the two causes multiplied by their causal power minus the intersection of the causes multiplied by both causal powers:

$$P(e) = P(c) \cdot p_c + P(a) \cdot p_a - P(c) \cdot P(a) \cdot p_c \cdot p_a.$$

Therefore the probability of the effect E conditional upon an observation of cause C— that is, $P(c) = 1$—is

$$P(e|c) = p_c + P(a|c) \cdot p_a - P(a|c) \cdot p_c \cdot p_a \quad 1$$

The probability of the effect given that the observable cause C is absent—that is, $P(c) = 0$—is

$$P(e|\sim c) = P(a|\sim c) \cdot p_a \quad 2$$

Equations 1 and 2 hold irrespective of whether the observed cause C and the unobserved cause A are dependent, $P(a|c) \neq P(a|\sim c)$, or independent, $P(a|c) = P(a|\sim c)$. Both Equation 1 and Equation 2 have at least two parameters that cannot be directly estimated on the basis of the observed relation between C and E. Thus, neither the probability nor the causal power of the unobserved cause can be directly inferred from the observable data.

Power PC theory makes the additional assumption that different causes of the same effect are independent of each other—that is, the theory assumes that the observed and the unobserved causes are not statistically related, $P(a|c) = P(a|\sim c) = P(a)$. This assumption allows it to derive estimates for the causal power of the observable causes even if there are other unknown causes generating the same effect. Based on this assumption Equations 1 and 2 can be simplified into

$$P(e|c) = p_c + P(a) \cdot p_a - P(a) \cdot p_a \cdot p_c \qquad 1'$$

The probability of the effect given that the observable cause C is absent—that is, $P(c) = 0$—is

$$P(e| \sim c) = P(a) \cdot p_a \qquad 2'$$

Inserting 2' into 1' yields

$$P(e|c) = p_c + P(e| \sim c) - P(e| \sim c) \cdot p_c \qquad 1''$$

which can be rearranged into the well-known formula for generative causal power

$$p_c = \frac{P(e|c) - P(e| \sim c)}{(1 - P(e| \sim c))}. \qquad 3; \text{ power formula}$$

What inferences can be made about the unobserved cause? The independence assumption of Power PC theory implies that the probability of the unobserved cause stays the same regardless of whether the observed cause has occurred or not. Moreover, Equation 2' implies that the causal power of the unobserved cause and its probability have to be at least as big as the probability of the effect in the absence of the observed cause, $p_a \geq P(e|\sim c)$ and $P(a) \geq P(e|\sim c)$). Equations 1' and 2' provide additional constraints for the two unknown parameters. Equation 2' requires that the product of the estimated probability and the

causal power of the unobserved cause has to equal the observable probability of the effect in the observable cause's absence. In sum, Power PC theory like other causal Bayes net theories assumes independence between causes and provides constraints for the probability and causal power of unobserved causes. This assumption is necessary to make precise inferences about the power of observed variables. However, these theories may also drop this assumption if it seems unwarranted. In the next section we give some examples for inferences that are possible without assuming independence.

Inferring unobserved causes

In this section we present two formal Bayesian analyses of potential inferences about an unobserved cause, which do not rely on the assumption of independence. The first analysis is based on probability calculus and concerns inferences about the probability and strength of a unobserved cause based on a set of observed data. The second analysis deals with inferences based on single observations of a given cause and an effect. The two analyses show that observable causal relations normatively allow some inferences to be drawn about unobserved causes, even if no independence among the causes is assumed. Readers not interested in the formal details may prefer to skip this section. The results of the analyses are summarized in the next section.

The first analysis is based on the causal model depicted in Figure 1. Two causes, C and A, one of which is not observable (A), are assumed to influence a joint effect E. Based on the chain rule of probability theory, the joint probabilities of the three events can be factorized as follows:

$$P(E, A, C) = P(E|A, C)*P(A, C)$$

While the joint probability of the two observable events $P(E, C)$ can be estimated on the basis of the observable events, neither the probability of the effect conditional on the pattern of the observed and unobserved causes, $P(E|A,C)$, nor the joint probability of the observed and unobserved cause, $P(A, C)$, can be estimated. Thus, additional assumptions have to be made. There is one popular assumption that is frequently made with causal Bayes nets (Jensen, 1997; Pearl, 1988), which is the so called noisy-or assumption. This assumption informally states (a) that each cause deterministically causes the effect unless its impact is intercepted by an inhibitor, and (b) that the inhibitors are independent of each other. Note that it is not assumed that the causes are independent. For example, if there are two causes of a common effect, and both are present, then either the first cause generates the effect or the second cause generates the effect or both do. Thus, the effect will only fail to occur if both causes are inhibited. Formally

$$P(e|a.c) = 1 - (1 - P(e|{\sim}a.c)) \cdot (1 - P(e|a.{\sim}c))$$

Based on the noisy-or rule the joint probability of cause and effect co-occurring can be calculated by

$$
\begin{aligned}
P(e.c) &= P(e|a.c) \cdot P(a|c) \cdot P(c) \\
&\quad + P(e|{\sim}a.c) \cdot P({\sim}a|c) \cdot P(c) \\
&= \{1 - [1 - P(e|{\sim}a.c)] \cdot [1 - P(e|a.{\sim}c)]\} \\
&\quad \cdot P(a|c) \cdot P(c) + P(e|{\sim}a.c) \cdot P({\sim}a|c) \cdot P(c)
\end{aligned}
$$

Conditionalized on the presence of the observable cause C, the following equation results:

$$
\begin{aligned}
P(e|c) &= \{[1 - [1 - P(e|{\sim}a.c)] \\
&\quad \cdot [1 - P(e|a.{\sim}c)]\} \cdot P(a|c) \qquad 4 \\
&\quad + P(e|{\sim}a.c) \cdot P({\sim}a|c)
\end{aligned}
$$

The probability of the effect occurring on its own can also be calculated:

$$
\begin{aligned}
P(e.{\sim}c) &= P(e|a.{\sim}c) \cdot P(a|{\sim}c) \cdot P({\sim}c) \\
&\quad + P(e|{\sim}a.{\sim}c) \cdot P({\sim}a|{\sim}c) \cdot P({\sim}c)
\end{aligned}
$$

According to the noisy-or assumption absent causes never lead to the effect—that is, $P(e|{\sim}$

$a.{\sim}c) = 0$. Therefore

$$P(e.{\sim}c) = P(e|a.{\sim}c) \cdot P(a|{\sim}c) \cdot P({\sim}c)$$

Conditional on the absence of the observable cause C, this equation can be further simplified into

$$P(e|{\sim}c) = P(e|a.{\sim}c) \cdot P(a|{\sim}c) \qquad 5$$

It should be noted that thus far no assumption about the statistical relation between the observable cause and the unobserved cause has been made. However, Equations 4 and 5 also show that no precise inferences about the probability and causal strength of the unobserved cause can be drawn on the basis of the observable events alone. There are at least two unknown parameters in each of these equations, which refer to the conditional probabilities that involve the unobservable cause. Nevertheless, Equations 4 and 5 do provide constraints for the possible causal strength and probability of the unobserved cause. In particular the probability of the effect in the absence of the observed cause provides a rather simple constraint. As Equation 5 shows, this probability represents a lower boundary for the probability of the unobserved cause in the observable cause's absence, $P(a|{\sim}c) \geq P(e|{\sim}c)$, and for the probability that this cause generates the observable effect on its own, which corresponds to its causal power, $P(e|a.{\sim}c) \geq P(e|{\sim}c))$. Thus, even if no precise inferences about the parameters of unobserved causes can be drawn this analysis shows that there are numeric boundaries for plausible inferences. The more often the effect occurs on its own, the more often the unobserved cause has probably been present and the stronger its causal impact upon the visible effect will be.

The second analysis shows that at least approximate inferences about the presence of the unobserved cause A can be drawn by observing the presence or absence of the cause C and effect E on individual trials. There are four possible patterns of events that might be observed: cause C and effect E both being present $(e.c)$, cause C being present without the effect $({\sim}e.c)$, the effect being present without the observable cause

$(e.{\sim}c)$, and both events being absent $({\sim}e.{\sim}c)$. From a Bayesian perspective the question is whether it is more likely for each of these four possible observations that an unobserved cause A is present (a) or that it is absent $({\sim}a)$. Using Bayes' theorem the probability of the unobserved cause being present can be calculated as

$$P(A|E,\ C) = \frac{P(E|A,\ C) \cdot P(A|C)}{P(E|C)}.$$

Given that the presence of both cause C and the effect E are being observed, the posterior odds for an unobserved cause to be present can be calculated by

$$\frac{P(a|e.c)}{P({\sim}a|e.c)} = \frac{P(e|a.c)}{P(e|{\sim}a.c)} \cdot \frac{P(a|c)}{P({\sim}a|c)} \qquad 6$$

(i.e., posterior odds = likelihood ratio ·

prior odds)

Let us first consider the likelihood ratio: The relevant question is whether the probability of the effect is higher given both the unobserved and the observed cause are present or higher given only the observable cause is present—that is, whether $P(e|a.c) > P(e|{\sim}a.c)$. If the unobserved cause is assumed to have a positive causal influence upon the effect, then the effect is more likely if both causes are present than if only one cause is present, $P(e|a.c) > P(e|{\sim}a.c)$. Therefore, an observation of both the cause and the effect makes the presence of an unobserved cause more likely. Nevertheless, no definite prediction is possible without taking into account the prior odds. As long as $P(a|c)$ is equal or bigger than $P({\sim}a|c)$, the prior odds are larger than or equal to one, which implies that the presence of the unobserved cause is more likely than its absence. This means that as long as we have reason to assume that the presence of an unobserved cause is a priori equally likely or more likely than its absence, its presence should be predicted if a cause and its effect are both being observed.

We now turn to the second possible pattern of events. If only the cause is observed without the effect then the posterior odds of the unobserved cause are given by

$$\frac{P(a|{\sim}e.c)}{P({\sim}a|{\sim}e.c)} = \frac{P({\sim}e|a.c)}{P({\sim}e|{\sim}a.c)} \cdot \frac{P(a|c)}{P({\sim}a|c)} \qquad 7$$

If both causes have a positive causal influence then $P(e|a.c) > P(e|{\sim}a.c)$ and therefore $P({\sim}e|a.c) < P({\sim}e|{\sim}a.c)$. Thus, an observation of a cause without its effect makes the presence of an unobserved cause less likely. Again a guess about the prior odds is needed to arrive at a definite judgement.

However, it is important to note that the prior odds are identical in all cases in which the cause is observed. Regardless of whether $e.c$ or ${\sim}e.c$ is being observed, the prior odds are $P(a|c)\,/\,P({\sim}a|c)$ (see Equations 6 and 7). This implies that the posterior odds of the unobserved cause are higher in cases in which both cause and effect are observed than in cases in which only the cause is observed no matter what the prior odds are. Thus, even if no definite estimates are possible without specific assumptions about the prior probabilities of the unobserved cause, the posterior odds should differ.

If the effect is observed without the observable cause, the posterior odds are calculated as

$$\frac{P(a|e.{\sim}c)}{P({\sim}a|e.{\sim}c)} = \frac{P(e|a.{\sim}c)}{P(e|{\sim}a.{\sim}c)} \cdot \frac{P(a|{\sim}c)}{P({\sim}a|{\sim}c)} \qquad 8$$

Thus, as long as the unobserved cause has a spositive influence, $P(e|a.{\sim}c) > P(e|{\sim}a.{\sim}c)$, this observation makes the presence of the unobserved cause more likely. However, an even more distinct prediction is possible based on the often-stated causal principle that nothing happens without a cause ("nihil fit sine causa", Audi, 1995). Based on this principle, $P(e|{\sim}a.{\sim}c)$ should equal zero, which implies that the unobserved cause has to be present for sure. Thus, an observation of an effect without any visible cause makes the presence of an unobserved cause necessary.

Finally, if neither the cause nor its effect is present, the posterior odds of the unobserved cause are

$$\frac{P(a|\sim e.\sim c)}{P(\sim a|\sim e.\sim c)} = \frac{P(\sim e|a.\sim c)}{P(\sim e|\sim a.\sim c)} \cdot \frac{P(a|\sim c)}{P(\sim a|\sim c)}$$ 9

If the effect never happens without any cause then $P(\sim e|\sim a.\sim c) = 1$. Thus, an observation of neither cause nor effect implies that it is less likely that the unobserved cause has happened. Again, for a definite prediction assumptions about the prior odds have to be made. However, as in the cases in which the observable cause is present, the prior odds are the same in all cases in which the observable cause is absent (see Equations 8 and 9). The prior odds of the unobserved cause given an observation of either $e.\sim c$ or $\sim e.\sim c$ are $P(a|\sim c)$ / $P(\sim a|\sim c)$. This implies that the posterior odds of the unobserved cause are lower when none of the events is observed than when the effect is observed by itself.

How can the prior odds be estimated? As we have shown in the first analysis the observable probability of the effect in the cause's absence provides a lower boundary for the probability of the unobserved cause, $P(a|\sim c) = 1 - P(\sim a|\sim c) \geq P(e|\sim c)$. Thus, after observing several trials at least the prior odds for cases in which the observable cause is absent can be estimated from the data.

The two analyses provided in this section show that even if no assumption of independence among the observed and the unobserved causes of a common effect is made, it is possible to derive some approximate inferences about the unobserved cause. This is true for individual trials as well as for complete data sets. Thus, informed guesses about unobserved causes can be made. For these analyses only probability calculus and Bayes' theorem were used. Consequently causal Bayes net theories can be adapted to cases in which the assumption of independence of causes seems unwarranted.

Summary

Current theories of causal learning consider unobserved causes and make assumptions that allow it to make inferences about these causes. Associative theories assume that an unobserved cause (i.e., the constant background) is always present and therefore independent of observable causes. Causal Bayes net theories including the special case of Power PC theory typically assume that different causes are independent of each other. This assumption allows these theories to make precise estimates about unobserved causes. However, despite the fact that these theories in general assume independence among different causes of a joint effect, these theories can also model situations in which the independence assumption does not hold. The analyses in the previous section have shown that in the case of dependence between observable and unobservable causes (i.e., confounding) it is normatively not possible to derive precise quantitative inferences about the probability and strength of the unobserved causes. Nevertheless it is possible to use Bayesian inferences to provide reasonable estimates. Even if no assumptions about dependence are made, the probability of the effect in the absence of the cause marks a lower boundary for the probability of the unobserved cause in the observable cause's absence, $P(a|\sim c) \geq P(e|\sim c)$.

Associative as well as causal Bayes net theories agree that $P(e|\sim c)$ is to a certain extent indicative of the causal strength of the unobserved cause. But whereas associative theories generally regard this probability as a valid indicator, Power PC and other causal Bayes net theories view this conditional probability as a lower boundary of the causal strength of the unobserved cause.

Causal Bayes net theories are also able to make specific predictions for different patterns of observations by using Bayesian inferences about unobserved causes (see previous section for details). If a cause and an effect are both observed it is more likely that an unobserved second cause is also present than when the cause is observed without an effect, $P(a|e.c) \geq P(a|\sim e.c)$. The existence and presence of an unobserved cause is certain if an effect is observed without any visible cause,

$P(a|e.\sim c) = 1$. If neither cause nor effect is observed, the presence of an unobserved cause is unlikely.

Experimental evidence

A number of researchers have provided evidence that people can and do infer the existence of unobserved causes. For example, children and adults infer the unobserved mental causes (e.g., desires and beliefs) of other people's actions (Gopnik & Wellman, 1994; Wellman, 1990). People also assume that there is an essential unobserved entity in categories, which has been speculated to play the role of a unobserved common cause of the observable features of category members (Gelman, 2003; Medin & Ortony, 1989; Rehder, 2003; Rehder & Hastie, 2001). In scientific reasoning people often infer unobserved entities to account for the observed events (Gopnik & Meltzoff, 1997; Keinath & Krems, 1999; Krems & Johnson, 1995). An example for recent studies on unobserved causes is a series of experiments conducted by Gopnik and colleagues (Gopnik et al., 2004; Kushnir et al., 2003). In one of their studies children were presented a stick-ball machine where they saw two balls moving together up and down for four times. Next an experimenter moved each ball by hand, which did not have any visible effect on the other ball. Children were asked to give an explanation. In accordance with causal Bayes net theories children as young as $4\frac{1}{2}$ years were able to reason that neither ball is the cause of the other so that there must have been an unobserved common cause that makes the two balls move together. These and other results show that children (and adults) are able to correctly infer the presence of an unobserved cause from a mixture of observations and interventions.

Our focus differs from these studies, however. Whereas Gopnik and colleagues (2004) were mainly interested in the induction of the presence of an unobserved common cause of multiple effects, our goal is to study inferences about the probability and the causal strength of unobserved causes that are known to exist. Moreover, whereas previous studies have focused on unobserved common causes of multiple observed effects, our experiments explore inferences about common-effect structures in which one cause is unobserved.

To the best of our knowledge only one study has thus far investigated some of these questions. Luhmann and Ahn (2003) have confronted participants with a single causal relation consisting of one observable cause and one observable effect (see also Ahn, Marsh, & Luhmann, in press). They showed that many participants were willing to judge the causal strength of unobserved causes that they had never observed during causal learning. In their first experiment Ahn and colleagues also found that the estimated causal influence of the unobserved causes declined when their number increased (the observable causal relation was kept constant). In a second study Luhmann and Ahn manipulated the probability of the observable effect when the observable cause was absent. It turned out that participants judged the causal strength of a single unobserved cause to be higher if $P(e|\sim c)$ was .5 than if it was zero. This finding is consistent with the theoretical accounts introduced above. Unfortunately, no estimates for the dependency between the observable and the unobserved cause were collected in these experiments. Therefore it is not possible to differentiate between an associative and a Bayesian account.

In an unpublished experiment (summarized in Ahn et al., in press) participants' inferences about the unobserved cause's presence were measured on each learning trial. It turned out that participants assumed the unobserved cause to be present when the effect had occurred on its own and to be absent when neither the visible cause nor the effect had occurred. This finding is in accordance with the predictions derived from a Bayesian analysis.

With the experiments presented in this paper we intended to go beyond these previous findings. In addition to causal strength estimates, we also collected assessments of the probability of the unobserved cause in the presence and absence of the observed cause and effect. We used a variety of methods to measure people's assumptions about the interdependence between observed and unobserved causes in different task contexts.

OUTLINE OF EXPERIMENTS

The aim of the following two experiments was to explore what assumptions participants make about the presence and causal strength of an unobserved cause in a trial-by-trial learning task and to test whether these assumptions conform to the predictions of any of the discussed theoretical models. In both experiments participants learned about the causal relation between an observable cause and an effect. In addition, participants were told that there was one other possible but unobserved cause of the effect. Participants never received any further information about the unobserved cause beyond this hint.

The statistical relation between the observable cause and the effect was manipulated in two experiments. In Experiment 1 the contingency between the observable cause and the effect was kept constant while the causal power varied across conditions. In Experiment 2 causal power was kept constant while the contingency varied. We used this manipulation to investigate whether participants would base their estimates of causal strength on the contingency between cause and effect or on the causal power of the cause, which could be inferred from the observations if independence amongst causes is assumed. Previous research yielded mixed evidence about this issue. While some researchers found support for the use of causal power (Buehner & Cheng, 1997; Buehner, Cheng, & Clifford, 2003) others found support for the use of contingencies (Lober & Shanks, 2000). Since we were interested in causal strength estimates, we were interested in finding out whether learners are sensitive to contingencies or causal power when estimating causal strength.

The manipulation of the statistical relation between the observable cause and the effect should also affect participants' guesses about the unobserved cause's strength. As we have outlined in the Introduction, the probability of the effect in the observable cause's absence is an indicator of the unobserved cause's strength and provides a lower boundary. Thus, the estimated causal strength should rise in parallel to the probability of the effect in the absence of the observed cause.

We also manipulated whether participants could only passively observe the cause and the effect (Experiment 1), or whether they could actively intervene and decide when the cause should be present or absent (Experiment 2). Mere observations without interventions do not permit it to make strong assumptions about the interdependence between the alternative causes. Either is possible, dependence or independence. Thus, participants may assume that the observed and the unobserved causes are dependent. In contrast, interventions should typically generate independence. Since the presence or absence of unobserved causes is unknown, deliberately setting a cause normally creates independence between the two causes (see Pearl, 2000; Spirtes et al., 1993; Woodward, 2003, for theoretical analyses of interventions). Therefore participants should assume independence (see Gopnik et al., 2004; Hagmayer, Sloman, Lagnado, & Waldmann, in press; Sloman & Lagnado, 2005; Waldmann & Hagmayer, 2005, for psychological evidence).

We used two different tasks to assess participants' estimates of the probability of the unobserved cause: First, participants were asked to guess on each learning trial whether the unobserved cause was present or absent. Then, at the end of the learning session we requested additional summary estimates. Both measures were used to assess participants' assumptions about independence between observed and unobserved causes. By making several predictions in a series of trials participants generate patterns of alternative causes, which allow analysis of the dependence between the causes that participants implicitly generate. It is known in the literature on learning that participants tend to match the probability of events when generating sequences (see reviews by Hernstein, 1997; Myers, 1976; Vulkan, 2000). Therefore we hypothesized that participants' predictions would mirror their assumptions about the probability of the unobserved cause. Participants' final overall estimates are more explicit; they are based on summary information stored in memory. We were interested in whether these two types of measures would yield similar estimates, or whether they would diverge. Since the online predictions are based on single cases, it may well be that these estimates focus on different aspects of the data from those focused on by the summary statements (see Catena, Maldonado, & Cándido, 1998, for an example of such a dissociation in the domain of causal strength estimation). For causal strength assessments summary estimates are, in our view, the more relevant evidence for independence assumptions as both are collected at the end of the learning phase.

EXPERIMENT 1

Participants' task in the first experiment was to learn about the causal relation between a microbe infecting flowering plants and the discoloration of their bloom. In addition, participants were requested to draw inferences about the presence and causal influence of a second but unobserved type of microbe, which may also affect the plant's coloration. This first experiment investigated observational learning—that is, participants could only observe whether a flower was infected and discoloured; they were not able to intervene themselves. Two experimental factors were manipulated: The first factor was the strength of the causal relation between the observable microbe and the discoloration of three types of plants. This factor was manipulated within subjects in a counterbalanced order. Contingencies between infection and discoloration were kept constant, but the two conditional probabilities $P(e|c)$ and $P(e|\sim c)$ were increased across conditions. This increase has two implications: (a) it implies an increasing causal power of the observable cause, and (b) it implies a higher probability or stronger causal strength of the second unobserved microbe because the probability of discoloration in the absence of an infection by the observable microbe increased.

As a second factor, which was manipulated between subjects, the learning procedure was manipulated: In two experimental conditions participants were requested to make predictions about the unobserved cause on each learning trial. In one

of these conditions ("prediction after effect") participants received information about the presence of the first microbe and the effect and then had to predict the presence of the unobserved microbe. This information should allow them to make more informed guesses about the unobserved cause (see the analysis in the section on inferring unobserved causes). Summarizing our analyses in the Introduction, participants should be quite sure that the unobserved microbe is present if the observable microbe is absent but the flower is discoloured. They should also feel confident that the unobserved cause is absent if neither the observable cause nor the effect has occurred. If cause and effect were both present, learners should predict the unobserved cause to be present more often than if the cause was present but the effect was missing. No feedback was provided about the unobserved cause.

In the second experimental condition ("prediction before effect") participants had to make their guess after observing the presence or absence of the observable cause, but before being informed about the occurrence of the effect. Thus, they were first informed about the presence or absence of the cause in each trial, and then they were asked to guess whether the unobserved cause was present without receiving feedback about the alternative unobserved cause. Only after they had made their prediction were they informed whether the effect had occurred at this particular trial or not. In contrast to the "prediction after effect" condition this condition does not allow specific inferences to be made about the unobserved cause's presence on an individual trial. Participants' inferences of the unobserved cause prior to effect information can only be guesses based on observed frequencies of the effect in the absence of the observable cause in past trials. As we have outlined above, the probability of the effect in the absence of the cause provides a lower boundary of the base rate of the unobserved cause. Therefore participants should use the trials in which the observed cause is absent to infer the probability of the unobserved cause. Assuming independence they should adapt their predictions for the trials in which the observed cause is present to this probability. If they did that, they would generate independence between the causes. A third control condition presented the learning data without requesting trial-by-trial predictions.

After observing the causal relation participants were requested to rate the causal strength of the observed as well as of the unobserved microbe. They were asked to estimate the probability of the second microbe being present, when the first microbe was present and when the first microbe was absent. Both participants' online inferences during learning and their final estimates were used to calculate their assumptions about the dependence between the two alternative causes.

Method

Participants and design

A total of 36 students from the University of Göttingen, Germany, participated in the experiment and were randomly assigned to one of the three learning conditions.

Materials and procedure

Participants were first instructed to learn about the causal relation between a fictitious microbe ("colorophages") and the discoloration of flowers. They were also told that there was only one other possible cause of the effect, an infection with another fictitious microbe ("mamococcus"), which was currently not observable. Next participants were presented a stack of index cards providing information about individual flowers. The front side of each index card showed whether the flower was infected by colorophages or not, and the backside informed about whether the flower was discoloured or not. Then participants were instructed about the specific learning procedure in their condition. In the "prediction before effect" condition participants were first shown the front side of the card, then they had to guess whether the flower was also infected by the other unobserved microbe, and finally the card was turned around by the experimenter revealing whether the flower was in fact discoloured or not. In contrast, in the second experimental

condition ("prediction after effect") the card was turned around after the presentation of the front side revealing the presence or absence of discoloration. Then the participants were asked to make their guesses about the unobserved cause. Guesses were secretly recorded without giving any feedback. In the third, the control, condition the cards were simply shown and turned around by the experimenter. No inferences about the unobserved cause were requested.

After each learning phase participants were asked to rate the strength of the causal influence of the observed and the unobserved cause on a scale ranging from 0 ("no causal influence") to 100 ("deterministic causal influence, i.e., the cause always yields the effect"). Participants were also asked to estimate how many of 10 flowers that were infected with the observed microbe were also infected with the other microbe, and how many of 10 flowers that were not infected with the observed microbe were instead infected with the other microbe. No feedback was provided about these assessments.

Three data sets were constructed in a manner that the contingency ΔP was held constant across all sets, whereas both $P(e|\sim c)$ and causal power were rising. Each data set consisted of 20 cases. The data sets and their statistical properties are shown in Table 1. All three data sets were shown to every participant in a within-subjects design. Different data sets were introduced as data from different species of flowers. It was pointed out to participants that the effectiveness of the microbes might vary depending on the species. The order of the presented data sets was counterbalanced.

Table 1. *Data sets shown in Experiment 1 and their statistical properties*

Observations	Data set 1	Data set 2	Data set 3	Statistics	Data set 1	Data set 2	Data set 3
$e.c$	6	8	10	$P(c)$	.50	.50	.50
$\sim e.c$	4	2	0	$P(e|c)$	.60	.80	1.0
$e.\sim c$	1	3	5	$P(e|\sim c)$	.10	.30	.50
$\sim e.\sim c$	9	7	5	ΔP	.50	.50	.50
Sum	20	20	20	Power p_c	.56	.71	1.0

Table 2. *Results of Experiment 1: Mean ratings of causal influence for observed and unobserved causes*

Condition	Causal strength: Observed cause			Causal strength: Unobserved cause		
	Data Set 1	Data Set 2	Data Set 3	Data Set 1	Data Set 2	Data Set 3
"Before effect"	57.5 (22.2)	68.3 (15.9)	78.3 (19.9)	50.5 (30.7)	48.3 (23.7)	46.7 (27.1)
"After effect"	64.1 (29.1)	70.8 (21.1)	77.9 (23.7)	34.2 (22.3)	61.7 (33.0)	73.8 (27.1)
Control	57.5 (19.1)	75.8 (12.4)	84.2 (16.2)	43.3 (25.6)	38.3 (21.7)	54.2 (19.3)

Note: Standard deviations in parentheses.

Results

First the estimated causal influence of the observed and the unobserved causes was analysed. Table 2 shows the mean ratings. Overall the descriptive means indicate increasing estimates for both causes. Separate analyses of variance for each cause with learning condition (before effect, after effect, control) as a between-subjects factor and data set (1, 2, 3) as a within-subjects factor were conducted. The analysis for the observed cause revealed a significant increase in causal strength ratings, $F(2, 66) = 12.7$, $MSE = 296.6$, $p < .01$, while the other main effect and the interaction failed to reach significance ($Fs < 1$). This pattern of results supports the predictions of Power PC theory, as the contingency between the cause and the effect remained constant across conditions. The analysis for the unobserved cause also resulted in a significant main effect of the factor data set, $F(2, 66) = 4.92$, $MSE = 408.1$, $p < .05$, which indicated that with increasing $P(e|{\sim}c)$ participants tended to assume a stronger causal strength of the unobserved cause. This result conforms to the predictions of all theoretical accounts discussed in the Introduction.

The interaction between data sets and learning condition also turned out to be significant,

$F(4, 66) = 4.55$, $MSE = 408.1$, $p < .05$. The observed increase was strongest in the "prediction after effect" condition followed by the control condition. This interaction can be explained by the different affordances of the three learning conditions. In the "prediction after effect" condition participants were sensitized to the possible presence and causal strength of the unobserved cause more than in the other two conditions. As we have shown in the Introduction, observing both cause and effect in a single trial allows informed predictions regarding the unobserved cause to be derived. No such predictions were possible in the other two conditions. In the "prediction before effect" condition participants lacked the information necessary to make an inference, which might have signalled to them that it is impossible to draw any inferences. In the control condition, they were never asked about the unobserved cause during learning.

Secondly, participants' implicit assumptions about the dependence between the causes were analysed. The trial-by-trial predictions of the unobserved cause in the presence and absence of the target cause were transformed into conditional frequencies and combined into subjective contingencies, $\Delta P = P(a|c) - P(a|{\sim}c)$.[1] This procedure

---

[1] We used the following formulae to derive $P_{gen}(a|c)$ and $P_{gen}(a|{\sim}c)$ from the observed frequencies with which different patterns of events were predicted:

$$P_{gen}(a|c) = [P_{gen}(a.e.c) + P_{gen}(a.{\sim}e.c)]/$$

$$[P_{gen}(a.e.c) + P_{gen}({\sim}a.e.c) + P_{gen}(a.{\sim}e.c) + P_{gen}({\sim}a.{\sim}e.c)]$$

$$P_{gen}(a|{\sim}c) = [P_{gen}(a.e.{\sim}c) + P_{gen}(a.{\sim}e.{\sim}c)]/$$

$$[P_{gen}(a.e.{\sim}c) + P_{gen}({\sim}a.e.{\sim}c) + P_{gen}(a.{\sim}e.{\sim}c) + P_{gen}({\sim}a.{\sim}e.{\sim}c)]$$

Table 3. *Results of Experiment 1: Mean generated and estimated dependencies of observed and unobserved causess*

	Generated dependence			Estimated dependence		
Condition	Data Set 1	Data Set 2	Data Set 3	Data Set 1	Data Set 2	Data Set 3
"Before effect"	.33 (.377)	.08 (.549)	−.22 (.273)	.30 (.252)	.06 (.360)	−.03 (.337)
"After effect"	.17 (.237)	.18 (.396)	−.29 (.204)	−.01 (.318)	.00 (.341)	−.23 (.470)
Control	—	—	—	.14 (.271)	.12 (.269)	.13 (.234)

Note: Values represent contingencies. Standard deviations in parentheses.

was based on the assumption that participants' predictions would reflect their underlying probability estimates due to probability matching. On the left side of Table 3 the mean contingencies that were generated online are listed. Participants' final ratings of the conditional frequency of the unobserved cause in the presence and absence of the observed cause were also transformed into subjective contingencies. Means are shown on the right hand side of Table 3. An analysis of variance of the generated contingencies with the between-subjects factor "learning procedure" and the within-subjects factor "data set" yielded a significant trend from positive to negative assessments, $F(2, 44) = 22.1$, $MSE = 749.8$, $p < .01$. No other main effect or interaction was found. Thus, the negative trend proved to be independent of the learning condition. The estimated contingencies showed a similar negative trend, $F(2, 66) = 4.2$, $MSE = 753.9$, $p < .05$. They also differed slightly across learning conditions, $F(2, 33) = 2.8$, $MSE = 1,646.4, p < .10$ but the interaction failed to reach significance.

To follow up these results more closely, generated and estimated contingencies were compared to an assumption of independence—that is, the empirically obtained contingencies were tested for deviations from zero using one-sample t tests. The analyses showed that the contingencies generated online were significantly above zero if $P(e|{\sim}c)$ was .1 (Data Set 1) and significantly below zero if $P(e|{\sim}c)$ was .5 (Data Set 3).

The pattern for the final summary estimates differed from the pattern for the generated dependencies. In comparison to an assumption of independence, only marginally significant deviations

were found for most of the estimates. The estimates for Data Set 1 in the "prediction before effect" condition were the only exception. These rather small deviations are consistent with an assumption of independence. This result points to a dissociation between online and post hoc assessments. While participants generated a positive dependence when the effect had never occurred in the absence of the observed cause and a negative dependence when it had occurred fairly often in the absence of the observable cause, the final summary estimates hovered around independence.

In a third analytical step the predictions regarding the unobserved cause, which participants made online on individual trials, were analysed. For this analysis the patterns of events generated in the online judgements were transformed into subjective probabilities of the unobserved cause conditional upon the patterns of the observed events. This means that they were transformed into probabilities of A conditional on both cause C and effect D, $P_{gen}(A|C, F)$, in the "prediction after effect" condition and into probabilities of A conditional on C, $P_{gen}(A|C)$, in the "prediction before effect" condition. Table 4 shows the mean conditional probabilities derived from the generated patterns. Note that in Data Set 3 participants never observed the effect to be absent when the observable cause was present. The probabilities in the "prediction after effect" condition conformed fairly well to the theoretical predictions derived in the Introduction. Participants judged the unobserved cause to be much more likely when the effect had occurred in the observable cause's absence than when neither cause nor effect had

Table 4. *Results of Experiment 1: Mean probabilities of unobserved cause generated by participants conditional upon each pattern of observations*

"Before effect" condition

Data Set 1		Data Set 2		Data Set 3	
$P_{gen}(a|c)$	$P_{gen}(a|\sim c)$	$P_{gen}(a|c)$	$P_{gen}(a|\sim c)$	$P_{gen}(a|c)$	$P_{gen}(a|\sim c)$
.66 (.22)	.32 (.20)	.50 (.35)	.53 (.26)	.27 (.16)	.48 (.21)

"After effect" condition

Data Set 1				Data Set 2				Data Set 3			
$P_{gen}(a|e.c)$	$P_{gen}(a|\sim e.c)$	$P_{gen}(a|e.\sim c)$	$P_{gen}(a|\sim e.\sim c)$	$P_{gen}(a|e.c)$	$P_{gen}(a|\sim e.c)$	$P_{gen}(a|e.\sim c)$	$P_{gen}(a|\sim e.\sim c)$	$P_{gen}(a|e.c)$	$P_{gen}(a|\sim e.c)$	$P_{gen}(a|e.\sim c)$	$P_{gen}(a|\sim e.\sim c)$
.40 (.34)	.21 (.35)	.92 (.29)	.07 (.12)	.52 (.43)	.29 (.40)	.92 (.15)	.05 (.16)	.44 (.38)	—	1.0 (0.0)	.02 (.06)

Note: Standard deviations in parentheses.

occurred. In fact, participants in this condition were almost certain that the unobserved cause was present, when the observable cause was absent, $P_{gen}(a|{\sim}c.e) > .90$, and absent otherwise, $P_{gen}(a|{\sim}c.{\sim}e) < .10$. An analysis of variance with the two within-subjects factors "data set" (1, 2, 3) and "presence of effect" (present vs. absent) yielded a highly significant main effect of the factor involving the effect's presence, $F(1, 11) = 347.0$, $MSE = 0.042$, $p < .01$. No other effect turned out to be significant. Participants' predictions were less clear cut when the observable cause was present. At least the descriptive differences pointed in the right direction. Participants considered the unobserved cause to be more likely when the observable cause and the effect had occurred than when only the observable cause had occurred without the effect. However, an analysis of variance with the two within-subjects factors "data set" (1 vs. 2) and "presence of effect" (present vs. absent) yielded no significant effect of the factor "presence of effect", $F(1, 11) = 2.59$, $MSE = 0.208$, $p = .14$. Increasing the statistical power of the experiment might confirm the expected difference (see Experiment 2). Nevertheless, participants' inferences exhibit a surprising grasp of the inferences that can be drawn from the individual patterns of events.

A rather awkward pattern resulted in the "prediction before effect" condition. Contrary to our predictions participants did not predict the unobserved cause to be present more often, when the probability of the effect in the observable cause's absence rose. They rather predicted the unobserved cause to be present less often in the observables cause's presence when the causal impact of the observable cause increased. In contrast to the "prediction after effect" condition it seems that participants had no clue how to derive predictions about the unobserved cause in this condition.

Overall the results from Experiment 1 contradicted some of the theoretical assumptions made by the currently predominant theories of causal learning. Participants assumed neither that the unobserved cause was always present nor that the two causes were independent (at least in the online judgements). This finding challenges

associative theories, Power PC theory, and other causal Bayes net theories, which assume independence of causes. However, we already have pointed out that an independence assumption is not necessary for Power PC theory and causal Bayes net theories in general. Causal Bayes net theories including Power PC theory can model dependence between observed and unobserved causes. Therefore, even if participants' answers did not conform to the independence assumption, their answers still might be coherent with modified versions of these theories. To be coherent participants' estimates would have to honour the constraints imposed by the learning data. The most important constraint is that the product of the causal power (or causal strength) of the unobserved cause and the probability of the unobserved cause in the absence of the observed cause must equal the probability of the effect in the absence of the observed cause.

To find out whether participants honour this constraint we used their causal strength and their final summary ratings of the unobserved cause to recalculate the probability of the effect E when cause C was absent:

$$P_{rec}(e|{\sim}c)$$
$$= \text{causal strength rating} A^* \text{rating } P(a|{\sim}c).$$

The recalculated probabilities and the actually observed probabilities are shown in Table 5. It can be seen that the recalculated probabilities in the "prediction after effect" condition were surprisingly close to the actually observed probabilities. In contrast, the recalculated probabilities in the other two conditions were inaccurate. Since these ratings were collected at the end of the learning phase the necessary information to make accurate summary estimates was available to learners in all conditions. However, it seems that participants had to be sensitized by the learning procedure to the presence and causal strength of the unobserved cause to be able to derive coherent estimates. The procedure in the "prediction after effect" condition required participants in each trial to think about the unobserved cause, and it provided participants with the right

Table 5. *Recalculated conditional probabilities of the effect in the absence of the observable cause*

Condition	Data Set 1		Data Set 2		Data Set 3	
	Recalculated	Observed	Recalculated	Observed	Recalculated	Observed
"Before effect"	.13 (.13)		.25 (.19)		.24 (.17)	
"After effect"	.14 (.15)	.10	.26 (.26)	.30	.43 (.28)	.50
Control	.14 (.10)		.21 (.20)		.21 (.14)	

Note: Calculations are based on the probabilities and causal strength parameters estimated by participants. Power PC theory is used to integrate these estimates. See text for more details. Standard deviations in parentheses.

information to be able to do so. Without this information participants' guesses showed some systematicity but they did not conform very well to the observed data. Thus, simply asking participants to think about unobserved causes on each trial—as we did in the "prediction before effect" condition—was clearly not sufficient.

An interesting novel finding is the dissociation between online judgements and final summary judgements. Although the online judgements show deviations from the independence assumption, the final judgements are consistent with this assumption. Apparently, online judgements were driven by other aspects of the data than the summary estimates. We discuss this point more closely in the General Discussion. This finding supports normative theories of power estimation (e.g., Power PC theory) that hypothesize that people default to an independence assumption. These theories might argue that the online judgements are less relevant than the final estimates, as power estimates are typically not made online but rather on the basis of a learning sample. If people retrospectively make the independence assumption when assessing power, their estimates should correspond to the predictions of normative theories (i.e., Power PC theory). This point is reinforced by the fact that learners' estimates seemed to mirror causal power rather than contingencies.

EXPERIMENT 2

In Experiment 1 participants could only passively observe the occurrence of a cause and an effect.

Mere observations do not rule out the possibility that the observed cause is in fact related to a second unobserved, confounding cause. It might have been the case that flowers were more often infected by both microbes than by only one. Such dependence might have even been plausible for some participants. To make independence more salient, we switched from observations to interventions in Experiment 2. In this experiment we allowed participants to arbitrarily manipulate the observable cause. Since these random interventions cannot be based on the presence or absence of the unobserved cause, they are more likely to be independent from the unobserved cause (see Hagmayer et al., in press; Meder, Hagmayer, & Waldmann, 2005; Waldmann & Hagmayer, 2005). Therefore, learning from interventions should make independence between alternative causes more salient than should learning from observations. We speculated that learners may be more prone to assume independence between alternative causes if they are allowed to freely manipulate the observable cause.

Participants in this second experiment were instructed to imagine being a captain on a pirate ship firing his battery at a fortress. Their task was to assess their own hit rate—that is, the causal strength of their actions upon the fortress. A second ship, which also fired at the fortress but was occluded from participants' view, served as the unobserved cause. Participants had to decide whether to fire or not on each trial. Only a limited number of shells were provided to ensure that all participants received equivalent data despite the fact that they arbitrarily set the cause themselves.

The same two factors as those in the first experiment were manipulated. Learning conditions were again varied between subjects. In the two experimental conditions participants either had to guess whether the other ship had fired during the current trial before they were informed about the occurrence of an explosion in the fortress ("prediction before effect"), or they had to predict the other ship's action after they had learned whether the fortress was hit ("prediction after effect"). In a third control condition no predictions were requested. At the end of the learning phase all participants were requested to give explicit estimates of the probability of the unobserved cause conditional upon the manipulated cause. They also had to rate the causal strength of the observed and of the unobserved cause.

As a second factor the data sets presented to participants were varied as a within-subjects variable. The order of the data sets was counterbalanced as in the first experiment. Again the conditional probability of the effect in the presence and absence of the cause was raised across conditions. In contrast to Experiment 1, in which contingencies were kept constant, we now kept causal power constant. Therefore we expected participants to rate the causal strength of the manipulated cause to be the same in all conditions. However, we again expected that the estimated probability and causal strength of the unobserved cause would rise in parallel to the probability of the effect in the absence of the observable cause.

Method

Participants and design

A total of 60 students from the University of Göttingen, Germany, participated and were randomly assigned to one of the three learning conditions.

Materials and procedure

This second experiment was run on a computer. First, participants were instructed to imagine being a captain on a pirate ship trying to invade fortresses in the Caribbean. Therefore they were firing at a fortress with their ship's battery. A second friendly ship, not visible from the captain's current position, allegedly also fired at the fortress. Participants were told that they had the chance to fire 30 salvos at the fortress on 60 occasions. Their task was to assess how often their own battery would hit the fortress. On each trial participants were first asked whether they wanted to fire a salvo until they used up their shells. In the "prediction before effect" condition they were next asked to predict whether the other ship had fired on this occasion or not. No feedback was provided. Then learners observed whether a causal effect (a blast within the fortress) had occurred or not. In the "prediction after effect" condition participants were informed after their intervention whether an explosion at the fortress had occurred or not, and then had to predict whether the other ship had also fired on this occasion. Again no feedback was given. In the control condition participants only decided whether to fire and then observed the causal effect.

After completing the 60 trials participants were asked to rate how often their salvos would hit the fortress if the other ship had stopped firing. Participants gave their answer on a scale ranging from 0 (= "never") to 100 (= "always"). They also had to estimate how often the other ship's battery would hit the fortress if they had stopped firing themselves. The same rating scale was used again. Participants were also asked how many of the 30 times they had fired had the other ship fired as well and how often within the set of 30 trials in which they had not fired had the other ship fired instead. No feedback was provided. Participants were then told that they had successfully captured the fortress and sailed on to the next. Before the next data set was shown, it was emphasized that the environmental conditions at the new fortress were completely different, so that other success rates might result.

Three new data sets consisting of 60 cases each were constructed. Each was constructed in a way that the contingency between the observed cause and the effect decreased across the data sets, whereas the causal power remained constant. Table 6 shows the conditional probabilities that were used to generate the data for each participant

Table 6. *Conditional probabilities used to generate the three data sets of Experiment 2*

	Data Set 1	Data Set 2	Data Set 3
$P(e|c)$	.70	.80	.90
$P(e|\sim c)$	.00	.33	.67
ΔP	.70	.47	.23
Power p_c	.70	.70	.70

in the three data set conditions. Each set was generated individually for each participant. This means that the data sets were not fixed in advance like in Experiment 1 but that the presence of the effect was determined on each trial anew using the probabilities shown in Table 6. For example, if a participant in the Data Set 1 condition chose to fire, the computer reported a causal effect with a probability of $P = .7$. As in Experiment 1 the order of the data sets was counterbalanced across participants.

Results

First participants' estimates of causal strength of the manipulated and the unobserved cause were analysed. Mean ratings for all conditions are shown in Table 7. An analysis of variance of the causal strength ratings of the manipulated cause with learning condition as a between-subjects factor and data sets as a within-subjects factor yielded no significant effects. This result is in accordance with the predictions of Power PC theory because causal power was kept constant across data sets. The same analysis conducted for the causal strength estimates concerning the unobserved cause yielded two significant main effects.

As in Experiment 1 the estimated causal influence rose across the three data sets, $F(2, 114) = 65.7$, $MSE = 408.2$, $p < .01$. This finding is consistent with all theories considered in the Introduction. There was also a significant difference between learning conditions, $F(2, 57) = 4.06$, $MSE = 591.8$, $p < .05$. Participants in the "prediction after effect" condition rated the causal strength of the unobserved cause to be higher than that in the other two conditions. This result may be a consequence of the learning procedure in this condition, which drew participants' attention to the possible influence of the unobserved cause. Remember that participants in this condition had to predict the other cause's presence based on their own action and the occurrence of the effect. Therefore every time the effect had occurred without the participant's intervention, the participant should have concluded that the other cause must have been present. No such predictions were required in the other two conditions, which might be the reason why participants in these conditions may have overlooked at least some of the crucial cases in which the effect had occurred on its own.

In a second step participants' implicit assumptions about the dependence between the manipulated and the unobserved cause were analysed. Thus again, the conditional frequencies generated by participants during their trial-by-trial predictions were translated into conditional probabilities and subtracted to yield contingencies. The resulting subjective dependencies are listed in Table 8. Supporting the results of Experiment 1, participants tended to generate a negative dependence between the causes. With one exception (Data Set 1 in the "prediction after effect" condition) all

Table 7. *Results of Experiment 2: Mean ratings of causal influence of observed and unobserved causes*

Condition	Causal strength: Observed cause			Causal strength: Unobserved cause		
	Data Set 1	Data Set 2	Data Set 3	Data Set 1	Data Set 2	Data Set 3
"Before effect"	67.7 (22.7)	65.1 (20.9)	68.0 (18.6)	27.3 (23.3)	44.8 (20.6)	65.8 (20.3)
"After effect"	70.0 (29.1)	61.4 (17.2)	62.0 (32.5)	36.0 (26.6)	57.9 (17.0)	81.6 (13.1)
Control	66.9 (15.8)	63.6 (11.8)	71.2 (17.6)	33.9 (32.7)	50.6 (21.2)	76.3 (16.8)

Note: Standard deviations in parentheses.

Table 8. *Results of Experiment 2: Mean generated and estimated dependencies of observed and unobserved causes*

	Generated dependence			Estimated dependence		
Condition	Data Set 1	Data Set 2	Data Set 3	Data Set 1	Data Set 2	Data Set 3
"Before effect"	−.24 (.319)	−.33 (.380)	−.29 (.438)	−.04 (.203)	.08 (.256)	−.08 (.306)
"After effect"	−.03 (.300)	−.20 (.276)	−.35 (.258)	−.13 (.341)	−.11 (.304)	−.01 (.589)
Control	—	—	—	.10 (.366)	.09 (.314)	−.06 (.339)

Note: Values represent contingencies. Standard deviations in parentheses.

generated dependencies deviated significantly from zero. An analysis of variance with data set and learning conditions as factors yielded a significant main effect of data set, $F(2, 76) = 6.97$, $MSE = 510.1$, $p < .01$ and a significant interaction, $F(2, 76) = 3.57$, $MSE = 510.1$, $p < .05$. The dependence became more negative when participants had received effect information before their predictions but remained at the same negative level when they made their predictions before being informed about the effect. In contrast to the generated dependencies in the online judgements the estimated dependencies in the final summary judgements did not statistically differ from each other and from zero. Thus, as in the first experiment, there was a clear dissociation between online and final summary judgements. Whereas the online judgements showed deviations from the independence assumption, the final estimates corresponded to it.

In a third analytical step we again analysed the trial-by-trial online predictions more closely. As in Experiment 1, the generated patterns were transformed into subjective probabilities of the unobserved cause conditional upon the manipulated cause, $P_{gen}(A|C)$, in the "prediction before effect" condition and probabilities conditional upon patterns of the observed cause and the effect, $P_{gen}(A|C,E)$, in the "prediction after effect" condition. The results are shown in Table 9. As in Experiment 1 it is important to note that Data Set 1 contained no cases in which the effect occurred in the absence of the manipulated cause. Overall the results were similar to those in Experiment 1. The probabilities generated in the "prediction after effect" condition again conformed

to the implications of a Bayesian analysis. Participants predicted the unobserved cause to be present with a very high probability when the observable cause was absent in the effect's presence and predicted it with a rather low probability when both cause and effect were absent. An analysis of variance with the two within-subject factors "data set" (2 vs. 3) and "presence of effect" (present vs. absent) yielded a strong main effect of the presence of the effect, $F(1, 19) = 115.4$, $MSE = 0.071$, $p < .01$, while all other effects were insignificant. Participants also differentiated between the cases in which both cause and effect were present and the cases in which the cause was present without generating the effect. In accordance with the Bayesian predictions participants inferred the unobserved cause with a higher probability in the first than in the second case. An analysis of variance with the two within-subjects factors "data set" and "presence of effect" confirmed the significance of this difference, $F(1, 19) = 7.50$, $MSE = 0.111$, $p < .05$. The probabilities generated by participants in the "prediction before effect" condition show a uniform pattern. Learners predicted the unobserved cause to be present more often when the observed cause was absent than when it was present. There was apparently no difference between the three data sets. Recall that in this condition participants had to make their prediction before receiving information about the effect, which did not allow them to draw specific inferences for individual cases. Nevertheless, participants should have adapted their predictions to the observable probability of the effect in the observable cause's presence, which defines a lower boundary for the probability of the unobserved cause. This conditional

Table 9. *Results of Experiment 2: Mean probabilities of unobserved cause generated by participants conditional upon each pattern of observations*

"Before effect" condition

	Data Set 1		Data Set 2		Data Set 3	
	$P_{gen}(a|c)$	$P_{gen}(a|{\sim}c)$	$P_{gen}(a|c)$	$P_{gen}(a|{\sim}c)$	$P_{gen}(a|c)$	$P_{gen}(a|{\sim}c)$
	.37 (.24)	.61 (.26)	.36 (.24)	.69 (.24)	.40 (.24)	.69 (.26)

"After effect" condition

	Data Set 1				Data Set 2				Data Set 3			
	$P_{gen}(a|e.c)$	$P_{gen}(a|{\sim}e.c)$	$P_{gen}(a|e.{\sim}c)$	$P_{gen}(a|{\sim}e.{\sim}c)$	$P_{gen}(a|e.c)$	$P_{gen}(a|{\sim}e.c)$	$P_{gen}(a|e.{\sim}c)$	$P_{gen}(a|{\sim}e.{\sim}c)$	$P_{gen}(a|e.c)$	$P_{gen}(a|{\sim}e.c)$	$P_{gen}(a|e.{\sim}c)$	$P_{gen}(a|{\sim}e.{\sim}c)$
	.39 (.22)	.29 (.21)	—	.40 (.29)	.42 (.21)	.26 (.30)	.99 (.04)	.39 (.32)	.41 (.24)	.18 (.25)	.98 (.05)	.29 (.29)

Note: Results concerning the "before effect" condition are shown in the upper half of the table, results concerning the "after effect" condition are shown in the lower half. Standard deviations in parentheses.

Table 10. *Recalculated conditional probabilities of the effect in the absence of the observable cause*

	Data Set 1		Data Set 2		Data Set 3	
Condition	Recalculated	Observed	Recalculated	Observed	Recalculated	Observed
"Before effect"	.13 (.13)		.20 (.12)		.42 (.22)	
"After effect"	.17 (.19)	.00	.35 (.17)	.33	.55 (.21)	.67
Control	.10 (.15)		.24 (.13)		.55 (.18)	

Note: Calculations are based on the probabilities and causal strength parameters estimated by participants. Power PC theory is used to integrate these estimates. Standard deviations in parentheses.

probability increased across trials. Therefore we expected to find a difference between the data sets at least for trials in which the observable cause was absent. As in Experiment 1 participant's predictions showed no sensitivity to this implication.

Finally, we again investigated whether participants' final ratings honoured the constraints imposed by causal Bayes net theories and Power PC theory. The estimated probabilities and causal strength estimates were used to recalculate the probability of the effect in the absence of the observable cause. If participants were sensitive to the constraints imposed by these theories, the values should closely resemble the observed conditional probabilities. The results are shown in Table 10. It can be seen that participants tended to honour the constraints. As in Experiment 1 the best performance was found in the "prediction after effect" condition in which participants (a) were asked about the unobserved cause on each occasion, and (b) had the information available that allowed them to make informed guesses.

GENERAL DISCUSSION

All current theories of causal reasoning consider unknown causes. However, there is no agreement about the correct way to model inferences about such causes. The aim of this paper was to empirically investigate the assumptions that learners make about unobserved causes to provide constraints for theories of causal learning. In two experiments we requested participants to learn a single causal relation between an observable

cause and an effect that, according to our instructions, could also be caused by an unobserved cause. Participants never received any feedback about this unobserved cause. Nevertheless, we asked them to assess the relation between the observed and the unobserved cause and the causal strength of both the observed and the unobserved cause upon the effect.

Associative theories predict that the estimated causal influence of the observed cause should correspond to the observed contingency between the observed cause and the effect. Power PC theory and other causal Bayes net accounts, on the other hand, predict that the estimated causal influence of a cause should correspond to its causal power—that is, its capacity to produce the effect in the absence of all other potential causes. The results of both experiments supported Power PC theory over an associative account. Participants' estimates conformed to the pattern predicted by causal power (see also Buehner et al., 2003).

All theoretical accounts agree that the causal strength of the unobserved cause has to be at least as high as the probability of the effect in the observable cause's absence, $P(e|{\sim}c)$. However, whereas associative theories would predict that the estimated causal influence equals this probability, Power PC theory and other causal Bayes net accounts predict that this probability just marks the lower boundary of the admissible values of causal strength. We found evidence in both experiments that the estimates of causal strength of the unobserved cause increased proportional to $P(e|{\sim}c)$. This finding replicates previous results (Luhmann & Ahn, 2003) and is in accordance with all theories that were discussed in the Introduction. However, we also found that the estimates were consistently higher than $P(e|\sim c)$. This result favours causal Bayes net theories over an associative account.

Associative theories assume that an unobserved cause is permanently present. This assumption ensures that the unobserved cause is independent of the observed cause, which allows the causal strength of both causes to be estimated. Causal Bayes net theories including Power PC theory are more flexible and allow the analysis of situations in which the unobserved cause can be present or absent. If independence is assumed, the causal power of observable causes can be precisely determined even when no information about the unobserved cause is available (see the power formula). In this case the probability of the unobserved cause and its causal strength are both constrained by the observable conditional probabilities, especially the probability of the effect in the observable cause's absence, $P(e|\sim c)$, which marks the lower boundary. In none of the experiments was evidence found that participants assumed that the unobserved cause was permanently present.

However, the results also did not unanimously support the independence assumption usually made by causal Bayes net accounts. In both experiments we found an interesting dissociation between participants' online and final summary judgements of the causes' interdependence. While their final estimates about the relation between the observed and the unobserved cause were consistent with an assumption of independence, their predictions for individual trials were not. In Experiment 1 (observational learning) participants generated a positive dependence if the effect only rarely occurred on its own, but a negative dependence if it occurred fairly often without any apparent cause. In Experiment 2 (interventional learning) participants generated a negative dependency throughout. This implies that participants thought that the unobserved cause had occurred more often when the observable cause was absent than when it was present. This finding is remarkable because interventions should ensure that the manipulated cause occurs independently of all unobserved causes.

There are several possible explanations for this unexpected finding of a negative dependency in online judgements. One reviewer speculated that the observed dependency might be due to the characteristics of the task. Predictions for individual trials require translating subjective probabilities into binary judgements. Such a translation process might generate a bias towards dependency. While we cannot rule out this possibility it seems unlikely to us. Our analyses are based on findings of an extensive literature that people tend to match probabilities when generating sequences of events (see Hernstein, 1997; Myers, 1976; Vulkan, 2000, for overviews). This assumption is supported by the fact that the predictions that were based on observed patterns of cause and effect ("prediction after effect" condition) closely mirrored the predictions derived from a Bayesian analysis. There was no sign of a bias in these judgements.

It is important to recall that the results concerning the online predictions clearly differed between the two learning conditions. The predictions made before information about the presence of the effect was revealed ("prediction before effect" condition) hardly showed any systematic relation to the data sets. The tendency to predict the unobserved cause less often when the observable cause was already present may be grounded in people's reluctance to accept overdetermination of an effect. Since one cause suffices to explain an effect, assuming a second unobserved cause is not necessary. A second related intuition is that events which are not causally related rarely occur simultaneously by chance. Thus, it seems unlikely that the observed and the unobserved cause co-occur. This would also explain an overall tendency to generate a negative dependency in this condition.

The tendency to create an increasingly negative dependency in the "prediction after effect" condition showed that participants in this condition were sensitive to the statistical properties of the data sets. In both experiments participants almost every time predicted the presence of the unobserved cause when the effect had occurred on its own. In addition, participants tended to assume its absence when neither the observable cause nor the effect had occurred. When the observed cause and the effect were present participants ascribed a slightly higher probability to the unobserved cause than when the observed cause had occurred without the effect. However, the overall probability assigned to the unobserved cause was medium to low in both cases and varied only slightly across conditions. These findings for the individual patterns of observations explain why participants tended to generate an increasingly negative dependency in the "prediction after effect" condition across data sets. Across the data sets the number of trials in which the effect occurred on its own increased. Since participants assumed that some cause must be responsible for the observed effect, the rising number of these cases led to more predictions of the unobserved cause across data sets—that is, the probability of the unobserved cause in the observed cause's absence, $P_{gen}(a|{\sim}c)$, rose substantially. In addition, the number of trials in which cause and effect co-occurred also increased across data sets. However, this trend only slightly increased the frequency of predictions of the unobserved cause in the observed cause's presence because participants ascribed only a slightly higher probability to the unobserved cause in the presence of both cause and effect than in trials when the cause was present by itself (see above). Therefore $P_{gen}(a|c)$ rose only slightly. As a consequence a negative trend was observed across data sets. Thus, the finding of an increasingly negative dependency might be just a sign of participants' Bayesian reasoning about individual trials that neglects the statistical properties of the whole sequence of events.

While participants' online judgements deviated significantly from independence, their final summary estimates did not. This dissociation provides an interesting challenge for theories on causal learning (see also Catena et al., 1998, for a similar dissociation regarding causal strength estimates). As we have outlined in the previous paragraphs the dependence generated in the online judgements is probably due to the way the predictions were derived for each individual case. Summary estimates, however, most likely do not focus on individual cases but on larger samples of cases. More research is needed to explore the processes underlying this interesting dissociation.

What are the implications of these findings for causal Bayes net theories and Power PC theory? Since these theories model strength estimates obtained at the asymptote of learning, summary judgements at the end of learning may be the more valid indicator of participants' assumptions about unobserved causes at this point of learning. These estimates did not on average deviate from independence, which is consistent with Power PC theory.

Even if the online judgements were viewed as the more valid indicator of people's intuitive assumption about dependence, causal Bayes net theories or Power PC theory are not refuted. Both theories may drop this assumption, however, at the cost of making causal power no longer precisely estimable. Causal Bayes net theories can model cases in which unobserved and observed causes are dependent. In this case, these theories provide constraints for consistent estimates. We used participants' final estimates to find out whether the estimates honour these constraints. The most important constraint is that the probability of the effect in the absence of the unobserved cause equals the product of the probability of the unobserved cause in the absence of the observed cause and the causal power of the unobserved cause, $P(e|{\sim}c) = P(a|{\sim}c)p_a$ (see Equations 2 and 5). Participants' estimates in fact tended to honour this constraint. Thus, even if independence was not assumed by learners, their estimates were coherent with a rational Bayesian analysis.

What are the implications of these findings for the debate between associative and cognitive theories of causal learning? Our findings clearly challenge associative theories (see Shanks, 2007) because participants proved capable of drawing systematic inferences about the presence and causal strength of cues that remained unobservable throughout learning. This finding supports the assumption of rational theories of causal learning (e.g., Power PC theory) that people represent causal learning tasks as situations in which unobservable causes and observed causes jointly generate the observed effects within a common-effect model. By contrast, associative theories claim that observed causes compete with the constantly present and observable context without separately considering unobservable causal events. Our results add to other findings reported in this volume, which show that participants use the observable information to draw rational inferences about observable and unobservable causal events and are sensitive to the structure of causal models (see Booth & Buehner, 2007; Cobos, López, & Luque, 2007; De Houwer, Vandorpe, & Beckers, 2007; Vandorpe, De Houwer, & Beckers, 2007).

To sum up, our results contradict the assumption of associative theories that learners assume the constant presence of alternative, unobserved causes. The results about the independence assumption made by Bayesian theories are mixed. Whereas the online estimates violated independence, occasionally in the direction of a positive, more often in the direction of a negative correlation, the summary estimates were on average close to independence. Moreover, a Bayesian analysis revealed that the estimates were rational and were consistent with Bayesian constraints. These analyses provide further convincing evidence for the usefulness of a Bayesian analysis of causal learning.

REFERENCES

Ahn, W.-K., Marsh, J. K., & Luhmann, C. C. (in press). Dynamic interpretations of covariation data. In A. Gopnik & L. Schulz (Eds.), *Causal learning: Psychology, philosophy, and computation.* Oxford, UK: Oxford University Press.

Audi, R. (1995). *The Cambridge dictionary of philosophy.* Cambridge, MA: Cambridge University Press.

Booth, S. L., & Buehner, M. J. (2007). Asymmetries in cue competition in forward and backward blocking designs: Further evidence for causal model theory. *Quarterly Journal of Experimental Psychology, 60,* 387–399.

Buehner, M. J., & Cheng, P. W. (1997). Causal induction: The power PC theory versus the Rescorla–Wagner model. In P. Langley & M. G. Shafto (Eds.), *Proceedings of the Nineteenth Annual Conference of the Cognitive Science Society* (pp. 55–60). Hillsdale, NJ: Lawrence Erlbaum Associates, Inc.

Buehner, M. J., Cheng, P. W., & Clifford, D. (2003). From covariaton to causation: A test of the assumption of causal power. *Journal of Experimental Psychology: Learning, Memory, and Cognition, 29,* 1119–1140.

Catena, A., Maldonado, A., & Cándido, A. (1998). The effect of frequency of judgement and the type of trials on covariation learning. *Journal of Experimental Psychology: Human Perception & Performance, 24,* 481–495.

Cheng, P. W. (1997). From covariation to causation: A causal power theory. *Psychological Review, 104,* 367–405.

Cobos, P. L., López, F. J., & Luque, D. (2007). Interference between cues of the same outcome depends on the causal interpretation of the events. *Quarterly Journal of Experimental Psychology, 60,* 369–386.

Danks, D. (2003). Equilibria of the Rescorla–Wagner model. *Journal of Mathematical Psychology, 47,* 109–121.

Danks, D. (in press). Causal learning from observations and manipulations. In M. Lovett & P. Shah (Eds.), *Thinking with data.* Mahwah, NJ: Lawrence Erlbaum Associates, Inc.

De Houwer, J., Vandorpe, S., & Beckers, T. (2007). Statistical contingency has a different impact on preparation judgements than on causal judgements. *Quarterly Journal of Experimental Psychology, 60,* 418–432.

Gelman, S. (2003). *The essential child. Origins of essentialism in everyday thought.* Cambridge, MA: Oxford University Press.

Glymour, C. (2001). *The mind's arrow. Bayes nets and graphical causal models in psychology.* Cambridge, MA: MIT Press.

Gopnik, A., Glymour, C., Sobel, D. M., Schulz, L. E., Kushnir, T., & Danks, D. (2004). A theory of causal learning in children: Causal maps and Bayes nets. *Psychological Review, 111,* 3–32.

Gopnik, A., & Meltzoff, A. N. (1997). *Words, thoughts and theories.* Cambridge, MA: MIT Press.

Gopnik, A., & Wellman, H. M. (1994). The theory theory. In L. Hirschfeld & S. Gelman (Eds.), *Mapping the mind: Domain specificity in cognition and culture* (pp. 257–293). New York: Cambridge University Press.

Griffiths, T. L., & Tenenbaum, J. B. (2005). Structure and strength in causal induction. *Cognitive Psychology, 51*, 285–386.

Hagmayer, Y., Sloman, S. A., Lagnado, D. A., & Waldmann, M. R. (in press). Causal reasoning through intervention. In A. Gopnik & L. Schulz (Eds.), *Causal learning: Psychology, philosophy, and computation.* Oxford, UK: Oxford University Press.

Hernstein, R. J. (1997). *The matching law.* Cambridge, MA: Harvard University Press.

Jensen, F. V. (1997). *An introduction to Bayesian networks.* London: Springer.

Keinath, A., & Krems, J. F. (1999). Anomalous data integration in diagnostic reasoning. In A. Bagnara (Ed.), *Proceedings of the 1999 European Conference on Cognitive Science* (pp. 213–218). Siena, Italy: Consiglo Nationale delle Ricerche.

Krems, J. F., & Johnson, T. (1995). Integration of anomalous data in multi causal explanations. In J. D. Moore & J. F. Lehman (Eds.), *Proceedings of the Seventeenth Annual Conference of the Cognitive Science Society* (pp. 277–282). Hillsdale, NJ: Lawrence Erlbaum Associates, Inc.

Kushnir, T., Gopnik, A., Schulz, L., & Danks, D. (2003). Inferring hidden causes. In P. Langley & M. G. Shafto (Eds.), *Proceedings of the Twenty-fifth Annual Conference of the Cognitive Science Society.* Mahwah, NJ: Lawrence Erlbaum Associates, Inc.

Lober, K., & Shanks, D. R. (2000). Is causal induction based on causal power? Critique of Cheng (1997). *Psychological Review, 107*, 195–212.

Luhmann, C. C., & Ahn, W.-K. (2003). Evaluating the causal role of unobserved variables. In P. Langley & M. G. Shafto (Eds.), *Proceedings of the Twenty-fifth Annual Conference of the Cognitive Science Society.* Mahwah, NJ: Lawrence Erlbaum Associates, Inc.

Meder, B., Hagmayer, Y., & Waldmann, Y. (2005). Doing after seeing. In B. G. Bara, L. Barsalou, & M. Bucciarelli (Eds.), *Proceedings of the Twenty-Seventh Annual Conference of the Cognitive Science Society.* Mahwah, NJ: Lawrence Erlbaum Associates, Inc.

Medin, D. L., & Ortony, A. (1989). Psychological essentialism. In S. Vosniadou & A. Ortony (Eds.), *Similarity and analogical reasoning* (pp. 179–195). Cambridge, UK: Cambridge University Press.

Myers, J. L. (1976). Probability learning and sequence learning. In W. K. Estes (Ed.), *Handbook of learning and cognitive processes: Approaches to human learning and motivation* (pp. 171–205). Hillsdale, NJ: Lawrence Erlbaum Associates, Inc.

Pearl, J. (1988). *Probabilistic reasoning in intelligent systems: Networks of plausible inference.* San Francisco, CA: Morgan Kaufmann.

Pearl, J. (2000). *Causality: Models, reasoning, and inference.* Cambridge, MA: Cambridge University Press.

Rehder, B. (2003). A causal-model theory of conceptual representation and categorization. *Journal of Experimental Psychology: Learning, Memory, and Cognition, 29*, 1141–1159.

Rehder, B., & Hastie, R. (2001). Causal knowledge and categories: The effects of causal beliefs on categorization, induction, and similarity. *Journal of Experimental Psychology: General, 130*, 323–360.

Rescorla, R. A., & Wagner, A. R. (1972). A theory of Pavlovian conditioning: Variations in the effectiveness of reinforcement and non-reinforcement. In A. H. Black & W. F. Prokasy (Eds.), *Classical conditioning II. Current research and theory* (pp. 64–99). New York: Appleton-Century-Crofts.

Shanks, D. R. (1987). Acquisition functions in contingency judgment. *Learning and Motivation, 18*, 147–166.

Shanks, D. R. (2007). Associationism and cognition: Human contingency learning at 25. *Quarterly Journal of Experimental Psychology, 60*, 291–309.

Shanks, D. R., Holyoak, K. J., & Medin, D. L. (1996). *The psychology of learning and motivation: Vol. 34. Causal learning.* San Diego, CA: Academic Press.

Sloman, S. A., & Lagnado, D. A. (2005). Do we "do"? *Cognitive Science, 29*, 5–39.

Spirtes, P., Glymour, C., & Scheines, R. (1993). *Causation, prediction and search.* New York: Springer.

Tenenbaum, J. B., & Griffiths, T. L. (2003). Theory-based causal inference. In T. K. Leen, T. G. Dietterich, & V. Tresp (Eds.), *Advances in neural information processing systems* (Vol. 15, pp. 35–42). Cambridge, MA: MIT Press.

Vandorpe, S., De Houwer, J., & Beckers, T. (2007). Outcome maximality and additivity training also influence cue competition in causal learning when learning involves many cues and events. *Quarterly Journal of Experimental Psychology, 60*, 356–368.

Vulkan, N. (2000). An economist's perspective on probability matching. *Journal of Economic Surveys, 14*, 101–118.

Waldmann, M. R., & Hagmayer, Y. (2001). Estimating causal strength: The role of structural knowledge and processing effort. *Cognition, 82*, 27–58.

Waldmann, M. R., & Hagmayer, Y. (2005). Seeing vs. doing: Two modes of accessing causal knowledge. *Journal of Experimental Psychology: Learning, Memory, and Cognition, 31,* 216–227.

Wasserman, E. A., Elek, S. M., Chatlosh, D. L., & Baker, A. G. (1993). Rating causal relations: Role of probability in judgments of response–outcome contingency. *Journal of Experimental Psychology: Learning, Memory, and Cognition, 19,* 174–188.

Wellman, H. M. (1990). *The child's theory of mind.* Cambridge, MA: MIT Press.

White, P. A. (2003). Making causal judgments from the proportion of confirming instances: The pCI rule. *Journal of Experimental Psychology: Learning, Memory, and Cognition, 29,* 710–727.

Woodward, J. (2003). *Making things happen. A theory of causal explanation.* Oxford, UK: Oxford University Press.

THE QUARTERLY JOURNAL OF EXPERIMENTAL PSYCHOLOGY
2007, 60 (3), 356–368

Outcome maximality and additivity training also influence cue competition in causal learning when learning involves many cues and events

Stefaan Vandorpe and Jan De Houwer

Ghent University, Ghent, Belgium

Tom Beckers

University of Leuven, Leuven, Belgium

Recent evidence shows that outcome maximality (e.g., De Houwer, Beckers, & Glautier, 2002) and additivity training (e.g., Lovibond, Been, Mitchell, Bouton, & Frohard, 2003) have an influence on cue competition in human causal learning. This evidence supports the idea that cue competition is based on controlled reasoning processes rather than on automatic associative processes. Until now, however, all the evidence for controlled reasoning processes comes from studies with rather simple designs that involved only few cues and events. We conducted two experiments with a complex design involving 24 different cues. The results showed that outcome maximality and additivity training had an influence on cue competition but that this influence was more pronounced for forward cue competition than for retrospective cue competition.

In human causal learning tasks, participants are presented with combinations of cues that are said to be potential causes of certain outcomes. After this learning stage, they are asked to assess for each cue separately to what extent it causes the outcome. Cue competition in human causal learning refers to the fact that the causal judgement about a target cue X is not only determined by the contingency between X and the outcome but also by the contingency between the outcome and an alternative cue A with which X co-occurred during the learning stage.

The most well-known cue competition effect is forward blocking (e.g., Dickinson, Shanks, & Evenden, 1984). In a forward blocking design, AX+ trials (cues A and X presented together and followed by the outcome) are preceded by A+ trials (cue A presented alone and followed by the outcome). Forward blocking refers to the fact that causal judgements for cue X in such a design will be lower than those when only AX+ trials are presented. Backward blocking (e.g., Shanks, 1985) refers to the same effect but the order of trials is reversed (AX+ trials precede the

Correspondence should be addressed to Stefaan Vandorpe, Department of Psychology, Ghent University, Henri Dunantlaan 2, B-9000 Gent, Belgium. E-mail: stefaan.vandorpe@UGent.be

Stefaan Vandorpe and Tom Beckers are postdoctoral researchers for the Fund for Scientific Research (FWO–Flanders, Belgium). We thank Klaus Melchers for providing us with a copy of the pictures that he used in his studies and Peter Lovibond and Michael Waldmann for their comments on an earlier draft of the paper.

http://www.psypress.com/qjep

DOI:10.1080/17470210601002561

A+ trials). Another cue competition effect is reduced overshadowing (e.g., De Houwer, Beckers, & Glautier, 2002). In a reduced overshadowing design, BY+ trials are preceded by B− trials (cue B presented alone and not followed by the outcome). Reduced overshadowing refers to the effect that causal judgement for cue Y will be higher than that when no B− trials precede the BY+ trials. Finally, release from overshadowing (e.g., Larkin, Aitken, & Dickinson, 1998) is the same effect as reduced overshadowing but the order of trials in the experimental design is reversed (BY+ trials precede the B− trials). Several studies on cue competition (e.g., Aitken, Larkin, & Dickinson, 2001; Chapman & Robbins, 1990; Dickinson & Burke, 1996; Melchers, Lachnit, & Shanks, 2004) combine A+, B−, AX+, and BY+ trials in their experimental design and compare the causal judgements of cues Y and X as a measure of cue competition. The difference in causal judgement between cues Y and X is called forward cue competition when A+ and B− trials precede the AX+ and BY+ trials and is called retrospective cue competition when the trial order is reversed.

Since the studies of Dickinson et al. (1984) and Shanks (1985), several associative models (e.g., Miller & Matzel, 1988; Rescorla & Wagner, 1972; Wagner, 1981) that were originally developed to explain animal conditioning have also been applied to human causal learning (e.g., Dickinson & Burke, 1996; Van Hamme & Wasserman, 1994; see Dickinson, 2001). This application of associative models to human causal learning has two foundations. First, the procedures of animal conditioning and human causal learning are very similar. Animals and humans are both faced with a series of trials in which certain stimuli (conditioned stimuli or cues) are followed by other stimuli (unconditioned stimuli or outcomes). The result of these trials is a change in behaviour. For example, in a typical fear conditioning study with animals, rats are faced with a tone followed by an electric shock. This results in an increased fear reaction upon presentation of the tone. In human causal learning, participants are presented with combinations of causes and

effects, and the change in behaviour is a changed causal judgement. Second, cue competition effects that were originally demonstrated in animal conditioning (e.g., forward blocking; see Kamin, 1969) were also found in human causal learning (e.g. Dickinson et al., 1984; Shanks, 1985). As a result of the similarity between the procedures of animal conditioning and human causal learning tasks and the observation that robust effects in animal conditioning can also be found in human causal learning, associative models of animal conditioning became increasingly popular in explaining human causal learning.

The core feature of associative models of animal conditioning and human causal learning is that the underlying processes are automatic and bottom-up. They do not include assumptions about the possible impact of controlled, top-down reasoning processes in human causal learning. Recently, however, increasing evidence suggests that cue competition is due to controlled reasoning processes (e.g., Lovibond, 2003; Lovibond, Been, Mitchell, Bouton, & Frohard, 2003; Waldmann, 2000; Waldmann & Walker, 2005; see De Houwer, Beckers, & Vandorpe, 2005, for a review). For example, Beckers, De Houwer, Pineño, and Miller (2005) found that additivity training of cues (see Lovibond et al., 2003, for similar results) and outcome maximality (see De Houwer et al., 2002; Vandorpe, De Houwer, & Beckers, 2005, and Wu & Cheng, 1999, for related results) influenced cue competition in human causal learning. When cues were explicitly pretrained to have additive effects on the outcome (i.e., when two pretraining cues T1 and T2 were presented together the outcome was more intense than when cue T1 and cue T2 were presented on their own) forward blocking was stronger than when cues were explicitly pretrained to have nonadditive effects (i.e., the pretraining cues T1 and T2 presented together caused the same intense outcome as when the cues were presented on their own). Furthermore, when the outcome on A+ and AX+ trials occurred with a maximal intensity (e.g., with an intensity of 10/10, De Houwer et al., 2002), forward blocking was weaker than when the outcome on A+ and

AX+ trials occurred with a submaximal intensity (e.g., with an intensity of 10/20).

Whereas existing associative models cannot explain the influence of additivity pretraining and outcome maximality on forward blocking (see Beckers et al., 2005, for a detailed discussion), these effects are compatible with higher order reasoning models of causal learning (e.g., De Houwer & Beckers, 2003; De Houwer et al., 2002; Lovibond et al., 2003; Waldmann, 2000; Waldmann & Walker, 2005). These models assume that participants come to a causal judgement by controlled reasoning processes. We can distinguish two broad levels of inference steps. The first level is the formation of premises. In the case of blocking, one has to make the premises that "A causes the outcome" and "A and X together cause the outcome". In the case of reduced overshadowing or release from overshadowing, one has to make the premises that "B does not cause the outcome" and "B and Y together cause the outcome". The second level is the derivation of a conclusion about the causal status of the target cue based on the premises. In the case of blocking, one can infer that X is not a cause of the outcome if A is the cause of the outcome, but only if (a) it can be verified that X adds nothing to the effect of A, and (b) cues have additive effects. If these conditions are not met (e.g., if A already causes the effect to a maximal extent or if one does not believe that cues have additive effects), the causal status of cue X is unsure, and X will receive a rating near the midpoint of the rating scale. Hence, blocking should occur only when the conditions for drawing the inference are met. Because manipulations of outcome maximality and additivity pretraining influence the extent to which the conditions are met, these manipulations should have an influence on blocking. In the case of reduced overshadowing or release from overshadowing, one can infer that cue Y is the cause of the outcome if B is not a cause of the outcome, independently of whether the outcome occurs to a maximal extent on BY+ trials or whether cues have additive effects or not. As a consequence, outcome maximality and additivity pretraining should have no influence on reduced overshadowing or release from overshadowing. These predictions have been confirmed (e.g., Beckers et al., 2005; De Houwer et al., 2002; Lovibond et al., 2003).

There is, however, an important caveat in the available evidence for the role of controlled reasoning processes in cue competition in human causal learning (see De Houwer et al., 2005, for a review). Until now, all studies that provided evidence for a higher order reasoning account of cue competition involved only very few cues and events. For instance, in the studies of De Houwer et al. (2002) that provided the first evidence for the effects of outcome maximality, there were only four events (A+, Z−, AX+, KL+), which were each presented at least 10 times. With such designs, participants can easily keep track of the different events and have ample opportunity to engage in controlled reasoning. Under these conditions, cue competition might indeed be based on reasoning and be sensitive to factors such as outcome maximality. Some researchers have pointed out that cue competition effects can be found even in situations where controlled reasoning processes are unlikely to take place. For instance, Le Pelley and McLaren (2003; also see Dickinson & Burke, 1996; Larkin et al., 1998; Wasserman & Berglan, 1998) found significant cue competition in a study in which 16 different cues were used, and 16 different compound stimuli were presented. They argued that the large number of cues "helped to ensure a large memory load, hopefully preventing subjects from basing their ratings on inferences made from explicit episodic memories. . . . Instead subjects should have to rely on associative processes to provide a more "automatic" measure of causal efficacy for each cue" (Le Pelley & McLaren, 2003, p. 74; also see Dickinson, 2001, p. 23). Also other authors (e.g., Waldmann & Walker, 2005) have argued that certain conflicting results in human contingency learning might be due to differences in the complexity of the design used. The aim of our studies was therefore to test whether we could find evidence for controlled reasoning processes in complex designs that involve many cues and events.

We did this by manipulating outcome maximality (maximal versus submaximal outcome, Experiment 1) and additivity pretraining (additive versus nonadditive pretraining, Experiment 2) within a complex design that consists of 24 different cues during the learning stage. If we still find an effect of these manipulations, it would strongly suggest that reasoning does play an important role even when the learning task is complex.

The design of our experiments was based on the design of Melchers et al. (2004; see Table 1), which is one of the most complex designs that has so far been used in causal learning studies. Melchers et al. used a food allergy paradigm wherein cues are foods, and the outcome is an allergic reaction. In order to measure retrospective cue competition, AB+, CD+ (first learning stage) and A+, C− (second learning stage) trials were presented. Retrospective cue competition corresponded to the mean causal rating of D minus the mean causal rating of B. In addition, E+, G− (first learning stage) and EF+, GH+ (second learning stage) trials were presented. This allows one to measure forward cue competition by subtracting the mean causal rating of F from the mean causal rating of H. Finally, there were also filler items (IJ−, K−, I−, KL−). To further increase the complexity of the design, Melchers et al. (2004) assigned two foods to each cue (i.e., two different foods allocated to cues A up to L), resulting in a design consisting of 24 different names of foods and 24 different events (e.g., two different A+ trials). In order to measure not only forward and retrospective cue competition but also the specific cue competition effects forward and backward blocking, reduced overshadowing and release from overshadowing, we made a modification to this original design of Melchers et al. Instead of two different IJ− and two different KL− trials, we only presented one IJ− event and one KL− event. The other nonreinforced IJ− and KL− event was reversed into reinforced trials, indicated by the XY+ and WZ+ trials in Table 1. As such, forward blocking can be measured by the mean causal rating of W and Z minus the causal rating of F, backward blocking by the mean causal rating of X and Y minus the causal rating of B, reduced overshadowing by the causal rating of H minus the mean causal rating of W and Z, and release from overshadowing by the causal rating of D minus the mean causal ratings of X and Y. As a consequence of our modification to the original design of Melchers et al., there were two different cues allocated to cues A up to H, but only one different food to the other cues. This resulted in a design with 24 cues and 22 different events.

EXPERIMENT 1

In our first experiment, we manipulated outcome maximality in a similar manner to that in the studies of De Houwer et al. (2002) but now used the more complex design described above. In the nonceiling condition, the outcome (allergic reaction) occurred with a submaximal intensity of 10/20 while in the ceiling condition the outcome occurred with a maximal intensity of 10/10.

Method

Participants

A total of 32 first-year psychology students at Ghent University participated for course credit. They were randomly assigned to the ceiling and no-ceiling conditions.

Table 1. *Design of the experiments*

	First stage	Second stage
Retrospective cue competition	AB+, CD+	A+, C−
Forward cue competition	E+, G−	EF+, GH+
Control cues	XY+	WZ+
Fillers	IJ−, K−	I−, KL−

Note: All letters refer to different foods. There were two different foods allocated to the letters A to H, while only one food to the other letters. This resulted in a design with 24 cues and 22 events. The "+" stands for occurrence of the outcome, which was an allergic reaction, and the "−" for nonoccurrence of the outcome.

Design, stimuli, and material

The design (see Table 1) was based on that of Melchers et al. (2004). In the first learning stage, AB+, CD+, E+, G−, XY+, IJ−, and K− trials were presented. In the second learning stage, A+, C−, EF+, GH+, WZ+, I−, and KL− trials were presented. Two different foods were assigned to cues A up to H, while only one food was assigned to the other cues. This resulted in a complex design with 24 cues and 22 events— 17 cues and 11 events in each learning stage. Each stage consisted of four blocks. Within each block, every event was presented twice, resulting in 22 trials per block—88 in each stage and 176 in the entire experiment. The sequence of trials within each block was randomized. There were no breaks between blocks or stages. The cues were presented as coloured pictures of foods against a white background, with the name of the food under the picture in a black colour. The following foods were used (translated from Dutch): apples, avocado, bananas, blueberries, broccoli, carrots, cherries, coffee, eggs, fish, grapes, ice-cream, kiwi, lemon, meat, mushrooms, nuts, pears, peppers, popcorn, potatoes, strawberries, toast, and tomatoes. As outcomes, the messages "allergic reaction: 10/20" (no-ceiling condition) and "allergic reaction: 10/10" (ceiling condition) were presented in a black colour under the picture and the name of the food. If the food was not followed by the outcome, the message "allergic reaction: 0/20" (or 0/10 in the ceiling condition) was presented.

The task was presented on a Pentium I PC and implemented using a custom made Inquisit program. Four different allocations of the foods to the different cues were used and were counterbalanced across participants.

Procedure

At the beginning of the experiment, the learning instructions appeared on the screen (see Appendix for full instructions). Participants were asked to imagine that they were a medical doctor who was treating a patient suffering from allergic reactions after eating certain foods. Their task was to determine for each food separately to what extent it caused an allergic reaction in the patient. After reading the learning instructions, participants could press a key to start the learning stage that consisted of 176 trials. Each trial started with the presentation of one or two foods. After 2,000 ms, information about the intensity of the allergic reaction was added at the bottom of the screen during 3,000 ms. The intertrial interval (ITI) was 3,000 ms. After presentation of all learning trials, participants were asked to judge for each food how likely it was to cause an allergic reaction on a scale from 1 to 9, where 1 stands for "never causes an allergic reaction" and "9" for "always causes an allergic reaction". On each test trial, the picture and corresponding name of a food was presented in the centre of the screen, and participants could made their causal rating by a click with the mouse on a digit of a Likert rating scale. The scale was presented underneath the picture and name of the food. The presentation of the foods was randomized for each participant separately. The ITI between two test trials was 1,000 ms.

Results

The causal ratings for the cues of importance are given in Table 2. First, we analysed the causal ratings for cues B, F, D, and H in order to investigate the influence of outcome maximality on forward and retrospective cue competition. Secondly, we also looked at the influence of outcome maximality on the specific cue competition effects. The ratings of cues B, F, D, and H were analysed by a 2 (type: blocked cues B and F versus reduced overshadowing cues D and H) × 2 (order: forward cues F and H versus backward cues B and D) × 2 (condition: no-ceiling versus ceiling condition) analysis of variance (ANOVA) with type and order as within-subject variables and condition as between-subject variable. This analysis revealed a main effect of type, $F(1, 30) = 270.89$, $p < .001$, a significant Type × Order interaction, $F(1, 30) = 9.13$, $p < .01$, and a marginally significant Type × Condition interaction, $F(1, 30) = 3.29$, $p = .08$. Also, the three-way Type × Order × Condition interaction was almost significant, $F(1, 30) = 4.06$, $p < .06$. In

Table 2. *Mean causal ratings for the blocked cues B and F, the reduced overshadowing cues D and H, and the mean of the control cues W and Z and X and Y in Experiment 1*

	B		F		D		H		WZ		XY	
	M	SE	M	SE	M	SE	M	SE	M	SE	M	SE
No-ceiling	2.69	0.74	1.34	0.19	8.28	0.52	9.59	0.31	5.53	0.28	4.69	0.48
Ceiling	4.03	0.66	3.81	0.53	9.31	0.31	9.63	0.28	6.06	0.38	6.66	0.51

order to clarify these interactions we analysed the Type × Condition interaction for each order separately and the Type × Order interaction for each condition separately.

Concerning forward cue competition, the Type (cue F versus cue H) × Condition ANOVA revealed a main effect of type, $F(1, 30) = 327.45$, $p < .001$, and an interaction of type with condition, $F(1, 30) = 9.84$, $p < .01$. The interaction demonstrates that forward cue competition was stronger in the no-ceiling condition. Furthermore, paired-sample t tests showed that forward cue competition was significant in both conditions, $t(15) = 24.37$, $p < .001$, and $t(15) = 8.31$, $p < .001$, for the no-ceiling and ceiling condition, respectively. Finally, independent-samples t tests showed that the causal rating of the blocked cue F was affected by condition, $t(30) = 4.39$, $p < .001$, but not the causal rating of the reduced overshadowing cue H, $t(30) < 1$.

Concerning backward cue competition, the Type (cue B versus cue D) × Condition ANOVA revealed a main effect of type, $F(1, 30) = 107.48$, $p < .001$, but no interaction with condition, $F(1, 30) < 1$. Independent-samples t tests showed that the differences in causal ratings between conditions for cues B and D failed to reach significance, $t(30) = 1.35$, $p > .15$, $t(30) = 1.69$, $p > .10$, respectively.

The Type × Order interaction was significant in the no-ceiling condition, $F(1, 15) = 14.68$, $p < .01$, but not in the ceiling condition, $F(1, 15) < 1$. The interaction of type with order in the no-ceiling condition demonstrates that forward cue competition was significantly stronger than retrospective cue competition.

We also looked to see whether there were differences in specific cue competition effects

between conditions (see Figure 1). Independent-samples t tests revealed a significant difference in forward blocking between conditions, $t(30) = 2.88$, $p < .01$. This was not the case for backward blocking, reduced overshadowing, and release from overshadowing, ts < 1.10.

Discussion

Experiment 1 investigated whether outcome maximality still had an influence on cue competition in a complex design. The results showed that the most important influence was a significant decrease of the causal rating of the forward blocked cue F when the outcome was submaximal.

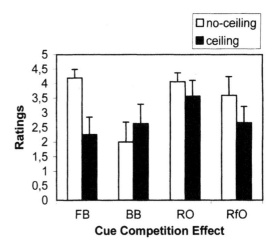

Figure 1. *Forward blocking, backward blocking, reduced overshadowing, and release from overshadowing in Experiment 1. White bars represent the competition effects for the no-ceiling condition, and dark bars represent the competition effects for the ceiling condition. Error bars represent standard errors of the mean. FB stands for forward blocking, BB for backward blocking, RO for reduced overshadowing, and RfO for release from overshadowing.*

As a result of this significant decrease, forward cue competition and forward blocking were significantly stronger in the no-ceiling condition than in the ceiling condition. The manipulation of outcome maximality did not have a significant influence on the causal rating of the backward blocking cue B, and as a result retrospective cue competition and backward blocking were not significantly different between ceiling conditions. Finally, the significant decrease of the causal rating of cue F but not of cue B in the no-ceiling condition resulted in stronger forward cue competition than retrospective cue competition in the no-ceiling condition.

The results of forward cue competition were in line with higher order reasoning accounts of human causal learning. According to these accounts, the decrease in the causal ratings of the forward blocked cue F in the no-ceiling condition is due to the fact that participants can infer the noncausal status of F with certainty in the no-ceiling condition (note that the mean causal rating for cue F is near 1, the lowest possible value) while the causal status of cue F is unsure in the ceiling condition. Outcome maximality, however, should not influence ratings for the reduced overshadowing cue H because participants can infer with certainty on GH+ trials that H has to be the cause of the outcome if G is not a cause of the outcome (an assumption that participants can make on the basis of the G− trials), irrespective of whether the outcome on GH+ trials is maximal or submaximal.

Higher order reasoning accounts, however, also predict similar results for retrospective cue competition—that is, a significant decrease in the backward blocking cue B in the no-ceiling condition and no significant differences between conditions for the causal rating of the release from overshadowing cue D. Although the results were in line with the latter prediction, no significant difference between conditions was found for the mean causal rating of cue B. We return to this finding in the General Discussion.

One might be surprised that we still found substantial blocking in the ceiling condition. Such a finding seems to contradict the fact that under these conditions, participants should be unsure about the causal status of the blocked cue, and hence no blocking should be found. However, previous research (Vandorpe et al., 2005, Exp. 2) showed that also in a simple design some participants reason that X is not a cause of the outcome, even if the outcome is merely present on A+ and AX+ trials. These participants thus seem to ignore the possibility that the effect of X was hidden because of ceiling effects. It is likely that some participants also failed to take into account this factor in the present study, especially given the high load imposed by the complex design. When faced with a complex design, it might indeed be easier to simply ignore the possibility of ceiling effects because this removes uncertainty and allows one to classify blocked stimuli as noncauses. Waldmann (2000) pointed at a second reason for why blocking can be found under ceiling conditions. He speculated that participants might infer that the control cues have intermediate causal strength while the causal strength of the blocked cue could range between zero and deterministic strength. Participants could express this difference by giving different causal ratings, notwithstanding that they are aware that they do not have enough evidence to determine the causal status of the blocked cue and the overshadowing control cues. Another reason why blocking might have occurred in the ceiling and additive conditions is that participants pay less attention to the cues that are redundant as information processing becomes more complex. This latter possibility fits well within associative models that assign a crucial role to attentional processes (e.g., Kruschke, 2001, Kruschke & Blair, 2000; Mackintosh, 1975) or could point to attentional processes that interfere with the induction of appropriate premises (see De Houwer et al., 2005). Finally, the possibility remains that the blocking effect in the ceiling condition was due to associative processes like those described in the Rescorla–Wagner model (Rescorla & Wagner, 1972). It would be interesting for further research to investigate these different possibilities.

EXPERIMENT 2

In Experiment 2, we investigated the influence of additivity pretraining within a complex design. In the additive condition, participants were pretrained with the following events: T1 and T2 presented on their own and followed by an allergic reaction with an intensity of 5; T1 and T2 presented together and followed by an allergic reaction with an intensity of 10; T3 followed by an allergic reaction with an intensity of 5; and T4 followed by no allergic reaction. The pretraining stage in the nonadditive condition differed in two ways from the pretraining stage in the additive condition. The presentation of foods T1 and T2 together was followed by an allergic reaction with an intensity of 5, and the presentation of food T3 was followed by an allergic reaction with an intensity of 10. The reason why the intensity of the allergic reaction was 10 and not 5 on T3+ trials is that there would otherwise be a confound between the influence of nonadditivity training (T2 adds nothing to the effect of T1 alone) and an influence of outcome maximality (if the intensity of the allergic reaction on T3+ trials was 5, this would be the maximal outcome ever experienced by the participants). The foods allocated to the pretraining cues were different from the foods allocated to the cues used in the learning stage.

Method

Participants
A total of 30 first-year psychology students at Ghent University participated for course credit. They were randomly assigned to the additive or nonadditive condition.

Design, stimuli, materials, and procedure
We only mention the differences compared to Experiment 1. First, the part of the instructions of Experiment 1 (see Appendix) starting at "Note that if the patient ate two different foods ..." and ending with the last sentence of the first full paragraph of the instructions was

dropped. Furthermore, after the sentence "You will also receive information about whether the patient showed an allergic reaction or not", we added the phrase "and information about the intensity of the allergic reaction". Second, before the learning stage, a pretraining stage was added. In the additive condition, participants were presented T1+, T2+, T1T2++, T3+, and T4−, where the + stands for occurrence of the outcome with an intensity of 5 and the + + for occurrence of the outcome with an intensity of 10. In the nonadditive condition, participants were pretrained with T1+, T2+, T1T2+, T3++, and T4−. The foods cheese, wine, pineapple, and corn were allocated to the four training cues. Each food was allocated once to each cue, and this allocation was matched with the four different allocations of the foods to the learning cues. Finally, all outcomes that were presented during the learning stage had an intensity of 5. Note that no information was given about the maximum intensity that could be measured (i.e., the upper limit of the intensity scale) because we did not want to confound possible effects of outcome maximality and additivity training.

Results

The causal ratings for the cues of importance are given in Table 3. Just like in Experiment 1, the ratings for cues B, F, D, and H were analysed using a 2 (type: blocked cues B and F versus reduced overshadowing cues D and H) × 2 (order: forward cues F and H versus backward cues B and D) × 2 (condition: additive versus nonadditive condition) ANOVA with type and order as within-subject variables and condition as between-subject variable. This analysis revealed a main effect of type, $F(28) = 80.40$, $p < .001$, an interaction effect of type and condition, $F(1, 28) = 12.81$, $p = .001$, and an interaction effect of type and order, $F(1, 28) = 5.56$, $p < .05$. None of the other effects reached significance, $Fs < 1.2$. Forward cue competition and retrospective cue competition were both significant in the additive condition, $t(14) = 8.29$, $p < .001$, and $t(14) = 7.70$, $p < .001$, respectively, and in the

Table 3. *Mean causal ratings for the blocked cues B and F, the reduced overshadowing cues D and H, and the mean of the control cues W and Z and X and Y in Experiment 2*

	B		F		D		H		WZ		XY	
	M	SE	M	SE	M	SE	M	SE	M	SE	M	SE
Additive	2.87	0.42	1.87	0.40	7.60	0.67	8.23	0.54	4.97	0.39	4.87	0.53
Nonadditive	5.03	0.56	5.00	0.55	6.97	0.72	7.83	0.65	5.80	0.41	5.87	0.40

nonadditive condition, $t(14) = 4.77, p < .001$, and $t(14) = 2.13, p = .051$, respectively. More importantly, forward and retrospective cue competition were both stronger in the additive condition than in the nonadditive condition, $t(28) = 3.64, p = .001$, and $t(28) = 2.56, p < .05$. Forward cue competition was also stronger than retrospective cue competition in the additive condition, $t(14) = 2.44, p < .05$, but not in the nonadditive condition, $t(14) = 1.07, p > .30$. Finally, independent-samples t tests revealed that the causal ratings for the forward blocked cue B and for the backward blocked cue F were affected by additivity, $t(28) = 3.09, p < .01$, and $t(28) = 4.59, p < .001$, respectively. This was not the case for the causal ratings for the reduced overshadowing cue H, $t(28) < 1$, and the release from overshadowing cue D, $t(28) < 1$.

As in Experiment 1, we also looked to see whether specific cue competition effects were affected by additivity condition (see Figure 2). Independent-samples t tests revealed a significant difference in forward blocking between conditions, $t(28) = 3.00, p < .01$, and a marginally significant difference in reduced overshadowing, $t(28) = 1.75, p < .10$. The differences in backward blocking and unovershadowing failed to reach significance, $t(28) = 1.64, p > .10, t(28) = 1.65, p > .10$, respectively.

cue B decreased significantly when cues were pretrained to have additive effects. This was not the case for the reduced overshadowing cue H and the release from overshadowing cue D. As a result of the decrease of the causal ratings for cues B and F, forward and retrospective cue competition were stronger in the additive than in the nonadditive condition. Similar to Experiment 1, forward cue competition was stronger than retrospective cue competition in the additive condition but not in the nonadditive condition. Also in line with Experiment 1, only forward blocking was significantly affected by condition.

The results of forward and retrospective cue competition were fully in line with higher order

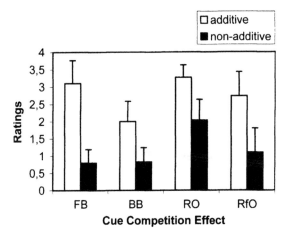

Figure 2. *Forward blocking, backward blocking, reduced overshadowing, and release from overshadowing in Experiment 2. White bars represent the competition effects for the additivity condition, and dark bars represent the competition effects for the nonadditivity condition. Error bars represent standard errors of the mean. FB stands for forward blocking, BB for backward blocking, RO for reduced overshadowing, and RfO for release from overshadowing.*

Discussion

In Experiment 2, we investigated whether manipulating outcome additivity had an influence on cue competition in a complex design. The results showed that the mean causal rating for the forward blocked cue F and the backward blocked reasoning accounts of human causal learning. According to these accounts, participants will infer that the blocked cues B and F are noncausal when they can verify that both cues add nothing to the effect of an alternative cue with which they were presented together, provided that they assume that cues have additive effects. In line with this latter qualification, causal ratings for cue B and F were significantly higher when the additivity assumption was violated by pretraining than when the additivity assumption was confirmed by pretraining. The causal status of the reduced overshadowing cues, however, was not affected by outcome additivity. When one cue never causes the outcome when presented alone (cue C or G) but is followed by the outcome when presented together with another cue (cue D or H), one can infer that the latter cue has to be the cause of the outcome, irrespective of whether cues have additive or nonadditive effects.

One aspect of the results that does not seem to be in line with higher order reasoning models is the fact that reduced overshadowing tended to be smaller in the nonadditivity condition than in the additivity condition. A closer look at the data revealed that this was mainly due to the effect of condition on the mean causal ratings of the control cues W and Z (an increase of .8) rather than to an effect of condition on the mean causal rating of the reduced overshadowing cue H (a decrease of .4, see Table 3). Also the backward control cues X and Y increased with 1.0 in the nonadditivity condition relative to the additivity condition. A possible explanation for this slight increase in causal ratings of the control cues is that the chance for the control cues to cause an allergic reaction with an intensity of 5 is .75 in the nonadditive condition (either both cause an allergic reaction with an intensity of 5 or only one does) while in the additive condition the chance to cause an allergic reaction of 5 is .50 (only one control cue can cause an allergic reaction of 5). The chance of being causal for a reduced overshadowing cue, however, is always 1, irrespective of whether cues have additive effects or not. Because the difference between the chance for a control cue to be causal and the chance for a

reduced overshadowing control to be causal to be smaller in the nonadditive condition than in the additive condition, a smaller reduced overshadowing effect in the nonadditive condition could have occurred. Note that the higher causal ratings of the control cues cannot account for the significant difference in forward blocking. On the contrary, the higher causal ratings of the control cues in the nonadditive condition allow, if anything, more blocking whereas blocking was significantly lower in the nonadditive condition.

GENERAL DISCUSSION

We investigated whether outcome maximality and additivity pretraining had an influence on cue competition in complex designs. The results showed that forward cue competition and forward blocking were indeed smaller when the intensity of the outcome was maximal and when cues were explicitly pretrained to have nonadditive effects than when the intensity of the outcome was submaximal and when cues were explicitly pretrained to have additive effects. Also the causal rating of the forward blocked cue F but not the causal rating of the reduced overshadowing cue H was affected by both outcome maximality and additivity pretraining. Retrospective cue competition and the causal rating of the backward blocked cue B, on the other hand, were significantly influenced by additivity training but not by outcome maximality.

The results that we found for forward cue competition are in line with higher order reasoning accounts of human causal learning. According to these accounts (e.g. Lovibond et al., 2003; Waldmann & Walker, 2005) one cannot infer the causal status of a blocked cue X when the outcome on A+ and AX+ trials is always fully present, whereas one can infer that cue X is noncausal when the outcome occurs to the same submaximal intensity on these trials, provided that one assumes that cues have additive effects (e.g., De Houwer et al., 2002). In line with these hypotheses, causal ratings of the blocked cue were lower and forward blocking stronger when the outcome occurred with the same submaximal intensity than when the outcome had the highest possible intensity (Experiment 1) and when cues were pretrained to have additive effects than when they were trained to have nonadditive effects (Experiment 2). Importantly, the causal status of a reduced overshadowing cue Y can always be inferred with certainty, irrespective of whether the outcome occurs to a maximal or submaximal intensity on B− and BY+ trials and irrespective of whether cues have additive or nonadditive effects. In line with this logic, the causal status of the reduced overshadowing cue H was not affected by outcome maximality and additivity pretraining.

The results of retrospective cue competition were less unequivocally in favour of higher order reasoning accounts of human causal learning. On the one hand, the results of Experiment 2 were in line with the predictions of these accounts. That is, causal ratings of the backward blocked cue B but not the release from overshadowing cue D were affected by nonadditivity pretraining. On the other hand, the causal rating of the backward blocked cue B was not significantly affected by the manipulation of outcome maximality in Experiment 1. However, both the influence of outcome maximality and additivity pretraining were more pronounced for forward cue competition than for retrospective cue competition. One could explain these observations by assuming that backward driven inferences are more difficult to make than forward driven inferences. There is indeed evidence from the reasoning literature (Evans, Newstead, & Byrne, 1993, pp. 233–234) and from studies with children (Bindra, Clarke, & Shultz, 1980) that processing information in a backward direction is more difficult than processing information in a forward direction. As we explained in the Introduction, drawing a valid inference involves several steps (i.e., formulating the premises, deriving a conclusion that takes into account assumptions about additivity).

As a consequence of the higher cognitive load for retrospective inferences, some participants may have failed to take into account assumptions about additivity.

The fact that we found evidence for controlled reasoning processes within a complex design does not mean that complexity itself cannot affect controlled reasoning processes. In a recent study at our laboratory (Vandorpe & De Houwer, 2006), we manipulated the complexity of the design (simple versus complex condition). The results showed that retrospective cue competition but not forward cue competition was smaller in the complex condition. It was concluded that retrospective but not forward reasoning processes were affected by the complexity manipulation. Instead of manipulating the complexity of the design, one can also affect the influence of controlled reasoning processes on cue competition by asking participants to perform a secondary task during the learning task. Recent studies indeed found that blocking[1] decreased within a simple design when participants had to perform a secondary task (Waldmann & Walker, 2005) or when the difficulty of the secondary task was increased (De Houwer & Beckers, 2003). In sum, what the studies of Vandorpe and De Houwer, Waldmann and Walker, and De Houwer and Beckers suggest is that cue competition effects are due to controlled reasoning processes and that these effects decrease when controlled reasoning processes are affected by an increasing load on working memory capacity.

One could argue that we still found an effect of reasoning because the task was not complex enough. Undoubtedly one can create even more complex tasks, and we cannot exclude the possibility that the manipulations would not eliminate the effect of reasoning processes in these tasks. What we can conclude, however, is that controlled reasoning processes cannot simply be dismissed a priori as a source of cue competition effects in

---

[1] A higher order reasoning account predicts small or no blocking effects when the outcome always occurs on A+ and AX+ trials. However, Waldmann and Walker (2005) compared the causal rating of the blocked cue X with the causal rating of cue A, and in the study of De Houwer and Beckers (2003) the outcome occurred with a submaximal intensity. As a consequence, strong blocking effects occurred in the easy task conditions.

studies with complex designs. Our data also show that reasoning processes still play a role in designs of similar complexity as in studies that have been assumed to prevent controlled reasoning processes (e.g., Le Pelley & McLaren, 2003). Hence, previous evidence for cue competition effects in studies with complex designs cannot simply be regarded as evidence for associative models of cue competition. Instead, even with complex designs, researchers need to check whether reasoning processes operate.

REFERENCES

Aitken, M. R .F., Larkin, M. J. W., & Dickinson, A. (2001). Re-examination of the role of within-compound associations in the retrospective revaluation of causal judgements. *Quarterly Journal of Experimental Psychology, 54B*, 27–51.

Beckers, T., De Houwer, J., Pineño, O., & Miller, R. R. (2005). Outcome additivity and outcome maximality influence cue competition in human causal learning. *Journal of Experimental Psychology: Learning, Memory, and Cognition, 31*, 238–249.

Bindra, D., Clarke, K. A., & Shultz, T. R. (1980). Understanding predictive relations of necessity and sufficiency in formally equivalent "causal" and "logical" problems. *Journal of Experimental Psychology: General, 109*, 422–443.

Chapman, G. B., & Robbins, S. J. (1990). Cue interaction in human contingency judgment. *Memory & Cognition, 18*, 537–545.

De Houwer, J., & Beckers, T. (2003). Secondary task difficulty modulates forward blocking in human contingency learning. *Quarterly Journal of Experimental Psychology, 56B*, 345–357.

De Houwer, J., Beckers, T., & Glautier, S. (2002). Outcome and cue properties modulate blocking. *Quarterly Journal of Experimental Psychology, 55B*, 3–25.

De Houwer, J., Beckers, T., & Vandorpe, S. (2005). Evidence for the role of higher-order reasoning processes in cue competition and other learning phenomena. *Learning & Behavior, 33*, 239–249.

Dickinson, A. (2001). The 28th Bartlett memorial lecture: Causal learning: An associative analysis. *Quarterly Journal of Experimental Psychology, 54B*, 3–25.

Dickinson, A., & Burke, J. (1996). Within-compound associations mediate the retrospective revaluation of causality judgements. *Quarterly Journal of Experimental Psychology, 49B*, 60–80.

Dickinson, A., Shanks, D., & Evenden, J. (1984). Judgement of act-outcome contingency: The role of selective attribution. *Quarterly Journal of Experimental Psychology, 36A*, 29–50.

Evans, J. St. B. T., Newstead, S. E., & Byrne, R. M. J. (1993). *Human reasoning: The psychology of deduction.* Hove, UK: Lawrence Erlbaum Associates Ltd.

Kamin, L. J. (1969). Predictability, surprise, attention, and conditioning. In R. M. Church (Ed.), *Punishment and aversive behaviour* (pp. 279–296). New York: Appleton-Century-Crofts.

Kruschke, J. K. (2001). Toward a unified model of attention in associative learning. *Journal of Mathematical Psychology, 45*, 812–863.

Kruschke, J. K., & Blair, N. J. (2000). Blocking and backward blocking involve learned inattention. *Psychonomic Bulletin & Review, 7*, 636–645.

Larkin, M. J. W., Aitken, M. R. F., & Dickinson, A. (1998). Retrospective revaluation of causal judgements under positive and negative contingencies. *Journal of Experimental Psychology: Learning, Memory, and Cognition, 24*, 1331–1352.

Le Pelley, M. E., & McLaren, I. P. L. (2003). Learned associability and associative change in human causal learning. *Quarterly Journal of Experimental Psychology, 56B*, 68–79.

Lovibond, P. F. (2003). Causal beliefs and conditioned responses: Retrospective revaluation induced by experience and by instruction. *Journal of Experimental Psychology: Learning, Memory, and Cognition, 29*, 97–106.

Lovibond, P. F., Been, S.-L., Mitchell, C. J., Bouton, M. E., & Frohardt, R. (2003). Forward and backward blocking of causal judgement is enhanced by additivity of effect magnitude. *Memory and Cognition, 31*, 133–142.

Mackintosh, N. J. (1975). A theory of attention: Variations in the associability of stimuli with reinforcement, *Psychological Review, 82*, 276–298.

Melchers, K. G., Lachnit, H., & Shanks, D. (2004). Within-compound associations in retrospective revaluation and in direct learning: A challenge for comparator theory. *Quarterly Journal of Experimental Psychology, 57B*, 25–54.

Miller, R. R., & Matzel, L. D. (1988). The comparator hypothesis: A response rule for the expression of associations. In G. H. Bower (Ed.), *The psychology of learning* and motivation: Vol. 22. Advances in research and theory (pp. 51–92). San Diego, CA: Academic Press.

Rescorla, R. A., & Wagner, A. R. (1972). A theory of Pavlovian conditioning: Variations in the effectiveness of reinforcement and nonreinforcement. In A. H. Black & W. F. Prokasy (Eds.), Classical conditioning II: Current research and theory (pp. 64–99). New York: Appleton.

Shanks, D. R. (1985). Forward and backward blocking in human contingency judgement. Quarterly Journal of Experimental Psychology, 37B, 1–21.

Vandorpe, S., & De Houwer, J. (2006). A comparison of cue competition in a simple and a complex design. Acta Psychologica, 122, 234–246.

Vandorpe, S., De Houwer, J., & Beckers, T. (2005). Further evidence for the role of inferential reasoning in forward blocking. Memory & Cognition, 33, 1047–1056.

Van Hamme, L. J., & Wasserman, E. A. (1994). Cue competition in causality judgements: The role of nonpresentation of compound stimulus elements. Learning & Motivation, 25, 127–151.

Wagner, A. R. (1981). SOP. A model of automatic memory processing in animal behavior. In N. E. Spear & R. R. Miller (Eds.), Information processing in animals: Memory mechanisms (pp. 5–47). Hillsdale, NJ: Lawrence Erlbaum Associates, Inc.

Waldmann, M. R. (2000). Competition among causes but not effects in predictive and diagnostic learning. Journal of Experimental Psychology: Learning, Memory, and Cognition, 26, 53–76.

Waldmann, M. R., & Walker, J. M. (2005). Competence and performance in human causal learning. Learning & Behavior, 33, 211–229.

Wasserman, E. A., & Berglan, I. R. (1998). Backward blocking and recovery from overshadowing in human causal judgement: The role of within-compound associations. Quarterly Journal of Experimental Psychology, 51B, 121–138.

Wu, M., & Cheng, P. W. (1999). Why causation need not follow from statistical covariation: Boundary conditions for the evaluation of generative and preventative causal powers. Psychological Science, 10, 93–97.

APPENDIX

Learning instructions for the no-ceiling condition (translated from Dutch; in the ceiling condition, the maximal intensity on the penultimate line of the first paragraph is replaced by 10).

This experiment is about how people learn relations between different events. Try to imagine that you are a doctor. One of your patients suffers from allergic reactions after eating certain foods. To discover which foods lead to an allergic reaction, the patient has eaten specific foods on different days and this was followed by a test on whether an allergic reaction occurred. In a moment, you will see the results of these daily allergy tests one by one on the screen. On each trial, you will first see what the patient had eaten that day. On some days, he only ate one food; on other days he ate two different foods. Look carefully each time to what the patient ate that day. You will also receive information about whether the patient showed an allergic reaction or not. Use this information to determine for each food separately whether it leads to an allergic reaction in your patient. Note that if the patient ate two different foods and there was an allergic reaction, you do not know which of the two foods was responsible for the allergic reaction. But you will always get information about the total intensity of the allergic reaction, as caused by all consumed foods. If the intensity is zero, this means that there is no allergic reaction; if the intensity is greater than zero, this means that there is an allergic reaction. Note that the maximal intensity that can be measured corresponds to an intensity of 20. You have to determine for each food separately to which extent it causes an allergic reaction in the patient.

First you will see information about 176 allergy tests. After that, you will have to judge for each food the extent to which you think it is a cause of an allergic reaction in the patient. Notice that only the presented information can help you. The task is to determine to which extent the foods cause an allergic reaction in this specific patient. Your personal experiences with the foods or occasional knowledge about the properties of the foods are not relevant and cannot help you. Only the presented information matters.

THE QUARTERLY JOURNAL OF EXPERIMENTAL PSYCHOLOGY
2007, 60 (3), 369–386

Interference between cues of the same outcome depends on the causal interpretation of the events

Pedro L. Cobos, Francisco J. López, and David Luque

University of Málaga, Spain

In an interference-between-cues design, the expression of a learned Cue A → Outcome 1 association has been shown to be impaired if another cue, B, is separately paired with the same outcome in a second learning phase. In the present study, we assessed whether this interference effect is mediated by participants' previous causal knowledge. This was achieved by having participants learn in a diagnostic situation in Experiment 1a, and then by manipulating the causal order of the learning task in Experiments 1b and 2. If participants use their previous causal knowledge during the learning process, interference should only be observed in the diagnostic situation because only there we have a common cause (Outcome 1) of two disjoint effects, namely cues A and B. Consistent with this prediction, interference between cues was only found in Experiment 1a and in the diagnostic conditions of Experiments 1b and 2.

In daily life causal relationships have to be inferred from data collected from a huge variety of different contexts (whether physical or temporal). In such circumstances, a crucial task for our cognitive system is to determine whether or not what we have learned in one context is valid in another one. In other words, our cognitive system has to evaluate whether the data sets coming from two (or more) different contexts have to be integrated to calculate the causal relationship between events or whether each data set has to enter into different computations to calculate causal relationships that are valid in one context but not in others. Thus, an important question in the causal learning field is to understand the circumstances in which people assume that what has been learned in one context is applicable in another one, as well as the circumstances in which people do not hold this assumption.

In our view, the study of retrospective interference in learning experiments can make important contributions to address the above questions. In an interference experiment, the expression of a previously learned relationship between a cue (or antecedent event), A, and an outcome (or consequent event), O1 (A–O1 relationship), is hindered if another relationship (e.g., A–O2, or B–O1) is learned in a later training phase[1].

---

[1] We should term this effect as retroactive interference to distinguish it from the proactive interference effect. Since we will only focus on the former, the term "interference" should be interpreted, hereafter, in the narrow sense of retroactive interference.

Correspondence should be addressed to Dr. Pedro L. Cobos, Departamento de Psicología Básica, Campus de los Teatinos, Universidad de Málaga, Málaga 29071, Spain. E-mail: p_cobos@uma.es

The research described here was supported by research grant from Junta de Andalucía (HUM-0105) from Spain. David Luque has been supported by F.P.I. fellowships also from Junta de Andalucía (Ref.: 4381).

We would like to thank Julián Almaraz, Fernando Blanco, Helena Matute, and Miguel A. Vadillo for their helpful comments on the experiments presented here.

369

DOI:10.1080/17470210601000961

There is extensive evidence, both from human and from animal learning experiments, that interference is not due to unlearning of the A-O1 relationship. It is well known that the expression of this relationship can recover almost completely if certain contextual cues (whether physical or temporal) are manipulated. For instance, if the A-O1 relationship is learned in Context X, and the second relationship is learned in Context Y, the expression of the former is recovered if participants are tested with A in Context X as well as in a new context (Bouton, 1993; García-Gutiérrez & Rosas, 2003a, 2003b; Pineño & Matute, 2000; Rosas & Bouton, 1998; Rosas, Vila, Lugo, & López, 2001; Vadillo, Vegas, & Matute, 2004). This recovery is also observed if a time delay is interpolated between the second training phase and the test phase (Bouton, 1993; Pavlov, 1927; Rosas & Bouton, 1998; Rosas et al., 2001). Thus, rather than unlearning the relationship learned in the first phase, people seem to behave as if what is learned in each phase were not valid in the other one. Moreover, contextual cues (whether physical or temporal) seem to play a crucial role in determining what relationship is pertinent at the present moment. But why is it that people tend to restrict the validity of each data set to different contexts in interference experiments?

At first glance, it could be thought that interference occurs because participants learn two conflicting predictive relationships. This could be the case in interference-between-outcomes treatments where participants learn that Cue A predicts Outcome 1 during the first training phase and Outcome 2 (or no outcome) during the subsequent training phase. These two conflicting relationships render Cue A ambiguous as it predicts either Outcome 1 or Outcome 2 but never both at the same time. But the idea of two conflicting predictive relationships does not apply so well in the case of interference between different cues of the same outcome (interference between cues hereafter). Table 1 shows a typical experimental design of interference between cues. This type of interference consists in the

Table 1. *Experimental design for interference between different cues of the same outcome*

| Experimental conditions | Training phases | | Test phase |
	Phase 1 Context X	Phase 2 Context Y	Context Y
Same outcome	A → O1	B → O1	A?
	C → O3	C → O3	
Different outcome	A → O1	B → O2	A?
	C → O3	C → O3	

Note: Letters A–C and numbers stand for cues and outcomes, respectively; O refers to outcome; letters X and Y stand for different contexts.

decrease of the expression of the A-O1 relationship learned in the first phase caused by the learning of a relationship between a different cue (i.e., Cue B) and the same outcome (i.e., Outcome 1) in a later phase. Because in this case there is no obvious conflict between the relationships learned —each cue only predicts one outcome— interference between cues has challenged current learning theories of interference and, thus, has recently attracted the attention of learning researchers.

Interference between cues, recently observed in predictive learning studies, had been found much earlier in the verbal learning tradition (Abra, 1967; Cheung & Goulet, 1968; Keppel, Bonge, Strand, & Parker, 1971; Schwartz, 1968). In predictive learning, the evidence for interference between cues comes mainly from human studies (see, for example, Escobar, Pineño, & Matute, 2002; Matute & Pineño, 1998; Ortega & Matute, 2000; Pineño, Ortega, & Matute, 2000), though there is also evidence for interference between cues from animal experiments (Escobar, Arcediano, & Miller, 2001; Escobar, Matute, & Miller, 2001; Escobar & Miller, 2003). As mentioned above for other forms of interference, interference between cues extinguishes or decreases whenever participants are tested with A either in a novel context or in the context in which the A-O1 relationship was learned (Matute & Pineño, 1998; Pineño et al., 2000; Pineño & Matute,

2000).[2] Thus, in an interference-between-cues treatment, rather than unlearning the A-O1 relationship, participants again seem to behave as if what is learned in one phase were not valid in the other.

Interference between cues has mainly been addressed by means of associative theories of learning. Although there are several associative explanations, most of them are inspired to a greater or lesser extent by Bouton's (1993) theory for interference between outcomes in animal learning (for more details, see Escobar et al., 2002; Matute & Pineño, 1998; Miller & Escobar, 2002). Without going into specific details concerning these explanations, overall, they build on the following two main ideas. First, interference occurs if two learned associations have a common element in a common temporal location (whether the cue or the outcome location), in which case such associations are learned separately. Second, the context in which a given association is acquired has the capacity of priming such association in detriment of others that share a common element with the previous one. Consequently, if two associations have a common cue or outcome, our cognitive system tends to diminish the validity of each association in the context in which the other was learned. According to these assertions, interference between cues occurs because: 1) the associations learned in the first and the second training phases have the outcome as a common element; 2) the context for the test is the same (or almost the same) as for the second training phase.[3]

Whereas almost all of the existing explanations for interference between cues originate from an associative framework, we propose that interference may be better understood from the viewpoint of what could be termed as causal reasoning theories, such as Causal Bayes Nets (Glymour, 2001; Gopnik et al., 2004; Sloman & Lagnado, 2004) and Causal Model Theory (Waldmann & Holyoak, 1992). This constitutes a novelty in the research on interference because, as far as we know, no attempt has been made to apply causal reasoning theories (CR theories hereafter) to explain interference, even though most of the experiments with humans have been framed within scenarios that are clearly susceptible of a causal interpretation.

Our CR account of interference between cues is based on two main assumptions: 1) people tend to give a causal interpretation to cues and outcomes; 2) they use their previous causal knowledge to infer the causal structure underlying the observed data. Regarding the causal interpretation, our hypothesis is that interference between cues is observed because cues and outcomes are interpreted as effects and causes, respectively, i.e., people perceive their task as a diagnostic learning task. According to this assumption, in an experiment of interference between cues, participants in the same-outcome condition learn that Cause 1 produces Effect A during the first phase and Effect B during the second phase (see the design in Table 1). Regarding the second assumption, we propose that people use structural knowledge about cause-effect relationships to infer the causal structure underlying the observed data. Such knowledge may be conceived of as a sort of intuitions about the probability distribution of events that should be expected given a specific causal model. If the expected distribution does not fit the observed probability distribution, the entertained causal model is rejected and substituted by

---

[2] Here, we use the term "context" in a wide sense to refer to a constant background or cue, a discrete cue immediately preceding a training trial, or to a temporal locus.

[3] Interference between cues has also been found without the use of different physical contexts or contextual cues to help participants differentiate between the two subsequent training phases (see, for example, Escobar et al., 2002). Based on this evidence, some authors have claimed that interference between cues could be explained by recency of the competing B-O1 association at the time of test (Ortega & Matute, 2000; Pineño et al., 2000). However, these results are also consistent with stating that the temporal context at the time of test, which is more similar to the temporal context of Phase 2 than to the temporal context of Phase 1, is priming the competing B-O1 over the A-O1 association.

another causal model. The application of this process may eventually lead to the postulation of hidden causes to improve the fit between the observed and the expected probability distribution.

What are the consequences of these assumptions in a design of interference between cues? If the learning task is given a diagnostic interpretation, the first thing to notice is that the probability distribution of events in the same-outcome condition is not compatible with a single-cause model (see Table 1). If Cause 1 were the only relevant cause explaining effects A and B, then, keeping constant the presence of Cause 1, there should be independence between the occurrence of A and of B. But this expectation is contradicted by the data since, given the presence of Cause 1, there is a highly negative correlation between its effects, i.e., A and B are disjoint effects. To explain this negative correlation, participants have to reject the single-cause model, and have to postulate the existence of a hidden causal factor that interacts with Cause 1, thereby producing either Effect A or Effect B (see also Hagmayer & Waldmann, 2007, in this issue for further information about inferences about unobserved causes from a causal Bayes net perspective). Such a causal factor works as an enabling or disabling condition that limits the capacity of Cause 1 to produce each effect. On this basis, the fact that Cause 1 systematically generates Effect A during Phase 1 and Effect B during Phase 2 can be accounted for by assuming that the hidden causal factor has one value in one phase and another value in the other phase. Given that there is no temporal or physical separation between the test trial and the trials of Phase 2, the hidden causal factor is assumed to be in the same state as in Phase 2. Such a state enables Cause 1 to produce Effect B, but not Effect A. Thus, when participants are tested with A, they are uncertain about the occurrence of Cause 1, even though they know of no other alternative cause that could have produced the effect.

When we say that participants in the same-outcome condition might be postulating a hidden causal factor we do not mean that they might necessarily be entertaining a specific hypothesis about what factor could explain the disjoint effects of Cause 1. People might simply be assuming that something unknown has changed from one phase to another that makes Cause 1 produce a different effect. This is likely to be the case in those circumstances in which people lack domain specific causal knowledge to imagine a plausible account of the data. Interference experiments are, in general, an example of such circumstances.

As a consequence of postulating a hidden causal factor in the same-outcome condition, contextual cues (whether temporal or physical) become causally relevant through the different status of the hidden causal factor that they signal. According to our CR account of interference between cues, contextual cues acquire causal significance because they are the only cues that inform participants about the state of the hidden causal factor. This could be the reason why contextual manipulations exert such a great influence on the extent to which interference is observed (for more on this, see the General Discussion).

Things are quite different in the control (different-outcome) condition: Cause 1 produces Effect A and Cause 2 produces Effect B during Phases 1 and 2, respectively. The data provided are consistent with single-cause models (i.e., one per causal relationship) so that no hidden causal factor needs to be assumed. Therefore, there is no reason to confine the validity of the calculations to a restricted training phase. Thus, when participants in the control condition are tested with A, they should be more confident that Cause 1 has occurred than participants in the same-outcome condition.

A critical prediction from our CR account is that interference between cues should not be observed in a predictive situation, i.e., if cues and outcomes are interpreted as causes and effects, respectively. In a predictive situation, participants in the same-outcome condition would learn that Cause A produces Effect 1 during Phase 1, and that Cause B produces the same effect during Phase 2 (see Table 1). Both relationships could be explained by single-cause models (one per relationship) because each cause only produces one effect. The fact that there are two events causing the same effect does not require the postulation of a hidden causal factor which affects the capacity of each cause to produce the effect. Thus, there is nothing in the causal structure of the data that should prevent participants from generalising the knowledge acquired in Phase 1 to Phase 2. Consequently, participants' responses to Cue A at test in the same-outcome condition should not differ from those in the control condition.

A relevant fact consistent with our prediction is that there is no evidence (that we are aware of) of interference between cues in predictive (cause-effect) learning tasks. The available evidence of interference between cues comes, generally, from studies in which the learning task can reasonably be interpreted in the diagnostic direction (we will return to this in the General Discussion).

From an associative framework, no asymmetry between predictive and diagnostic situations is expected. Associative learning mechanisms are thought to be blind to the causal role played by cues and outcomes. Therefore, according to associative learning theories (see above), interference between cues should be observed both in predictive and in diagnostic situations.

In summary, according to our CR account of interference between cues, interference should be found in diagnostic but not in predictive situations. According to associative theories, equivalent interference should be obtained in predictive and diagnostic situations.

Interestingly, the manipulation of the causal role of events has been shown to have an influence on cue interaction effects, but in the opposite way (López, Cobos, & Caño, 2005; Tangen & Allan, 2004; Van Hamme, Kao, & Wasserman, 1993; Waldmann, 2000, 2001; Waldmann & Holyoak, 1992). Specifically, there is evidence showing cue interaction effects in predictive but not in diagnostic conditions. Such asymmetries are consistent with CR theories and are again not predicted by associative theories. Note that there is no conflict between the predictions derived from our CR account concerning interference between cues and the asymmetry predicted from CR theories concerning cue interaction effects because each prediction is based on different principles.

The aim of our study was to find out whether or not interference between cues is affected by the causal role of cues and outcomes. For this, we created a predictive condition in which cues and outcomes played the role of causes and effects, respectively, and a diagnostic condition in which cues and outcomes played the role of effects and causes, respectively. Observing a higher interference between cues in the diagnostic than in the predictive condition would lend support to our CR account. Alternatively, if the interference effects in the predictive and in the diagnostic conditions are not significantly different, the results would be consistent with associative theories.

Our first purpose was to replicate the interference between cues by using a learning task framed in a causal scenario susceptible to be defined in either a diagnostic or a predictive direction with minimal changes. To test whether our task was suitable to obtain interference between cues in the first place, in Experiment 1a all participants learned the task in the diagnostic direction, as both theoretical accounts predict interference between cues in this causal order condition. Since a reliable interference effect was obtained in Experiment 1a, Experiment 1b was conducted to find out whether such effect was modulated by the manipulation of the causal order of the learning task. Thus, in Experiment 1b participants were divided into two groups, one of which learned in a predictive condition whereas the other learned in a diagnostic condition. Finally, Experiment 2 was carried out to improve some methodological aspects of Experiments 1a and 1b, and to rule out alternative explanations to our CR account of the results.

EXPERIMENT 1A

The purpose of Experiment 1a was to find out whether our learning task was suitable to induce and replicate the interference between cues previously obtained with other learning tasks. According to Escobar et al. (2002), some tasks have proven to be rather insensitive to interference between cues. Thus, we tried to develop a sensitive procedure to induce interference effects. One procedural measure that could help induce interference is providing a clear and different context for each training phase. Evidence coming from interference-between-outcomes experiments shows that the interference effect is stronger when contextual cues other than the temporal locus are added to help discriminate between the two training phases (Rosas & Bouton, 1998; Rosas et al., 2001; Vadillo et al., 2004). Thus, participants were trained in Context X during Phase 1 and in Context Y during Phase 2. Each context consisted of a series of cues that remained unchanged along each training phase. To favour the interference effect, the test trial took place in Context Y, i.e., in the same context as the interfering training phase. In addition, because both the associative and our CR accounts predict the interference effect in diagnostic situations, all participants in the present experiment learned in the diagnostic condition.

Method

Participants, design, and apparatus
Thirty eight psychology undergraduate students from University of Málaga took part in the present experiment for course credits. They were randomly assigned to one of the two experimental conditions shown in Table 1. The task was performed on IBM-PC compatible computers in semi-isolated individual cubicles.

Procedure
Participants started by reading the instructions on the computer screen placed in one of the ten cubicles in the laboratory. The instructions contained detailed explanations of the learning task described here. The learning task was a variation of the spy-radio task developed by Pineño et al. (2000) to obtain interference between cues. The main distinctive feature of our learning task concerns the causal scenario. We designed a causal scenario that could be defined in both causal order conditions with minimal changes. In our task, participants were asked to imagine that they were physicists working for the Red Cross organisation in a very poor area of Central Africa. Due to

hunger, members of certain tribes had begun to eat a series of plants, some of which were poisonous. On each trial, participants had to guess whether or not a hypothetical patient had eaten a poisonous plant and, if so, they had to administer a certain amount of antidote to prevent the poisoning symptoms. If the patient had eaten a poisonous plant, then participants could gain as many points as antidote units were administered. Such units could be administered by repeatedly pressing the space bar or by keeping it pressed for a period of time. Rather than the poisonous plants, patients could have eaten either an anomalous or an innocuous plant. Administering the antidote to a patient who had eaten the anomalous plant caused her/him to be intoxicated, and, thus, participants lost as many points as antidote units were given. Eating this plant had no effect when the antidote was not administered. Finally, administering the antidote when the patient had eaten an innocuous plant had no effect, and, thus, participants neither gained nor lost points. Participants were encouraged to gain as many points as possible.

Instructions stated that the ingestion of each type of plant caused different changes in the patient's body pH that could be detected thanks to a special sort of litmus paper that could take on one of three different colours: brown, yellow, or blue. Thus, each litmus-paper colour was the effect of having eaten a different type of plant. Participants had to decide, on each trial, the amount of antidote that had to be administered from knowing what colour the litmus paper took on. After responding, participants received information about the outcome which consisted of three different messages: (a) a photo of the plant including its name and the category label (poisonous, anomalous, and innocuous); (b) the amount of points gained or lost on the current trial; (c) the points accumulated throughout the training session.

In the same-outcome condition, each litmus-paper colour played the role of one of the cues in the design shown in Table 1. Cues A and B indicated that the patient had eaten the same poisonous plant, i.e., Plant 1, whereas Cue C indicated that the patient had eaten an anomalous plant, i.e.,

Plant 3. The different-outcome condition was identical except that Cue B indicated that the patient had eaten an innocuous plant, Plant 2. Because Cue A indicated the ingestion of the poisonous plant, good acquisition would involve a high response rate (a great amount of antidote units) in the presence of Cue A. An interference effect would be observed if the number of responses at test were lower in the same-outcome condition than in the different-outcome condition.

The instructions stressed the importance of: (a) maintaining attention throughout the entire learning task; (b) gaining as much points as possible; (c) placing the hands on the keyboard in a specific fixed position to prevent participants from seeking the response key during the task. At the end of the instructions, participants were invited to ask the experimenter all possible questions about the task. Once all questions were resolved, participants went into the learning task which consisted of two learning phases plus an additional test trial at the end. In each training phase, participants were presented with hypothetical patients from one of two tribes: "ULUS" and "GANTUAS". These tribes played the role of the contexts X and Y displayed in Table 1. The assignment of these roles to each tribe was counterbalanced across participants. During Phase 1, all participants were exposed to ten A-O1 trials intermixed with ten C-O3 trials. Then participants received ten B-O1 trials intermixed with ten C-O3 trials during Phase 2 in the same-outcome condition, whereas participants in the different-outcome condition received ten B-O2 trials intermixed with ten C-O3 trials during Phase 2. The order of trial presentation was randomised with the constraint of disallowing more than two consecutive presentations of the same trial type. The test trial was not marked to participants and consisted of an additional A-O1 trial after the last trial of Phase 2. The context for the test trial was the same as for Phase 2, i.e., Context Y. The abstract cues A through C were assigned to the different litmus-paper colours according to a counterbalancing procedure. Outcomes 1, 2 and 3 were the poisonous, the innocuous, and the anomalous plant, respectively. Also according to a counterbalancing

procedure, the three different plants were assigned corresponding plant photos labelled "Dobe", "Yamma", and "Kollin".

On each trial, the message "In the case of Patient #, the colour the litmus paper took on was" appeared at the top centre of the screen. Just below, a small rectangle filled with the corresponding colour was displayed. The colour was visible for 3.5 s only. After that time, the rectangle was filled with the same colour as the background, i.e., grey colour. Participants could administer the antidote by pressing the space bar while the litmus-paper colour was visible. After the colour disappeared, pressing the space bar had no effect on the amount of antidote given anymore. A scrollbar at the bottom centre of the screen indicated the amount of antidote that was being administered. If the spacebar was held pressed, the scrollbar face moved smoothly from left to right. The position of the face was translated into a number of antidote units from 1 through 100 displayed in a small textbox on the right of the scrollbar. The initial position of the face on each trial was the left extreme of the scrollbar, which corresponded with zero antidote units. Once the 3.5 s for the cue presentation had elapsed, participants received information about the outcome. The outcome included a photo of the plant with its corresponding name together with an indication of the type of plant (poisonous, anomalous, and innocuous) displayed in a small rectangle on the left of the scrollbar. Besides this, a message conveying the number of points won or lost was displayed in a small textbox just above the scrollbar. If the hypothetical patient was poisoned, the message displayed was "you win # points"; if the patient had eaten the anomalous plant, the message was "you lose # points"; if the patient had eaten the innocuous plant, the message was "you neither win nor lose points". The points referred to in the message were the amount of antidote units given by the participant. These points were added or subtracted to the accumulated points displayed in a small textbox located at the top right of the screen, at the same height as the litmus paper. The outcome information remained on the screen until participants pressed the 'X' on the keyboard. Then all the outcome information was removed except the accumulated points, and the next trial followed 2 s later. Throughout, information about the context was displayed in a big rectangle as wide as the screen width at the centre of the screen. The message "ULUS (or GANTUAS) TRIBE" appeared in big size letters within the rectangle. The rectangle was filled either with red or with green colour depending on the training phase. The assignment of each colour to each phase was counterbalanced across participants. The context was displayed as a constant background that remained unchanged throughout the entire training phase.

Results and discussion

To ensure that only the data from those participants who paid attention to the task and showed a reasonable discriminative acquisition were include in the analysis, we decided to select those participants who met a certain learning criterion. Accordingly, participants in all the experiments were selected if the total responses to Cue C were less than 100 and the total score was higher than the mean minus two standard deviations at the end of Phase 1. As a result, 25 participants from the initial sample were selected for data analysis: 10 were from the same-outcome condition, and 15 were from the different-outcome condition.

Table 2 shows the mean response rate to Cue A at test. A one-tailed t-test was performed on participants' responses revealing a significantly lower response rate for the same-outcome group than for the different-outcome group, $t(23) = 3.8$, $p < .001$, indicating interference between cues.

The purpose of finding out whether our preparation was sensitive to interference between cues

has been successfully achieved. It seems that the causal scenario together with the use of different contexts for each training phase have been particularly effective in favouring the interference effect. This is an interesting result because interference between cues has shown to be somewhat elusive. For example, Lipp and Dal Santo (2002) have reported several failures to observe interference between cues even when using a task that had produced interference before (Ortega & Matute, 2000). It remains to be shown, however, what the role of causal order is in inducing the interference effect.

EXPERIMENT 1B

After showing that our learning task can be used to induce interference between cues, Experiment 1b was conducted to test whether the effect can be modulated by the causal order of the task. Thus, we had two groups in this experiment: (a) a diagnostic group, similar to Experiment 1a; (b) a predictive group who received the information in a cause-effect order on each trial. According to our CR account, interference should only be observed in the diagnostic condition. According to associative theories, interference should be equivalent in both conditions.

Method

Participants, design, and apparatus
Seventy two psychology undergraduate students from University of Málaga took part in the present experiment for course credits. They were randomly assigned to four equally sized experimental groups ($N = 18$ for each group): a same-outcome predictive (SO-PR), a different-outcome

Table 2. *Means and standard errors from Experiments 1a, 1b, and 2*

	Exp. 1a	Exp. 1b		Exp. 2	
Causal order	Diagnostic	Diagnostic	Predictive	Diagnostic	Predictive
Group SO	23.7 (8.62)	45.71 (7.09)	57 (5.84)	31.17 (7.39)	54.95 (4.36)
Group DO	61.5 (5.76)	64.27 (3.18)	53.27 (3.76)	53.17 (4.42)	55.05 (4.08)

Note: SO and DO stand for same outcome and different outcome, respectively; standard errors are shown in parentheses.

predictive (DO-PR), a same-outcome diagnostic (SO-DG), and a different-outcome diagnostic (DO-DG) group. The task was performed using the same apparatus as for Experiment 1a.

Procedure

The procedure was identical to Experiment 1a except for some minimal changes regarding the predictive groups. Participants in these groups received the same causal scenario and the same cover story as participants in the diagnostic groups. However, they had to learn to decide the amount of antidote to be given from knowing what plant the patient ate (the cause of the patients' symptoms) instead of knowing what colour the litmus paper took on (the effect of the type of plant eaten). As in the diagnostic conditions, the cues, the contexts, and the outcomes were displayed at the top, at the centre, and at the bottom of the screen, respectively. The same plant photos and names that played the role of outcomes in Experiment 1a played the role of cues for the predictive groups. Specifically, each photo included a fictitious name for the plant, and was displayed, on each trial, for the same amount of time as cues in the diagnostic condition. The outcomes presented to participants were identical to those presented to the diagnostic groups except that a rectangle filled in with the corresponding litmus-paper colour was displayed on the left of the scrollbar instead of the plant photo. This rectangle was accompanied by the category label (poisonous, anomalous, or innocuous) for the plant eaten. Colours blue, yellow, and brown were used as litmus-paper colours. An equivalent counterbalancing scheme as in Experiment 1a was adopted for cues, outcomes, and contexts.

Results and discussion

Sixty three participants were selected for data analysis as a result of applying the learning criterion described above: 16 from the SO-PR group, 15 from the DO-PR group, 17 from the SO-DG group, and 15 from the DO-DG group. Meeting the learning criterion did not correlate with any of the manipulated factors, as the number of

participants eliminated in each group was almost identical (2 from the SO-PR, 3 from the DO-PR, 1 from the SO-DG, and 3 from the DO-DG group).

Table 2 shows the mean response rate to Cue A at test for each group. A 2 (group: same-outcome group vs. different-outcome group) × 2 (causal order: predictive vs. diagnostic) analysis of variance yielded a significant interaction between group and causal order, $F(1, 59) = 4.26$, $p = .043$, $MSE = 457.68$. The remaining effects were non significant (largest $F = 1.9$, $p > .17$). A look at the means reveals that the difference between the same-outcome and the different-outcome group was considerably greater in the diagnostic than in the predictive condition. Moreover, the difference is in line with an interference effect in the diagnostic condition, whereas, if anything, there is a small trend in the opposite direction in the predictive condition. Thus, the interaction seems to mean that the interference between cues was observed in the diagnostic but not in the predictive condition. This interpretation was confirmed by an analysis of the simple effects of group in each level of causal order. The effect of the factor group was significant in the diagnostic condition, $F(1, 59) = 6.00$, $p = .017$, $MSE = 457.68$, but not in the predictive condition, $F(1, 59) < 1$, $MSE = 457.68$.

In summary, in Experiment 1b we have replicated the interference effect of Experiment 1a in the diagnostic group, and we have found evidence that the interference effect is influenced by the causal interpretation of the task. As predicted by our CR account, and at odds with associative theories' predictions, interference was found when cues and outcomes were interpreted as effects and causes, respectively, but not when they were interpreted as causes and effects.

Although the results of Experiment 1b suggest that interference between cues can be influenced by people's previous causal knowledge, some aspects of the procedure could raise doubts about our CR explanation. First, it could be argued that participants in the predictive group were not informed about the absence of Cue A in B-O1 trials, whereas this information was implicit for participants in the diagnostic group because presenting the litmus paper in one colour necessarily implies that it did not take on the other colours. This difference could inspire different explanations of why interference was only found in the diagnostic group. For example, participants might have assumed the presence of Cue A in B-O1 trials unless otherwise indicated. Since the presence of Cue A was implicitly negated in the diagnostic condition, only participants in the predictive condition would have actually made this assumption. This would have had a consequence similar to training the A-O1 relationship in Phase 2 (or in Context Y), which explains why interference was not observed. From an associative point of view, we could say that the representation of Cue A could have been elicited in B-O1 trials by way of a backward association with Outcome 1, resulting in a sort of mediated learning in Context Y analogous to mediated conditioning in animals.

A second criticism could be that, in both causal order conditions, the outcome included information about the category label of the plant. Such category label could be easily understood as an essential property of the plant. Thus, for the predictive group, this category label informed participants about an essential property of the cue. This could be viewed as an aid to generalise responding to A from Phase 1 to the test phase because the essential properties of plants or whatever object are not supposed to change from one context to another. This would explain the absence of interference in the predictive group. Contrarily, in the diagnostic condition, the category label included as part of the outcome did not refer to an essential property of the cue (the litmus paper) but to an essential property of another part of the outcome (the plant). Thus, participants in the diagnostic condition were not induced to generalise from Phase 1 to the test phase to the same extent as participants in the predictive group.

EXPERIMENT 2

Experiment 2 was conducted to achieve two main purposes. First, we changed some aspects of the

procedure to overcome the shortcomings referred to above. Second, we intended to replicate the asymmetry observed in Experiment 1b to obtain more compelling evidence of the influence of the causal interpretation of the task on the interference effect.

To overcome the problem of implicitly informing participants about the absence of Cue A in B-O1 trials in the diagnostic but not in the predictive condition, we made two changes. First, participants in both causal order conditions were explained through instructions that there were three chemical reagents of different colours, instead of a unique litmus paper, that could react as a consequence of the type of plant eaten. Thus, each trial informed about the reagent altered in a hypothetical case, and participants had to learn which reagent was altered as a consequence of eating each type of plant. Second, the instructions for the diagnostic group stated that, on each trial, participants would be presented with the only reagent altered. The reagents not presented were not altered. The same strategy was used regarding the information about the plant eaten in the predictive condition. Instructions stated that, on each trial, participants would be presented with the only plant eaten. The plants not presented were not eaten by the hypothetical patients. All this was explicitly stated on each trial. This way, both causal order groups were equivalent regarding the information received about absent cues on each trial.

To solve the problem related to presenting the category label, we decided to eliminate this information from the outcome in both causal order conditions. Instead, information about the state of the patient as a consequence of having eaten the plant was added as part of the outcome.

Method

Participants, design, and apparatus
Ninety nine psychology undergraduate students from University of Málaga took part in the present experiment for course credits. They were randomly assigned to four groups resulting in the following distribution: $N = 26$ for group

SO-PR, $N = 24$ for group DO-PR, $N = 24$ for group SO-DG, and $N = 25$ for group DO-DG. The task was performed on the same apparatus as in the previous experiments.

Procedure

The procedure was identical to Experiment 1b except for the following aspects. As said before, each trial informed about the only chemical reagent that had been altered, and about the only plant eaten by the hypothetical patient. Thus, on each trial, participants in the diagnostic condition could read the message "In the case of Patient # the only reagent altered was" at the top of the screen. As in the previous experiments, a rectangle filled with the corresponding reagent colour was displayed below the message. The information about the plant eaten was displayed at the bottom left of the screen and consisted of a plant photo and a fictitious name at the top of the photo. In the predictive condition, participants could read the message "In the case of Patient #, the only plant eaten was" at the top of the screen on each trial. Below the message, the corresponding plant photo was displayed, accompanied by a fictitious name. The rectangle representing the reagent was displayed at the bottom left of the screen below the message "Reagent altered". In both causal order conditions, a message indicating the state of the patient as a consequence of having eaten the plant was added as part of the outcome. This message was displayed in the same small textbox as the points won or lost by the participant. If the patient had eaten a poisonous plant, the message was "poisoned patient"; if the plant eaten was anomalous, the message was "sensitised patient"; and if the plant eaten was innocuous, the message was "healthy patient". The meaning of these terms was clearly stated to participants through instructions.

Results and discussion

Seventy eight participants were selected for data analysis according to the same learning criterion as in the previous experiments: 22 from the SO-PR group, 21 from the DO-PR group, 17 from the SO-DG group, and 18 from the DO-DG group. The number of participants whose data did not enter the analysis was distributed across groups as follows: 4 from the SO-PR, 3 from the DO-PR, 7 from the SO-DG, and 7 from the DO-DG group. Because the percentage of participants selected from the predictive group was higher than from the diagnostic group, we performed a chi-square test for independence between causal order and being selected or not. The analysis revealed that the distribution of participants per cell did not significantly depart from an independence distribution [$\chi = 3.1439 < \chi_{.05}(1) = 3.841$]. In other words, the probability of being selected did not significantly differ between participants in the predictive and in the diagnostic groups.

Table 2 shows the mean response rate to Cue A at test for each group. A 2 (group: same-outcome group vs. different-outcome group) × 2 (causal order: predictive vs. diagnostic) analysis of variance yielded a significant effect of group, $F(1, 74) = 4.75$, $p = .033$, $MSE = 495.31$, a significant effect of causal order, $F(1, 74) = 6.41$, $p = .013$, $MSE = 495.31$, and a significant interaction between group and causal order, $F(1, 74) = 4.67$, $p = .034$, $MSE = 495.31$. A look at the means reveals a clear trend toward an interference effect in the diagnostic group, whereas the means in the predictive group are almost identical. This was confirmed by an analysis of the simple effects of group within each causal order condition. The effect of group was significant in the diagnostic condition, $F(1, 74) = 8.54$, $p = .005$, $MSE = 495.31$, but not in the predictive condition, $F(1, 74) < 1$, $MSE = 495.31$. The significant and robust interference effect found in the diagnostic condition clearly explains the main effects of group and causal order.

According to these results, we have achieved the main purposes pursued in this experiment. First, we have replicated the interaction between causal order and group found in Experiment 1b. Like in that experiment, the interference effect was observed in the diagnostic but not in the predictive condition. Second, we have shown that neither of the two procedural aspects of Experiment 1b that were changed in Experiment 2 can explain the interaction between group and causal order. Specifically, the interaction did not vanish due to (1) making explicit the absence of cues in the two causal order conditions, nor by (2) eliminating the category label for the plant from the outcome. Thus, the results found in this experiment add more compelling evidence for the influence of the causal interpretation of the task and of previous causal knowledge on interference between cues. Such results cannot be accounted for by associative learning theories because, as previously mentioned, these theories do not differentiate between predictive and diagnostic processing of the cue-outcome relationships.

GENERAL DISCUSSION

Summary and comments on alternative explanations

According to our CR account, interference between different cues of the same outcome takes place as a consequence of the causal interpretation of the learning task together with the use of previous causal knowledge. If the task is interpreted as a diagnostic learning task, participants need to postulate the existence of some hidden causal factor with different states for each training phase to explain why Cause 1 produces Effect A in Phase 1 and Effect B in Phase 2. The state of the hidden cause would enable or disable the capacity of Cause 1 to produce either A or B. Interference would occur because participants assume, when tested on Cue A, that the hidden causal factor is in a state that does not allow Cause 1 to produce Effect A. From our CR account it is predicted that interference between cues should not be observed if the task is given a predictive interpretation, i.e., if cues and outcomes are interpreted as causes and effects, respectively. Experiments 1a through 2 were intended to provide evidence consistent with this prediction. The purpose of Experiment 1a was to find out whether interference between cues could be

obtained with a new learning task framed within a causal scenario that allowed for both predictive and diagnostic learning with minimal changes. For this, all participants learned in a diagnostic condition, and different contextual cues were used for each training phase. Since we were successful at inducing the interference effect, the causal order was manipulated in Experiment 1b to test whether the interference effect is influenced by the causal interpretation of the task. The data analysis yielded a significant interaction between causal order and interference that resulted from the interference effect being significant in the diagnostic but not in the predictive condition. Finally, the results of Experiment 1b were replicated in Experiment 2 after changing two aspects of the procedure to rule out some alternative explanations. Experiment 2 provided additional evidence of the influence of causal knowledge on interference between cues. Overall, the results of Experiments 1b and 2 are consistent with our CR account, and cannot be accounted for by associative learning theories.

A possible objection to Experiments 1b and 2 could be that the stimuli used as cues and outcomes in the diagnostic condition were different to those used in the predictive condition. For example, in the diagnostic condition, the cues consisted of coloured rectangles, whereas in the predictive condition, they consisted of plant photos labelled with fictitious names. It could be argued that learning to discriminate between familiar colours is not the same as learning to discriminate between unknown plant-photos labelled with fictitious names. For one thing, in the latter case, participants have to discriminate between more complex stimuli consisting of a greater amount of features than in the former case. But if this difference were important enough to explain participants' responses at test, it should also have a detectable influence on, for example, the acquisition of discrimination over the course of training. After all, the test trial was one more training trial at the end of the learning task. The data concerning response acquisition in Experiment 2 contradict this prediction. Figure 1 shows the response rate per trial for each cue-outcome pairing in

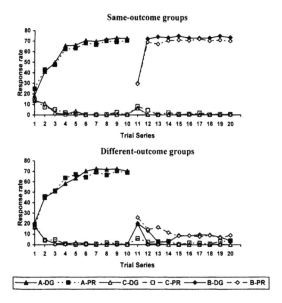

Same-outcome groups

Different-outcome groups

| ▲ A-DG | ▪ ⋯ A-PR | △ C-DG | ▢ C-PR | ◆ B-DG | ◇ B-PR |

Figure 1. *Response-rate curves for each group and for each cue along the training phases of Experiment 2.*

each training phase. It shows that the acquisition curve in the diagnostic group was virtually identical to that in the predictive group. The results of the statistical analyses confirmed this impression. We first averaged responses to each cue along each training phase in three trial blocks. The first, second, and third block comprised trials 1 through 4, 5 through 7, and 8 through 10, respectively.[4] We conducted separate analyses for each phase and each cue. In Phase 1, for Cue A, a 2 (group: same-outcome group vs. different-outcome group) × 2 (causal order: predictive vs. diagnostic) × 3 (trial block 1 vs. trial block 2 vs. trial block 3) analysis of variance with trial block as a within-subjects factor yielded a significant effect of trial block, $F(2, 148) = 179.31$, $p < .001$, $MSE = 91.31$. None of the remaining effects were significant (all $Fs < 1$). The same analysis of variance on participants' responses to Cue C yielded a significant effect of trial block, $F(2, 148) = 50.00$, $p < .001$, $MSE = 18.79$.

None of the remaining effects were significant (all $Fs < 1$). Consequently, the predictive and the diagnostic groups were not significantly different regarding the acquisition of the discrimination between Cues A and C along Phase 1. Because responses to Cue C did not differ between the predictive and the diagnostic groups in Phase 1, the same statistical analysis was only performed on responses to B in Phase 2. This analysis yielded a significant effect of group, $F(1, 74) = 545.60$, $p < .001$, $MSE = 363.35$, a significant effect of trial block, $F(2, 148) = 3.41$, $p < .036$, $MSE = 72.15$, and a significant interaction between group and trial block, $F(2, 148) = 25.47$, $p < .001$, $MSE = 72.15$. All of the remaining effects were non-significant (largest $F = 1.50$, $p > .24$). The interaction between trial block and group is hardly surprising if we take into account the different meaning of Cue B for each group. What really matters, however, is that causal order was not involved in any of the significant effects found. Thus, the predictive group did not differ from the diagnostic group regarding the acquisition of responses to B along Phase 2. In summary, the use of different stimuli as cues and outcomes in the predictive and the diagnostic groups did not produce any detectable influence on participants' response rates to any cue along the training phases of Experiment 2.[5] Moreover, the difference in stimuli did not influence participants' responses to A at test in the different-outcome group either. Consequently, given that the use of different stimuli did not significantly affect participants' responses in any of the multiple cases in which it could potentially have had an influence, it is very unlikely that such use of different stimuli could account for the interaction found in Experiments 1b and 2 between causal order and interference.

An alternative explanation of our results is that the calculation of the conditional Δp (Cheng & Holyoak, 1995; Cheng & Novick, 1990) in the same-outcome condition gives a value of 1 for

---

[4] The first block was allowed to include one more trial than the other two blocks to compensate for the greater response variability that is usually observed during the first training trials.

[5] The same analysis on participants' responses in Experiment 1b yielded virtually the same results.

the Cause A → Effect 1 causal relationship in the predictive condition, and a value of .5 for the corresponding Cause 1 → Effect A causal relationship in the diagnostic condition. In contrast, in the different-outcome condition, the value for Δp is 1 in both causal order conditions. This could explain the interaction found between causal order and the interference effect. Notice that, as our CR account, this explanation assumes that interference between cues is influenced by the causal interpretation of events because the conditional Δp is always computed in the cause-effect direction regardless of the order in which information is presented. The main difference between both accounts is that the latter assumes that, in the same-outcome diagnostic condition, B-O1 trials of Phase 2 are taken into account to compute the Cause 1 → Effect A causal relationship. In contrast, our CR account states that participants should estimate that Phases 1 and 2 differ with respect to a hidden causal factor. Thus, neither the B-O1 trials should enter into the calculation of the Cause 1 → Effect A causal relationship, nor vice versa. In other words, participants should estimate that what is learned in Phase 2 does not generalise to Phase 1, and that what is learned in Phase 1 does not generalise to Phase 2. The main problem with the alternative Δp explanation is that it turns out to be implausible in the light of the evidence provided in other studies. Specifically, such explanation is incompatible with studies showing that interference between cues vanishes when certain contextual manipulations are made (Matute & Pineño, 1998; Pineño & Matute, 2000; Pineño et al., 2000), or when a delay is introduced between the second training phase and the test (Pineño et al., 2000). There is also evidence that interference between cues vanishes when A-O1 and B-O1 trials are intermixed in a single training phase (Pineño et al., 2000). Even though this result is not necessarily incompatible with the alternative Δp explanation, it poses an additional difficulty. In contrast, as we will see in the next paragraphs, our CR account is highly consistent with these findings.

Explaining the main findings of previous studies on interference between cues from the CR account

An interesting point of the CR explanation developed in this article is that it provides a parsimonious account for the main findings in research on interference between cues. In this respect, there are three points worth mentioning. First, the data obtained to date are consistent with the prediction that interference between cues should be found in the diagnostic rather than in the predictive direction. Apart from our learning task, there are only three tasks that have been used to obtain interference between cues, even though with different frequency and success. The most frequently and successfully used is the spy-radio task (Castro, Ortega, & Matute, 2002; Escobar et al., 2002; Pineño & Matute, 2000; Pineño et al., 2000). In this task, participants have to rescue as many refugees as possible in a war zone plagued with hidden mines by repeatedly pressing the space bar to place the refugees in a series of trucks. The coloured lights of a spy radio, which play the role of cues, tell the state of the road (free of mines, mined, or closed) on each trial. In this case, the causal scenario is very likely to induce participants to interpret the coloured lights of the spy radio as effects of the state of the road on some kind of detector device. After all, people are very familiar with the existence of mine detectors and devices that can detect metals or other sort of materials. In any case, it is very unlikely for participants to have attributed any causal power to the illumination of the lights to produce one road state or another. A similar analysis could be made regarding the Martians task (Lipp & Dal Santo, 2002; Matute & Pineño, 1998; Ortega & Matute, 2000), and, to a lesser extent, the Air-Force task (Escobar et al., 2002: Experiment 1). In any case, there is no evidence for interference in learning tasks framed in a clear predictive causal scenario.

A second feature of interference between cues is its tendency to vanish when some contextual manipulations are made. As said in the introduction, in whatever sense the term "context" may be used (see Footnote 2), results from different studies converge in that interference between cues decreases (or disappears) if the test takes place in a different context than that of the second training phase (Matute & Pineño, 1998; Pineño & Matute, 2000; Pineño et al., 2000). From our CR account, the reason for this is that the context comes to be causally relevant in the same-outcome condition when the learning task is given a diagnostic interpretation. As said in the introduction, the causal relevance of the context lies in its informative value for the different states of the hidden causal factor that enables Cause 1 to produce either Effect A or B. Thus, if the test phase takes place in the same context as Phase 2, participants infer that the hidden causal factor is in the state which enables Cause 1 to produce Effect B rather than A. If the context changes from Phase 2 to the test phase, there are two possibilities: (a) some participants might infer that the hidden causal factor has also changed to the state which enables Cause 1 to produce effect A; (b) others might be uncertain about the state of the hidden causal factor. In both cases, however, an increase in the response rate to A at test should be expected with respect to when participants are tested in the same context as for the second training phase.

Finally, a third point regarding previous studies on interference between cues that deserves our attention is, as mentioned above, the absence of interference when A-O1 and B-O1 trials are intermixed in a single training phase (see Pineño et al., 2000, Experiment 2). According to our CR account, if participants learn in a diagnostic situation, they should also infer the existence of a hidden causal factor to explain why Cause 1 produces Effects A and B in a disjoint manner. However, contrary to what is the case when participants are trained in two different phases, the context would be the same for both trial types, and, thus, it would not convey any information about the state of the hidden causal factor. At the same time, because of the training regime, participants would get used to expect rapid successive changes in the state of the hidden causal factor. Thus, when participants are tested with A, they

can be sure that Cause 1 has occurred, and no interference effect should be observed.

In light of these considerations, it seems that our CR account is highly consistent with the main findings on interference between cues. However, this does not mean that the effects of interference between cues found in previous studies are necessarily caused by the processes envisaged by CR theories. It could well be that associative and CR processes are both responsible for interference between cues. In fact, interference between cues has also been found in studies with animals, who are not supposed to enjoy the competencies postulated by CR theories (but see Beckers, Miller, De Houwer, & Urushihara, 2006). At the same time, the idea that both associative and CR processes could be responsible for a common learning phenomenon is gaining increasing acceptance as a consequence of evidence obtained in other experimental paradigms (Cobos, López, Caño, Almaraz, & Shanks, 2002; Le Pelley, Oakeshott, & McLaren, 2005; López et al., 2005; Price & Yates, 1995; Tangen & Allan, 2004). Consequently, rather than invalidating the associative explanations, the experiments reported here show the viability of alternative accounts of interference between cues based on CR processes. In future studies, both theoretical approaches should be borne in mind when offering an account of the empirical phenomena obtained.

Extending the CR approach to interference between different outcomes of the same cue

A straightforward consequence of our account is that the same CR processes responsible for the interference between cues found in our experiments might also be responsible, at least in some circumstances, for interference between different outcomes of the same cue. In fact, the causal structure of the data for the same-outcome diagnostic condition used in our experiments is the same as for the interference groups of experiments on interference between outcomes. The most typical studies on interference between outcomes in humans have used causal learning tasks in which a given cause, Cue A, is paired with one effect during Phase 1 (Outcome 1), and with another effect (or the absence of the previous one) during Phase 2 (García-Gutiérrez & Rosas, 2003a, 2003b; Matute, Vegas, & De Marez, 2002; Rosas et al., 2001; Vadillo et al., 2004). Thus, according to our CR account of interference between cues, participants should infer the existence of a hidden causal factor that interacts with the target cause, Cue A, to produce either O1 (during Phase 1) or O2 (during Phase 2). Again, the context present in each phase would serve as a signal of the different states of the hidden factor. Interference would occur if the context present at test is the same as (or similar to) the context of Phase 2 because, in such a case, participants would infer that the hidden causal factor is in the state that enables Cue A to produce O2 but not O1. Because associative theories also predict interference between outcomes, it turns out that, to extend our CR account to this kind of interference, we need to empirically discriminate between these different explanations. We are currently working on a design of interference between outcomes that will allow for such discrimination.

CONCLUDING COMMENTS

The results obtained in our study are consistent with studies showing the influence of causal knowledge on cue-interaction effects in causal learning experiments. Some of these studies, as in our case, have searched for asymmetries between predictive and diagnostic situations regarding cue-interaction effects as a means to provide evidence supporting CR theories (López et al., 2005; Tangen & Allan, 2004; Waldmann, 2000, 2001; Waldmann & Holyoak, 1992; Waldmann & Walker, 2005). In this sense, our research may be viewed as an extension of these strategies and findings to the area of interference between cues. But at the same time, our study differs in a relevant respect that goes beyond the experimental paradigm used or the phenomenon tackled here. Most of the studies on cue-interaction effects have focussed on how people distinguish between true and spurious causal relationships.

At odds with this, our study has focussed on how people calculate causal structure from the probability distribution of events, and how the inferred causal structure determines whether or not the data collected in one context generalise to another one. Some advocates of causal Bayes nets have claimed that calculating causal structure is at the core of causal learning and may be viewed as the main use for causal knowledge (Griffiths & Tenenbaum, 2005; Sloman & Lagnado, 2004).

Finally, we hope to have shown the relevance of the interference between cues phenomenon to the study of causal learning. The main idea we have tried to pursue throughout the experimental work reported here was to show that understanding causal learning requires an understanding of how people assess whether or not the evidence gathered in one context generalises to other contexts. Our experiments have shown that interference paradigms may be a useful tool for such understanding. Thus, we think that future causal learning research will greatly benefit from more empirical work on interference effects. In line with this, a relevant research question would be to evaluate whether similar results to those reported here are obtained using a different interference paradigm like that involved in the effect of interference between different outcomes.

REFERENCES

Abra, J. C. (1967). Time changes in the strength of forward and backward associations. *Journal of Verbal Learning & Verbal Behavior, 6,* 640–645

Beckers, T., Miller, R. R., De Houwer, J., & Urushihara, K. (2006). Reasoning rats: Forward blocking in Pavlovian animal conditioning is sensitive to constraints of causal inference. *Journal of Experimental Psychology: General, 135,* 92–102.

Bouton, M. E. (1993). Context, time, and memory retrieval in the interference paradigms of Pavlovian learning. *Psychological Bulletin, 114,* 80–99.

Castro, L., Ortega, N., & Matute, H. (2002). Proactive interference in human predictive learning. *International Journal of Comparative Psychology, 15,* 55–68.

Cheng, P. W., & Holyoak, K. J. (1995). Complex adaptive systems as intuitive statisticians: causality, contingency, and prediction. In J. A. Meyer & H. Roitblat (Eds.), *Comparative approaches to cognition* (pp 271–302). Cambridge, MA: The MIT Press.

Cheng, P. W., & Novick, L. R. (1990). A probabilistic contrast model of causal induction. *Journal of Personality and Social Psychology, 58*, 545–567.

Cheung, C. G., & Goulet, L. R. (1968). Retroactive inhibition of R–S associations in the A–B, B–C, C–B paradigms. *Journal of Experimental Psychology, 76*, 327–328.

Cobos, P. L., López, F. J., Caño, A., Almaraz, J., & Shanks, D. R. (2002). Mechanisms of predictive and diagnostic causal induction. *Journal of Experimental Psychology: Animal Behavior Processes, 28*, 331–346.

Escobar, M., Arcediano, F., & Miller, R. R. (2001). Conditions favoring retroactive interference between antecedent events (cue competition) and between subsequent events (outcome competition). *Psychonomic Bulletin & Review, 8*, 691–697.

Escobar, M., Matute, H., & Miller, R. R. (2001). Cues trained apart compete for behavioral control in rats: Convergence with the associative interference literature. *Journal of Experimental Psychology: General, 130*, 97–115.

Escobar, M., & Miller, R. R. (2003). Timing in retroactive interference. *Learning & Behavior, 31*, 257–272.

Escobar, M., Pineño, O., & Matute, H. (2002). A comparison between elemental and compound training of cues in retrospective revaluation. *Animal Learning & Behavior, 30*, 228–238.

García-Gutiérrez, A., & Rosas, J. M. (2003a). Context change as the mechanism of reinstatement in causal learning. *Journal of Experimental Psychology: Animal Behavior Processes, 29*, 292–310.

García-Gutiérrez, A., & Rosas, J. M. (2003b). Empirical and theoretical implications of additivity between reinstatement and renewal after interference in causal learning. *Behavioural Processes, 63*, 21–31.

Glymour, C. (2001). *The mind's arrows: Bayes nets and graphical causal models in psychology*. Cambridge, MA: MIT Press.

Gopnik, A., Glymour, C., Sobel, D. M., Schulz, L. E., Kushnir, T., & Danks, D. (2004). A theory of causal learning in children: Causal maps and Bayes nets. *Psychology Review, 111*, 1–30.

Griffiths, T. L., & Tenenbaum, J. B. (2005). Structure and strength in causal induction. *Cognitive Psychology, 51*, 354–384.

Hagmayer, Y & Waldmann, M. R. (2007). Inferences about unobserved causes in human contingency learning. *Quarterly Journal of Experimental Psychology, 60*, 330–355.

Keppel, G., Bonge, D., Strand, B. Z., & Parker, J. (1971). Direct and indirect interference in the recall of paired associates. *Journal of Experimental Psychology, 88*, 414–422.

Le Pelley, M. E., Oakeshott, S. M., & McLaren, I. P. L. (2005). Blocking and unblocking in human causal learning. *Journal of Experimental Psychology: Animal Behavior Processes, 31*, 56–70.

Lipp, O. V., & Dal Santo, L. A. (2002). Cue competition between elementary trained stimuli: US miscuing, interference, and US omission. *Learning & Motivation, 33*, 327–346.

López, F. J., Cobos, P. L., & Caño, A. (2005). Associative and causal reasoning accounts of causal induction: Symmetries and asymmetries in predictive and diagnostic inferences. *Memory & Cognition, 33*, 1388–1398.

Matute, H., & Pineño, O. (1998). Stimulus competition in the absence of compound conditioning. *Animal Learning & Behavior, 26*, 3–14.

Matute, H., Vegas, S., & De Marez, P. J. (2002). Flexible use of recent information in causal and predictive judgments. *Journal of Experimental Psychology: Learning, Memory, and Cognition, 28*, 714–725.

Miller, R. R., & Escobar, M. (2002). Associative interference between cues and between outcomes presented together and presented apart: An integration. *Behavioural Processes, 57*, 163–185.

Ortega, O., & Matute, H. (2000). Interference between elementally trained stimuli can take place in one trial. *Learning & Motivation 31*, 323–344.

Pavlov, I. P. (1927). *Conditioned reflexes*. London: Clarendon Press.

Pineño, O., & Matute, H. (2000). Interference in human predictive learning when associations share a common element. *International Journal of Comparative Psychology, 13*, 16–33.

Pineño, O., Ortega, N., & Matute, H. (2000). The relative activation of the associations modulates interference between elementally trained cues. *Learning and Motivation, 31*, 128–152.

Price, P. C., & Yates, J. F. (1995). Associative and rule-based accounts of cue interaction in contingency judgment. *Journal of Experimental Psychology: Learning, Memory, and Cognition, 21*, 1639–1655.

Rosas, J. M., & Bouton, M. E. (1998). Context change and retention interval have additive, rather than interactive, effects after taste aversion extinction. *Psychonomic Bulletin & Review, 5,* 79–83.

Rosas, J. M., Vila, N. J., Lugo, M., & López, L. (2001). Combined effect of context change and retention interval on interference in causality judgment. *Journal of Experimental Psychology: Animal Behavior Proceses, 27,* 153–164.

Schwartz, M. (1968). Effect of stimulus class on transfer and RI in the A–B, A–C paradigm. *Journal of Verbal Learning & Verbal Behavior, 7,* 189–195.

Sloman, S., & Lagnado, D. (2004). Causal invariance in reasoning and learning. In Brian H. Ross (Ed.), *The psychology of learning and motivation* (Vol. 44, pp. 287–325). San Diego, CA: Academic Press.

Tangen, J. M., & Allan, L. G. (2004). Cue-interaction and judgments of causality: contributions of causal and associative processes. *Memory & Cognition, 32,* 107–124.

Vadillo, M. A., Vegas, S., & Matute, H. (2004). Frequency of judgment as a context-like determinant of predictive judgments. *Memory & Cognition, 32,* 1065–1075.

Van Hamme, L. J., Kao, S.-F., & Wasserman, E. A. (1993). Judging interevent relations: from cause to effect and from effect to cause. *Memory & Cognition, 21,* 802–808.

Waldmann, M. R. (2000). Competition among causes but not effects in predictive and diagnostic learning. *Journal of Experimental Psychology: Learning, Memory, and Cognition, 26,* 53–76.

Waldmann, M. R. (2001). Predictive versus diagnostic causal learning: evidence from an overshadowing paradigm. *Psychonomic Bulletin and Review, 8,* 600–608.

Waldmann, M. R., & Holyoak, K. J. (1992). Predictive and diagnostic learning within causal models: asymmetries in cue competition. *Journal of Experimental Psychology: General, 121,* 222–236.

Waldmann, M. R., & Walker, J. M. (2005). Competence and performance in causal learning. *Learning & Behavior, 33,* 211–229.

THE QUARTERLY JOURNAL OF EXPERIMENTAL PSYCHOLOGY
2007, 60 (3), 387–399

Asymmetries in cue competition in forward and backward blocking designs: Further evidence for causal model theory

Samantha L. Booth and Marc J. Buehner

Cardiff University, Cardiff, UK

A hallmark feature of elemental associative learning theories is that multiple cues compete for associative strength when presented with an outcome. Cue competition effects have been observed in humans, both in forward and in backward blocking procedures (e.g., Shanks, 1985) and are often interpreted as evidence for an associative account of human causal learning (e.g., Shanks & Dickinson, 1987). Waldmann and Holyoak (1992), however, demonstrated that cue competition only occurs in predictive, and not diagnostic, learning paradigms. While unexplainable from an associative perspective, this asymmetry readily follows from structural considerations of causal model theory. In this paper, we show that causal models determine the extent of cue competition not only in forward but also in backward blocking designs. Implications for associative and inferential accounts of causal learning are discussed.

This paper contributes to an ongoing debate between associative theories (e.g., Dickinson, 2001; Shanks & Dickinson, 1987; Shanks & Lopez, 1996) and causal model theory (e.g., Waldmann, 2000, 2001; Waldmann & Holyoak, 1992, 1997; Waldmann, Holyoak, & Fratianne, 1995; for an overview of the debate, see Shanks, Holyoak, & Medin, 1996). The research presented here concerns *cue competition*, a phenomenon originally reported in animal conditioning (Kamin, 1969), but subsequently also found in human causal learning (e.g., Shanks, 1985). As the term suggests, cue competition occurs when two or more cues compete to predict the same outcome. Several experimental paradigms can give rise to cue competition; in a standard *blocking paradigm*,

for example, participants learn that Cue A leads to an outcome (A+). In a second phase, a redundant cue, B, is paired with A and the outcome (AB+). In Kamin's (1969) experiment rats were presented with a light followed by a shock (A+), followed by a phase where a light and tone presented simultaneously signalled a shock (AB+). Less conditioned fear to the tone was found in these rats than in a control group of rats who received only the AB+ trials.

An associative learning analysis of cue competition

The Rescorla–Wagner model (Rescorla & Wagner, 1972; RWM henceforth) was developed

Correspondence should be addressed to Marc J. Buehner, School of Psychology, Cardiff University, Tower Building, Park Place, Cardiff, CF10 3AT, UK. E-mail: BuehnerM@Cardiff.ac.uk

This paper is based on a final year undergraduate research project conducted by the first author and supervised by the second author. We thank Duncan Brumby for assistance in collecting data and Mark Haselgrove for running RWM simulations.

387

DOI:10.1080/17470210601000839

to explain animal conditioning phenomena such as cue competition and consists of an error-correcting algorithm. According to this model:

$$\Delta V_{CS} = \alpha_{CS} \cdot \beta_{US} \cdot (\lambda_{US} - \sum V)$$

learning consists of reducing the discrepancy between the actual outcome, λ, and the expected outcome, as given by the sum of associative strengths of all cues present in that trial, ΣV; α and β are learning rate parameters representing the salience of the conditioned stimulus (CS) and unconditioned stimulus (US). RWM can explain cue competition as follows: At the end of the first phase, the shock was fully predictable by the light (A). In other words, there was no discrepancy between expected and actual outcome at any time during the subsequent phase, when the tone (B) was paired with the light (A), and this compound was followed by shock (AB+). Consequently, B accrued very little associative strength. In the control group, in contrast, both light and tone accrued equal amounts of associative strength. Cue competition has also been reported in human causal judgement experiments (e.g., Chapman & Robbins, 1990; Shanks, 1985, 1991; Shanks & Dickinson, 1987), prompting Shanks and Dickinson to suggest that the processes underlying human causal learning can be explained by associative models, such as RWM.

In backward blocking, participants first learn that a compound is followed by an outcome (AB+). Subsequently, they observe one of the elements in isolation, followed by the outcome (A+). In other words, the order of learning phases is reversed relative to the standard design. Again, cue competition is said to occur, when the associative strength of B decreases due to the subsequent presentation of A+ , relative to a control group who did not experience subsequent A+ trials. Shanks (1985) reported cue competition

in a backward blocking design and demonstrated that it is due to a retrospective change in judgements rather than forgetting of contingency information (see also De Houwer, 2002, for a discussion about the role of retrospective inferences in blocking in general).

The original RWM cannot account for backward blocking as the learning rule only applies to cues that are present in a given trial and cannot retrospectively change the associative strength of absent cues. However, Van Hamme and Wasserman (1994) extended RWM by allowing α to take on negative values to represent absent cues. This modification means that associative strengths of cues will decrease on trials where the outcome occurs in the absence of that cue.

Cue competition in causal model theory

Waldmann and Holyoak (1992) demonstrated an interesting asymmetry of cue competition in predictive versus diagnostic tasks. In a predictive task, people learn about cause → effect relations. If multiple causes are involved in a common-effect structure, causes compete for explanatory strength. Consider an allergy detection tasks: If shrimp is already known to produce nausea, subsequent experience that a meal of walnuts and shrimp together also leads to nausea will not necessarily lead us to believe that walnuts are inducing nausea. Cue competition occurs: The outcome, nausea, is already fully explained by shrimp. Walnuts may or may not cause the outcome; their causal status is unknown, leading to considerably reduced causal attribution.[1] The situation changes, however, when one considers diagnostic learning, where people learn about effect ← cause relations. In common-cause structures, where one cause produces several effects, the effects should not compete for explanatory strength. One can

---

[1] Note that according to this account, full blocking (i.e., a zero rating of the redundant cue) would not be expected to occur; uncertainty about the causal status of R is reflected by a reduced rating near the midpoint of the scale (i.e., "weak blocking"). Recent research has shown that full blocking is the result of additional inferential processes (e.g., Beckers et al., 2005; Lovibond, Been, Mitchell, Bouton, & Frohardt, 2003) and occurs only when participants make additional assumptions about cue-additivity or outcome-maximality.

conceivably learn that headache is a symptom of a particular disease; if subsequent experience reveals that rash and headache both occur with the disease we readily learn that both are symptoms of the disease. Furthermore, we can use the information that both headache and rash are associated with the disease to diagnose it.

Causal model theory proposes that people are sensitive to causal structure and employ different learning strategies depending on whether learning is predictive or diagnostic. Associative learning theory, in contrast, is insensitive to such higher order structural consideration. Instead, it assigns cue and outcome labels to events according to the temporal order that they are presented in, regardless of whether events are causes or effects.

In Waldmann and Holyoak's Experiment 3 (1992) participants in both the predictive and diagnostic conditions received the same stimuli throughout the experiment, the only difference being the causal role of the cues specified in the instructions. In Phase 1 participants received on/off information on three buttons located in a room called A and had to learn to predict the status of an alarm. In the predictive condition, instructions stated that the buttons (potential causes) were being switched on and off to test which buttons turned on the alarm (the effect). In the diagnostic condition, the alarm (the cause) was being switched on and off to work out which buttons (potential effects) signalled that it was on. Obviously, these instructions imply that the temporal order of occurrence of buttons and alarm was reversed between predictive and diagnostic conditions. For the participants, however, the temporal order in which they received information was the same: In both conditions, they were first presented with information about the buttons in Room A, followed by information about the status of the alarm. Participants learnt that one button (cue P) was a perfect predictor of the alarm status. In a subsequent learning phase a second room, B, was introduced, containing a fourth button (redundant cue R), which was also a perfect predictor of the alarm status. Predictiveness ratings collected throughout the study found cue competition for the redundant cue in the predictive but not the diagnostic condition.

Scope

Waldmann and Holyoak's (1992) conclusions have subsequently been questioned, with some reports claiming to have found cue competition between effects (Matute, Arcediano, & Miller, 1996; Shanks & López, 1996). However, Waldmann and Holyoak (1997) showed that these studies did not properly convey the directionality of the causal structures to participants, which would explain why cue competition occurred. Waldmann (2000, 2001) has since extended the original findings to various other experimental paradigms and scenarios, suggesting that asymmetries in cue competition are a robust feature of human causal learning.

Interestingly, no research has been carried out so far to find out whether these asymmetries also hold in a backward blocking design. Although more cognitive resources are required in backward than forward designs (due to the retrospective adjustment of causal beliefs), the same asymmetries should be obtained. Because some researchers (Shanks & López, 1996) have questioned the reliability of Waldmann and Holyoak's (1992) original study, we first replicated the forward blocking procedure from their original Experiment 3. We then proceeded to reverse the order of learning phases, resulting in a backward blocking procedure.

EXPERIMENT 1: FORWARD BLOCKING DESIGN

Method

Participants

A total of 48 students from Cardiff University, aged between 18 and 28 years, participated, to partially fulfil a course requirement or to receive £5.

Procedure and materials

The experiment was programmed in PsyScope (Cohen, MacWhinney, Flatt, & Provost, 1993) and ran on two computers, located in separate cubicles. The materials were based on Waldmann and Holyoak's Experiment 3 (1992) and involved learning the relations of various cues with one outcome. For participants in the predictive condition, initial instructions referred to three cues as potential causes of one effect, whereas in the diagnostic condition, instructions referred to the same cues as effects of one common cause (see Appendices A and B for full instructions).

Three identical buttons labelled "1", "2", and "3" were presented in a box on the top half of the computer screen that was labelled "Room A". On each trial, buttons were ON or OFF, and participants had to predict (by pressing Y/N) whether the alarm was ON or OFF. Corrective feedback was presented for 2 seconds in the centre of the screen following each response. At the end of Phase 1 participants were asked to rate the predictiveness of each button with respect to the state of the alarm individually on a scale of 0 to 10.

After participants provided ratings for all three cues, new instructions introduced an additional fourth cue. In the predictive condition, this cue was introduced as yet another potential cause that could turn the alarm on; in the diagnostic condition, it was referred to as another signal, indicating the state of the alarm. For both groups, instructions then stated that trials would continue as before, except that the screen would now be split into Room A and Room B, and that participants would be asked for ratings of the predictiveness of each button at two points throughout learning (see Appendices A and B).

The screen in Phase 2 contained an additional box in the bottom half of the screen, labelled "Room B". The box for Room B was the same size as that for Room A and contained a button, identical to the three others and located in the centre of the box, labelled "4".

Design

A mixed design manipulated *causal condition* (predictive vs. diagnostic) between participants. Each participant provided ratings for four cues (P, C, U, and R). In Phase 1, 48 trials provided information about three cues. One cue (C) was constant

and always set as off. Another (P) was a perfect predictor of the correct yes–no response and was on for 24 trials and off for the other 24. A third (U) was uncorrelated with the yes–no response and was therefore on 12 times when cue P was on, but also on 12 times when cue P was off. The labels P, U, and C are only used in the report; there was no reference to them in the experimental procedure. The assignment of cues C, P, and U to Buttons 1, 2, and 3 was counterbalanced.

In Phase 2 the redundant predictor (R) was introduced. R was always on when P was on, and off when P was off; it was therefore also a perfect predictor of the correct response. Phase 2 consisted of two sets of 48 trials, with the buttons programmed to appear on and off within each set of 48 trials according to the same format as that used in Phase 1, except that R was programmed to be on whenever P was on. The order of learning trials was random in both phases.

Results and discussion

We adopted a significance level of .05 for all statistical analyses. Figure 1 shows the mean predictiveness ratings for the three cues presented during Phase 1 and for the four cues presented in Phase 2, with ratings averaged across the two measurements collected. In line with our intentions, cue P was established as the best predictor for the status of the alarm during Phase 1, receiving mean ratings of 8.29 ($SD = 2.97$) and 8.88 ($SD = 2.31$) in the predictive and diagnostic conditions, respectively. The constant and uncorrelated cues C and U received low predictiveness ratings for both conditions. A one-way repeated measures analysis of variance (ANOVA) on predictiveness ratings in Phase 1 with the factor *cue* corroborated this observation: There was a main effect of cue, $F(2, 92) = 32.19$, $MSE = 13.60$ only, and no main effect of or interaction with causal condition (predictive vs. diagnostic).

During Phase 2, P still received high predictiveness ratings in both conditions, $M = 8.96$, $SD = 2.18$ in the predictive, and $M = 9.04$, $SD = 2.08$ in the diagnostic conditions. The redundant cue R was rated lower in the predictive

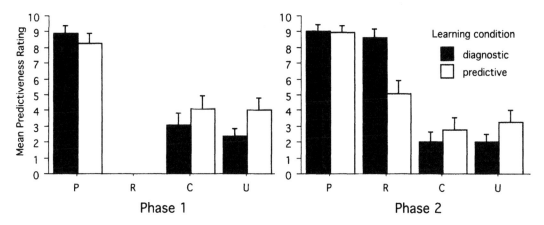

Figure 1. *Forward blocking: Mean predictiveness ratings for predictive and diagnostic conditions in Phase 1 and Phase 2 for the perfect predictor cue (P), the redundant predictive cue (R), the constant cue (C), and the uncorrelated cue (U).*

($M = 5.10$, $SD = 3.89$) than in the diagnostic condition ($M = 8.58$, $SD = 2.73$). Ratings for P and R were compared using a 2 × 2 mixed ANOVA, with cues as the within-subjects and causal condition as the between-subjects variables. Significant main effects were found for both causal condition, $F(1, 46) = 8.10$, $MSE = 9.4$, and cues, $F(1, 46) = 17.39$, $MSE = 6.42$. Results also yielded a significant Cue × Causal Condition interaction, $F(1, 46) = 10.79$, $MSE = 6.42$, with R receiving higher ratings in the diagnostic condition than in the predictive condition.[2]

Therefore cue competition occurred in the predictive but not in the diagnostic condition, replicating Waldmann and Holyoak's (1992) original findings.[3] To further test differences between predictive and diagnostic learning, Experiment 2 investigates cue competition in a backward blocking design. Recall that RWM in its original formulation cannot predict cue competition in backward designs. Although the modified RWM

(Van Hamme & Wasserman, 1994) can, it still cannot distinguish between diagnostic and predictive tasks. In line with causal model theory, we predicted that cue competition will occur only in the predictive and not in the diagnostic condition.

EXPERIMENT 2: BACKWARD BLOCKING DESIGN

Experiment 2 was identical to Experiment 1, except that the order of learning phases was reversed. The instructions were changed where necessary.

Method

Participants
A total of 48 students from Cardiff University, aged between 18 and 22 years, participated either to partially fulfil a course requirement or to receive £5.

---

[2] In order to make our analyses comparable to those of Waldmann and Holyoak (1992), we averaged ratings during Phase 2. Contrary to Waldmann and Holyoak's experiments, however, entering time of rating into the analysis of our data revealed a significant main effect of time of rating, $F(1, 46) = 6.86$, $MSE = 2.47$, in addition to the main effects of cues, causal condition, and the Cues × Causal Condition interaction. Inspection of the data revealed that ratings generally increased from the first to the second time. Conducting the ANOVA on the ratings from the second time only produces an even stronger pattern of results: a main effect of cues, $F(1, 46) = 9.98$, and a Cues × Causal Condition interaction, $F(1, 46) = 44.0$, $MSE = 7.19$, with the main effect of causal condition failing to reach significance, $F(1, 46) = 3.57$, $MSE = 10.81$.

[3] Strictly speaking, our (and Waldmann & Holyoak's, 1992) design lacks the adequate control group to demonstrate the absence of cue competition in the diagnostic condition (e.g., see Shanks & López, 1996). This is entirely inconsequential for our purposes, however. What matters is the asymmetry in cue competition between predictive and diagnostic learning, not its absolute size.

Materials and procedure

The materials were identical to those of Experiment 1, except that the order of learning phases was reversed. This meant that information for both Room A and Room B was provided in Phase 1 of this experiment. To ensure that the absence of Room B in Phase 2 was adequately explained whilst maintaining the distinction between the diagnostic and predictive conditions, the scenarios were adapted slightly (see Appendices C and D). Participants in both groups first worked on two sets of 48 learning trials. Predictiveness ratings for all four cues were prompted after each set was completed. Participants then received another set of instructions on the screen, notifying them that information about Cue 4 would no longer be available in the subsequent trials (see Appendices C and D). Participants then worked on another 48 learning trials, presenting information about cues C, P, and U only. At the end, however, they had to provide ratings for all four cues.

Results and discussion

Data for 1 participant in the predictive condition was lost due to a computer error. The predictive and diagnostic groups thus comprise data from 23 and 24 participants, respectively. Figure 2 shows the mean predictiveness ratings for all four cues in the predictive and diagnostic conditions during Phase 1 (averaged across the two measurements) and Phase 2.[4]

Cues R and P received the highest ratings in Phase 1. A repeated measures ANOVA on ratings in Phase 1 found a main effect of cue only, $F(3, 135) = 39.20$, $MSE = 9.71$, and no main effect or interaction associated with causal condition. The main manipulation check for the backward blocking procedure is to ensure that

cues P and R received identical ratings in Phase 1. Paired samples t tests failed to detect a difference between predictiveness ratings for these cues, $t(22) = 1.22$, and $t(23) = 0.60$, for the predictive and diagnostic conditions, respectively.

In Phase 2, ratings for R dropped compared to Phase 1, with the reduction being more pronounced in the predictive condition ($M = 2.46$; $SD = 3.28$) than in the diagnostic condition ($M = 5.44$; $SD = 4.50$). In contrast, ratings for P remained high, $M = 9.96$, $SD = 0.21$ in the predictive, and $M = 9.54$, $SD = 2.04$ in the diagnostic condition. A 2(causal condition) × 2 (cues) mixed ANOVA of ratings for cues P and R corroborated these observations. A significant main effect was found for causal condition, $F(1, 43) = 4.57$, $MSE = 7.98$, as well as a significant effect of cues, $F(1, 43) = 76.79$, $MSE = 9.83$. These effects were qualified by a Cues × Causal Condition interaction, $F(1, 43) = 6.66$, $MSE = 9.83$.

An omnibus 2 (causal condition) × 2 (cues) × 2 (phase) ANOVA revealed main effects of cue, $F(1, 43) = 44.10$, $MSE = 7.48$, and phase, $F = (1, 43) = 10.66$, $MSE = 6.82$, as well as a Phase × Cues, $F(1, 43) = 83.89$, $MSE = 5.11$, and a Phase × Cues × Causal Condition interaction, $F(1, 43) = 8.70$, $MSE = 5.11$.[5] Although the absence of cue R in Phase 2 led to a general reduction in its rating, this reduction was more pronounced in the predictive than in the diagnostic condition. Thus, asymmetry of cue competition for predictive compared to diagnostic learning, first demonstrated by Waldmann and Holyoak (1992) and replicated in a number of other forward learning paradigms (Waldmann, 2000, 2001), is also reliable in backward learning procedures.

One might be concerned that the asymmetry is not as large in backward as in forward blocking. We conducted a cross-experimental comparison on the ratings of cues P and R in Phase 2. A

---

[4] Comparable to Experiment 1, ratings increased between the first and second time that they were prompted, $F(1, 43) = 9.32$, $MSE = 2.37$.

[5] Conducting the ANOVA with the terminal ratings from Phase 1, rather than the averaged ratings, produces exactly the same pattern of results: main effects of cues, $F(1, 41) = 42.05$, $MSE = 7.14$, and phase, $F(1, 41) = 14.92$, $MSE = 7.48$, as well as a Phase × Cues, $F(1, 43) = 72.61$, $MSE = 5.34$, and a Phase × Cues × Causal Condition interaction, $F(1, 43) = 10.35$, $MSE = 5.34$. The degrees of freedom from this analysis are lower, because for 2 participants the computer failed to record terminal ratings in Phase 1.

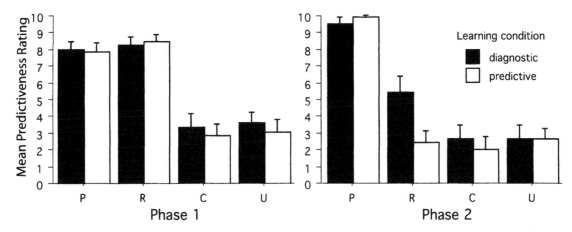

Figure 2. *Backward blocking: Mean predictiveness ratings for predictive and diagnostic conditions in Phase 1 and Phase 2 for the perfect predictor cue (P), the redundant predictive cue (R), the constant cue (C), and the uncorrelated cue (U).*

mixed ANOVA with the factors phase order, causal condition, and cues revealed main effects of cues, $F(1, 89) = 90.98$, $MSE = 8.07$, causal condition, $F(1, 89) = 12.43$, $MSE = 8.72$, and the crucial Cues × Causal Condition interaction, $F(1, 89) = 16.69$, $MSE = 8.07$. In addition to these effects, which demonstrate asymmetry of cue competition between predictive and diagnostic learning, there was a main effect of phase order, $F(1, 89) = 6.22$, $MSE = 8.72$, qualified by a Phase Order × Cues interaction, $F(1, 89) = 19.05$, $MSE = 8.07$, indicating that Phase 2 ratings for R were generally lower in the backward than in the forward blocking paradigm. Importantly, however, phase order did not interact with any effects associated with causal condition—for example, $F(1, 89) < 0.001$, $MSE = 8.07$, for the Phase Order × Cues × Causal Condition interaction, which suggests that the asymmetry of cue competition between predictive and diagnostic learning is equally strong in backward as in forward learning.

GENERAL DISCUSSION

The main purpose of this paper was to test whether asymmetries in cue competition (Waldmann, 2000, 2001; Waldmann & Holyoak, 1992)—previously established in forward learning procedures only—also extend to a backward learning paradigm. An implicit assumption of causal model theory, or any inferential account of cue competition in causal learning (e.g., see Beckers et al., 2005; De Houwer, 2002; Lovibond et al., 2003; see also Vandorpe, De Houwer, & Beckers, 2007) is that the order of learning phases is inconsequential for the occurrence of cue competition. In contrast, the order in which stimuli are encountered is crucial for associative learning theories. Indeed, the first demonstration of cue competition in a backward learning predictive causal learning task (Shanks, 1985) caused serious embarrassment for the RWM as an adequate account of human causal learning. As is often the case, adding an additional degree of freedom allowed the model to survive this blow (Van Hamme & Wasserman, 1994). While the so-modified RWM can account for cue competition in backward and forward blocking designs, it still lacks sensitivity to causal structure. Our demonstration of asymmetries in cue competition in a backward blocking design is clearly at variance with any associative model of causal learning, including the modified RWM. In contrast, it adds to the growing support for an inferential account of causal learning, as first proposed by Waldmann and Holyoak.

Retrospective inferences and asymmetries in underlying assumptions

Retrospective inferences concerning the redundant cue are vital in explaining asymmetries in cue competition: Waldmann (2000) found that participants in a forward blocking diagnostic task inferred that the redundant cue had already occurred in Phase 1 although information about it was not provided until Phase 2. Although participants were not asked about this, we can assume that participants in our Experiment 1 made analogous retrospective inferences about the redundant cue. In Experiment 2 it would appear that participants in the diagnostic, but not the predictive, condition inferred that R was still present during Phase 2, although information about it was no longer available.

One could argue that the selective occurrence of retrospective and prospective inferences about the presence of unobserved cues in diagnostic, but not predictive, learning would allow an associative account to explain asymmetries in cue competition: In the forward design, diagnostic Phase 2 instructions might result in a mental replay of Phase 1, with R present on all reinforced trials; likewise, in the backward design, Phase 2 instructions would result in R still being assumed to be present on all reinforced trials, even though no feedback about R is provided. These mental simulations concerning the presence of R would allow R to retrospectively gain (forward blocking) or retain (backward blocking) associative strength in diagnostic, but not predictive, learning tasks.

While lacking parsimony and scientific elegance, this argument carries intuitive appeal and thus needs to be evaluated. What would such a concession mean for an associative account? Participants were not explicitly instructed to mentally simulate the presence of R at each trial of the diagnostic conditions. We propose that sensitivity to causal structure led them, at the time of providing their rating, to infer that R would have been present each time P was present. Our predictive conditions involved a common effect, the diagnostic conditions a common cause structure (see Figure 3). Selective inferences in diagnostic but

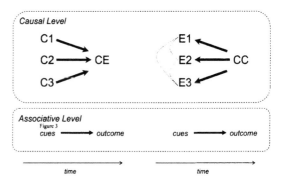

Figure 3. In a common effect causal structure (left) multiple causes independently produce a single effect. In a common cause causal structure (right) one cause simultaneously produces multiple effects. Whereas multiple causes (left) compete for explanatory strength, multiple effects (right) are spuriously correlated and thus do not compete for explanatory strength.

not predictive conditions that R would still have been ON even when no information about it was available are only possible by recruiting these structural assumptions. In fact, if R were thought to have not *occurred* (as opposed to *occurred* but not *observed*), its diagnostic value would indeed be poorer than P's, and asymmetries in cue competition would no longer be predicted (cf. De Houwer, 2002). Crucially, however, associative theories cannot represent such structural complexities: They simply capture cue–outcome learning; assigning cues to causes and outcomes to effects, or vice versa, falls outside their scope. Trying to shoehorn structural information into theories that inherently cannot represent such knowledge is equivalent to accepting that causal learning involves much more than merely tracking associations.

Asymmetries in cue competition need not necessarily rule out that causal learning recruits associative learning processes. One could well imagine a hybrid model, where higher level structural and lower level associative processes complement each other (for more detailed discussion of hybrid accounts, see Pineño & Miller, 2007). Yet another approach would be to propose a dual-systems account, where one (associative) system tracks associations, while another (statistical) system integrates acquired information. Collins and Shanks (2002), for instance, have suggested that procedural details (e.g., whether participants are repeatedly probed for causal ratings throughout learning, or are asked to provide a single judgement at the end of learning) determine which system is recruited for a task: They found that multiple ratings throughout learning gave rise to a recency effect (i.e., participants weight information towards the end of learning more heavily), while a single terminal rating led to a normative, integrative rating, not subject to any biases. Associative accounts readily predict recency effects, but statistical accounts cannot, unless one makes additional assumptions about task demands. Dennis (2004) however, challenged Collins and Shanks's results on methodological grounds and found integrative ratings even when participants were probed after every trial, thus seriously undermining the credibility of a dual-systems account. More specifically, Dennis found a slight primacy effect (i.e., trials occurring early in learning were weighted more than later trials), which is exactly opposite to Collins and Shanks's results and furthermore completely unexplainable by associative algorithms. Primacy effects, while not predicted by simple contingency-based accounts either, fit with a statistical account of belief updating (see also Dennis & Ahn, 2001; Marsh & Ahn, 2006).

Furthermore, other research has demonstrated that standard associative algorithms—whether as part of a hybrid or a dual-systems model—are incapable of representing causal strength as an unbound variable (Holyoak & Hummel, 2000) independent of covariation (Buehner, Cheng, & Clifford, 2003). In our opinion, unless these problems are surmounted, statistical, inferential approaches to causal learning remain the only plausible alternative.

REFERENCES

Beckers, T., De Houwer, J., Pineño, O., & Miller, R. R. (2005). Outcome additivity and outcome maximality influence cue competition in human causal learning. *Journal of Experimental Psychology: Learning, Memory, and Cognition, 31*, 238–249.

Buehner, M. J., Cheng, P. W., & Clifford, D. (2003). From covariation to causation: A test of the assumption of causal power. *Journal of Experimental Psychology: Learning, Memory, and Cognition, 29*, 1119–1140.

Chapman, G. B., & Robbins, S. J. (1990). Cue interaction in human contingency judgment. *Memory and Cognition, 18*, 537–545.

Cohen, J. D., MacWhinney, B., Flatt, M., & Provost, J. (1993). Psyscope: An interactive graphic system for designing and controlling experiments in the psychology laboratory using Macintosh computers. *Behavior Research Methods, Instruments and Computers, 25*, 257–271.

Collins, D. J., & Shanks, D. R. (2002). Momentary and integrative response strategies in causal judgment. *Memory and Cognition, 30*, 1138–1147.

De Houwer, J. (2002). Forward blocking depends on retrospective inferences about the presence of the blocked cue during the elemental phase. *Memory and Cognition, 30*, 24–33.

Dennis, M. J. (2004). *Primacy in causal strength judgments: The effect of initial evidence for generative versus inhibitory relationships.* New Haven, CT: Yale University.

Dennis, M. J., & Ahn, W.-K. (2001). Primacy in causal strength judgments: The effect of initial evidence for generative versus inhibitory relationships. *Memory & Cognition, 29*, 152–164.

Dickinson, A. (2001). Causal learning: An associative analysis. *Quarterly Journal of Experimental Psychology, 54B*, 3–25.

Holyoak, K. J., & Hummel, J. E. (2000). The proper treatment of symbols in a connectionist architecture. In E. Dietrich & A. Markman (Eds.), *Cognitive dynamics: Conceptual change in humans and machines* (pp. 229–263). Mahwah, NJ: Erlbaum.

Kamin, L. J. (1969). Predictability, surprise, attention and conditioning. In B. A. Campbell & R. M. Church (Eds.), *Punishment and aversive behavior.* New York: Appleton Century Crofts.

Lovibond, P. F., Been, S. L., Mitchell, C. J., Bouton, M. E., & Frohardt, R. (2003). Forward and backward blocking of causal judgment is enhanced by additivity of effect magnitude. *Memory and Cognition, 31*, 133–142.

Marsh, J. K., & Ahn, W.-K. (2006). Order effects in contingency learning: The role of task complexity. *Memory & Cognition, 34*, 568–576.

Matute, H., Arcediano, F., & Miller, R. R. (1996). Test question modulates cue competition between causes and between effects. *Journal of Experimental Psychology: Learning, Memory, and Cognition, 22,* 182–196.

Pineño, O. & Miller, R. R. (2007). Comparing associative, statistical, and inferential reasoning account of human contingency learning. *Quarterly Journal of Experimental Psychology, 60,* 310–329.

Rescorla, R. A., & Wagner, A. R. (1972). A theory of pavlovian conditioning: Variations in the effectiveness of reinforcement and nonreinforcement. In A. H. Black & W. F. Prokasy (Eds.), *Classical conditioning II: Current theory and research* (pp. 64–99). New York: Appleton-Century Crofts.

Shanks, D. R. (1985). Forward and backward blocking in human contingency judgement. *Quarterly Journal of Experimental Psychology, 37B,* 1–21.

Shanks, D. R. (1991). Categorization by a connectionist network. *Journal of Experimental Psychology: Learning, Memory, and Cognition, 17,* 433–443.

Shanks, D. R., & Dickinson, A. (1987). Associative accounts of causality judgment. In G. H. Bower (Ed.), *Psychology of learning and motivation: Advances in research and theory* (Vol. 21, pp. 229–261). San Diego, CA: Academic Press.

Shanks, D. R., Holyoak, K. J., & Medin, D. L. (Eds.). (1996). *The psychology of learning and motivation*: Vol. 34. Causal learning. San Diego, CA: Academic Press.

Shanks, D. R., & López, F. J. (1996). Causal order does not affect cue selection in human associative learning. *Memory & Cognition, 24,* 511–522.

Vandorpe, S., De Houwer, J., & Beckers, T. (2007). Outcome maximality and additivity training also influence cue competition in causal learning when learning involves many cues and events. *Quarterly Journal of Experimental Psychology, 60,* 356–368.

Van Hamme, L. J., & Wasserman, E. A. (1994). Cue competition in causality judgments: The role of non-presentation of compound stimulus elements. *Learning and Motivation, 25,* 127–151.

Waldmann, M. R. (2000). Competition among causes but not effects in predictive and diagnostic learning. *Journal of Experimental Psychology: Learning, Memory, and Cognition, 26,* 53–76.

Waldmann, M. R. (2001). Predictive versus diagnostic causal learning: Evidence from an overshadowing paradigm. *Psychonomic Bulletin & Review, 8,* 600–608.

Waldmann, M. R., & Holyoak, K. J. (1992). Predictive and diagnostic learning within causal models: Asymmetries in cue competition. *Journal of Experimental Psychology: General, 121,* 222–236.

Waldmann, M. R., & Holyoak, K. J. (1997). Determining whether causal order affects cue selection in human contingency learning: Comments on Shanks and López (1996). *Memory & Cognition, 25,* 125–134.

Waldmann, M. R., Holyoak, K. J., & Fratianne, A. (1995). Causal models and the acquisition of category structure. *Journal of Experimental Psychology: General, 124,* 181–206.

APPENDIX A

Predictive instructions for Experiment 1

Phase 1

PETER W. HAS JUST STARTED TO WORK AT A BANK IN ROOM A. IN THE EVENING HE IS EXPECTED TO SWITCH ON THE ALARM, BUT UNFORTUNATELY NOBODY HAS TOLD HIM WHICH BUTTONS TURN ON THE ALARM, SO HE TRIES SEVERAL BUTTONS.

Trials will be presented individually providing information on whether different buttons are on or off. The buttons will be GREEN when they are ON and BLUE when they are OFF. Using the information provided, after each trial a prediction is required as to whether the alarm is on or off.

IF YOU BELIEVE THAT THE ALARM IS ON, PLEASE PRESS THE "Y" KEY ON THE KEYPAD. IF YOU BELIEVE THAT THE ALARM IS OFF, PLEASE PRESS THE "N" KEY.

Corrective feedback will be given after each response stating either correct or incorrect.

At the end you will be asked to rate the predictiveness of each button individually (i.e., the extent to which each button predicts the status of the alarm) on a scale of 0 (not a predictor) to 10 (perfect predictor). It is therefore important that you focus on all the information provided in each trial.

Response time is unimportant, so please take as much time as you need to make your response.

WHEN YOU ARE READY TO BEGIN THE EXPERIMENT, PLEASE PRESS THE SPACE BAR.

Phase 2

MARY B. HAS STARTED WORK AT THE BANK ON THE SAME DAY AS PETER W. SHE WORKS IN A DIFFERENT ROOM, ROOM B, AND BECAUSE SHE IS UNAWARE OF PETER'S ATTEMPTS, SHE SIMULTANEOUSLY TRIES TO SWITCH ON THE ALARM. SEVERAL BUTTONS ARE LOCATED IN HER ROOM, BUT ONLY INFORMATION ABOUT ONE WILL BE PROVIDED.

Trials will be presented as before. The screen will be split into Room A and Room B by a line and the rooms will be labelled. Again, after each trial a prediction is required as to whether the alarm is on or off.

IF YOU BELIEVE THAT THE ALARM IS ON, PLEASE PRESS THE "Y" KEY ON THE KEYPAD. IF YOU BELIEVE THAT THE ALARM IS OFF, PLEASE PRESS THE "N" KEY.

Corrective feedback will be given after each response stating either correct or incorrect.

At two points you will be asked to rate the predictiveness of each button individually (i.e., the extent to which each button predicts the status of the alarm) on a scale of 0 (not a predictor) to 10 (perfect predictor). It is therefore important that you focus on all the information provided in each trial.

Response time is unimportant, so please take as much time as you need to make your response.

Please feel free to ask any questions before you begin.

WHEN YOU ARE READY TO BEGIN THE EXPERIMENT, PLEASE PRESS THE SPACE BAR.

APPENDIX B

Diagnostic instructions Experiment 1

Phase 1

PETER W. HAS JUST STARTED WORK AT A BANK IN ROOM A. IN THE EVENING HE HAS TO CHECK THAT THE ALARM IS ON. HE HAS BEEN TOLD THAT THE STATE OF THE ALARM IS SIGNALLED BY CERTAIN BUTTONS, BUT UNFORTUNATELY NOBODY HAS TOLD HIM WHICH BUTTONS SIGNAL THAT THE ALARM IS ON. PETER W. THEREFORE EXPERIMENTALLY SWITCHES THE ALARM ON AND OFF AND CHECKS WHICH BUTTONS ARE ON.

Trials will be presented individually providing information on whether different buttons are on or off. The buttons will be GREEN when they are ON and BLUE when they are OFF. Using the information provided, after each trial a prediction is required as to whether the alarm is on or off.

IF YOU BELIEVE THAT THE ALARM IS ON, PLEASE PRESS THE "Y" KEY ON THE KEYPAD. IF YOU BELIEVE THAT THE ALARM IS OFF, PLEASE PRESS THE "N" KEY.

Corrective feedback will be given after each response stating either correct or incorrect.

At the end you will be asked to rate the predictiveness of each button individually (i.e., the extent to which each button predicts the status of the alarm) on a scale of 0 (not a predictor) to 10 (perfect predictor). It is therefore important that you focus on all the information provided in each trial.

Response time is unimportant, so please take as much time as you need to make your response.

Please feel free to ask any questions before you begin.

WHEN YOU ARE READY TO BEGIN THE EXPERIMENT, PLEASE PRESS THE SPACE BAR.

Phase 2

MARY B. HAS STARTED WORK AT THE BANK ON THE SAME DAY AS PETER W. SHE WORKS IN A DIFFERENT ROOM, ROOM B, AND BECAUSE SHE IS UNAWARE OF PETER'S ATTEMPTS, SHE SIMULTANEOUSLY TRIES TO WORK OUT WHICH BUTTONS SIGNAL THAT THE ALARM IS ON. SEVERAL BUTTONS ARE LOCATED IN HER ROOM BUT ONLY INFORMATION ABOUT ONE WILL BE PROVIDED.

Trials will be presented as before. The screen will be split into Room A and Room B by a line and the rooms will be labelled. Again, after each trial a prediction is required as to whether the alarm is on or off.

IF YOU BELIEVE THAT THE ALARM IS ON, PLEASE PRESS THE "Y" KEY ON THE KEYPAD. IF YOU BELIEVE THAT THE ALARM IS OFF, PLEASE PRESS THE "N" KEY.

Corrective feedback will be given after each response stating either correct or incorrect.

At two points you will be asked to rate the predictiveness of each button individually (i.e., the extent to which each button predicts the status of the alarm) on a scale of 0 (not a predictor) to 10 (perfect predictor). It is therefore important that you focus on all the information provided in each trial.

Please feel free to ask any questions before you begin.

WHEN YOU ARE READY TO BEGIN THE EXPERIMENT, PLEASE PRESS THE SPACE BAR.

APPENDIX C

Predictive instructions for Experiment 2

Phase 1

PETER W. AND MARY B. HAVE JUST STARTED TO WORK AT A BANK IN SEPARATE ROOMS. PETER W. WORKS IN ROOM A AND MARY B. IN ROOM B. IN THE EVENING, BOTH PETER AND MARY HAVE TO SWITCH THE BANK'S ALARM ON AS PART OF THEIR WORK, BUT UNFORTUNATELY NOBODY HAS TOLD THEM WHICH BUTTONS TURN ON THE ALARM. THEREFORE, TOGETHER, THEY EXPERIMENTALLY SWITCH BUTTONS ON AND OFF IN THEIR OWN ROOMS AND THEN CHECK IF THE ALARM IS ON. SEVERAL BUTTONS ARE LOCATED IN MARY'S ROOM, BUT ONLY INFORMATION ABOUT ONE WILL BE PROVIDED.

Trials will be presented individually providing information on whether different buttons are on or off. The buttons will be GREEN when they are ON and BLUE when they are OFF. The screen will be split into Room A and Room B by a line and the rooms will be labelled. Using the information provided, after each trial a prediction is required as to whether the alarm is on or off.

IF YOU BELIEVE THAT THE ALARM IS ON, PLEASE PRESS THE "Y" KEY ON THE KEYPAD. IF YOU BELIEVE THAT THE ALARM IS OFF, PLEASE PRESS THE "N" KEY.

Corrective feedback will be given after each response stating either correct or incorrect.

At two points you will be asked to rate the predictiveness of each button individually (i.e., the extent to which each button predicts the status of the alarm) on a scale of 0 (not a predictor) to 10 (perfect predictor). It is therefore important that you focus on all the information provided in each trial.

Response time is unimportant, so please take as much time as you need to make your response.

Please feel free to ask any questions before you begin.

WHEN YOU ARE READY TO BEGIN THE EXPERIMENT, PLEASE PRESS THE SPACE BAR.

Phase 2

MARY HAS QUIT HER JOB IN THE BANK AND PETER IS LEFT IN CHARGE ALONE TO SWITCH THE ALARM ON. NO REPLACEMENT HAS YET BEEN FOUND FOR MARY, AND THUS NOBODY PRESSES BUTTONS IN ROOM B ANYMORE. PETER CONTINUES HIS EFFORTS TO FIND OUT WHICH BUTTONS IN HIS ROOM, ROOM A, TURN THE ALARM ON.

Trials will be presented as before, *except information will no longer be provided for Room B*. Again, after each trial a prediction is required as to whether the alarm is on or off.

IF YOU BELIEVE THAT THE ALARM IS ON, PLEASE PRESS THE "Y" KEY ON THE KEYPAD. IF YOU BELIEVE THAT THE ALARM IS OFF, PLEASE PRESS THE "N" KEY.

Corrective feedback will be given after each response stating either correct or incorrect.

At the end you will be asked to rate the predictiveness of each button *in Rooms A and B individually* (i.e., the extent to which each button predicts the status of the alarm) on a scale of 0 (not a predictor) to 10 (perfect predictor). It is therefore important that you focus on all the information provided in each trial.

Response time is unimportant, so please take as much time as you need to make your response.

Please feel free to ask any questions before you begin.

WHEN YOU ARE READY TO BEGIN THE EXPERIMENT, PLEASE PRESS THE SPACE BAR.

APPENDIX D

Diagnostic instructions for Experiment 2

Phase 1

PETER W. AND MARY B. HAVE JUST STARTED TO WORK AT A BANK IN SEPARATE ROOMS. PETER W. WORKS IN ROOM A AND MARY B. IN ROOM B. IN THE EVENING, BOTH HAVE TO CHECK THAT THE BANK'S ALARM IS ON AS PART OF THEIR WORK. THEY HAVE BEEN TOLD THAT THE STATE OF THE ALARM IS SIGNALLED BY CERTAIN BUTTONS, BUT UNFORTUNATELY NOBODY HAS TOLD THEM WHICH BUTTONS SIGNAL THAT THE ALARM IS ON. THEREFORE, TOGETHER, THEY EXPERIMENTALLY SWITCH THE ALARM ON AND OFF AND THEN CHECK WHICH BUTTONS ARE ON IN THEIR OWN ROOMS.

SEVERAL BUTTONS ARE LOCATED IN MARY'S ROOM, BUT ONLY INFORMATION ABOUT ONE WILL BE PROVIDED.

Trials will be presented individually providing information on whether different buttons are on or off. The buttons will be GREEN when they are ON and BLUE when they are OFF. The screen will be split into Room A and Room B by a line and the rooms will be labelled. Using the information provided, after each trial a prediction is required as to whether the alarm is on or off.

IF YOU BELIEVE THAT THE ALARM IS ON, PLEASE PRESS THE "Y" KEY ON THE KEYPAD. IF YOU BELIEVE THAT THE ALARM IS OFF, PLEASE PRESS THE "N" KEY.

Corrective feedback will be given after each response stating either correct or incorrect.

At two points you will be asked to rate the predictiveness of each button individually (i.e., the extent to which each button predicts the status of the alarm) on a scale of 0 (not a predictor) to 10 (perfect predictor). It is therefore important that you focus on all the information provided in each trial.

Response time is unimportant, so please take as much time as you need to make your response.

Please feel free to ask any questions before you begin.

WHEN YOU ARE READY TO BEGIN THE EXPERIMENT, PLEASE PRESS THE SPACE BAR.

Phase 2

MARY HAS QUIT HER JOB IN THE BANK AND PETER IS LEFT IN CHARGE ALONE TO CHECK THAT THE ALARM IS ON. NO REPLACEMENT HAS YET BEEN FOUND FOR MARY, AND THUS NOBODY CHECKS THE BUTTONS IN ROOM B ANYMORE. PETER CONTINUES HIS EFFORTS TO FIND OUT WHICH BUTTONS IN HIS ROOM, ROOM A, SIGNAL THAT THE ALARM IS ON.

Trials will be presented as before, *except information will no longer be provided for Room B*. Again, after each trial a prediction is required as to whether the alarm is on or off.

IF YOU BELIEVE THAT THE ALARM IS ON, PLEASE PRESS THE "Y" KEY ON THE KEYPAD. IF YOU BELIEVE THAT THE ALARM IS OFF, PLEASE PRESS THE "N" KEY.

Corrective feedback will be given after each response stating either correct or incorrect.

At the end you will be asked to rate the predictiveness of each button *in Rooms A and B individually* (i.e., the extent to which each button predicts the status of the alarm) on a scale of 0 (not a predictor) to 10 (perfect predictor). It is therefore important that you focus on all the information provided in each trial.

Response time is unimportant, so please take as much time as you need to make your response.

Please feel free to ask any questions before you begin.

WHEN YOU ARE READY TO BEGIN THE EXPERIMENT, PLEASE PRESS THE SPACE BAR.

THE QUARTERLY JOURNAL OF EXPERIMENTAL PSYCHOLOGY
2007, 60 (3), 400–417

A dissociation between causal judgement and the ease with which a cause is categorized with its effect

Chris J. Mitchell
University of New South Wales, Sydney, New South Wales, Australia

Evan Livesey
Cambridge University, Cambridge, UK

Peter F. Lovibond
University of New South Wales, Sydney, New South Wales, Australia

The associative view of human causal learning argues that causation is attributed to the extent that the putative cause activates, via an association, a mental representation of the effect. That is, causal learning is a human analogue of animal conditioning. We tested this associative theory using a task in which a fictitious character suffered from two allergic reactions, rash (O_1) and headache (O_2). In a conditioned inhibition design with each of these two outcomes ($A-O_1/AX-$ and $B-O_2/BY-$), participants were trained that one herbal remedy (X) prevented O_1 and that the other (Y) prevented O_2. These inhibitory properties were revealed in a causal judgement summation test. In a subsequent categorization task, X was most easily categorized with O_1, and Y with O_2. Thus, the categorization data indicated an excitatory $X-O_1$ and $Y-O_2$ association, the reverse of the inhibitory relationship observed on the causal judgement measure. A second experiment showed that this pattern of excitation and inhibition is dependent on intermixed $A-O_1$ and $AX-$ trials. These results are problematic for the standard application of associative activation theories to causal judgement. We argue instead that the inhibition revealed in the causal judgement task reflects inferential reasoning, which relies, in part, on the ability of the cue in question to excite a representation of the outcome, as revealed in the categorization test.

More than 20 years ago, Dickinson, Shanks, and Evenden (1984) suggested that causal judgements made by humans might result from the same psychological mechanisms as those responsible for conditioning in nonhuman animals: associative learning. For example, when a person suffers a headache after eating chocolate, the attribution "chocolate causes headache" might be made. According to the associative view, this causal attribution directly reflects an association between the mental representations of the cause (chocolate) and the effect (headache). In other words, causal efficacy is attributed to chocolate because, when chocolate is presented, it activates (by association) the mental representation of the headache. Subsequent research has provided support for the associative view; many animal learning phenomena, thought to result from an

---

Correspondence should be addressed to Chris Mitchell, School of Psychology, University of New South Wales, Sydney NSW 2052, Australia. E-mail: Chris.Mitchell@unsw.edu.au

DOI:10.1080/17470210601002512

associative mechanism, are also observed in human causal learning. These phenomena include negatively accelerated learning curves (Shanks, López, Darby, & Dickinson, 1996), blocking (Chapman & Robbins, 1990), and conditioned inhibition (Karazinov & Boakes, 2004).

Blocking is probably the most extensively studied of the human causal learning phenomena. In this procedure, participants receive pairings of one cue, A, with an outcome (A+), and then a compound of that cue and a second cue, B, is also followed by the outcome (AB+). The causal rating of cue B on test is often lower than that of a control cue, D, trained in compound with a non-pretrained cue C (CD+). A common associative explanation for blocking is that the outcome on AB+ trials is unsurprising—it is predicted by the pretrained cue A, and thus no learning takes place on AB+ trials. In the control condition, neither C nor D receives pretraining, and thus the outcome is surprising on CD+ trials, and learning about both cues takes place. The observation of blocking in both nonhuman conditioning studies (e.g., Kamin, 1969) and human causal judgement studies (Chapman & Robbins, 1990) has been taken as strong support for the idea that a common learning mechanism is responsible for conditioning and causal judgements. Specifically, because the modal view of blocking in animals is the associative view, blocking in humans has been taken as support for the associative view of human causal judgements.

The alternative to this view, which has been proposed in different forms by a number of theorists (De Houwer, Beckers & Glautier, 2002; Lovibond, Been, Mitchell, Bouton & Frohardt, 2003; Waldman, 2000), is that causal judgements involve high-level inferential reasoning processes and the application of flexible rules. Further studies of the blocking phenomenon have provided evidence in favour of this account. For example, in the A+/AB+ design above, cue B can be reasoned by inference to be noncausal, but only if an outcome larger than that observed on A+ trials is possible (++). If this larger outcome is possible, participants can reason that, were B causal (B+), then the presence of B would enhance the magnitude of the outcome (AB++) relative to when A is presented alone (A+). In the A+/AB+ design described above, the outcome on AB trials is not larger than that on A alone trials; thus, B can be reasoned to be noncausal. That is, blocking will be observed. Of course, in blocking, if the outcome on A+ trials is the maximum possible (it is at ceiling), then the outcome on AB trials could not be larger than that on A alone trials. Under these circumstances, the AB+ trials are uninformative—it cannot be concluded that B is noncausal—so strong blocking will not be observed. Evidence that human participants engage in inferential reasoning comes from the finding that, consistent with the analysis above, blocking is strong only when the outcome is not the maximum possible on AB+ trials (De Houwer et al., 2002; Lovibond et al., 2003). In other words, B is more likely to be given a low causal rating when it can be inferred to be noncausal. Therefore, the finding of blocking in human causal judgements does not, in itself, provide evidence in favour of the associative view.

The present paper aims to test the inferential view against the associative view by examining another phenomenon drawn from animal conditioning: conditioned inhibition. However, before we proceed further, it is necessary to define more clearly what we mean by the "associative view". The term associative learning can take at least two quite different meanings. First, this idea can be taken to refer to the straightforward empirical finding that humans can detect an association between a cue and an outcome in the environment. This definition of associative learning does not specify a particular learning mechanism. As we have argued, one might become aware of an associative relationship in the environment as a result of a deductive inference, or some other high-level reasoning process. The second meaning of associative learning is much narrower and refers to a specific psychological mechanism that has been proposed to be responsible for causal judgements in humans and conditioned responding in animals. According to this meaning, an association is a link between two mental representations, such that activation of one representation is able to trigger activation in the second representation.

In the present paper, we use "associative learning" to refer to the second of the above meanings—that is, the psychological mechanism of mental connections between representations. According to this view, when a cue is judged to cause an outcome it is because presentation of that cue elicits (by association) activation of the mental representation of the outcome. This association between the two events is then directly translated into a causal rating. The alternative inferential view allows that associations, in some sense of the term, will form between mental representations such that the one can bring to mind the other. However, according to this view, although contiguous pairings of a cue and an outcome will allow the observer to recall that the cue "went with" the outcome, the causal attribution (that the cue causes the outcome) requires a further inferential step. This inferential processing of the association between the cue and outcome is a top-down cognitive process that recruits information from a whole variety of sources such as verbal rules and causal models. In summary, the associative view allows that associations can be directly translated into causal judgements, whereas the inferential view requires further top-down processing for an association to be expressed as a causal relationship. We return to this argument in the General Discussion.

Over the past two years we have conducted a series of experiments in our laboratory in an effort to establish whether causal judgements of cues do indeed directly reflect associative activation of the outcome representation. In one set of studies we examined blocking (Mitchell, Lovibond, Minard, & Lavis, 2006). We arranged for a fictitious Mr X to suffer from a range of fictitious allergic reactions (daryosis, xianethis, etc.) after consuming different foods. Thus, in the blocking design (A+ then AB+), Mr X might eat radish and suffer from daryosis and then consume a meal of radish and pizza and suffer from daryosis. On test, participants were required to respond in two different ways. First they were asked to remember which outcome

(daryosis, xianethis, etc.) followed the consumption of each food and then to what extent the food caused that outcome. We found blocking in causal judgements; causal ratings of B were lower than those of the control cue D (trained in compound with the nonpretrained cue C). More importantly, we also found blocking on the memory measure; participants were less accurate in recalling which outcome followed B than which followed D. Thus, consistent with the associative view, it would appear that blocking in causal judgement sometimes reflects a failure of the target cue to activate the outcome with which it was paired.

On the other hand, the experiments by De Houwer et al. (2002) and Lovibond et al. (2003) showing reasoning effects in blocking suggest that blocking is not always due to a failure to encode a cue–outcome association. According to the inferential view, because the same cue–outcome memories can give rise to different inferences (when combined with other information), causal judgements and cue–outcome recall might not always show the same pattern of responding. For example, in blocking, participants might very well recall that cue B was followed by the outcome on AB+ trials (B activates the outcome representation), but reason that B is not causal because A was present on that trial, and no increase in the size of the outcome was observed.

We conducted a second series of experiments that suggested that causal judgements do not always reflect the degree to which the cue in question is able to activate the representation of the outcome (Mitchell, Lovibond, & Gan, 2005). We used the same fictitious allergies and foods as those in Mitchell et al. (2006). The experimental design included a blocking contingency (A+/ AB+) and a protection from overshadowing contingency (C−/CD+). In protection from overshadowing, because C does not produce the outcome when presented alone, D is the likely cause of the outcome that follows the CD compound. In associative terminology, C is less able to compete with D for associative strength.

However, cue competition is not the only possible outcome of the A+/AB+/C−/CD+ design according to associative theory. In fact, the reverse phenomenon, mediated learning, is also possible (e.g., Holland, 1990). Thus, rather than failing to learn about B due to the presence of A (blocking) participants might actually learn a stronger B− unconditioned stimulus (US) association by virtue of the presence of A. One account of mediated learning is as follows. On AB+ trials, two associations form, one between B and the US and a second between B and A. As a result, B is able to activate the US via two routes on test: directly, as a result of its pairing with the US and indirectly via its ability to activate A (Hall, 1996).[1] This second process would give B an advantage over D because A, the associate of B (but not C, the associate of D) is paired with the US when presented alone.

Therefore, in Mitchell et al.'s (2005) study, an associative account can be given for the observation of either cue competition or mediated learning on the causal judgement and the cued recall (US activation) task. What the associative account has difficulty explaining is any dissociation between the effects observed on the two measures. In fact, the outcome that followed B (on AB+) trials was better recalled than that which followed D (on CD+ trials)—mediated learning—but B was judged to be less causal than D—blocking. It was concluded that, although the outcome was more strongly activated by cue B than cue D, participants were able to reason that cue D was more causal than cue B.

The measure of activation in these studies is the degree to which participants are able to remember which outcome followed each cue. We argued that good outcome recall must be accompanied by activation of the outcome representation, and so this recall measure is an index of activation. However, defenders of the associative view may argue that our dissociation reflected the operation of two separate systems: an associative learning mechanism and an episodic memory system. In order to test whether causal judgements directly reflect the ability of the cue to activate the

outcome representation, what is needed is a nonepisodic measure of outcome activation.

In fact, using quite different stimuli, Hall, Mitchell, Graham, and Lavis (2003) have demonstrated a dissociation between causal judgements and performance on a categorization task, a measure of association that does not require episodic memory. Of course, measures of memory such as ease of categorization are never "process pure" (e.g., Jacoby, Toth, Yonelinas, & Debner, 1994). That is, participants may use episodic and nonepisodic memory to help them categorize stimuli together. However, unlike cued recall, two associated stimuli can be more easily categorized together without deliberate recollection of the episodes in which they were presented together (in which the association was learned).

In Hall et al.'s (2003) procedure, shape–nonsense-word pairings were intermixed with pairings of the same shape and a colour patch. For example, a red colour patch followed the presentation of a triangle on some trials, and the nonsense word "wug" followed the same triangle on other trials. Two tests were then given. First, participants were required to categorize the colours and nonsense words together. When red and wug were preceded by the same triangle, red and wug were very easily categorized together. It would appear that the two stimuli preceded by the same shape during training became associated with one another (mediated learning) and that this association transferred to the subsequent categorization task. Following the categorization task, Hall et al. (2003, Exp. 4) asked participants to rate which of two nonwords was prevented from appearing by the colour presented on the screen. For example, participants were asked to decide which of the nonsense words "wug" or "zif" would be prevented by the appearance of the colour red. Participants tended to respond that red would more likely prevent wug than zif. Thus, although mediated learning between red and wug was revealed on the categorization task, an inhibitory (preventative) causal relationship

---

[1] This is not the only account of all types of mediated learning (see Rizley & Rescorla, 1972).

was expressed between these same two stimuli on the causal judgement task.

This experiment provides strong evidence that causal judgements do not directly reflect associative activation. However, the experiment was designed to investigate acquired equivalence, not causal learning. As a result, the causal question on test, "which nonsense word did this colour prevent", was a surprise to participants. There was no reason for participants to encode the training trials in causal terms, and the stimuli (shapes, colours, and nonsense words) certainly did not lend themselves to a causal interpretation. Dickinson (2001) has shown that the causal scenario is critical in determining whether cue competition is observed, and it might also be critical in determining whether mediated learning or conditioned inhibition is observed in Hall et al.'s (2003) design.

In the present experiments we tested whether associations between cues and outcomes, as measured on a categorization task, would dissociate from ratings in a causal judgement task. Our interpretation of the associative model of causal judgements suggests that causal judgements reflect the ability of a cue to activate, via an associative link, the outcome representation. If this is the case, then whatever associative relationship between cue and outcome is revealed in the categorization task will also be revealed in the causal judgement task. In an A+/AX− design, cue X might inherit associative strength from A, and therefore, according to the associative theory, X should then be judged causal (mediated learning). Alternatively, X might demonstrate inhibitory properties with respect to the outcome on the categorization task and would therefore be expected to reveal these properties on the causal judgement task. As Karazinov and Boakes (2007) pointed out, inferential reasoning would not generally lead participants to conclude that X caused the outcome in the A+/AX− design, the most natural inference being that X prevented the occurrence of the outcome. Thus, even if an X− outcome association is revealed on the categorization task, the inferential model predicts that conditioned inhibition will be observed in a causal judgement task. That is, a dissociation

between performance on the categorization and causal judgement tasks might be observed.

EXPERIMENT 1

The design of the present experiment followed from Hall et al.'s studies (2003, Exp. 4) but used the common "allergist" causal judgement task. In this task, Mr X consumed a range of foods and "herbal remedies", following which he suffered from a rash, a headache, or no allergic reaction. It was arranged for Mr X to suffer one of the outcomes (O_1) on consumption of one food (A) and the second outcome (O_2) on consumption of a second food (B). Intermixed with these $A-O_1$ and $B-O_2$ pairings were trials on which foods A and B were presented in combination with two of the herbal remedies, X and Y respectively, but no outcome followed (AX− and BY−). We assessed the relationship between X and O_1 and between Y and O_2 in two ways. First, participants were given a causal judgement task, in the form of a forced-choice summation test, and then they were given a categorization task.

The summation test required the use of two further excitatory cues, C and D, which were paired with O_1 and O_2 respectively. On test, participants were required to choose which of two compounds, CX or CY, would most likely result in the outcome O_1 and which of DX and DY would most likely result in outcome O_2. The choice of CX over CY would indicate an excitatory relationship between X and O_1 because C and X combined to produce more activation of the outcome than did C and Y. The choice of CY over CX would indicate an inhibitory relationship between X and O_1 (a similar analysis applies to DX and DY).

For the subsequent categorization task, participants were split into two groups—consistent and inconsistent. Every participant was required to learn the correct response assignment, a left or right key press, to the cues, X, Y, O_1, and O_2. In group consistent, cues X and O_1 were assigned to the left response, and cues Y and O_2 to the right response. In group inconsistent, cues Y and O_1 were assigned to the left response, and cues X and O_2 to the right response. Participants learnt the correct response assignments through feedback (correct/incorrect) following every response. To the extent that X and O_1 (and Y and O_2) are associated, performance in group consistent should be superior to performance in group inconsistent. To the extent that there exists an inhibitory relationship between X and O_1 (and between Y and O_2), performance in group consistent should be poorer than that in group inconsistent.

As outlined above, either an excitatory association (mediated by cues A and B) or an inhibitory association will form between X and O_1 and between Y and O_2, according to associative theory. Therefore, it is not possible to predict which of group consistent or inconsistent will show better performance in the categorization task. However, a dissociation between the categorization measure and the causal judgement measure would represent a challenge to associative theory, because according to this view, both measures reveal the workings of the same associative mechanism.

Method

Participants

Participants were 20 undergraduate psychology students from the University of New South Wales, who volunteered to take part in this experiment in return for course credit.

Apparatus and stimuli

Testing was conducted on a personal computer. A program written in Visual Basic was used to present all of the instructions and experimental trials and to record responses, which were made via the computer mouse. There were seven training cues and two allergic reaction outcomes in all. Food cues A–D were avocado, milk, bread, and peanuts. The herbal remedies X–Z were chamomile, echinacea, and ginseng. The allergic reactions O_1 and O_2 were rash and headache. Finally, the two responses used in the categorization test phase, R_1 and R_2, were keys A and L on the computer keyboard. All cues and responses

were randomly assigned to elements in the experimental design for each participant.

The food cues and food–remedy compounds were presented in the centre of the computer screen in a blue 36-point font. Beneath these cues appeared three buttons, "no reaction", "headache", and "rash". When participants clicked on one of these buttons, the true outcome of that trial was revealed on a new page. On this page, outcomes O_1 and O_2 appeared in a red 36-point font, or the words "no reaction" appeared in a green font.

Design

The design of Experiment 1 is presented in Table 1. There were two training phases: element and compound. In the element training phase, food cues A and B were paired eight times with O_1 and O_2, respectively. Eight additional presentations of herbal remedy Z were given with no outcome (Z−). In the compound phase, a further 12 pairings of both A–O_1 and B–O_2 contingencies were given. Cues A and B were also presented 24 times each in compound with herbal remedies X and Y, respectively, without any outcome (AX− and BY−). There were 12 further Z− trials, and cue Z was also presented in compound with A and B, followed by the outcome that followed A and B when presented alone (AZ–O_1 and BZ–O_2). Finally, 12 presentations of each of C–O_1 and D–O_2 were given.

In summary, a positive contingency was trained between A and O_1 and between B and O_2. A negative contingency was trained between X and O_1 and between Y and O_2. Neither outcome was contingent on presentations of cue Z. Finally, a positive contingency was trained between cue C and O_1 and between cue D and O_2.

Participants then received two types of test: a summation test followed by a categorization test. In the summation test, two compounds were presented, and participants were required to choose which compound would most likely result in a specified outcome (see Table 1). Cue A was presented in compound with remedies X and Y, and participants were required to choose which of the two compounds (AX or AY) would most likely

Table 1. *Design of Experiment 1*

		Phase	
Training		*Test*	
Element	Compound	Summation	Categorization
$A-O_1$ (8)	$A-O_1$ (12)	AX vs. AY: O_1 (2)	*Group consistent*
$B-O_2$ (8)	$B-O_2$ (12)	BX vs. BY: O_2 (2)	R1: O_1 (8)
$Z-$ (8)			R1: X (8)
	$AX-$ (24)	CX vs. CY: O_1 (2)	R2: O_2 (8)
	$BY-$ (24)	DX vs. DY: O_2 (2)	R2: Y (8)
	$Z-$ (12)	AX vs. AZ: O_1 (2)	*Group inconsistent*
	$AZ-O_1$ (12)	BY vs. BZ: O_2 (2)	R1: O_1 (8)
	$BZ-O_2$ (12)	AY vs. AZ: O_1 (2)	R1: Y (8)
		BX vs. BZ: O_2 (2)	R2: O_2 (8)
	$C-O_1$ (12)		R2: X (8)
	$D-O_2$ (12)	CX vs. CZ: O_1 (2)	
		DY vs. DZ: O_2 (2)	
		CY vs. CZ: O_1 (2)	
		DX vs. DZ: O_2 (2)	

Note: Letters A–D refer to food cues, and X–Z to herbal remedies. Outcomes (O_{1-2}) were allergic reactions of rash and headache. Numbers in parentheses indicate the number of trials of each type. There were four blocks of training trials in the element phase; each contingency was presented twice in each block. There were six blocks of training in the compound phase; each contingency was presented either twice (for a total of 12 trials) or four times (for a total of 24 trials). Trials were randomly intermixed in the summation phase. There were four blocks of trials in the categorization phase; the four stimuli were presented twice in each block.

result in O_1. Similarly, cue B was presented with X and Y, and participants were required to choose which compound was more likely to produce O_2. This constituted a direct test of the contingencies learned in training between AX and O_1 and BY and O_2, respectively. In the critical transfer test, compounds CX and CY were presented, and participants were required to choose which was more likely to produce O_1. Similarly, compounds DX and DY were presented, and participants were required to choose which was more likely to produce O_2. In the remaining summation tests, the remedies X and Y were compared to the remedy Z in their ability to prevent the outcomes that might otherwise have occurred in the presence of all food cues A–D. All food–remedy combinations were tested twice in the summation phase.

In the categorization test, participants were required to learn four response assignments. In group consistent, R_1 was assigned to X and O_1, and the second response R_2 was assigned to Y

and O_2. In group inconsistent, R_1 was assigned to Y and O_1, and R_2 was assigned to X and O_2. Each stimulus was presented eight times in the categorization phase. The speed and accuracy of learning these response assignments were recorded.

Procedure

Participants were instructed to assume the role of an allergist and to determine the extent to which particular foods caused, and the herbal remedies prevented, allergic reactions in the hypothetical patient "Mr. X". An example of a training trial in which Mr X ate tomatoes was presented. The options (stomach-ache, fever, and no reaction) were presented on the buttons at the bottom of the screen, and, once participants clicked on one of the buttons, it was revealed that Mr X suffered from a stomach-ache. A second similar example trial revealed that Mr X suffered no reaction to tomatoes and horse radish. Participants were instructed that the training trials would be similar to the example trials and to press the space bar to move from one trial to the next. A 2-s delay followed the space-bar press before the initiation of the following trial. Finally, participants were asked to read each food out loud as it was presented and were told to take their time making their predictions. There were 156 training trials in total, and no indication was given to participants of the progression from one training phase to another.

Once the training trials were completed, participants were told that they would be required to make some judgements about the foods and herbal remedies. On each summation test trial, participants were asked, "Which of the following do you think MORE likely to be followed by a rash [or headache]?" Below this question appeared two compound cues, for example AX on the left and AY on the right. Participants were required to make their choice by clicking on one of the compound stimuli. This choice was indicated by a purple square that surrounded that compound stimulus. In addition, as the choice was made, a confidence scale appeared below the two compound stimuli marked "completely certain" at the left-most end and "completely uncertain" at the right-most end. No other anchors appeared on the scale. Participants were required to indicate the certainty of their previous choice by clicking on the scale. Participants could change their choice of compound or estimate of certainty as often as they wished.

The categorization test immediately followed the summation test. Participants were asked to categorize individual stimuli into two groups. They were told that, on each trial, the name of either a remedy or an allergic reaction would appear and that they were to press either the "A" or the "L" key (left or right) in response. They were told that they would not know which responses to make at first, but that they would learn which response was correct through the feedback given. The feedback, "correct" or "wrong", was given on each trial, after the presentation of the stimulus and the response. Both the speed and the accuracy of the responses were recorded.

Results

Summation

The results of the summation test, collapsed across the two groups, are presented in Figure 1. The bars represent participants' beliefs that consumption of foods A–D was more likely to produce an allergic reaction (O_1 or O_2) in the presence of herbal remedy Y than X. Specifically, the high percentage of choices of Y over X in the A–O_1 condition indicates that participants thought O_1 was more likely to follow food A when that food was presented in compound with Y than when it was presented in compound with X. That is to say, remedy X was thought more likely than Y to prevent the outcome (O_1) that might otherwise have occurred as a result of food A. The reverse was true in the B–O_2 condition; the percentage of choices of Y over X was very low in this condition, suggesting that Y was more likely than X to prevent the outcome (O_2) that might otherwise have occurred as a result of food B. A set of orthogonal contrasts was tested using a multivariate, repeated measures model (O'Brien & Kaiser, 1985) in this and all subsequent statistical analyses. The significance level was set at $p < .05$.

A contrast comparing the percentage of choices of Y over X in condition A–O_1 to that in condition B–O_2 confirmed that choices of

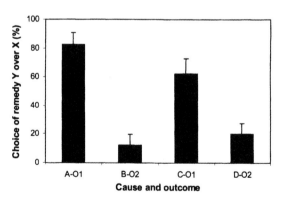

Figure 1. *Results of the forced-choice causal judgement task in Experiment 1. Scores indicate choice of remedy Y over remedy X as more likely to produce the outcome shown (O_1 or O_2) when presented in compound with the cue shown (A–D). Error bars indicate SEMs.*

Y were higher in condition $A-O_1$ than in condition $B-O_2$, $F(1, 19) = 32.67$. This difference between choices of Y over X in conditions $A-O_1$ and $B-O_2$ was mirrored in conditions $C-O_1$ and $D-O_2$. Cue compound CY was thought more likely to produce O_1 than was CX, and DX was thought more likely to produce O_2 than was DY. That is, participants chose Y significantly more often in the $C-O_1$ condition than in the $D-O_2$ condition, $F(1, 19) = 7.95$.

The remaining summation tests (not shown in the figure) compared compounds of foods A–D and remedy Z with compounds of the same foods and remedies X and Y. Because Z was not shown to prevent any allergic reaction in the present experiment, it was anticipated that participants would expect any outcome to be more likely in the presence of this ineffective remedy than either of the effective remedies X or Y. This was overwhelmingly the case, with compounds including Z chosen over those containing X or Y on 91.25% of test trials. In addition, the confidence data revealed that choices in which Z was compared to X or Y were made with greater confidence than those in which X and Y were compared to each other, $F(1, 19) = 8.80$. It was clear to our participants that any given outcome was more likely when the food was presented in compound with the ineffective remedy Z than with either of the other remedies X or Y.

Categorization

The accuracy data for the categorization test are presented in Figure 2. The filled squares indicate performance in the consistent group, and the open squares indicate performance in the inconsistent group. Performance appears to be equivalent in groups consistent and inconsistent at the start of training, but increases more sharply in group consistent than in group inconsistent across Trials 1–3. The difference between the two groups is then maintained throughout the remainder of the test. A contrast comparing overall performance in groups consistent and inconsistent was significant, $F(1, 18) = 7.75$. In addition, there was a significant linear trend across trials, $F(1, 18) = 16.95$. However, there

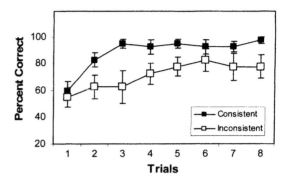

Figure 2. *Percentage of correct responding for groups consistent and inconsistent on the categorization task in Experiment 1. Scores are averaged across all four stimuli, X, Y, O_1, and O_2, and across all participants within each group, for each of the eight trials on this test. Error bars indicate SEMs.*

was no interaction between the grouping factor and the linear trend ($F < 1$). The average response latency for group consistent was 1,038 ms, and for group inconsistent it was 1,044 ms. This similarity in latencies indicates that the superiority of group consistent on the accuracy measure was not achieved at the expense of speed.

Discussion

The present experiment provides very good evidence for inhibition in causal judgements. Because the test for inhibition is outcome specific, the Y cue provides a good control condition for the inhibitory relationship between X and O_1. In particular, absolute exposure to cues X and Y, and whether that exposure occurred in compound or as an element, is exactly equated. In our strict interpretation of associative theory, causal judgements reflect the ability of the cue to activate the representation of the outcome. According to this view, X and O_1 (and Y and O_2) should be especially difficult to categorize together; cue X is able to inhibit activation of O_1 and thus should be more easily associated with O_2. In fact, the reverse was observed. Group consistent were required to categorize X and O_1 together, and performance in this group was superior to that in group inconsistent who were required to categorize X and O_1 apart. We take these data to argue against the associative view of causal judgements.

EXPERIMENT 2

The present experiment replicated Experiment 1 and, in addition, investigated the impact of manipulating the order of element ($A-O_1$ and $B-O_2$) and compound (AX and BX) trials. Experiment 1 used a design in which element trials were intermixed with compound trials. Intermixed training of this kind has been found to be necessary to observe strong conditioned inhibition in rats (Yin, Barnet, & Miller, 1994). Perhaps intermixed training is also necessary to produce inhibition in human causal judgements. To test this idea, we arranged for three groups to receive training similar to that given in Experiment 1, but varied the order in which the trials were presented. Group mixed received intermixed trials of $A-O_1$ and AX−, and of $B-O_2$ and BY−, just as in Experiment 1. Group forward received all $A-O_1$ and $B-O_2$ trials prior to AX− and BY− trials. Group backward received all of their $A-O_1$ and $B-O_2$ trials subsequent to AX and BY trials.

Within an inferential model, causal judgements require memories for cue−outcome relationships (associations), but a further step beyond just recollection that a particular cue "goes with" a particular outcome is necessary to infer cause. What does the inferential model predict with respect to the manipulation of trial order in the present experiment? Of course, participants might assess the causal status of X and Y on test only, in which case no differences between the three groups should be observed (they all receive the same training trials). However, participants have the additional opportunity to evaluate the causal status of the critical cues X and Y on AX and BY trials in groups mixed and forward, but not in group backward. For example, on an AX− trial, if participants recall that A was followed by O_1 when presented alone, participants can infer an inhibitory relationship between X and O_1—that "X prevents O_1". This process is expected to be easier in group mixed than in group forward; $A-O_1$ trials will be more recent on any given AX− trial in group mixed and therefore more easily recalled. Furthermore, this process cannot take place in group backward because the $A-O_1$ relationship has not yet been learnt on AX− trials.

We have argued that the categorization test assesses the very simple relationship between X and O_1, that X "goes with" O_1, whatever the causal relationship between this cue and outcome. However, the summation test, because it is a causal judgement measure, assesses the specific nature of this relationship in causal terms. Because knowing that X goes with O_1 is necessary to infer that X prevents O_1 and not O_2, it follows that manipulations that produce stronger mediated learning in the categorization test will show stronger inhibition in the summation test. Thus, we expect group mixed to show stronger (opposing) effects on both tasks than would group forward, and we do not anticipate any effects to be observed in group backward. Of course, the summation and categorization tests may not be of equivalent sensitivity to the differences between the three groups; thus, an exact match of effect strength in the two tasks is unlikely. However, across the three groups, the rank order of the strength of the mediated learning in the categorization task should not differ from the rank order of the strength of inhibition on the summation task.

It is difficult to assess the prediction made by associative theory across these three groups. Although Yin et al. (1994) found inhibition only following intermixed training, the negative contingency between X and O_1 and between Y and O_2 is present in all three groups. Thus, inhibition may be observed in all three groups. However, it is possible that inhibition relies on maintenance of the excitatory strength of elements A and B on AX− and BY− trials; any extinction of A and B across AX− and BY− trials would be expected to weaken the inhibitory relationship between X and Y and outcomes O_1 and O_2. Group forward would then be expected to show weaker conditioned inhibition than group mixed, and group backward would not be expected to show inhibition at all (A and B have no associative strength on AX– and BY– trials in group backward). However, no formal theory of associative learning requires that group mixed but not group forward should demonstrate conditioned inhibition. What one can say is that, to the extent that associative theorists argue that human causal learning resembles animal conditioning, inhibition is most likely to be observed in group mixed.

Overall, associative models view mediated learning and inhibition to be opposites. Manipulations that enhance one effect, all things being equal, will reduce the other. The inferential view makes a quite different prediction; the inference that a cue inhibits an outcome requires that the cue is able to activate the representation of the outcome. Thus, increases in the cue–outcome "association" (mediated learning) will, under the appropriate circumstances, enhance the learning of inhibition.

Method

Participants

The participants were 60 undergraduate psychology students from the University of New South Wales, who volunteered to take part in this experiment in return for course credit. Participants were randomly assigned to one of three groups at the start of testing; groups mixed, forward, and backward.

Apparatus and stimuli

The apparatus and stimuli were the same as those in Experiment 1.

Design

The experimental design for the training of groups mixed and forward are presented in Table 2; group backward is described below. The contingencies were the same in each group, but the order varied. Groups mixed received two identical phases of training in which nine contingencies were trained in an intermixed fashion: $A-O_1$, $AX-$, $B-O_2$, $BY-$, $C-O_1$, $D-O_2$, $Z-$, $AZ-O_1$, and $BZ-O_2$. Each phase comprised six identical blocks of trials in which each contingency appeared once or twice (the number of each kind of trial

Table 2. *Training blocks in Experiment 2*

Group	Phase 1	Phase 2
Mixed	$A-O_1$ (12)	$A-O_1$ (12)
	$AX-$ (12)	$AX-$ (12)
	$B-O_2$ (12)	$B-O_2$ (12)
	$BY-$ (12)	$BY-$ (12)
	$C-O_1$ (6)	$C-O_1$ (6)
	$D-O_2$ (6)	$D-O_2$ (6)
	$Z-$ (12)	$Z-$ (12)
	$AZ-O_1$ (6)	$AZ-O_1$ (6)
	$BZ-O_2$ (6)	$BZ-O_2$ (6)
Forward	$A-O_1$ (24)	$AX-$ (24)
	$B-O_2$ (24)	$BY-$ (24)
	$C-O_1$ (6)	$C-O_1$ (6)
	$D-O_2$ (6)	$D-O_2$ (6)
	$Z-$ (24)	$Z-$ (12)
	$AZ-O_1$ (6)	$AZ-O_1$ (6)
	$BZ-O_2$ (6)	$BZ-O_2$ (6)

Note: Letters A–D refer to food cues, and X–Z to herbal remedies. Outcomes (O_{1-2}) were allergic reactions of rash and headache. Numbers in parentheses indicate the number of trials of each type. There were six blocks of training trials in each phase; each contingency was presented once, twice, or four times in each block. Group backward received exactly the same training as group forward but the order of Phases 1 and 2 was reversed.

presented in each phase appears in parentheses in Table 2).

Group forward received different training trials in each phase. In Phase 1, participants were trained with the $A-O_1$ and $B-O_2$ contingencies. In Phase 2, participants were trained with the $AX-$ and $BY-$ contingencies. The remaining contingencies ($C-O_1$, $D-O_2$, $Z-$, $AZ-O_1$ and $BZ-O_2$) were the same across the two phases and the same as those in group mixed. Group backward received identical training to that in group forward, except that the two phases were reversed. Thus, the $AX-$ and $BY-$ contingencies were presented before the $A-O_1$ and $B-O_2$ contingencies.

Following the two training phases, all three groups received the same summation and categorization tests as those given to participants in Experiment 1. As a result, a total of six groups of participants were used. Half of the participants in the three groups, mixed, forward, and backward, were given a consistent response assignment in the categorization test, and the other half an inconsistent response assignment.

Procedure

The procedure was the same as that in Experiment 1.

Results

Summation

Figure 3 shows the percentage of choices of Y over X when these two cures were presented in compound with A and B to produce outcomes O_1 and O_2, respectively. Just as in Experiment 1, participants were required to judge which of AX and AY was more likely to produce outcome O_1 and whether BX or BY was more likely to produce outcome O_2.

Averaged across groups, AY and BX were chosen more often than AX or BY to produce outcomes O_1 and O_2, respectively, $F(1, 57) = 93.26$. An interaction contrast comparing the size of this effect in group mixed with the other two groups was also reliable, $F(1, 57) = 4.48$. That is, the choice of AY and BX over AX and BY was more marked following the intermixed training schedule than the forward and backward schedules combined. However, group forward did not differ from group backward in its choice of AY and

BX, $F(1, 54) = 1.78$. Although these interaction analyses revealed differences in the size of the inhibition effect across groups, simple effects analyses showed that participants given all three training orders chose compounds AY and BX over AX and BY; the effect was observed in group mixed, $F(1, 19) = 53.34$, group forward, $F(1, 19) = 31.97$, and group backward, $F(1, 19) = 14.21$.

Figure 4 shows the percentage of choices of Y over X when these two cures were presented in compound with the transfer exciters C and D to produce outcomes O_1 and O_2, respectively. Participants were required to judge which of CX and CY was more likely to produce outcome O_1 and which of DX or DY was more likely to produce outcome O_2. Averaged across groups, CY and DX were chosen more often than CX or DY to produce outcomes O_1 and O_2, respectively, $F(1, 57) = 30.53$. An interaction contrast comparing the size of this effect in group mixed with that in the remaining two groups was not reliable ($F < 1$). However, groups forward and backward did differ from one another in their choice of CY and DX, $F(1, 57) = 9.37$. Simple effects analyses showed that participants chose compounds CY and DX over CX and DY in group mixed, $F(1, 19) = 15.00$, and group forward, $F(1, 19) = 25.13$, but not group backward ($F < 1$).

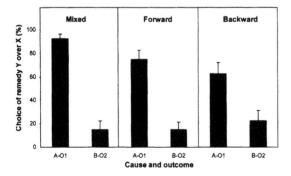

Figure 3. *Mean percentage choice of remedy Y over remedy X as most likely to produce O_1 or O_2 when presented in compound with A or B, respectively, in the forced-choice causal judgement task in Experiment 2. The leftmost, central, and rightmost panels indicate groups mixed, forward, and backward, respectively. Error bars indicate SEMs.*

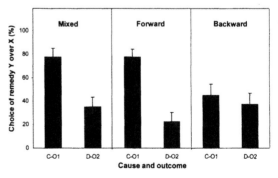

Figure 4. *Mean percentage choice of remedy Y over remedy X as most likely to produce O_1 or O_2 when presented in compound with C or D, respectively, in the forced-choice causal judgement task in Experiment 2. The leftmost, central, and rightmost panels indicate groups mixed, forward, and backward, respectively. Error bars indicate SEMs.*

The remaining summation tests (not shown in the figure) compared compounds of foods A–D and remedy Z with compounds of the same foods and remedies X and Y. Compounds including Z were chosen over those containing X or Y on 86.46% of test trials. In addition, these choices, in which Z was compared to X or Y, were made with greater confidence than those in which X and Y were compared to each other, $F(1, 57) = 23.35$. Thus, just as in Experiment 1, our participants were confident that any given outcome was more likely when the causal food was presented in compound with the ineffective remedy Z than with either of the other remedies X or Y.

Categorization

The accuracy data for the categorization test task are presented in Figure 5. From left to right, the three panels refer to groups given the intermixed, forward, and backward training orders, respectively. Filled squares represent the consistent groups, and open squares represent the inconsistent groups. There was a main effect of consistent versus inconsistent response assignment across all three groups; response accuracy was higher overall in consistent groups, $F(1, 54) = 4.65$. Examination of Figure 5 suggests a larger consistent/inconsistent difference in the

participants given the intermixed training than in the remaining participants. An interaction contrast confirmed this observation, $F(1, 54) = 6.28$. However, the size of the effect did not differ between participants given the forward and backward training trial orders, $F(1, 54) = 1.06$. Simple effects analyses revealed a consistent/inconsistent difference in group mixed, $F(1, 18) = 10.83$, but not in groups forward or backward (both $Fs < 1$). When all groups were combined, a linear trend was observed across trials, $F(1, 54) = 141.33$. This learning effect did not interact with the consistent/inconsistent response assignment within group mixed, $F(1, 18) = 1.11$, group forward, $F(1, 18) = 1.25$, or group backward, $F(1, 18) = 4.07$.

Average reaction time in group mixed consistent was 1,155.73 ms, and in group mixed inconsistent it was 1,249.88 ms. This difference, although not significant ($F < 1$), suggests that the superior accuracy in group mixed consistent was not achieved at the expense of speed. Responses were faster in group forward consistent (1,173.08 ms) than in group forward inconsistent (1,324.49 ms) but faster in group backward inconsistent (1,025.37 ms) than in group backward consistent (1,123.96 ms). Neither of these differences was significant ($F < 1$ in both cases).

Discussion

The first important finding of Experiment 2 is that the effect observed in Experiment 1 was replicated in group mixed. Secondly, differences were observed by manipulating trial order in the other two groups. These differences partially support the inferential view. The inferential view suggests that any weakening of the mediated learning effect in the categorization test will be accompanied by a reduction in the strength of the inhibition observed on the summation test. This prediction was broadly confirmed; intermixed training produced strong mediated learning and strong inhibition, and backward training produced neither effect.

However, contrary to our predictions, forward training showed strong inhibition, but no mediated learning. According to the inferential

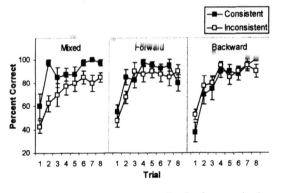

Figure 5. *Percentage of correct responding in the categorization task. Groups mixed, forward, and backward are presented in the leftmost, central, and rightmost panels, respectively. Scores are averaged across all four stimuli, X, Y, O_1, and O_2, and across all participants within the consistent and inconsistent groupings, for each of the eight trials on this test. Error bars indicate SEMs.*

view, inhibition of the kind observed in the present experiments is not possible in the absence of any association between X and O_1 and between Y and O_2. Perhaps the absence of mediated learning and presence of inhibition in group forward is due to a difference in sensitivity of the categorization and summation tests; the former relies on a between-group comparison, the latter a (potentially more sensitive) within-group comparison. In support of this account, there is a numerical advantage of forward consistent over forward inconsistent performance in the categorization test. A more sensitive within-subjects measure of association might allow the detection of mediated learning in this group. Overall though, the results support the inferential over the associative view. The dissociation between associative strength assessed by the categorization test and causal judgement assessed by the summation test suggest that causal judgements do not reflect directly the strength of a cue–outcome association.

GENERAL DISCUSSION

Participants learned that two different food cues A and B produced two different outcomes O_1 and O_2 in Mr. X, but that these cues did not produce any outcome when they were combined with herbal remedies X and Y, respectively (AX– and BY–). In addition, two further food–outcome relationships were trained, C with O_1 and D with O_2. A causal judgement summation test showed that participants had learnt that X and Y prevented the outcomes O_1 and O_2, respectively, that were otherwise produced by C and D. In a subsequent categorization task, participants found it easier to categorize X with O_1 than with O_2 and easier to categorize Y with O_2 than with O_1. This pattern suggests that X and O_1, and Y and O_2, were associated with each other. Associative learning models that consider causal judgement to derive from the ability of a cue to activate an outcome representation are inconsistent with this dissociation between performance on the categorization test and that on the summation test. The ease with which X and O_1 were categorized

together suggests that these two events were associated with each other. However, X was not judged to cause O_1, but to prevent it from occurring in the summation test. In Experiment 2, the dissociation was observed only when A–O_1 and AX– trials were intermixed during training. When A–O_1 trials preceded AX– trials (forward training), X was judged to prevent O_1 on the summation task, but was no easier to categorize with O_1 than O_2. When AX– trials preceded A–O_1 trials (backward training), no effect was observed on either measure.

We have argued that the dissociation observed following intermixed training is difficult to account for within an associative framework because if causal judgement directly reflects associative strength, responding on the summation test should have reflected performance on the categorization test. However, one version of associative theory could potentially account for the data. Perhaps X and Y served as negative occasion setters for O_1 and O_2, but were themselves net excitors. That is, X and Y may have modulated the excitatory strength of C and D downwards when presented in compound with those excitors in the summation test, despite possessing the ability to weakly activate O_1 and O_2 when presented alone (as evidenced in the categorization test). Thus, the dissociation observed here may have resulted, not from the different tasks used, but because X and Y were presented alone in the categorization test (and demonstrated their excitatory properties) but in compound with another excitor in the summation test (demonstrating their modulatory properties).

Ruling out such an explanation is not a straightforward matter. However, we think it unlikely that the present data can be adequately accounted for in this way. Baeyens, Vervliet, Vansteenwegen, Beckers, Hermans, and Eelen (2004) found that negative occasion setters only modulate excitors that have been, themselves, subject to occasion setting by some other stimulus. Our transfer excitors C and D were not subject to occasion setting during training, but merely paired with outcomes O_1 and O_2. This suggests that X and Y, which were able to reduce responding to

C and D, were inhibitors of O_1 and O_2; if they were occasion setters, their modulatory properties would not have transferred to C and D. Our interpretation is also consistent with Baeyens et al.'s finding that conditioned inhibition is observed only when the cues A and X are presented simultaneously (as was the case in the present experiments) and that occasion setting occurs when the cues are presented sequentially (X → A). Therefore, our cues X and Y appear to have the properties of net inhibitors, not negative occasion setters with net excitatory strength.

Our interpretation of the present data is that, during training, participants learnt that cue X "goes with" outcome O_1 and that cue Y "goes with" outcome O_2. It is this simple, "associative" knowledge that determined performance on the categorization test. However, a further inferential step was required for inhibition to be observed. Participants were presumably aware that the associative relationship between X and Y on the one hand, and O_1 and O_2 on the other, was mediated by A and B. Thus, although X "brought to mind" O_1, it is also clear that, in the presence of A, O_1 occurred unless X was present. Thus, when X was presented on test, participants recalled O_1, but inferred that the relationship between X and O_1 was preventative in nature. The relationship between X and O_1 is similar to that between hospitals and illness—it is associative, but it is not causal. Of course, in order for a preventative relationship between a cue and an outcome to be inferred, it is necessary than some sort of associative relationship between the two events exists, otherwise it would be unclear as to which outcome the cue prevents. Thus, the present data are consistent with the idea that causal judgements are not a direct reflection of associative strength, but result from top-down inferential processes.

We anticipate three major objections from proponents of the associative view to the inferential view presented here. First, it is open to associative theorists to claim that our characterization of their position is overly narrow and restrictive. Second, it has often been commented that, unlike associative theory, there is no formal model of causal inferences, and thus specific predictions are not easy to derive. Third, Dickinson has claimed that associative theory is only applicable to highly complex causal scenarios in which it is not possible to reason about the relationships between the cues and outcomes. Associative theory would not be considered relevant to the present design because we used relatively few cues, and the design was quite simple. We address these three objections in turn.

First, not all associative learning theorists will accept that the associative approach, broadly construed, requires that outcome activation is translated directly into causal judgements. There are well-established associative theories that do not require such an assumption—for example, Miller's comparator hypothesis (Miller & Matzel, 1988). According to the comparator hypothesis, conditioned responding on test is determined by the associative strength of the target cue relative to any other cues that were present during training. For example, if the compound AB is followed by an outcome in training, responding to B on test will be determined by the associative strength of B relative to A. Thus, B might be strongly associated with the outcome, but little responding will be observed to B if A is even more strongly associated with that outcome.

Some form of comparator hypothesis might be able to account for the present data quite well (see Pineño and Miller, 2007, in this issue for a similar argument). The causal judgements made in the summation test might reflect the output of a comparator, whereas the categorization test might reflect more directly the associative strength of the target cue. That is, cues X and Y might be associated with outcomes O_1 and O_2, but when compared to their comparators A and B, produce performance that is consistent with an inhibitory relationship. Of course, this requires modification to the existing comparator model. It needs to be explained why the X–O_1 and Y–O_2 associations are directly expressed in behaviour in a categorization task, but are subject to the comparator process when expressed as causal ratings.

It is interesting to note that, although the comparator model is an associative model in the sense that associations are involved, the mechanism that produces cue competition and inhibition (the comparator) is distinctly nonassociative. In fact, the comparator mechanism would appear to be the opposite of an associative mechanism. In many respects it resembles a very simple version of the inferential process that we propose to account for the present data. However, as a model of inferential reasoning, the comparator is far too simple to account for other phenomena such as the effect of additivity training on blocking in causal judgements (Lovibond et al., 2003).

The second objection to the inferential view of causal judgements is that, unlike associative theory, there is no formal model of inferential reasoning that allows specific predictions to be made. The inferential view, according to this argument, might be viewed to be infinitely flexible and ultimately untestable. There are arguments to be made on both sides of this debate. On the one hand, it is not true to say that there are no testable models. There exist models of both inductive (e.g., Gopnik, Glymour, Sobel, Schulz, Kushnir, & Danks, 2004) and deductive reasoning (e.g., Johnson-Laird, 1983). However, it is also true to say that humans are able to entertain the idea of possible worlds in which events interact in bizarre and counterintuitive ways, and there seems to be no limit on this capacity. Therefore, no model that assumes a particular rule about the way in which events interact with one another (e.g., Rescorla & Wagner, 1972) will ever capture the whole range of human inferential reasoning capabilities.

However, to compare the inferential view and the associative view in this manner is to confuse two levels of analysis. What is at issue is not the testing of a single theory, but a class of theories. At this level of analysis, the associative account is no different from the inferential account—it does not provide a single coherent and testable theory. When causal judgements are analysed in associative terms, no single theory is being tested. Instead, there is a bewildering array of associative learning theories available to account for any given pattern of data. It is not even the case that all associative theories have a core set of predictions in common. Associative theories of one kind or another can account for blocking (e.g., Kamin, 1969) and its opposite, augmentation (Batsell, Paschall, Gleason, & Batson, 2001), a form of mediated learning. They can account for overshadowing (Pavlov, 1927) and its opposite, potentiation (Durlach & Rescorla, 1980). As we have already seen, they can also account for conditioned inhibition (Pavlov, 1927) and its opposite, second-order conditioning (Holland, 1990). At this level of analysis, it is clear that associative theory is (perhaps infinitely) flexible. Thus, the associative and inferential views are similar; they are highly flexible and can account for a wide variety of, sometimes contradictory, findings. This does not, however, suggest that they are untestable; the broad characteristics of associative and inferential views can be tested against one another. This is a different level of analysis, at which the availability of specific formal models of associative learning (or the absence of such models of inferential reasoning) is quite irrelevant.

The associative and inferential accounts have been compared in a number of recent experiments. Some findings are inconsistent with an associative account, and others are inconsistent with an inferential account. The effects of rules on cue competition (De Houwer et al., 2002; Lovibond et al., 2003; Mitchell & Lovibond, 2002) are inconsistent with the associative account. Similarly, dissociations between causal judgements and the associative knowledge on which they are based (Mitchell et al., 2005; the present data) are inconsistent with the associative account. However, other experiments have demonstrated phenomena more consistent with an associative mechanism. Le Pelley, Oakeshott, and McLaren (2005) recently observed unblocking in human causal judgements, an effect predicted by Mackintosh's (1975) model of associability. Also, Karazinov and Boakes (2007) observed second-order conditioning (a form of mediated learning) of causal judgements. We agree with these authors that these effects are unlikely to have resulted from an inferential process; in both cases, when participants were allowed the opportunity to engage in inferential reasoning, the putative associative effects were either eliminated or reversed. It is clear then, that it is possible to test the inferential view against the associative view.

These latter findings bring us to the third objection. Associative models of animal learning have been argued to be applicable to human causal learning only when the task is highly complex (Dickinson, 2001). This is particularly pertinent to the present procedure. We used only seven cues in total and many training trials. It is clear that participants should have no difficulty in remembering the exact relationship between each cue and its outcome, or engaging in top-down inferential reasoning about those relationships. Associative theory would, therefore, be considered by many not to be applicable to the inhibition effects observed in the present experiment. Despite the intuitive appeal of the complexity argument, the results of Karazinov and Boakes' (2007) studies, in which complexity was manipulated, further argue against the associative view of conditioned inhibition. Their conditioned inhibition effect was reversed when complexity was increased. Therefore, in order to study conditioned inhibition, it would appear that a relatively simple task must be used. This further supports an inferential cognitive account of conditioned inhibition in human causal judgements.

In summary, the present dissociation between causal judgements and the ease with which cues and outcomes are categorized together suggests that causal judgements do not directly reflect the degree to which cues activate outcome representations. In particular, participants in our present experiments appear to recall the manner in which the cue and outcome are associated—namely, that cue X was not associated with the outcome O_1 directly, but via cue A. This recollection allowed them to infer that, although X "went with" O_1, its causal relationship with that outcome was preventative. Taken together with research showing the role of rule application in blocking (De Houwer et al., 2002; Lovibond et al., 2003), and the absence of any direct evidence for inhibition or cue competition based on an associative mechanism, these results suggest that complex cue interaction effects in causal

judgement result from inferential processes. It remains to be seen whether inferential processes also contribute to the learning of simple cause–effect relationships.

REFERENCES

Baeyens, F., Vervliet, B., Vansteenwegen, D., Beckers, T., Hermans, D., & Eelen, P. (2004). Simultaneous and sequential feature negative discriminations: Elemental learning and occasion setting in human Pavlovian conditioning. *Learning and Motivation*, *35*, 136–166.

Batsell, W. R., Paschall, G. Y., Gleason, D. I., & Batson, J. D. (2001). Taste preconditioning augments odor-aversion learning. *Journal of Experimental Psychology: Animal Behavior Processes*, *27*, 30–47.

Chapman, G. B., & Robbins, S. J. (1990). Cue interaction in human contingency judgment. *Journal of Experimental Psychology: Memory and Cognition*, *18*, 537–545.

De Houwer, J., Beckers, T., & Glautier, S. (2002). Outcome and cue properties modulate blocking. *Quarterly Journal of Experimental Psychology*, *55A*, 965–985.

Dickinson, A. (2001). Causal learning: An associative analysis. *Quarterly Journal of Experimental Psychology*, *54B*, 3–25.

Dickinson, A., Shanks, D., & Evenden, J. (1984). Judgment of act–outcome contingency: The role of selective attribution. *Quarterly Journal of Experimental Psychology*, *36A*, 29–50.

Durlach, P. J., & Rescorla, R. A. (1980). Potentiation rather than overshadowing in flavor-aversion learning: An analysis in terms of within-compound associations. *Journal of Experimental Psychology: Animal Behavior Processes*, *6*, 175–187.

Gopnik, A., Glymour, C., Sobel, D. M., Schulz, L. E., Kushnir, T., & Danks, D. (2004). A theory of causal learning in children: Causal maps and Bayes nets. *Psychological Review*, *111*, 3–32.

Hall, G. (1996). Learning about associatively activated representations: Implications for acquired equivalence and perceptual learning. *Animal Learning & Behavior*, *24*, 233–255.

Hall, G., Mitchell, C. J., Graham, S., & Lavis, Y. (2003). Acquired equivalence and distinctiveness in human discrimination learning: Evidence for associative mediation. *Journal of Experimental Psychology: General, 132,* 266–276.

Holland, P. C. (1990). Event representation in Pavlovian conditioning: Image and action. *Cognition, 37,* 105–131.

Jacoby, L. L., Toth, J. P., Yonelinas, A. P., & Debner, J. A. (1994). The relationship between conscious and unconscious influences: Independence or redundancy? *Journal of Experimental Psychology: General, 123,* 216–219.

Johnson-Laird, P. N. (1983). *Mental models.* Cambridge, UK: Cambridge University Press.

Kamin, L. J. (1969). Predictability, surprise, attention and conditioning. In B. A. Campbell & R. M. Church (Eds.), *Punishment and aversive behavior* (pp. 279–296). New York: Appleton-Century-Crofts.

Karazinov, D. M., & Boakes, R. A. (2004). Learning about cues that prevent an outcome: Conditioned inhibition and differential inhibition in human predictive learning. *Quarterly Journal of Experimental Psychology, 57B,* 153–178.

Karazinov, D. M., & Boakes, R. A. (2007). Second-order conditioning in human predictive judgements when there is little time to think. *Quarterly Journal of Experimental Psychology, 60,* 448–460.

Le Pelley, M. E., Oakeshott, S. M., & McLaren, I. P. L. (2005). Blocking and unblocking in human causal learning. *Journal of Experimental Psychology: Animal Behavior Processes, 31,* 56–70.

Lovibond, P. F., Been, S., Mitchell, C. J., Bouton, M. E., & Frohardt, R. (2003). Forward and backward blocking of causal judgment is enhanced by additivity of effect magnitude. *Memory & Cognition, 31,* 133–142.

Mackintosh, N. J. (1975). A theory of attention: Variation in the associability of stimuli with reinforcement. *Psychological Review, 82,* 276–298.

Miller, R. R., & Matzel, L. D. (1988). The comparator hypothesis: A response rule for the expression of associations. In G. H. Bower (Ed.), *The psychology of learning and motivation* (Vol. 22, pp. 51–92). Orlando, FL: Academic Press.

Mitchell, C. J., & Lovibond, P. F. (2002). Backward and forward blocking in human electrodermal conditioning: Blocking requires an assumption of outcome additivity. *Quarterly Journal of Experimental Psychology, 55B,* 311–329.

Mitchell, C. J., Lovibond, P. F., & Gan, C. (2005). A dissociation between memory and causal judgments. *Psychonomic Bulletin & Review, 12,* 950–954.

Mitchell, C. J., Lovibond, P. F., Minard, E., & Lavis, Y. (2006). Forward blocking in human learning sometimes reflects the failure to encode a cue–outcome relationship. *Quarterly Journal of Experimental Psychology, 59,* 830–844.

O'Brien, R. G., & Kaiser, M. K. (1985). MANOVA method for analyzing repeated measures designs: An extensive primer. *Psychological Bulletin, 97,* 316–333.

Pavlov, I. P. (1927). *Conditioned reflexes.* London: Oxford University Press.

Pineño, O., & Miller, R. R. (2007). Comparing associative, statistical, and inferential reasoning accounts of human contingency learning. *Quarterly Journal of Experimental Psychology, 60,* 310–329.

Rescorla, R. A., & Wagner, A. R. (1972). A theory of Pavlovian conditioning: Variations in the effectiveness of reinforcement and nonreinforcement. In A. H. Black & W. F. Prokasy (Eds.), *Classical conditioning II: Current research and theory* (pp. 64–99). New York: Appleton-Century-Crofts.

Rizley, R. C., & Rescorla, R. A. (1972). Associations in second-order conditioning and sensory preconditioning. *Journal of Comparative & Physiological Psychology, 81,* 1–11.

Shanks, D. R., López, F. J., Darby, R. J., & Dickinson, A. (1996). Distinguishing associative and probabilistic contrast theories of human contingency judgment. In D. R. Shanks, K. Holyoak, & D. L. Medin (Eds.), *Causal learning* (pp. 265–311). San Diego, CA: Academic Press.

Waldmann, M. R. (2000). Competition among causes but not effects in predictive and diagnostic learning. *Journal of Experimental Psychology: Learning, Memory, & Cognition, 26,* 53–76.

Yin, H., Barnet, R. C., & Miller, R. R. (1994). Second-order conditioning and Pavlovian conditioned inhibition: Operational similarities and differences. *Journal of Experimental Psychology: Animal Behavior Processes, 20,* 419–428.

THE QUARTERLY JOURNAL OF EXPERIMENTAL PSYCHOLOGY
2007, 60 (3), 418–432

Statistical contingency has a different impact on preparation judgements than on causal judgements

Jan De Houwer and Stefaan Vandorpe

Ghent University, Ghent, Belgium

Tom Beckers

University of Leuven, Leuven, Belgium

Previous studies on causal learning showed that judgements about the causal effect of a cue on an outcome depend on the statistical contingency between the presence of the cue and the outcome. We demonstrate that statistical contingency has a different impact on preparation judgements (i.e., judgements about the usefulness of responses that allow one to prepare for the outcome). Our results suggest that preparation judgements primarily reflect information about the outcome in prior situations that are identical to the test situation. These findings also add to previous evidence showing that people can use contingency information in a flexible manner depending on the type of test question.

Most papers on human causal learning start with the statement that such learning is crucial from an evolutionary point of view. One of the often-cited advantages of learning the causal relation between a cue and an outcome is that it allows one to prepare for the outcome once the cue has been detected. But instead of directly examining how information about the occurrence of cues and outcomes influences preparatory responses, in most if not all studies, only responses related to the causal value of cues are registered. In this paper, we first point out that there are good reasons to assume that co-occurrence information has a different impact on preparatory responses than on causal responses. Afterwards, we present the data of two experiments that provide support for these predictions.

Existing research has demonstrated that judgements about the causal impact of a cue on an outcome depend heavily on the statistical contingency between the cue and the outcome (e.g., Allan, Siegel, & Hannah, 2007; Msetfi, Murphy, & Simpson, 2007; Wasserman, Elek, Chatlosh, & Baker, 1993; see Baker, Murphy, Vallée-Tourangeau, & Mehta, 2000, for a review). That is, causal judgements depend not only on the probability of the outcome when the cue is present, $P(O/C)$, but also on the probability of the outcome when the cue is absent, $P(O/\sim C)$. At the normative level, this finding can be explained in the following manner (e.g., Cheng, 1997). In principle, one can infer the causal effect of a cue C on an outcome O on the basis of the observed $P(O|C)$, but only if one is certain

Correspondence should be addressed to Jan De Houwer, Department of Psychology, Ghent University, Henri Dunantlaan 2, B-9000, Ghent, Belgium. E-mail: Jan.DeHouwer@UGent.be

Stefaan Vandorpe and Tom Beckers are Postdoctoral Researchers for the Research Foundation–Flanders (FWO-Vlaanderen).

DOI:10.1080/17470210601001084

that C is the only possible cause of O in those situations. In reality, it is most often difficult to exclude the possibility that a hidden alternative cause of O is present when C is present (also see Hagmayer & Waldmann, 2007). One possible solution to this problem is to compare the probability of the outcome in situations where C is present, $P(O|C)$, with the probability of the outcome in a focal set of situations that are identical apart from the fact that C is now absent, $P(O|{\sim}C)$. It is likely that any difference between these probabilities is due to the presence of C because the situations only differ with regard to the presence of C. Hence, comparing $P(O|C)$ with $P(O|{\sim}C)$ can be used to infer what would happen in a hypothetical situation where C is the only possible cause of O.

Whereas there are good reasons to assume that causal judgements should depend both on $P(O|C)$ and on $P(O|{\sim}C)$, one can argue that preparatory responses should not. Imagine that you are asked to prepare for a certain outcome in a test situation where cue C is present. From a normative perspective, whether you decide to prepare should be a function of the probability of the outcome in the actual test situation that you are in. This probability is determined by the combined causal effect of all causes that are present in the situation. Hence, an important difference between causal judgements and preparatory responses is that the former should reflect the effect of one cause in isolation from all other possible causes whereas the latter should reflect the combined effect of all causes that are present in the current situation. The most direct way to estimate the combined effect of all causes that are present in a test situation (and thus the probability of the outcome in that situation) is to determine the probability of the outcome in previous situations that are identical to the current situation. When the current situation is identical to a focal set of previous situations, this implies that the same set of causes is present in all those situations and thus that the observed probability of the outcome in those previous situations is likely to provide a good estimate of the probability of the outcome in the current test situation.

This analysis has important implications for predictions about the impact of statistical contingency on preparatory responses. Imagine a test situation in which a cue C is present. In such a situation, C can be considered as a potential cause of the outcome but the context might also contain hidden causes of the outcome. In order to estimate the probability of the outcome when C and those hidden causes are present, one can assess the probability of the outcome in previous identical situations—that is, situations where C and those hidden causes were assumed to be present. Hence, given the assumption that the same hidden causes are present in the current test situation as in previous situations where C was present, the need for preparatory responses can be determined on the basis of $P(O|C)$ only. If one can identify previous situations in which C was presented in the same context as that during test, there is no need to take into account $P(O|{\sim}C)$ because $P(O|C)$ provides a direct estimate of the combined effect of all causes that are present in the test situation (i.e., both C and the hidden causes). Preparatory responses in situations where a cue C is absent should, on the other hand, be primarily a function of $P(O|{\sim}C)$. When no cues are present, only hidden causes can be responsible for the outcome. Hence, one can estimate the probability of the outcome in a situation where no cues are present by looking at the probability of the outcome in previous situations where no cues are present. The accuracy of this estimate depends only on the assumption that the hidden causes that were operating in those previous situations are the same as those that are operating in the present situation. To summarize, the central idea in this paper is that, compared to causal judgements, preparatory responses should depend more on information about what happened in identical situations—that is, on $P(O|C)$ when the cue is present and on $P(O|{\sim}C)$ when the cue is absent—than on information about other situations.

We tested this idea in two experiments. The first experiment was a paper-and-pencil study in which participants were asked to recommend treatments for patients who had been tested for allergic reactions (i.e., the outcome) to mushrooms (i.e., the cue). On 10 occasions, the patient was tested 2 hours after eating mushrooms. In 10 other tests, the patient did not eat anything, and allergic reactions were registered after a waiting period of 2 hours. Each participant saw the test results of three fictitious patients and was asked the following questions for each patient: If the aim is to prevent the patient having allergic reactions, then (a) how important is it that the patient refrains from eating mushrooms? (b) how important is it that the patient takes an antiallergic medicine when he or she has not eaten anything? (c) how important is it that the patient takes an antiallergic medicine after he or she has eaten mushrooms? The first question probes the extent to which mushrooms are regarded as a cause of allergic reactions. If mushrooms do cause unwanted allergic reactions, it is indeed best to recommend an intervention in which the cause is removed (see Gopnik et al., 2004; Hagmayer & Waldmann, 2007). The second and third questions measured preparatory responses. Given the aim of preventing allergic reactions, taking an antiallergic medicine is a preparatory response that can prevent an upcoming allergic reaction (note that participants were informed that this was the only effect of the medicine and that it was therefore not a permanent cure). The second question probed for preparatory responses when the cue (i.e., mushrooms) was absent, and only hidden causes could have been present, whereas the third question indexed preparatory responses when the cue was present, and hidden causes could also have been present. For ease of expression, we refer to answers to the second question as the "cue-absent preparation judgements" whereas answers to the third question are called "cue-present preparation judgements".

One of the patients had an allergic reaction on all tests (10/10 patient), one patient had an allergic reaction only after eating mushrooms but never after eating nothing (10/0 patient), and one patient had an allergic reaction on half of the mushroom tests but not on the other tests (5/0 patient). In order to examine the impact of $P(O|\sim C)$ on judgements about the relation between mushrooms and allergic reactions, we looked at the difference between judgements for the 10/10 patient and the 10/0 patient. Based on our analysis, we predicted that the causal judgements for these patients should differ whereas the cue-present preparation judgements should not differ or at least to a lesser extent. Our design also allowed us to test the impact of $P(O|C)$ by comparing judgements for the 10/0 and 5/0 patients. Given that both causal and cue-present preparation responses should depend on $P(O|C)$, we expected that causal and cue-present preparation judgements for these patients should differ to the same extent. Finally, a comparison of the cue-present and cue-absent preparation judgements allowed us to test the more general idea that preparatory responses are based on situations that are similar to the situation in which the preparatory response is required. Specifically, preparatory responses in situations where a cue is absent should reflect $P(O|\sim C)$ whereas preparatory responses in situations where a cue is present should reflect $P(O|C)$. In order to test the generality of our findings, we also conducted a second experiment that was conceptually identical to Experiment 1. The main differences were that we used a different cover story and presented the contingency information in a trial-by-trial manner rather than in a summarized form.

EXPERIMENT 1

Method

Participants
A total of 51 second-year psychology students at Ghent University volunteered to participate. They were tested before the start of a lecture that took place in an large auditorium.

Materials and procedure
All instructions and information were presented in Dutch, but we only present the English translation. We constructed a booklet that contained one page for instructions and three

test pages, one test page for each fictitious patient. A translation of the instructions can be found in Appendix A. Basically, the instructions informed the participants that they should imagine being a physician who treats patients with allergic reactions. They would receive the dossiers of three different patients. Each dossier would contain information about two types of test. In one type of test, allergic reactions were registered 2 hours after the patient ate mushrooms. In the other type, the patient ate nothing, and allergic reactions were measured after a waiting period of 2 hours. Participants were then shown an example of a dossier. Each dossier had the format of a four-field table where the numbers on the left indicated the number of tests in which an allergic reaction occurred, and the numbers on the right corresponded to the number of tests in which no allergic reaction was found. The two numbers in the top row referred to tests where the patient had eaten mushrooms, the two numbers in the bottom row referred to tests where the patient ate nothing. Participants were informed that their task was to give advice to the patient with the aim of preventing as many allergic reactions as possible. They were told that it was not possible to cure the patient, but they could make two recommendations. The first one was to ask the patient to stop eating mushrooms. The second one was to ask the patient to take an antiallergenic medicine that could prevent upcoming allergic reactions. Participants were told that, just like a good physician, they should only give recommendations that according to them were actually useful for the patient. In order to allow participants to make graded recommendations, they could indicate on a scale from 1 (not important) to 10 (very important) how important it was that the patient would follow a specific recommendation. Participants also rated how sure they were of each advice on a scale from 1 (not sure) to 10 (very sure). These confidence ratings were added for exploratory reasons and are therefore not discussed further. Finally, participants were told that they should complete all ratings for one patient before moving on to the next patient.

Each of the other three pages of the booklet contained the dossier and rating scales for one patient. A first patient (10/10) had an allergic reaction in each of the 10 tests that involved eating mushrooms and in each of the 10 tests in which the patient ate nothing. A second patient (10/0) always had an allergic reaction after eating mushrooms but never when he or she did not eat anything. The third patient (5/0) had an allergic reaction on 5 of the 10 tests that involved eating mushrooms but not on the other tests. The order in which the three pages for the three patients appeared in the booklets was counterbalanced across participants. Underneath each dossier, six rating scales were printed, each ranging from 1 to 10. The first scale was accompanied by the question "How important is it that this patient no longer eats mushrooms?", the third one by the question "How important is it that this patient takes an antiallergic medicine after he/she did not eat anything?", and the fifth one by the question "How important is it that this patient takes an antiallergic medicine after he/she eats mushrooms?". The left end of these scales was labelled "not important", the right end as "very important". After each of these scales, there was a scale that was accompanied by the question "How sure are you that your score is accurate" with a rating of 1 corresponding to "very unsure" and a rating of 10 to "very sure". Participants gave their ratings by circling a number of the scale.

Results

Causal judgements versus cue-present preparation judgements

We first examined the judgements regarding the relation between mushrooms and allergic reactions by conducting an analysis of variance (ANOVA) with patient (10/10, 10/0, 5/0) and type of judgement (causal, cue-present preparation) as within-subjects variables. This analysis revealed a main effect of patient, $F(2, 100) = 40.05$, $p < .001$, and type of judgement, $F(1, 50) = 14.85$, $p < .001$, as well as an interaction between both variables, $F(2, 100) = 18.84$, $p < .001$. As can be inferred from Table 1, the interaction was due to the fact that variations in P(O|~C) (i.e., 10/10 vs. 10/0) had a different effect on the causal than on the cue-present preparation judgements whereas variations in P(O|C) (i.e., 10/0 vs. 5/0) did not or to a lesser extent.

To examine the effect of variations in P(O|~C) separately, we removed the data regarding the 5/0 patient from the ANOVA, thus leaving the variable "patient" with two levels (10/10 vs. 10/0). Again, the main effect of patient, $F(1, 50) = 46.98$, $p < .001$, the main effect of type of judgement, $F(1, 50) = 14.33$, $p < .001$, and the interaction, $F(1, 50) = 28.03$, $p < .001$, were significant. Planned comparisons showed that causal ratings for patient 10/10 were significantly lower than those for patient 10/0, $t(50) = 7.43$, $p < .001$. Although the interaction demonstrates that the effect of patient was significantly smaller for the cue-present preparation judgements than for the causal judgements, the cue-present preparation judgements were nevertheless also significantly lower for patient 10/10 than for patient 10/0, $t(50) = 2.50$, $p = .02$ (see Table 1).

We then examined the effect of variations in P(O|C) using an ANOVA with patient (10/0 vs. 5/0) and type of judgement (causal vs. cue-present preparation) as within-subjects variables. The main effect of patient was again significant, $F(1, 50) = 213.80$, $p < .001$, but the main effect of type of judgement was not, $F < 1$. More important, the interaction just failed to reach significance, $F(1, 50) = 3.94$, $p = .053$. Planned

Table 1. *Causal and preparation judgements as a function of patient in Experiment 1*

	Patient					
	10/10		10/0		5/0	
Type of judgement	M	SD	M	SD	M	SD
Causal	5.55	4.04	9.78	0.81	6.57	1.96
Cue-present preparation	8.51	2.96	9.49	1.46	6.96	1.87
Cue-absent preparation	8.34	2.92	1.12	0.38	1.51	1.72

comparisons showed that ratings for patient 10/0 were higher than those for patient 5/0, both for the causal judgements, $t(50) = 12.15$, $p < .001$, and for the cue-present preparation judgements, $t(50) = 9.78$, $p < .001$.

Cue-present versus cue-absent preparation ratings

An ANOVA with patient (10/10, 10/0, 5/0) and type of judgement (cue-present preparation, cue-absent preparation) as within-subjects variables revealed a main effect of patient, $F(2, 100) = 89.84$, $p < .001$, a main effect of type of judgement, $F(1, 50) = 574.30$, and an interaction between both variables, $F(2, 100) = 187.88$, $p < .001$. The latter effect shows that P(O|~C) (i.e., patient 10/10 vs. patient 10/0) had a larger effect on cue-absent preparation responses than on cue-present preparation responses, whereas the reverse was true for P(O|C) (i.e., patient 10/0 vs. patient 5/0; see Table 1).

We again examined the effect of P(O|~C) by dropping the ratings from patient 5/0 from the ANOVA. The main effect of patient (10/10 vs. 10/0) was significant, $F(1, 50) = 78.09$, $p < .001$, as was the main effect of type of judgement, $F(1, 50) = 439.68$, and the interaction between both variables, $F(1, 50) = 371.19$. As noted above, the effect of P(O|~C) on cue-present preparation judgements was significant, but much smaller than the effect on cue-absent preparation judgements, $t(50) = 16.96$, $p < .001$ (see Table 1).

The ANOVA for examining the effect of P(O|C) also showed a main effect of patient (10/0 vs. 5/0), $F(1, 50) = 34.66$, $p < .001$, a main effect of type of judgement, $F(1, 50) = 923.91$, $p < .001$, and an interaction, $F(1, 50) = 68.52$, $p < .001$. Whereas P(O|C) had a large effect on cue-present preparation judgements, $t(50) = 9.78$, $p < .001$, it did not have a significant effect on cue-absent preparation judgements, $t(50) = 1.59$, $p = .12$ (see Table 1).

Discussion

The results were largely in line with the predictions that we derived from our analysis: (a) Variations in P(O|~C) had a larger impact on causal judgements than on cue-present preparation judgements, (b) variations in P(O|C) had virtually the same strong impact on causal judgements and cue-present preparation judgements, (c) P(O|~C) had a larger impact on cue-absent preparation judgements than on cue-present preparation judgements, and (d) P(O|C) had a strong impact on cue-present preparation judgements but no impact on cue-absent preparation judgements. These findings confirm that, in contrast to causal judgements, preparation judgements are influenced most by what happened in situations that are identical to the situation for which the judgement is required. Having said this, we did find a small but significant influence of P(O|~C) on cue-present preparation judgements. According to our analysis, this effect should not have occurred.

EXPERIMENT 2

One could argue that the results of Experiment 1 arose because of specific elements of the procedure. For instance, information about the frequency of the four possible combinations of the presence of the cue and the presence of the outcome was presented in a table. This mode of presentation could have facilitated a flexible use of the contingency information. Furthermore, some aspects of the cover story that was used in Experiment 1 were rather unusual. For instance, participants might have had trouble understanding how it is possible that a patient can show an allergic reaction in all tests where he or she had not eaten anything. We therefore ran a second experiment that was identical to Experiment 1 except for the mode of presentation and the nature of the cover story.

In Experiment 2, participants were told that they would receive information about tests with certain chemical products. During each test, the product was placed either in an unheated test chamber or in a preheated test chamber. On each test, it was recorded whether the product inflamed (i.e., started burning). Hence, heating of the test chamber can be seen as the cue event and the inflammation of the chemical product as the outcome. As in Experiment 1, we manipulated P(O|C) and P(O|~C) and checked whether this influenced causal judgements ("To what extent is heating the room a cause of the inflammation?") and preparation judgements ("To what extent is it important to enable automatic fire extinguishers in order to prevent damage to the test chamber?"). One advantage of this cover story is that it is plausible that the outcome (inflammation of the chemical product) occurs without the cue event (heating of the test chamber). A second important change was that we now presented the contingency information on a trial-by-trial basis. On each trial, participants received information about one test situation in which the chamber could be heated (cue present) or not (cue absent), and the product could inflame (outcome present) or not (outcome absent).

Method

Participants
A total of 27 first-year psychology students at Ghent University took part in exchange for partial fulfilment of course requirements. All were native Dutch speakers.

Stimuli and materials
Three nonwords (BAYRAM, ENANWAL, SARICIK) were said to be the names of chemical products. The experiment was implemented using an Inquisit 1.32 program that was run on a Pentium IV PC with a 15-inch screen. Participants entered their ratings by using the mouse to click on a particular value of a 9-point rating scale. We created three versions of the computer program that differed only with regard to which nonwords were assigned to which contingency (10/10, 10/0, or 5/0). Across the three programs, each nonword was assigned once to each contingency.

Procedure
Participants were tested one by one. After signing an informed consent form, they were given instructions about the nature of the task (see Appendix B). They were told that they would

receive information about tests with three chemical products. During each test, one of the chemical products would be placed in a test chamber that was not preheated (and thus had a room temperature of 19 degrees Celsius) or in a test chamber that was heated until it reached a temperature of 50 degrees Celsius. On each test, it was checked whether the product inflamed (i.e., started burning). We also informed the participants that there would be 20 tests with each product, 10 of which would involve a preheated test chamber. They were told that after seeing all tests, they would be asked to answer certain questions. First of all, they would need to judge for each product the extent to which heating the chamber caused the inflammation of the product. The other two questions would focus on safety precautions. It was said that the test chamber was equipped with a fire extinguisher installation that was designed to prevent damage to the chamber. But the system only works when it is enabled. We informed the participants that they would need to judge for each product how important it was to enable the fire-extinguishing system when the product was put into a chamber that was heated and a chamber that was unheated. Finally, the participants were told that the experiment would last about 15 minutes.

After reading the instructions, 60 learning trials were presented in a random order. For product 10/10, there were 10 learning trials on which the product caught fire when in a preheated test chamber and 10 learning trials on which it inflamed when in an unheated test chamber. Product 10/0 inflamed on the 10 trials where the chamber was preheated but not on the 10 trials where the chamber was not heated. Product 5/0 caught fire on 5 of the 10 tests where the chamber was heated but in none of the tests where the chamber was not heated.

On each trial, a test set-up was presented in the top half of the screen. This included the message "Products used:", with the name of one product next to it. Underneath the message about the nature of the product, we presented the message "Test chamber:", with next to it "heated" or "not heated". Information about the result of the test was given 1,500 ms after the information about the design. This information consisted of the sentence "product inflames" in red letters (outcome present trial) or the sentence "product does not inflame" in white letters (outcome absent trial). Both the test set-up and the result of the test were presented together on the screen for an additional 5 s. The intertrial interval was 3 s. All verbal stimuli were presented on a black background in upper-case letters of the Arial Black font with font size 18. Note that all verbal information was presented in Dutch.

After the learning trials, instructions were presented about the test phase (see Appendix C). Participants were informed that they would be asked to answer three questions for each product. First, they would need to judge to what extent heating of the chamber was a cause of the inflammation of the product (causal judgement). They could do this by clicking on a number from 1 (not at all a cause) to 9 (a very important cause). The second and third question focused on the use of the fire extinguisher installation. Given the aim to avoid damage to the test chamber, participants judged how important it was to enable the installation when that product was placed in a preheated test chamber (cue-present preparation judgement) and when the product was placed in a test chamber that was not heated (cue-absent preparation judgement). In both cases, they could do so by clicking on a number from 1 (completely unimportant) to 9 (very important). Finally, participants were asked to always carefully read each test question so that they would be sure which question was asked about which product.

All products had to be rated with regard to one type of question (causal, cue-present preparatory, cue-absent preparatory) before the next type of question was presented. The order in which the questions of each type were presented was counterbalanced over participants (e.g., some first answered the causal question for each of the three products, then all cue-present preparation questions, and then all cue-absent preparation questions; for others, the cue-present preparation questions came first, followed by the causal questions and the cue-absent preparation questions; and so on). When translated from Dutch, the causal questions read "To what extent is heating the chamber a cause of the inflammation of xxxx?", the cue-present preparation judgements read "How important is it to enable the fire extinguisher installation if xxxx is placed in a heated room?", and the cue-absent preparation judgement read "How important is it to enable the fire extinguisher installation if xxxx is placed in an unheated room?", where xxxx was replaced by the name of a product. Each question appeared in white letters (bold Arial Black, font size 12) on a black background in the centre of the screen. The rating scale appeared simultaneous with and underneath the question within a white rectangle of 27.5 cm long and 2 cm high. The rating scale consisted of 10 interconnected squares with a number between 1 (left side) and 9 (right side) written on each square. Participants could enter their rating by clicking on one of the squares. The next question appeared 1 s after entering a rating.

Results

Causal judgements versus cue-present preparation judgements

An ANOVA with product (10/10, 10/0, 5/0) and type of judgement (causal, cue-present preparation) as within-subjects variables showed a main effect of product, $F(2, 52) = 10.39$, $p < .001$, a main effect of type of judgement, $F(1, 26) = 50.43$, $p < .001$, and a significant interaction between both variables, $F(2, 52) = 13.94$, $p < .001$. Table 2 shows that an increase in $P(O|\sim C)$ (i.e., 10/10 vs. 10/0) led to a decrease in causal judgements but did not affect cue-present preparation judgements, whereas a decrease in $P(O|C)$ (i.e., 10/0 vs. 5/0) led to a decrease in both causal and cue-present judgements.

In order to verify this interpretation of the interaction, we first dropped the data of the 5/0 product from the ANOVA. The main effect of product (10/10 vs. 10/0) was significant, $F(1, 26) = 15.85$, $p < .001$, as was the main effect of type of judgement (causal vs. cue-present preparation), $F(1, 26) = 41.05$, $p < .001$, and the interaction, $F(1, 26) = 16.82$, $p < .001$. Planned

Table 2. *Causal and preparation judgements as a function of product in Experiment 2*

| | Product | | | | | |
| | 10/10 | | 10/0 | | 5/0 | |
Type of judgement	M	SD	M	SD	M	SD
Causal	4.56	3.27	8.11	2.03	5.52	2.16
Cue-present preparation	8.41	1.58	8.56	1.25	6.67	2.27
Cue-absent preparation	8.56	1.12	2.85	2.69	2.37	2.29

comparisons showed that causal ratings for the 10/10 product were significantly lower than those for the 10/0 product, $t(26) = 4.54$, $p < .001$, whereas the cue-present preparation judgements did not differ, $t < 1$.

We then conducted an ANOVA with product (10/0 vs. 5/0) and type of judgement (causal vs. cue-present preparation) as within-subjects variables in order to examine the effect of $P(O|C)$. There was a main effect of product, $F(1, 26) = 22.42$, $p < .001$, and a main effect of type of judgement, $F(1, 26) = 11.23$, $p = .002$. The interaction, however, failed to reach significance, $F(1, 26) = 2.68$, $p = .11$. Both causal, $t(26) = 4.34$, and cue-present preparation judgements, $t(26) = 4.41$, $p < .001$, were significantly lower for the 5/0 product than for the 10/0 product.

Cue-present versus cue-absent preparation judgements

The ANOVA with product (10/10, 10/0, 5/0) and type of judgement (cue-present preparation, cue-absent preparation) as within-subjects variables showed a main effect of product, $F(2, 52) = 49.84$, $p < .001$, a main effect of type of judgement, $F(1, 26) = 173.19$, $p < .001$, and an interaction, $F(2, 52) = 35.07$, $p < .001$. Table 2 shows that a reduction in $P(O|\sim C)$ (i.e., 10/10 vs. 10/0) led to a reduction in cue-absent preparation judgements but did not affect cue-present preparation judgements. A reduction in $P(O|C)$ (i.e., 10/0 vs. 5/0), however, led to a reduction in cue-present preparation judgements but did not influence cue-absent preparation judgements.

We verified the differential effect of variations in $P(O|\sim C)$ by conducting an ANOVA with product (10/10 vs. 10/0) and type of judgement (cue-present preparation vs. cue-absent preparation) as within-subjects variables. The main effect of product, $F(1, 26) = 60.75$, $p < .001$, the main effect of type of judgement, $F(1, 26) = 98.19$, $p < .001$, and the interaction, $F(1, 26) = 64.38$, $p < .001$, were significant. As noted above, cue-present preparation judgements for the 10/10 product did not differ from those for the 10/0 product, $t < 1$, whereas cue-absent preparation judgements were lower for the 10/0 product than for the 10/10 product, $t(26) = 9.57$, $p < .001$.

An ANOVA with product (10/0 vs. 5/0) and type of judgement (cue-present preparation vs. cue-absent preparation) as within-subjects variables allowed us to examine the effect of variations in $P(O|C)$. The main effect of product, $F(1, 26) = 8.01$, $p < .01$, and the main effect of type of judgement, $F(1, 26) = 153.95$, $p < .001$, were significant. Although the interaction was only marginally significant, $F(1, 26) = 3.53$, $p = .07$, planned comparisons showed that $P(O|C)$ had a large effect on cue-present preparation judgements, $t(26) = 4.41$, $p < .001$, but no effect on cue-absent preparation judgements, $t < 1$.

Discussion

The results again confirmed the predictions: Variations on $P(O|\sim C)$ had a much bigger impact on causal judgements and cue-absent preparation judgements than on cue-present preparation judgements, whereas variations on $P(O|C)$ affected causal judgements and cue-present preparation judgements but not cue-absent preparation judgements. These results are thus in line with those of Experiment 1 and confirm that our findings generalize across different cover stories and different modes of presentation of the contingency information. One could argue that the present results are in fact even more convincing given that we now found

no effect of $P(O|\sim C)$ on cue-present preparation judgements.

GENERAL DISCUSSION

In the Introduction, we argued that the statistical contingency between a cue and an outcome should have a different impact on preparatory responses than on causal responses. Judgements about the usefulness of a preparatory response in a particular test situation should depend primarily on information about the probability and the nature of the outcome in previous situations that are assumed to be identical to the present one. When a cue is present, and hidden causes could also be present, decisions about whether to prepare for a certain outcome can be based on what happened in previous situations where the same cue was present—that is, $P(O|C)$. Likewise, when a cue is absent, and only hidden causes could be present, preparatory responses can be based on information about the probability and nature of the outcome in previous situations in which the cue was absent—that is, $P(O|\sim C)$. The validity of this approach hinges only on the assumption that the hidden causes that are present in the current situation are the same and operate in the same manner as those that were present in the previous situations. Judgements about whether a cue is a cause of the outcome should, however, depend on information about events in which the cue and hidden causes were present, $P(O/C)$, and situations in which the cue was absent, and only hidden causes could have been present, $P(O/\sim C)$. It is necessary to consider the latter information because it can provide insight into whether the outcome on cue-present trials was actually caused by the cue or by hidden causes that could have also been present on the cue-present trials.

In two experiments that used different cover stories (allergic reactions in Experiment 1 vs. inflammation of chemical products in Experiment 2) and different modes of presentation (all information at once in a table in Experiment 1 vs. information presented trial by trial in Experiment 2), we found direct evidence for the claim that statistical contingency has a different impact on causal judgements than on preparation judgements. In those experiments, variations in $P(O|\sim C)$ had more impact on causal judgements than on cue-present preparatory judgements (i.e., judgements about the importance of a preparatory response when the cue was present, and hidden causes were assumed to be present). It is important to note that this finding is not due to the fact that preparation judgements are less sensitive to experimental manipulations than are causal judgements. This alternative explanation is incompatible with the fact that $P(O|C)$ did have virtually the same impact on both types of judgement and the fact that $P(O|\sim C)$ did have a substantial impact on cue-absent preparation judgements (i.e., judgements about the importance of a preparatory response when the cue was absent and thus only hidden causes could have been operating). The latter finding supports also the idea that preparation judgements depend primarily on information about the probability of the outcome in situations that are assumed to be identical to the test situation: Cue-absent preparation judgements reflect only $P(O|\sim C)$ whereas cue-present preparation judgements are influenced most by $P(O|C)$. We are somewhat more prudent about our conclusions regarding cue-present preparation judgements because in Experiment 1, $P(O|\sim C)$ had a small but significant impact on cue-present preparation judgements. Note, however, that this effect was not replicated in Experiment 2 where a different cover story was used.

Until now we assumed that participants based their preparation judgements on their estimate of the relevant conditional probability—that is, $P(O|C)$ for cue-present preparation judgements and $P(O|\sim C)$ for cue-absent preparation judgements. However, there is also an alternative explanation for the observed correspondence between preparation judgements and conditional probabilities.[1] As we argued in the Introduction, the probability of an outcome in a given situation is a function of the combined effect of all causes of

the outcome that are present in that situation. This combined effect can be estimated not only by looking at the probability of the outcome in previous situations that are assumed to be identical to the current situation. An alternative is to estimate the causal effect of each assumed potential cause and then to predict the combined effect of all causes on the basis of these separate estimates. For instance, in the present experiments, participants could infer the causal effect of the assumed hidden causes on the basis of $P(O|\sim C)$ and the causal effect of C by comparing $P(O|C)$ with $P(O|\sim C)$. Based on these separate estimates, they could then predict what the combined causal effect of the assumed hidden causes and C would be and base their cue-present preparation judgements on this prediction.

Although we agree that this explanation is in line with the results, one could argue that it is not necessarily the most plausible one. First, estimating causal power and then combining the estimates is a more indirect and complex strategy than simply relying on appropriate conditional probabilities. Second, and more important, the latter strategy seems to depend on fewer assumptions than does the former one. For instance, in order to use $P(O|C)$ to predict the probability of the outcome in a test situation where C is present, one only needs to assume that the hidden causes and C operate in the same manner on all these trials. The validity of the indirect strategy also depends on this assumption, otherwise the estimates of the effect of each separate cause are not valid for the test situation. But the indirect strategy also depends on assumptions about how the effects of the different causes combine. For instance, the combined effect of two causes might correspond to the sum of the separate effects. But it is also possible that under certain conditions, the effect of both causes interact. In contrast, $P(O|C)$ is the result of the actual combined effect of all causes that are present, regardless of whether the different effects simply summed up or interacted. Assuming that people take into account these

---

[1] We thank Miguel Vadillo for pointing out this alternative explanation.

considerations, they should thus prefer to base their preparation judgements directly on the relevant conditional probability.

It is, however, likely that people will follow the indirect strategy when it is impossible to determine the relevant conditional probability. For instance, imagine that you have seen situations in which Cue A is present in a certain context (A trials), situations in which both Cue A and Cue B are present in the same context (AB trials), and situations in which only that context is present (context-only). You then need to prepare for the outcome in a test situation in which only Cue B is present. Because you have not yet experienced such a situation, it is impossible to determine the relevant conditional probability—that is, $P(O|B)$. However, one can arrive at a prediction of the probability of the outcome in such a situation by first estimating the causal effect of B and the causal effect of the hidden causes that are assumed to be present in the context. The effect of B can be estimated by comparing the probability of the outcome on A trials with the probability of the outcome on AB trials (e.g., Cheng, 1997; Cheng & Holyoak, 1995). The effect of assumed hidden causes can be assessed by looking at the probability of the outcome on context-only trials. Hence, preparatory responses to B should be influenced by situations in which B was not present (see Lovibond, 2003, and Mitchell & Lovibond, 2002, for evidence supporting this prediction). But it might be the case that if there have been prior situations in which B was present in the context without A, preparatory responses to B would be a function primarily of the probability of the outcome in these situations without much impact of A trials and context-only trials. This prediction can be tested in future research.

Although it is not yet entirely clear how people arrive at preparation judgements, this theoretical issue is independent from our empirical observation that contingency information has a different impact on preparation judgements than on causal judgements. However, one could argue that our empirical results regarding the preparation judgements are an artefact caused by the fact that the questions for the preparation judgements

contained a reference to a specific situation. For instance, the question for the cue-present judgement in Experiment 1 (i.e., "How important is it that the patient takes an antiallergic medicine after eating mushrooms?") referred to situations in which the patient had eaten mushrooms. This reference could as such have encouraged participants to take into account only information about the outcome in situations where the patient had eaten mushrooms. According to this argument, the results would have been different if we would have assessed preparation responses without explicitly referring to a specific situation. However, if the different results for preparation judgements and causal judgements were due to the fact that only the questions for preparation judgements referred to a specific situation, then one should predict that causal judgements would also be different if one would add a reference to a specific situation. But it seems unlikely that our results would have been different if we would have used the following question for causal judgements: "To what extent is eating mushrooms a cause of the allergic reaction *after the patient has eaten mushrooms?*".

One might argue that there is little difference between our preparatory questions and questions regarding the probability of the outcome in the presence or absence of a cue. However, asking participants to judge the usefulness of a preparatory response in the presence (absence) of a cue is not the same as asking that participant to judge the likelihood of the outcome in the presence of the cue. That is, the first question is more than a linguistic reformulation of the second one. It might seem obvious in hindsight that the preparatory response will be based on the likelihood of the outcome in the presence of the cue, but it is not a necessity. In our opinion, our results reveal the psychological (rather than linguistic) link between preparation and conditional probabilities.

The fact that contingency had a different effect on preparation judgements than on causal judgements also demonstrates that people's judgements about the relationship between events depends on the exact question that is used to probe their knowledge. The same point has already been made by Matute and colleagues (e.g., Matute, Arcediano, & Miller, 1996). Our studies are most similar to recent studies by Vadillo, Miller, and Matute (2005; also see Vadillo & Matute, 2007) who showed that manipulations of contingency had a different effect on causal judgements (i.e., to what extent a cue is a cause of an outcome) and predictive-value judgements (i.e., to what extent the cue is a good predictor of the outcome) than on prediction judgements (i.e., how likely it is that the cue will be followed by the outcome). In fact, just like cue-present preparation judgements, prediction judgements depended only on $P(O|C)$ and not on $P(O|\sim C)$.

Findings such as those of Vadillo et al. (2005) and the present findings do not only demonstrate that one has to pay close attention to the type of question that is used to examine associative learning in humans. They also point at a shortcoming of an important class of associative models of human associative learning according to which judgements about the relation between a cue and an outcome are based on the acquired strength of the association between the representations of the cue and the outcome (e.g., Dickinson & Burke, 1996; Rescorla & Wagner, 1972; Van Hamme & Wasserman, 1994; also see Pineño & Miller, 2007). These models account for the effect of contingency on causal judgements by postulating that the degree of contingency is reflected in the strength of the cue–outcome association. But because judgements can depend only on the acquired associative strength, all possible judgements about the cue–outcome relation should also be affected by the degree of contingency. Our results and those of Vadillo et al. (2005) clearly contradict that prediction. One could argue that associative models were designed to deal with situations in which contingency information is given on a trial-by-trial basis rather than in a summarized format. Hence, the validity of these models cannot be judged on the basis of the results of Experiment 1. However, we found similar effects in Experiment 2 in which contingency information was presented on a trial-by-trial basis.

As Vadillo and Matute (2007) point out, results regarding the impact of the type of judgement can be accommodated by associative models if these models are extended with a decision mechanism that is responsible for retrieving and combining those associations that are relevant for the required judgement or behaviour. However, this suggestion has important implications. It implies that behaviour is not a direct reflection of associative knowledge. Hence, it becomes difficult to draw conclusions regarding the properties of associative learning processes on the basis of behavioural effects because these effects could have been due to or influenced by the nonassociative decision mechanism (also see Miller & Matzel, 1988). It might well be that important learning phenomena (e.g., blocking and other cue competition phenomena) are not due to associative learning processes but to the operation of the decision mechanism (see De Houwer, Beckers, & Vandorpe, 2005). In line with the ideas of Vadillo et al. (2005; also see De Houwer, Thomas, & Baeyens, 2001, p. 865), we believe that information about different events or types of event is stored independently in memory, in the form of either memory instances (e.g., Medin & Schaffer, 1978) or simple Hebbian associations (e.g., Hebb, 1949). This stored information can then be retrieved and used in a flexible manner depending on the current requirements—for instance, the precise nature of the test question that is used. But regardless of the merits of this view, the idea that associative processes need to be supplemented with a decision mechanism opens up a range of new questions that need to be addressed in future research.

REFERENCES

Allan, L. G., Siegel, S., & Hannah, S. (2007). The sad truth about depressive realism. *Quarterly Journal of Experimental Psychology, 60*, 482–495.

Baker, A. G., Murphy, R. A., Vallée-Tourangeau, F., & Mehta, R. (2000). Contingency learning and causal reasoning. In R. R. Mowrer & S. B. Klein (Eds.),

Handbook of contemporary learning theories (pp. 255–306). Mahwah, NJ: Lawrence Erlbaum Associates, Inc.

Cheng, P. W. (1997). From covariation to causation: A causal power theory. *Psychological Review, 104*, 367–405.

Cheng, P. W., & Holyoak, K. J. (1995). Complex adaptive systems as intuitive statisticians: Causality, contingency, and prediction. In J.-A. Meyer & H. Roitblat (Eds.), *Comparative approaches to cognition* (pp. 271–302). Cambridge, MA: MIT Press.

De Houwer, J., Beckers, T., & Vandorpe, S. (2005). Evidence for the role of higher-order reasoning processes in cue competition and other learning phenomena. *Learning & Behavior, 33*, 239–249.

De Houwer, J., Thomas, S., & Baeyens, F. (2001). Associative learning of likes and dislikes: A review of 25 years of research on human evaluative conditioning. *Psychological Bulletin, 127*, 853–869.

Dickinson, A., & Burke, J. (1996). Within-compound associations mediate the retrospective revaluation of causality judgments. *Quarterly Journal of Experimental Psychology, 49B*, 60–80.

Gopnik, A., Glymour, C., Sobel, D. M., Schulz, L. E., Kushnir, T., & Danks, D. (2004). A theory of causal learning in children: Causal maps and Bayes nets. *Psychological Review, 111*, 3–32.

Hagmayer, Y., & Waldmann, M. R. (2007). Inferences about unobserved causes in human contingency learning. *Quarterly Journal of Experimental Psychology, 60*, 330–355.

Hebb, D. (1949). *The organization of learning.* Cambridge, MA: MIT Press.

Lovibond, P. F. (2003). Causal beliefs and conditioned responses: Retrospective revaluation induced by experience and by instruction. *Journal of Experimental Psychology: Learning, Memory, and Cognition, 29*, 97–106.

Matute, H., Arcediano, F., & Miller, R. R. (1996). Test question modulates cue competition between causes and between effects. *Journal of Experimental Psychology: Learning, Memory, and Cognition, 22*, 182–196.

Medin, D. L., & Schaffer, M. M. (1978). Context theory of classification learning. *Psychological Review, 85*, 207–238.

Miller, R. R., & Matzel, L. D. (1988). The comparator hypothesis: A response rule for the expression of associations. In G. H. Bower (Ed.), *The psychology of learning and motivation* (Vol. 22, pp. 51–92). San Diego, CA: Academic Press.

Mitchell, C. J., & Lovibond, P. F. (2002). Backward and forward blocking in human electrodermal conditioning: Blocking requires an assumption of outcome additivity. *Quarterly Journal of Experimental Psychology, 55B*, 311–330.

Msetfi, R. M., Murphy, R. A., & Simpson, J. (2007). Depressive realism and the effect of intertrial interval on judgements of zero, positive, and negative contingencies. *Quarterly Journal of Experimental Psychology, 60*, 461–481.

Pineño, O., & Miller, R. R. (2007). Comparing associative, statistical, and inferential reasoning accounts of human contingency learning. *Quarterly Journal of Experimental Psychology, 60*, 310–329.

Rescorla, R. A., & Wagner, A. R. (1972). A theory of Pavlovian conditioning: Variations in the effectiveness of reinforcement and nonreinforcement. In A. H. Black & W. F. Prokasy (Eds.), *Classical conditioning II: Current research and theory* (pp. 64–99). New York: Appleton.

Vadillo, M. A., & Matute, H. (2007). Predictions and causal estimations are not supported by the same associative structure. *Quarterly Journal of Experimental Psychology, 60*, 433–447.

Vadillo, M. A., Miller, R. R., & Matute, H. (2005). Causal and predictive-value judgments, but not predictions, are based on cue–outcome contingency. *Learning & Behavior, 33*, 172–183.

Van Hamme, L. J., & Wasserman, E. A. (1994). Cue competition in causality judgments: The role of non-presentation of compound stimulus elements. *Learning & Motivation, 25*, 127–151.

Wasserman, E. A., Elek, S. M., Chatlosh, D. L., & Baker, A. G. (1993). Rating causal relations: Role of probability in judgments of response–outcome contingency. *Journal of Experimental Psychology: Learning, Memory, and Cognition, 19*, 174–188.

APPENDIX A

Instructions of Experiment 1

Imagine that you are physician who treats patients with allergic reactions. You receive the dossiers of three different patients. Each dossier contains information about different tests. There are two test situations that were each repeated ten times.

Test situation A: The patient comes to the lab and there (s)he eats 100 grams of mushrooms. Two hours later, it is tested whether he/she shows an allergic reaction.

Test situation B: The patient comes to the lab and does not eat anything. Two hours later, it is tested whether he/she shows an allergic reaction.

Example dossier:

	Allergic reaction	No allergic reaction
Test situation A (patient eats mushrooms):	7	3
Test situation B (patient eats nothing):	2	8

In this example, the patient got an allergic reaction in 7 of the 10 times after eating mushrooms (Test situation 1) and after eating nothing, he/she got an allergic reaction 2 of the 10 times (Test situation 2).

On the basis of this information, you need to give advice to the patient. Your aim is to prevent as many allergic reactions as possible. Unfortunately, there are no means to cure the allergy. You can only give advice about the manner in which the patient can prevent allergic reactions. There are two possible types of advice.

You can advise the patient not to eat mushrooms again.
You can advise the patient to take an antiallergic medicine. Such a medicine stops upcoming allergic reactions.

For each advice, you need to indicate how useful the advice is to prevent that the patient will get an allergic reaction. As is appropriate for any good physician, the extent to which you give an advice should depend on the extent to which the advice is really useful for preventing allergic reactions in this patient. In order to allow you to nuance your advice, you can formulate it in terms of the degree to which it is important for the patient to follow the advice. You can do this by giving a score for 0 to 10 where 0 stands for "unimportant" and 10 stands for "very important". For each score, you also need to indicate how sure you are (0 = unsure; 10 = sure) that that score is an accurate reflection of how effective the treatment will actually be.

Please answer all questions on a page before turning over the page. Once you have turned a page you cannot go back.

APPENDIX B

Learning instructions in Experiment 2

In this task, you will receive information regarding tests that have been performed with certain chemical products, namely the products BAYRAM, ENANWAL, and SARICIK. In each test, one product was placed in a test chamber that was either not heated (and thus had a room temperature of 19 degrees Celsius) or that was heated to a temperature of 50 degrees Celsius. Each time it was checked whether the product inflamed (i.e., caught fire). There were 20 tests with each product. The chamber was heated in 10 of those tests; it was not heated in the other 10 tests.

After you have seen this information, you will be asked to answer certain questions. First of all, you have to indicate for each product the extent to which heating the chamber is a cause of the inflammation of the product. The two other questions are about taking security precautions. The test chamber is equipped with a fire extinguisher installation designed to prevent damage to the test chamber. The installation only works when it is enabled. You will have to decide for each product how important it is to enable the fire extinguisher installation when the chamber is heated and when the chamber is not heated. The entire task will last about 15 minutes.

APPENDIX C

Test instructions in Experiment 2

Now you will need to answer for each product 3 questions.

1. To which extent is heating of the test chamber a cause of the inflammation of that product? You can answer this question by clicking on a number from 1 to 9 where 1 stands for "not a cause at all" and 9 stands for "very important cause". So the higher the number that you click on, the more you think that heating of the chamber is a cause of the inflammation.
2. Given the goal to prevent damage to the test chamber, how important is it to enable the fire extinguisher installation when the product is placed in a heated chamber? Again you can answer by clicking a number between 1 and 9 where 1 now stands for "not important at all" and 9 stands for "very important". So the higher the number, the more important you think it is to enable the fire extinguisher installation.
3. Given the goal to prevent damage to the test chamber, how important is it to enable the fire extinguisher installation when the product is placed in an unheated chamber? As with question 2, you can answer by clicking a number between 1 and 9 where 1 now stands for "not important at all" and 9 stands for "very important". So the higher the number, the more important you think it is to enable the fire extinguisher installation.

It is very important that you read each question carefully so that you are sure which questions is asked about which product in which type of room.

Good luck.

THE QUARTERLY JOURNAL OF EXPERIMENTAL PSYCHOLOGY
2007, 60 (3), 433–447

Predictions and causal estimations are not supported by the same associative structure

Miguel A. Vadillo and Helena Matute

Universidad de Deusto, Bilbao, Spain

Studies performed by different researchers have shown that judgements about cue–outcome relationships are systematically influenced by the type of question used to request those judgements. It is now recognized that judgements about the strength of the causal link between a cue and an outcome are mostly determined by the cue–outcome contingency, whereas predictions of the outcome are more influenced by the probability of the outcome given the cue. Although these results make clear that those different types of judgement are mediated by some knowledge of the normative differences between causal estimations and outcome predictions, they do not speak to the underlying processes of these effects. The experiment presented here reveals an interaction between the type of question and the order of trials that challenges standard models of causal and predictive learning that are framed exclusively in associative terms or exclusively in higher order reasoning terms. However, this evidence could be easily explained by assuming the combined intervention of both types of process.

Although the study of human contingency learning is far from being a young field in psychology (Jenkins & Ward, 1965; Smedslund, 1963; Ward & Jenkins, 1965) and was extraordinarily stimulated during the 1980s (Allan & Jenkins, 1983; Dickinson, Shanks, & Evenden, 1984; Wasserman, Chatlosh, & Neunaber, 1983), few would deny that this area of investigation is now experiencing one of its most intense moments. Many of the resulting studies have focused on the distinction between two general, theoretical views of causal learning. One of these frameworks assumes that causal learning is mostly determined by higher order cognitive processes related to statistical reasoning (Allan, 1980; Cheng, 1997; Cheng & Novick, 1992) or deductive inference (De Houwer, Beckers, & Glautier, 2002; Lovibond, Been, Mitchell, Bouton, & Frohardt, 2003). The second framework, on the contrary, regards causal learning as the result of rather mechanistic associative processes, which automatically capture interevent contingencies without the need for a deliberate and conscious process of reasoning (Allan, 1993; Dickinson et al., 1984). The distinction between these two frameworks (see Shanks, 2007, for a comprehensive review) is

Correspondence should be addressed to Miguel A. Vadillo or Helena Matute, Departamento de Psicología, Universidad de Deusto, Apartado 1, 48080 Bilbao, Spain. E-mail: mvadillo@fice.deusto.es or matute@fice.deusto.es

Support for this research was provided by Grant PI–2000–12 from Departamento de Educación, Universidades, e Investigación of the Basque Government to H.M. M.A.V. was supported by an FPI fellowship from the Basque Government (Ref. BFI01.31). We would like to thank Jan De Houwer, Francisco López, and Pedro Cobos for their insightful discussions concerning the experiments presented here.

433

DOI:10.1080/17470210601002520

to some extent isomorphic to the more general distinction between conscious rule interpretation and intuitive processing (Smolensky, 1988) and also to the distinctions between rational inferences and intuitive inferences (Hinton, 1990) or between associative processing and rule-based processing (Sloman, 1996).

One of the many strategies that have been followed to distinguish between the associative and the higher order cognitive reasoning accounts of causal learning consists in manipulating the type of question used to request participants' judgements about the perceived degree of relationship between a cue (or cause) and an outcome (or effect). From a strict associative point of view, this manipulation should have no impact on judgements. Regardless of the wording of the question, judgements should be based on the strength of the association between the cue and the outcome that has been learned during the sequence of trials in which both events have or have not co-occurred (see Cobos, Caño, López, Luque, & Almaraz, 2000). However, if higher order reasoning processes are responsible for participants' judgements, manipulating the test question may have an effect: Different questions might induce participants to think that different statistical indexes should be computed to solve the task efficiently. Empirical research has shown that the precise wording of the test question does have an influence on judgements (Crocker, 1982; De Houwer, Vandorpe, & Beckers, 2007; Gredebäck, Winman, & Juslin, 2000; Matute, Arcediano, & Miller, 1996; Matute, Vegas, & De Marez, 2002; Pineño, Denniston, Beckers, Matute, & Miller, 2005; Vadillo, Miller, & Matute, 2005; White, 2003).

For example, Matute et al. (1996) exposed their participants to a cue competition paradigm known as relative-validity (Wagner, Logan, Haberlandt, & Price, 1968; Wasserman, 1974, 1990) and studied the impact of using different test questions to assess the degree of cue competition. In the relative-validity design, participants in the experimental group are exposed to two types of trial. In one type of trial, two cues, A and X, appear in a compound followed by the presentation of the outcome (AX+). In the other type of trial, a different compound, but with a common cue, is followed by no outcome (BX−). For participants in the control group, both compounds are followed by the outcome in half of the trials and are followed by no outcome in the other half (AX+, AX−, BX+, BX−). Although Cue X is followed by the outcome with a probability of .50 in both groups, participants in the experimental group tend to judge the X−outcome relationship lower than do participants in the control condition. What Matute et al. (1996) found was that this relative-validity effect appears when subjects are asked to rate whether Cue X is a cause or an indicator of the outcome, but vanishes when subjects are asked to rate to what extent Cue X and the outcome co-occurred.

In a similar vein, Gredebäck et al. (2000) showed that other cue competition effects do also depend on the type of question. In their Experiment 1 they used a cue competition design in which during the first phase in some trials Cue A was followed by the outcome (A+), and in the remaining trials Cue C was followed by no outcome (C−). Then, during the second phase, participants saw two compounds of cues, each one containing one of the previously trained cues together with a novel cue, and both compounds were always followed by the outcome (AB+ and CD+). In this design, cue competition is observed if judgements for B are lower than judgements for D. Gredebäck et al. (2000) found a significant cue competition effect when participants were asked about the predictive value of the cue, as well as when they were asked about the causal relationship between the cue and the outcome. However, the cue competition effect did not reach statistical significance when participants were asked about the probability of the outcome given the cue, nor when they were asked about the frequency of cue−outcome pairings. Similarly, in Experiment 2 they showed that the conditioned inhibition effect disappears if the test question asks either for conditional probabilities or for the frequency with which the two events co-occur.

Other experiments have shown that the type of question also has an effect in designs different from those of cue competition. In a recent set of experiments, Vadillo et al. (2005) looked for differences between causal judgements (judgements about the strength of the causal relation between the cue and the outcome), predictive-value judgements (judgements about the predictiveness of the cue—that is, the value of the cue as a predictor of the outcome), and what they called prediction judgements (judgements in which participants have to estimate how likely it is that the outcome will occur).[1] On the one hand, they found that both causal and predictive-value judgements tended to be based on the cue–outcome contingency, as measured by the statistical index Δp—that is, the difference between the probability of the outcome given the presence of the cue and the probability of the outcome given the absence of the cue; that is, $p(o|c) - p(o|\sim c)$. On the other hand, they found that prediction judgements were based on the probability of the outcome given the cue—that is, $p(o|c)$.

As we have argued, the type-of-question effect is interesting from a theoretical point of view because it is beyond the scope of several models of causal learning. For instance, this effect cannot be explained by associative models, which assume that people rely on the strength of cue–outcome associations whenever they are asked to rate the degree of relationship between a cue and an outcome. However, although the question effect is problematic for a purely associative view of causal learning, it does not exclude the possibility that associative mechanisms play some role in the learning of the cue–outcome relationship. The only thing it shows is that there must be some nonassociative processes involved at least in

the production of the response to different questions. In other words, associative processes might take part in what participants learn, even though they cannot wholly account for the flexible use that participants make of this acquired information (see Matute et al., 1996, 2002; Vadillo et al., 2005).

It is possible to develop an integrative view of causal, predictive-value, and prediction judgements that incorporates both associative mechanisms and reasoning processes. According to this view, some types of judgement can be regarded as being directly based on the strength of the cue–outcome association, while some others can be based on a combination of the cue–outcome and context–outcome associations. The decision of whether one or the other applies as a response to a given question is clearly nonassociative. However, the acquired knowledge that is used to construct that response would be, from this point of view, associative. For example, it is well known that the famous learning algorithm proposed by Rescorla and Wagner (1972) predicts that the asymptotic strength of the cue–outcome associations should be dependent on cue–outcome Δp (Chapman & Robbins, 1990; Danks, 2003; Wasserman, Elek, Chatlosh, & Baker, 1993).[2] Therefore, the judgements that have been shown to be dependent on Δp (causal judgements and predictive-value judgements; see Vadillo et al., 2005) could be a direct expression of the cue–outcome associative strength as computed by the Rescorla and Wagner (1972) learning algorithm. When making predictions, in contrast, participants should take into account all present cues that could be provoking the outcome, which means that both the cue–outcome and the

---

[1] In the prediction question used by Vadillo et al. (2005), participants had to estimate the likelihood of the outcome in the presence of the cue. Another possible prediction question would ask participants to predict the likelihood of the outcome in the absence of the cue (for an example of questions regarding what happens in the absence of the cue, see De Houwer et al., 2007). For the sake of simplicity, however, we always use the term prediction judgement as referring to what happens when the cue is present. Our assumption is that the results should, in general, be symmetrical for the cue-absent question.

[2] In fact, the predicted value of the asymptotic associative strength is exactly equal to Δp, if the learning rate parameter β is assumed to have the same value on outcome-present trials and on outcome-absent trials. When this constraint is met, the resulting algorithm is known as the restricted Rescorla–Wagner model (Lober & Shanks, 2000). If β has different values in outcome-present and outcome-absent trials, then the asymptotic value of the associative strength is no longer equal to Δp, but it is still dependent on this statistical index (higher levels of Δp lead to higher associative strengths).

context–outcome associations should be taken into account. It is easy to show that the asymptotic value of the addition of the cue's and context's associative strengths, as computed by the Rescorla–Wagner algorithm, is not dependent on Δp, but on $p(o|c)$, regardless of the saliences of the cue and the context (see Matute & Vadillo, 2005, for simulations illustrating this feature of the Rescorla–Wagner model). Thus, this would explain Vadillo et al.'s (2005) finding that prediction judgements, unlike causal and predictive-value judgements, are not dependent on cue–outcome contingency. Once it has been recognized that the effect of the type of question does not exclude the possible intervention of associative processes, the question is: Can we distinguish between this explanation, partly based on associative mechanism, and the alternative account exclusively framed in terms of higher order cognitive reasoning?

Although most higher order reasoning models do not usually include explicit algorithmic details (i.e., Cheng, 1997; Cheng & Novick, 1992; but see Cheng & Holyoak, 1995), it is commonly assumed that, from their point of view, what participants learn during the training experience is not associations between mental representations of the events, but some sort of mental model of a contingency table where the frequencies of each type of trial are stored. In situations where a single cue and a single training context are involved, it is assumed that participants store information about the frequency of four types of trial: trials in which both the cue and the outcome are present (type a trials); trials in which the cue is present but the outcome is absent (type b trials); trials in which the cue is absent but the outcome is present (type c trials); and trials in which both the cue and the outcome are absent (type d trials). An important feature of this view is that people are not supposed to keep information about the order in which they received these trials. That is, a participant having experienced 10 cue–outcome trials followed by 10 cue–no-outcome trials is supposed to acquire the same mental representation as that acquired by another participant having experienced 10

cue–no-outcome trials followed by 10 cue–outcome trials. Both of them should have stored a mental model with 10 Type a trials and 10 Type b trials.

Associative learning algorithms, on the contrary, are supposed to be highly sensitive to the precise order in which information was provided. Specifically, associative models generally assume that cue–outcome associations are constantly being updated as more information is provided. This means that the associative strength is strongly determined by the most recent contingencies. These models predict that, when contradictory information is received in different phases, what is learned in the last phase will overwrite what was learned previously, a process that has been called *catastrophic forgetting* (Hetherington & Seidenberg, 1989; Lewandowsky, 1991; McCloskey & Cohen, 1989; Ratcliff, 1990).

This differential prediction of higher order reasoning and associative accounts of causal learning is one of the best strategies that can be used to discriminate empirically between them (e.g., Chapman, 1991; López, Shanks, Almaraz, & Fernández, 1998). Thus, in the following experiment we use this trial-order strategy to assess the plausibility of a hybrid (partly associative and partly reasoning-based) account of causal and prediction judgements and test it against the explanation provided by standard higher order reasoning models.

Overview of the experiment

The major finding of Vadillo et al. (2005) was that prediction judgements were mostly determined by $p(o|c)$, whereas causal judgements were influenced by both $p(o|c)$ and $p(o|\sim c)$—that is, by Δp. Thus, predictions are only based on a and b trials, whereas causal judgements are based on a, b, c, and d trials. This means that manipulations affecting only c and d trials should have no impact on prediction judgements but should have an effect on causal judgements. Thus, if the order of c and d trials were manipulated while keeping the same order regarding a and b trials, prediction judgements should not be affected. But what pattern of causal judgements should we expect based on the different theoretical models? As we have just mentioned, from the point of view of higher order reasoning models, the order of trials should have no effect, and, therefore, causal judgements should be the same regardless of the order in which information about c and d trials were presented. On the contrary, associative models predict that varying the order of c and d trials should have an impact on causal judgements. Thus, according to our hypothesis, if causal judgements are based on the strength of the cue–outcome association as computed by the Rescorla–Wagner algorithm, then these judgements should be larger if most Type d trials are presented at the last phase of training than if most Type c trials are presented at that moment. Additionally, prediction judgements should not change depending on the order of c and d trials. This manipulation would affect the associative strength of the cue, but it would also affect the associative strength of the context in the opposite direction. Thus, if prediction judgements are based on the addition of the associative strength of the cue and the associative strength of the context, then manipulating the order of c and d trials should not have an effect on prediction judgements. It is only for causal judgements that we expect this manipulation to have some relevance.

Summarizing, both the associative account and the higher order reasoning account predict that the order of c and d trials should have no impact on prediction judgements. However, they make different predictions regarding whether such manipulation should have an effect on causal judgements. The associative account predicts a recency effect in causal judgements (i.e., causal judgements should be larger if most c trials are presented first, and most d trials are presented in the last training phase), whereas the higher order reasoning account predicts no trial-order effect.

These predictions were tested in this experiment with the design shown in Table 1. Two groups of participants were exposed to two phases of training. The probability of the outcome given the cue was set to .50 in both phases for both groups (15 a and 15 b trials were

presented in each phase in both conditions). However, the probability of the outcome in the absence of the cue was different in each training phase. For participants in group CD, most c trials were presented during the first training phase, and most d trials were presented during the second training phase. This resulted in a higher probability of the outcome in the absence of the cue during the first phase, $p(o|\sim c) = .83$, obtained with 25 c and 5 d trials, than during the second phase, $p(o|\sim c) = .17$, obtained with 5 c and 25 d trials. For participants in group DC, the order of these blocks of trials was reversed: Most d trials were presented during the first training phase, $p(o|\sim c) = .17$, obtained with 5 c and 25 d trials, and most c trials were presented during the second phase, $p(o|\sim c) = .83$, obtained with 25 c and 5 d trials. Despite this critical difference in the order of trials, participants in both groups were exposed to the same overall $p(o|c)$ and $p(o|\sim c)$ (both equal to .50) and also to the same overall Δp (equal to 0). According to higher order reasoning models of causal induction this should give rise to equal causal judgements and predictions in both groups. However, according to our associative perspective, prediction judgements should be identical but causal judgements should be more sensitive to the cue–outcome contingency of the second training phase. Given that c trials should reduce the strength of the cue–outcome association and that d trials should increase it, this model predicts a greater judgement when most d trials are presented in the last training phase (CD condition) than when most c trials are presented in that phase (DC condition).

Method

Participants and apparatus

The experiment was run simultaneously over the Internet and in traditional laboratory conditions (for recent reviews on Internet-based research, see Birnbaum, 2000; Gosling, Vazire, Srivastava, & John, 2004; Kraut et al., 2004). Concerning the Internet replication, 59 anonymous Internet users volunteered to take part in this experiment. These participants were randomly assigned to

Table 1. *Design summary of the experiment*

	Phase 1				Phase 2			
Group	Trial frequencies	$p(o|c)$	$p(o|\sim c)$	Δp	Trial frequencies	$p(o|c)$	$p(o|\sim c)$	Δp
CD	15a, 15b, 25c, 5d	.50	.83	−.33	15a, 15b, 5c, 25d	.50	.17	.33
DC	15a, 15b, 5c, 25d	.50	.17	.33	15a, 15b, 25c, 5d	.50	.83	−.33

one of the two experimental conditions, which resulted in 30 participants in group CD and 29 participants in group DC. In order to comply with ethical regulations for human research over the Internet (Frankel & Siang, 1999) we decided not to record any data without the consent of the participants. Thus, the conditions in which these participants performed the experiment are completely unknown to us. However, we controlled for the potential noisy data obtained through the Internet by running an additional pool of 67 participants in our laboratory. These were psychology students from Deusto University who took part in the experiment voluntarily. Random assignment of these laboratory participants to the two experimental conditions resulted in 35 participants in group CD and 32 in group DC. These students performed the experiment in a large computer room, where adjacent participants were seated at about 1.5 m apart from each other and were exposed to different experimental conditions. This double-location procedure allows us to check that the effects under study can be generalized to less controlled conditions than those of the laboratory, while making sure that the potential noise introduced by the Internet-based methodology is not affecting the results.

The experimental program was an adaptation of the allergy task that we commonly use in experiments on human contingency learning (Bárcena, Vadillo, & Matute, 2003). This program was

implemented in an HTML document dynamically modified with JavaScript, which allowed us to perform the experiment in any computer connected to the World Wide Web with a standard Internet browser.

Design and procedure

At the beginning of the experiment, participants were shown the following instructions on the computer's screen:

Imagine that you are a specialist who wants to study to what degree the consumption of a medicine causes, as a secondary effect, an allergic reaction. The medical records of a series of patients will be presented. You will first see a card that tells you whether a patient has taken the medicine. Once you have read it, you will see, on a second card, whether the patient did or did not develop the allergic reaction. After that, you will see the cards for the next patient, and so on. After seeing all the patients' records, you will have to assess the relationship between the medicine and the allergic reaction.

After having read these instructions, participants were exposed to a sequence of 120 trials. Each trial began with the presentation of a medical card where it could be read whether or not that trial's patient had taken a medicine called Dugetil. Below this card and on the same screen, participants were asked to predict, giving a *yes*/*no* response, whether this patient would develop an allergic reaction to the medicine.[3] After having entered their response for that trial, participants could see in another medical card, which was presented underneath the yes/no

---

[3] Although it is well known that a high frequency of judgements can induce a recency effect (Catena, Maldonado, & Cándido, 1998), previous studies have shown that frequent yes/no responses do not affect participant's ratings given at the end of the experiment in a numerical scale (see Matute et al., 2002). For instance, both Collins and Shanks (2002) and Matute et al. (2002) observed an absence of recency in a numerical judgement given at the end of the experiment, in spite of participants being requested to give this yes/no responses during training. The recency effect only appeared when the numerical judgement itself was requested with a high frequency during training. Thus, it is unlikely that our yes/no responses are affecting ratings given at the end of the experiment.

buttons, whether or not the patient had actually developed the allergic reaction (see Bárcena et al., 2003). In each trial, the patient could take the medicine and develop the allergy (Type *a* trial), take the medicine but not develop the allergy (Type *b* trial), not take the medicine but develop the allergy (Type *c* trial), or not take the medicine and not develop the allergy (Type *d* trial). During the experiment, participants in both conditions were exposed to 30 trials of each type, but the distribution of these trials was different for each group: Participants in group CD were first exposed to a set of 15 *a*, 15 *b*, 25 *c*, and 5 *d* trials and then, without any visible interruption, to a set of 15 *a*, 15 *b*, 5 *c*, and 25 *d* trials; participants in group DC were exposed to these two sets of trials in the reverse order.

After having seen the whole sequence of 120 trials, a different screen appeared on which participants were asked two questions that appeared simultaneously, one above the other (with the position of question counterbalanced across participants). Participants could answer these questions in any order and were allowed to change their ratings before finishing the experiment. One of the questions can be translated as *To what extent do you believe that Dugetil is the cause of the allergic reaction?* Participants were asked to respond to this question by clicking any point in an scale numbered from 0 to 100, with the opposite ends labelled as *It is definitely not the cause* and *It is definitely the cause*. The second question can be translated as *If a patient has taken Dugetil, to what extent do you believe that this patient will develop the allergic reaction?* Participants were asked to respond to this question in a separate scale, also numbered from 0 to 100, but with the opposite ends now labelled as *Definitely will not develop it* and *Definitely will develop it*. After having entered their judgements, participants were allowed either to change their ratings or to finish the experiment.

Although causal judgements should theoretically be requested with a bipolar rating scale ranging from −100 to 100 (because normative measures of causality, such as Δp, can adopt negative values), we decided to use a unidirectional scale from 0 to 100 in order to keep consistency with prediction judgements, which can never adopt negative values (i.e., an event cannot occur with a negative probability). In addition, it should be noted that in the present experiment we were more interested in detecting which type of judgement (causal or prediction) was affected by the order of *c* and *d* trials than in studying the precise values of the judgements given by participants in response to each question. Moreover, the use of a unidirectional scale keeps the procedure as consistent as possible with our previous studies (Vadillo et al., 2005).

Results

As the following analyses confirm, data gathered in the laboratory and over the Internet were not different from each other. Thus, data from both samples were collapsed. Figure 1 shows mean prediction and causal judgements at test collapsing both sets of data. The order of trials seems to have had no effect on prediction judgements, but causal judgements, on the contrary, have been affected systematically by this variable: As expected, causal judgements are higher in group CD than in group DC, suggesting a recency effect for these judgements.

These general impressions were confirmed by a 2 (type of question: causal vs. prediction) × 2

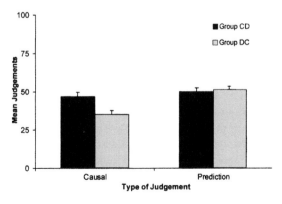

Figure 1. *Mean judgements at test given in response to the causal and prediction questions. Error bars represent the standard errors of the means.*

(group: CD vs. DC) × 2 (location: laboratory vs. Internet) mixed analysis of variance (ANOVA) performed on participants' judgements. This analysis yielded a main effect of the type of question, $F(1, 122) = 21.07$, $MSE = 282.49$, $p < .001$, and a marginally significant main effect of group, $F(1, 122) = 3.78$, $MSE = 465.95$, $p = .054$, as well as a significant interaction between type of question and group, $F(1, 122) = 9.6$, $MSE = 282.49$, $p < .005$. All main effects or interactions involving the location in which the experiment was run were nonsignificant, all Fs < 1; therefore, this factor was not used in subsequent analyses.

The interaction of the type of question and the trial order supports our hypothesis: Trial order effects are different for each question. A priori t test for independent samples confirmed that causal judgements were significantly higher in group CD than in group DC, $t(124) = 3.2$, $p < .01$, and that there was no significant difference between groups in prediction judgements, $t(124) = 0.39$, $p = .69$.

Discussion

These results indicate that the manipulation of the order of c and d trials gives rise to recency effects in causal judgements, whereas this manipulation has no effect on prediction judgements. In their present state, none of the most widely cited models of causal and predictive learning can explain this pattern of results without additional assumptions. On the one hand, the higher order reasoning account (Cheng, 1997; Cheng & Holyoak, 1995; Cheng & Novick, 1992) provides a partially satisfactory explanation for some of the evidence. For example, the lack of trial-order effects in prediction judgements is perfectly coherent with the predictions that one could draw from this theoretical perspective. Additionally, the fact that prediction and causal judgements follow different statistical indexes suggests that participants are aware of the differences between making predictions and assessing the strength of causal relations. This sensitivity to the subtle differences between the demands posed by a

prediction question and those posed by a causal question is certainly in line with the hypothesis that people act as intuitive statisticians and possess some abstract knowledge about statistical relations (Buehner & May, 2003; Waldmann, 2000; Waldmann & Holyoak, 1992). However, given that the order in which information is presented is not considered relevant (or given, at least, that its relevance has not been addressed) in these models, they remain unable to explain the trial-order effects that we observed in causal judgements (see also López et al., 1998).

On the other hand, it is equally difficult to propose a complete explanation of our results from a purely associative perspective. Associative mechanisms (e.g., Dickinson & Burke, 1996; Rescorla & Wagner, 1972; Van Hamme & Wasserman, 1994) could easily account for the recency effects observed in causal judgements, but they cannot explain the absence of recency in prediction judgements that was observed in the present study. Moreover, if judgements about a cue–outcome relationship are always based on the strength of the cue–outcome association then causal and prediction judgements should be equivalent, and manipulations affecting one of them should also affect the other (Cobos et al., 2000). This prediction is not supported by our data.

It seems, therefore, that a successful explanation of the present results cannot be framed exclusively in terms of higher order cognitive reasoning processes or in terms of associative processes. However, one need not conclude from this that both theoretical perspectives should be abandoned. Instead of that, one could simply regard them as incomplete but compatible accounts and try to find an integrative explanation borrowing concepts and ideas from both sets of theories. The hybrid framework that provided the starting point for this experiment is one of such possible accounts. According to our hypothesis, participants' basic learning of the cue–outcome relationship could be associative, but the subsequent use that participants make of this associative knowledge can be determined by higher order cognitive processes similar to those invoked by statistical

(Cheng, 1997; Cheng & Holyoak, 1995) and inferential (De Houwer, 2002; De Houwer & Beckers, 2002; De Houwer et al., 2002; Lovibond et al., 2003) reasoning accounts of human causal learning. In other words, participants can learn associations and use these associations in a more flexible way than that assumed by associative theories.

As we have discussed in the Introduction, one way of materializing this general perspective is by assuming that participants learn the cue–outcome contingency through an associative learning mechanism similar to the one proposed by Rescorla and Wagner (1972). Then, causal judgements are directly based on the strength of the cue–outcome association, whereas prediction judgements are based on the sum of the associative strengths of all the cues (including the context) that could cause the outcome at test. When $p(o|{\sim}c) > 0$, participants will probably perceive the context as a relevant causal factor, which can potentially contribute to the occurrence of the outcome. Thus, an accurate prediction of the outcome at test should be based not only on what is known about the cue (i.e., the cue–outcome association), but also on what is known about the context (i.e., the context–outcome association). In the Introduction, we have argued that, in situations involving the four trial types (a, b, c, and d) here manipulated, the summed associative strengths of the cue and the context are at asymptote equivalent to $p(o|c)$ and provide, therefore, an appropriate basis on which participants could base their prediction judgements.

This formal account of causal and prediction judgements provides a straightforward explanation of our pattern of results. A simulation of the conditions used in our groups CD and DC is shown in Figure 2. As can be seen there, if causal judgements are assumed to be based on the associative strength of the cue, as computed by the Rescorla–Wagner learning algorithm, then a strong recency effect is expected for these judgements; that is, causal judgements should be higher in condition CD than in condition DC. However, prediction judgements are assumed to be based on the sum of the associative strengths

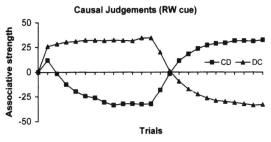

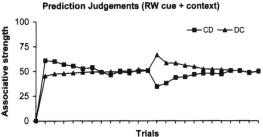

Figure 2. *Simulation of the Rescorla–Wagner model showing both the predicted associative strengths of the cue and the sum of the cue's and the context's associative strengths for conditions CD and DC. Learning rate parameters were assigned the following values: $\alpha_{Cue} = .8$, $\alpha_{Context} = .5$, $\beta_{Outcome} = .6$, and $\beta_{NoOutcome} = .6$. For each condition, 10,000 iterations with randomized trial orders within each phase were performed.*

of the cue and the context, and this sum is predicted to be similar for both groups, with only minor preasymptotic divergences in both phases. Thus, were prediction judgements based on these summed associative strengths, judgements would be equal in both trial-order conditions.

Note that the articulation of associative and reasoning processes could also be achieved by alternative formalizations. Here we have discussed how the present results could be explained assuming that the process of learning depends on an associative algorithm similar to the one described by Rescorla and Wagner (1972). However, we could also explain our results by assuming that learning is based on a simpler and more parsimonious associative mechanism like the one proposed by Bush and Mosteller (1951) or Hebb (1949). For example, the learning algorithm proposed by Bush and Mosteller (1951) is sensitive to $p(o|c)$ but not to Δp. If people learnt the cue–outcome association using such mechanism, then they would be able to make accurate predictions (though not accurate causal judgements) basing their judgements directly on the strength of the cue–outcome association. However, participants could easily give an accurate assessment of the causal relation by subtracting the associative strength of the context–outcome association from the associative strength of the cue–outcome association. This formalization, framed in terms of the Bush–Mosteller learning algorithm, is similar to some current accounts of flexibility in human causal judgements based on the comparator hypothesis (Miller & Matzel, 1988; see, for example, Beckers, De Houwer, Pineño, & Miller, 2005; Pineño et al., 2005) and is also similar to an earlier associative account of human causal learning proposed by Shanks and Dickinson (1987), according to which people learn an association between the cue–context configuration and the outcome and also an association between the context-alone configuration and the outcome; causal judgements would be based on the difference between these two associations.

Our explanation based on the Bush–Mosteller learning algorithm bears some resemblance to the one framed in terms of the Rescorla–Wagner learning model. In the account based on the Rescorla–Wagner model, causal judgements are a direct expression of the cue–outcome association, and prediction judgements are the sum of the cue–outcome and the context–outcome associations. However, in the account based on the Bush and Mosteller learning algorithm, prediction judgements are a direct expression of the cue–outcome association, and causal judgements subtract the strength of the context–outcome association from the strength of the cue–outcome association. With our present data we cannot favour one of these explanations over the other.

In the present paper we have focused on the effect of the type of question in contingency designs where only four types of trial are used (resulting from combining the presence or absence of the cue with the presence or absence of the outcome). However, researchers have observed that the type of question also affects cue competition effects. Usually, cue competition is stronger if participants are asked to assess the causal relationship between the cue and the outcome than if they are asked to predict the outcome based on the presence of the cue (Gredebäck et al., 2000), if they are asked to rate the degree with which the cue and the outcome co-occur (Matute et al., 1996), or if they are asked to rate the cue–outcome predictiveness (Gredebäck et al., 2000; Pineño et al., 2005). Cue competition is also stronger if cues and outcomes are presented as causes and effects than if they are described as predictors and outcomes (De Houwer et al., 2002; Pineño et al., 2005). These results are not easy to explain from our hypothesis based on the Rescorla–Wagner algorithm. We have proposed that causal and predictive-value judgements are based on the associative strength of the target cue, whereas predictions are based on the combined associative strengths of the target cue and the context. However, the joint associative strength of a blocked cue and the context will always be lower than the associative strength of a nonblocked control cue and the test context. In other words, blocking should be observed regardless of whether participants base their judgements on the associative strength of the target cues or on the combination of the associative strengths of the target cues with the context. Thus, blocking should be observed even if the test question (e.g., prediction question) or the instructions (e.g., predictive scenario) induce participants to combine the associative strengths of the cue and the context. In spite of this, the addition of the associative strength of the context might in some situations reduce the relative difference between the response to the blocked cue and the response to its corresponding control cue: If a blocked cue receives less associative strength than the control cue, then the blocked cue and the context together will also have less associative strength than the control cue and the context together, but their relative difference will be smaller. Thus, a reduction of blocking is expected if participants combine the associative strengths of the target cues with the associative strength of the context.

Although we have argued that the recency effect observed in causal judgements is difficult to explain by current higher order reasoning models, it could perhaps be explained from their perspective by assuming that participants store not only a mental representation of a contingency table during training, but also more detailed information about the order in which this information was provided. This alternative coding strategy would allow participants to selectively focus on the most recent information when making their causal ratings. Although this explanation may be valid for some simple experimental designs (e.g., acquisition–extinction), it is not clear whether participants can store information in that format in complex designs like the one used in this experiment, in which there are all types of trial in both training phases, and the trial-order manipulation refers only to c and d trials (which are probably less salient than a and b trials). And if participants are able to do so, it remains unclear which can be the nature of the learning process responsible for the formation of such mental representation. Additionally, in the absence of a formalized model incorporating these hypotheses one cannot easily make a priori predictions of how participants' behaviour would be in situations like those used in our procedure or in alternative paradigms. In fact, the development of such formalization is one of the most important future challenges of higher order reasoning models of causal induction (De Houwer, Beckers, & Vandorpe, 2005). Thus, although we cannot exclude the possibility that our results would be one day entirely explainable in terms of higher order processes alone, we prefer to emphasize their consistency with associative models until a more scientifically testable account of trial-order effects is offered in terms of reasoning.

In the present paper we have focused on the distinction between causal and prediction judgements. Of course, our analysis could be extended to other types of judgement. For example, Vadillo et al. (2005) made a distinction between prediction judgements (asking participants to predict the likelihood that the outcome will occur) and predictive-value judgements (asking participants to assess whether the cue is a good predictor of the outcome) and found that, unlike

prediction judgements, predictive-value judgements tended to be based on Δp. They concluded that the explanation given for causal judgements could be equally valid for predictive-value judgements. De Houwer et al. (2007) have also explored an alternative type of judgement, which they called preparatory judgements, in which participants were asked to prepare for the occurrence of the outcome if they thought that it would occur in a given trial. De Houwer et al. showed that preparatory judgements when the cue was presented (i.e., cue-present preparatory judgements) were less sensitive to Δp than were causal judgements, whereas they were strongly influenced by $p(o|c)$. Similarly, preparatory judgements in the absence of the cue were mostly determined by $p(o|\sim c)$. The similarities between the results observed when prediction questions and preparatory questions are used could be indicating that the mechanisms underlying prediction judgements are probably at the basis of preparatory behaviour as well.

Some of the results observed in the present experiment seem to contradict the results of Matute et al. (2002), who showed (a) that prediction questions are more sensitive to recency effects than are causal questions and (b) that requesting participant's judgements only at the end of the experiment produces an integration of all the information received or, in other words, prevents recency effects. Our results contradict (a) because in this experiment we observed a recency effect that affected only causal judgements (no recency was observed in prediction judgements), and they also contradict (b) because we observed this recency effect in causal judgements even though participants were only requested to give a single judgement at the end of the experiment. The absence of recency in prediction judgements in the present experiment is not really problematic: If these judgements are based solely on a and b trials, then there is no reason to expect recency in prediction judgements, unless the order of a and b trials is manipulated. Consistent with this, we did not observe trial-order effects in prediction judgements when only the order of c and d trials was manipulated. Therefore, with respect to (a), it is not surprising that causal judgements were more sensitive to recency effects than were prediction judgements in the present experiment.

An important difference between the present experiment and those reported by Matute et al. (2002), which could potentially account for the divergent results with respect to (b), is the degree of difficulty of the task used in both series of experiments. Whereas Matute et al. (2002) used a very simple acquisition–extinction design (see also Collins & Shanks, 2002, for a similar result using a slightly more complex trial-order manipulation), in the present experiment we used a rather complex design where the transition from the first to the second phase was relatively difficult to perceive and remember. Several researchers have noted that simpler processing occurs as the difficulty of the task increases (e.g., see Le Pelley, Oakeshott, & McLaren, 2005). Thus, quite possibly, the complexity of the task used in this experiment induced participants to enrol in simpler processing than that in Matute et al.'s (2002) experiments. An additional difference between both sets of experiments is that Matute et al. (2002) requested prediction judgements by presenting the question during a training or test trial (the cue and the target question were presented simultaneously), whereas we requested judgements by means of a questionnaire that was presented at the end of the experiment. This procedural difference might have also contributed to our finding recency with a single judgement at the end of the experiment.

We would not like to end the present paper without remarking on the similarities between the results observed in the laboratory and those observed over the Internet. The lack of a main effect of location or an interaction involving this factor indicates that the results were essentially the same for the Internet sample and for the laboratory sample, a result that confirms previous findings of other studies that also show a clear correspondence between traditional methodologies and Internet-based research (e.g., Buchanan & Smith, 1999; McGraw, Tew, & Williams, 2000; Steyvers, Tenenbaum, Wagenmakers, & Blum, 2003; Vadillo et al., 2005). These consistent similarities between experiments performed in the laboratory and experiments performed over the Internet encourage the still infrequent use of online experiments in our area.

REFERENCES

Allan, L. G. (1980). A note on measurement of contingency between two binary variables in judgement tasks. *Bulletin of the Psychonomic Society, 15*, 147–149.

Allan, L. G. (1993). Human contingency judgments: Rule based or associative? *Psychological Bulletin, 114*, 435–448.

Allan, L. G., & Jenkins, H. M. (1983). The effect of representations of binary variables on judgment of influence. *Learning and Motivation, 14*, 381–405.

Bárcena, R., Vadillo, M. A., & Matute, H. (2003). *Allergy task for Windows* [Computer program]. Available from http://www.labpsico.com

Beckers, T., De Houwer, J., Pineño, O., & Miller, R. R. (2005). Outcome additivity and outcome maximality influence cue competition in human causal learning. *Journal of Experimental Psychology: Learning, Memory, and Cognition, 31*, 238–249.

Birnbaum, M. H. (Ed.). (2000). *Psychological experiments on the Internet.* San Diego, CA: Academic Press.

Buchanan, T., & Smith, J. L. (1999). Using the Internet for psychological research: Personality testing on the World Wide Web. *British Journal of Psychology, 90*, 125–144.

Buehner, M. J., & May, J. (2003). Rethinking temporal contiguity and the judgment of causality: Effects of prior knowledge, experience, and reinforcement procedure. *Quarterly Journal of Experimental Psychology, 56A*, 865–890.

Bush, R. R., & Mosteller, F. (1951). A mathematical model for simple learning. *Psychological Review, 58*, 313–323.

Catena, A., Maldonado, A., & Cándido, A. (1998). The effect of the frequency of judgment and the type of trials on covariation learning. *Journal of Experimental Psychology: Human Perception and Performance, 24*, 481–495.

Chapman, G. B. (1991). Trial order affects cue interaction in contingency judgment. *Journal of Experimental Psychology: Learning, Memory, and Cognition, 17*, 837–854.

Chapman, G. B., & Robbins, S. J. (1990). Cue interaction in human contingency judgment. *Memory & Cognition, 18*, 537–545.

Cheng, P. W. (1997). From covariation to causation: A causal power theory. *Psychological Review, 104*, 367–405.

Cheng, P. W., & Holyoak, K. J. (1995). Complex adaptative systems as intuitive statisticians: Causality, contingency and prediction. In H. L. Roitblat & J.-A. Meyer (Eds.), *Comparative approaches to cognitive science* (pp. 271–302). Cambridge, MA: MIT Press.

Cheng, P. W., & Novick, L. R. (1992). Covariation in natural causal induction. *Psychological Review, 99*, 365–382.

Cobos, P. L., Caño, A., López, F. J., Luque, J. L., & Almaraz, J. (2000). Does the type of judgement required modulate cue competition? *Quarterly Journal of Experimental Psychology, 53B*, 193–207.

Collins, D. J., & Shanks, D. R. (2002). Momentary and integrative response strategies in causal judgment. *Memory & Cognition, 30*, 1138–1147.

Crocker, J. (1982). Biased questions in judgment of covariation studies. *Personality and Social Psychology Bulletin, 8*, 214–220.

Danks, D. (2003). Equilibria of the Rescorla–Wagner model. *Journal of Mathematical Psychology, 47*, 109–121.

De Houwer, J. (2002). Forward blocking depends on retrospective inferences about the presence of the blocked cue during the elemental phase. *Memory & Cognition, 30*, 24–33.

De Houwer, J., & Beckers, T. (2002). Higher-order retrospective revaluation in human causal learning. *Quarterly Journal of Experimental Psychology, 55B*, 137–151.

De Houwer, J., Beckers, T., & Glautier, S. (2002). Outcome and cue properties modulate blocking. *Quarterly Journal of Experimental Psychology, 55A*, 965–985.

De Houwer, J., Beckers, T., & Vandorpe, S. (2005). Evidence for the role of higher order reasoning processes in cue competition and other learning phenomena. *Learning & Behavior, 33*, 239–249.

De Houwer, J., Vandorpe, S., & Beckers, T. (2007). Statistical contingency has a different impact on preparation judgements than on causal judgements. *Quarterly Journal of Experimental Psychology, 60*, 418–432.

Dickinson, A., & Burke, J. (1996). Within-compound associations mediate the retrospective revaluation of causality judgements. *Quarterly Journal of Experimental Psychology, 49B*, 60–80.

Dickinson, A., Shanks, D. R., & Evenden, J. (1984). Judgement of act–outcome contingency: The role of selective attribution. *Quarterly Journal of Experimental Psychology, 36A*, 29–50.

Frankel, M. S., & Siang, S. (1999). *Ethical and legal aspects of human subjects research on the Internet.* [Report of a workshop convened by the American Association for the Advancement of Science, Program on Scientific Freedom, Responsibility, and Law, Washington, DC.] Retrieved May 9, 2005, from http://www.aaas.org/spp/dspp/sfrl/projects/intres/main.htm

Gosling, S. D., Vazire, S., Srivastava, S., & John, O. P. (2004). Should we trust web-based studies? A comparative analysis of six preconceptions about Internet questionnaires. *American Psychologist, 59*, 93–104.

Gredebäck, G., Winman, A., & Juslin, P. (2000). Rational assessments of covariation and causality. *Proceedings of the 22nd Annual Conference of the Cognitive Science Society* (pp. 190–195). Hillsdale, NJ: Lawrence Erlbaum Associates, Inc.

Hebb, D. O. (1949). *The organization of behavior: A neuropsychological theory.* New York: Wiley.

Hetherington, P. A., & Seidenberg, M. S. (1989). Is there "catastrophic interference" in connectionist networks? *Proceedings of the Eleventh Annual Conference of the Cognitive Science Society* (pp. 26–33). Hillsdale, NJ: Lawrence Erlbaum Associates, Inc.

Hinton, G. E. (1990). Mapping part-whole hierarchies into connectionist networks. *Artificial Intelligence, 46*, 47–75.

Jenkins, H. M., & Ward, W. C. (1965). Judgment of contingency between responses and outcomes. *Psychological Monographs, 79*, 1–17.

Kraut, R., Olson, J., Banaji, M., Bruckman, A., Cohen, J., & Couper, M. (2004). Psychological research online: Report of board of scientific affairs' advisory group on the conduct of research on the Internet. *American Psychologist, 59*, 105–117.

Le Pelley, M. E., Oakeshott, S. M., & McLaren, I. P. L. (2005). Blocking and unblocking in human causal learning. *Journal of Experimental Psychology: Animal Behavior Processes, 31*, 56–70.

Lewandowsky, S. (1991). Gradual unlearning and catastrophic interference: A comparison of distributed architectures. In W. E. Hockley & S. Lewandowsky (Eds.), *Relating theory and data:*

Essays on human memory in honor of Bennet B. Murdock (pp. 445–476). Hillsdale, NJ: Lawrence Erlbaum Associates, Inc.

Lober, K., & Shanks, D. R. (2000). Is causal induction based on causal power? Critique of Cheng (1997). *Psychological Review, 107*, 195–212.

López, F. J., Shanks, D. R., Almaraz, J., & Fernández, P. (1998). Effects of trial order on contingency judgments: A comparison of associative and probabilistic contrast accounts. *Journal of Experimental Psychology: Learning, Memory, & Cognition, 24*, 672–694.

Lovibond, P. F., Been, S.-L., Mitchell, C. J., Bouton, M. E., & Frohardt, R. (2003). Forward and backward blocking of causal judgment is enhanced by additivity of effect magnitude. *Memory & Cognition, 31*, 133–142.

Matute, H., Arcediano, F., & Miller, R. R. (1996). Test question modulates cue competition between causes and between effects. *Journal of Experimental Psychology: Learning, Memory, and Cognition, 22*, 182–196.

Matute, H., & Vadillo, M. A. (2005). *Inferring causality and making predictions: Some misconceptions in the animal and human learning literature.* [Paper presented at the Online Conference on Causality organized by the Institute for Cognitive Sciences at Lyon and the Université de Genève.] Retrieved July 21, 2005, from http://www.interdisciplines.org/causality/papers/16

Matute, H., Vegas, S., & De Marez, P. J. (2002). Flexible use of recent information in causal and predictive judgments. *Journal of Experimental Psychology: Learning, Memory, and Cognition, 28*, 714–725.

McCloskey, M., & Cohen, N. J. (1989). Catastrophic interference in connectionist networks: The sequential learning problem. In G. H. Bower (Ed.), *The psychology of learning and motivation* (Vol. 24, pp. 109–165). San Diego, CA: Academic Press.

McGraw, K. O., Tew, M. D., & Williams, J. E. (2000). The integrity of web-delivered experiments: Can you trust the data? *Psychological Science, 11*, 502–506.

Miller, R. R., & Matzel, L. D. (1988). The comparator hypothesis: A response rule for the expression of associations. In G. H. Bower (Ed.), *The psychology of learning and motivation* (Vol. 22, pp. 51–92). San Diego, CA: Academic Press.

Pineño, O., Denniston, J. C., Beckers, T., Matute, H., & Miller, R. R. (2005). Contrasting predictive and causal values of predictors and causes. *Learning & Behavior, 33*, 184–196.

Ratcliff, R. (1990). Connectionist models of recognition memory: Constraints imposed by learning and forgetting functions. *Psychological Review, 97*, 285–308.

Rescorla, R. A., & Wagner, A. R. (1972). A theory of Pavlovian conditioning: Variations in the effectiveness of reinforcement and nonreinforcement. In A. H. Black & W. F. Prokasy (Eds.), *Classical conditioning II: Current research and theory* (pp. 64–99). New York: Appleton-Century-Crofts.

Shanks, D. R. (2007). Associationism and cognition: Human contingency learning at 25. *Quarterly Journal of Experimental Psychology, 60*, 291–309.

Shanks, D. R., & Dickinson, A. (1987). Associative accounts of causality judgment. In G. H. Bower (Ed.), *The psychology of learning and motivation* (Vol. 21, pp. 229–261). San Diego, CA: Academic Press.

Sloman, S. A. (1996). The empirical case for two systems of reasoning. *Psychological Bulletin, 119*, 3–22.

Smedslund, J. (1963). The concept of correlation in adults. *Scandinavian Journal of Psychology, 4*, 165–173.

Smolensky, P. (1988). On the proper treatment of connectionism. *Behavioral and Brain Sciences, 11*, 1–74.

Steyvers, M., Tenenbaum, J. B., Wagenmakers, E.-J., & Blum, B. (2003). Inferring causal networks from observations and interventions. *Cognitive Science, 27*, 453–489.

Vadillo, M. A., Miller, R. R., & Matute, H. M. (2005). Causal and predictive-value judgments, but not predictions, are based on cue–outcome contingency. *Learning & Behavior, 33*, 172–183.

Van Hamme, L. J., & Wasserman, E. A. (1994). Cue competition in causality judgments: The role of nonpresentation of compound stimulus elements. *Learning and Motivation, 25*, 127–151.

Wagner, A. R., Logan, F. A., Haberlandt, K., & Price, T. (1968). Stimulus selection in animal discrimination learning. *Journal of Experimental Psychology, 76*, 171–180.

Waldmann, M. R. (2000). Competition among causes but not effects in predictive and diagnostic learning. *Journal of Experimental Psychology: Learning, Memory, and Cognition, 26*, 53–76.

Waldmann, M. R., & Holyoak, K. J. (1992). Predictive and diagnostic learning within causal models: Asymmetries in cue competition. *Journal of Experimental Psychology: General, 121*, 222–236.

Ward, W. C., & Jenkins, H. M. (1965). The display of information and the judgment of contingency. *Canadian Journal of Psychology, 19*, 231–241.

Wasserman, E. A. (1974). Stimulus-reinforcer predictiveness and selective discrimination learning in pigeons. *Journal of Experimental Psychology, 103*, 284–297.

Wasserman, E. A. (1990). Attribution of causality to common and distinctive elements of compound stimuli. *Psychological Science, 1*, 298–302.

Wasserman, E. A., Chatlosh, D. L., & Neunaber, D. J. (1983). Perception of causal relations in humans:

Factors affecting judgments of response–outcome contingencies under free-operant procedures. *Learning and Motivation, 14*, 406–432.

Wasserman, E. A., Elek, S. M., Chatlosh, D. L., & Baker, A. G. (1993). Rating causal relations: The role of probability in judgments of response–outcome contingency. *Journal of Experimental Psychology: Learning, Memory, and Cognition, 19*, 174–188.

White, P. A. (2003). Effects of wording and stimulus format on the use of contingency information in causal judgment. *Memory and Cognition, 31*, 231–242.

THE QUARTERLY JOURNAL OF EXPERIMENTAL PSYCHOLOGY
2007, 60 (3), 448–460

Second-order conditioning in human predictive judgements when there is little time to think

Danielle M. Karazinov and Robert A. Boakes
University of Sydney, Sydney, Australia

Associative accounts uniquely predict that second-order conditioning might be observed in human predictive judgements. Such an effect was found for cue X in two experiments in which participants were required to predict the outcomes of a series of training trials that included P+ and PX−, but only when training was paced by requiring participants to make a prediction within 3 s on each trial. In Experiment 1 training on P+ ended before training was given on PX−. In Experiment 2 trials with P+ , PX−, T+ and other cues were intermixed. In the unpaced group inhibitory learning was revealed by a summation test, TX versus TM, where M was a control stimulus. These results suggest either that pacing interferes with learning successive associations more than with learning simultaneous associations or that lack of time to think interferes with inferential processes required for this type of inhibitory learning.

Human predictive learning experiments seek to determine how humans make judgements about the relation that a particular cue holds with a particular outcome. In such experiments, participants might be given a series of trials in which different foods predict the presence or absence of an illness in a hypothetical person. After receiving this information, participants complete a test in which they are asked to rate the likelihood of the outcome given the presence of particular cues.

As discussed extensively in other articles in this issue (e.g., Shanks, 2007), there are at least two classes of theory that potentially explain the process that humans use when making such judgements. On the one hand, the normative or cognitive approach includes statistical models (e.g., Cheng & Novick, 1992; Cheng, Park, Yarlas, & Holyoak, 1996; Ward & Jenkins, 1965) as well as more general propositional reasoning. Statistical models propose that humans base their judgements on the contingency between the target cue and outcome. If there is a positive contingency between cue and outcome, humans will judge the cue to predict the presence of the outcome proportionally to that positive contingency, and if there is a negative contingency between cue and outcome, humans will judge the cue to prevent the outcome in proportion to that negative contingency. Finally, if there is a zero contingency, humans will judge the cue to be

Correspondence should be addressed to D. M. Karazinov, School of Psychology, University of Sydney, NSW 2006, Australia. E-mail: dannyk@psych.usyd.edu.au

We wish to thank Evan Livesey for programming the computer tasks for the experiments in this paper. This research was supported by an Australian Postgraduate Award and a Postgraduate Research Grant from the School of Psychology, University of Sydney to D.M.K. and a grant from the Australian Research Council to R.A.B.

DOI:10.1080/17470210601002488

unrelated to the outcome. Although amendments have been made to the basic statistical model in order to accommodate a wider range of effects (e.g., Cheng, 1997; Cheng & Novick, 1992), the basic principle of the statistical approach is always that a positive contingency draws a judgement of positive relation whereas a negative contingency draws a judgement of a negative relation.

The more general approach of propositional reasoning (e.g., De Houwer & Beckers, 2003; Lovibond, 2003; Michell & Lovibond, 2002) assumes that participants use deliberate logical reasoning to draw conclusions from the premises available in the given information. Like the statistical model described above, this approach is normative in nature but more loosely formulated. The basic assumption is that humans apply rules of logic and prior knowledge of causal systems to work out the relationship between the cue and outcome. Presumably, this would mean that, at the very least, cues always followed by the outcome would be judged to be positively causal, while cues never followed by the outcome might be either inhibitory or unrelated to the outcome.

The second class of theory is the associative learning approach (e.g., Dickinson, Shanks, & Evenden, 1984; Shanks, 1995, 2007). This approach proposes that human predictive judgements are based on the same mechanisms as is animal associative learning. In very basic terms, associative learning theory assumes that, when two stimuli are paired together, an association develops between them such that when one is presented, a representation of the other is elicited. There are various formal associative learning theories. Many incorporate some form of learning rule based on the notion of expectedness of the outcome. Most of these theories predict that learning increases to the degree that the outcome is surprising. Thus, when a cue is followed by an outcome, a positive association develops between the cue and the outcome until that outcome is fully predicted in such trials. Inhibitory associations develop when a cue is followed by the absence of an expected outcome.

Distinguishing between these two classes of model is difficult because, after learning has reached asymptote, the models make similar predictions for many types of learning task. However, at least one effect found in animal conditioning studies is not predicted by normative or inferential models, but is predicted by associative theories. The effect is second-order conditioning (SOC; e.g., Holland & Rescorla, 1975; Leyland & Mackintosh, 1978; Nairne & Rescorla, 1981; Rizely & Rescorla, 1972; Yin, Barnet, & Miller, 1994). This refers to the finding that a cue can acquire positive strength simply by being associated with a previously trained positive cue. Based on normative and inferential models, it is difficult to see how a stimulus can be judged as a cause or predictor of the outcome if the stimulus and outcome have never co-occurred. However, the associative approach can allow a second-order association if one accepts that cue–cue associations, as well as cue–outcome associations, occur in predictive judgement learning. To take a standard example from animal research, if a tone is first paired with a shock, and then a light is paired with the tone, a subsequent test may reveal that the light now elicits a fear response, even though it has never been directly paired with the shock (Rescorla, 1973).

An intriguing point noted by Pavlov (1927), Rescorla (1973), and Yin et al. (1994) in relation to animal learning research was that training with the same two types of trial can sometimes lead to SOC and at other times to conditioned inhibition. One of these trial types is the pairing of one cue, P, with the outcome (P+ trials) such that P becomes a positive predictor. The other type of trial involves combining cue P with another neutral cue, X, without a subsequent outcome (PX− trials). In a briefly reported fear conditioning experiment, of the kind given in the above example, Rescorla (1973) found that, regardless of whether P and X were presented simultaneously (PX) or in succession (X → P), X developed SOC early in training. However, after extensive training X was found to be inhibitory, although only in a group given simultaneous PX− trials. Yin et al. (1994) also used fear conditioning in rats and varied both number of trials and order of trial type to examine the conditions that would determine whether SOC or inhibitory learning occurs. SOC was found when there were only a few PX− trials, either when the P+ and PX− trials were intermixed or when they were given in consecutive blocks (i.e., P+ trials followed by PX− trials). Inhibition was obtained only when there were many PX− trials and when the two trial types were intermixed. These findings were taken to mean that a transient excitatory phase (SOC) precedes inhibitory learning under such conditions. If human predictive judgements reflect similar learning processes to those tapped by such animal conditioning experiments, then cue X in the design P+, PX− would be expected to undergo a brief SOC phase before becoming an inhibitor. Neither normative nor inferential models make such a prediction.

We recently conducted a number of experiments in which we varied the number of training trials within an intermixed P+ and PX− design (Karazinov, 2005). In these between-group experiments, eight trials each of P+ and PX− produced inhibition. However, neither two nor four trials of P+ and PX− produced any type of learning. Thus, simply using a small number of training trials did not produce SOC. The acquisition functions in this type of task (e.g., Karazinov & Boakes, 2004a) suggested that simply reducing the number of training trials might not be an effective way of producing preasymptotic learning because most changes occur within the first few trials. In essence, SOC should arise under conditions where some acquisition of the successive P+ and the simultaneous P−X associations takes place prior to acquisition of a strong successive PX− no-outcome association. This is possible if cue−no-outcome associations are slower to develop than cue−outcome associations. In the present experiments we examined whether such conditions might be produced by limiting the amount of time that participants spent on each training trial.

The experimental procedure made use of a computer-based task in which a hypothetical person ate different foods (cues) and suffered a migraine headache (outcome) after some of these foods. Participants were asked to predict whether or not this outcome would occur on each trial during both training and test phases of an experiment. In both experiments reported here, training included trials of P+, PX−, and T+ (transfer stimulus). In a subsequent test, X was presented both on its own and combined with T in a summation test (TX). The logic behind this test is that a necessary condition for judging a stimulus to be inhibitory is reduction of the conditioned response that would otherwise be elicited by an excitatory stimulus (T) other than the one it has been trained against (P); this criterion has been generally accepted in animal-based conditioning research since Rescorla (1969). Several previous studies using human participants have found evidence for inhibitory learning from a summation test given after training on intermixed P+, PX−, and T+ trials (e.g., Karazinov & Boakes, 2004a; Williams, 1996; Williams & Docking, 1995). However, the question of whether any positive strength can also be detected for X under these conditions—that is, SOC—does not appear to have been examined previously in experiments involving human participants.

EXPERIMENT 1

Experiment 1 used a two-group design in which both groups were given the same trials (see Table 1), and both were given identical self-paced tests. The only difference was that in the paced group a time limit of 3 s was imposed on the time that participants had to make a prediction on a training trial.

There were three phases in training, such that eight P+ trials were presented before the four PX− trials, as shown in Table 1. This training sequence was intended to increase the likelihood of obtaining SOC because it resembles the kind of design most commonly used to study SOC in animals (e.g., Nairne & Rescorla, 1981; Rizely & Rescorla, 1972). The three training phases in the experiment were not explicitly marked for participants, for whom the sequence of training trials was effectively seamless.

Table 1. *Design and mean test ratings for Experiment 1*

	Training cues				Ratings	
Blocks 1 & 2	Block 3	Block 4	Test cues	Unpaced group	Paced group
P+ (3)	P+ (2)	PX− (4)	X	21.4	30.9
T+ (2)	T+ (2)	LM− (4)	M	26.7	15.1
N− (2)	N− (2)	T+ (2)	TX	51.4	68.0
	FG+ (4)	N− (2)	TM	58.7	58.0
	FH− (4)	FG+ (4)	T	89.9	94.4
		FH− (4)	N	8.9	2.9
			C	40.7	42.9
			P	91.1	89.0

Note: For training cues, number of presentations is given in parentheses. Ratings on an ungraduated analogue scale were converted to a scale of 0 ("Migraine certain not to occur") to 100 ("Migraine certain to occur"). Each value corresponds to the test cue listed to its left and represents means over three test trials.

The control cue used was LM− . As indicated in Table 1, LM− was equivalent to PX− in every respect except that P+ was trained separately; thus, a higher rating for X than for M would indicate SOC. On test, the compounds TX and TM were intended to provide a summation test for inhibitory learning, indicated by a lower rating for TX than for TM (cf. Karazinov & Boakes, 2004b). Finally, the compounds FG+ and FH− were included in training to provide a further instance of cue interaction, but one unrelated to either SOC or inhibitory learning. Without including FG+ and FH−, the cues P+ and PX− would have been the only set of cues with a common cue and may have attracted extra attention. We have used compounds such as FG+ and FH− in previous experiments that included an overshadowing manipulation (Karazinov & Boakes, 2004b), but here they were introduced as filler cues and are not discussed further. Of the training cues, three were positive and four negative; two of the three single cues and one of the four compound cues were positive.

Method

Participants

A total of 59 first-year psychology students from the University of Sydney received course credit for taking part in the experiment. They were allocated to either the paced or the unpaced conditions according to the session they attended. Paced ($n = 30$) and unpaced ($n = 29$) participants were run in alternate sessions.

Procedure

A total of 1–12 participants were tested at a time in a single session of about 30 min. When participants arrived they were shown to a computer and were told that the experiment used a computer-based task about a person who suffers migraine headaches after eating certain foods.

Although the written instructions on the computer for paced groups were designed to inform them about the time restriction, it was thought that some participants in this condition might miss the first few trials if the instructions were not fully understood. Consequently, the experimenter demonstrated one training trial to every participant, pointing out the rapid pace of training trials for participants in the paced group. Participants then read the following instructions at their own pace:

We wish you to imagine that you are a doctor and that you want to discover what is causing a particular patient to have migraine attacks. You believe that some of the foods that patient is eating may be related to the occurrence of migraine attacks. In order to try and find out which foods are influencing migraines, you instruct the patient to consume particular foods on specific days and to record whether a migraine occurs or not. Your task is to look at these results and then try to determine whether any foods alter the likelihood of a migraine occurring. When you begin the simulation, you will be shown which foods have been consumed on a given day. A rating line will be presented on the screen. The rating line represents a scale from "Migraine certain NOT to occur" to "Migraine certain to occur". The midpoint represents a 50/50 chance that the outcome will/won't occur. You must make a prediction about whether you expect a migraine to occur by clicking on the line. An arrow will then mark the point that you have chosen. When you have made your prediction, you will be shown the information indicating whether a migraine occurred or not. Numerous days will be presented and the foods consumed will sometimes be repeated, so that your ability to predict whether a migraine will occur should improve. Please use the slider scale carefully, only use the extreme ends of the scale if you are absolutely certain that a migraine will or will not occur.

The instructions for the paced condition were amended to include the following: "You will be given 3 seconds to make a prediction. You can move the arrow once it is placed if you are not happy with its position. After 3 seconds a message will appear on the screen indicating whether a migraine occurred or not."

After participants had read these instructions, a screen appeared containing one button labelled "Display next food". Once this button had been pressed, the first training trial began. On each training trial the name of one (for single cues) or two (for compound cues) foods appeared in the top-centre of the screen, and below this appeared a horizontal scale. The left end of this scale was marked "Migraine certain not to occur", the right end "Migraine certain to occur", and a small vertical line marked the midpoint. No pointer was initially positioned on the scale. Instead, when a participant clicked on the scale, a red arrow appeared at that position. The red arrow could be repositioned by clicking on another point on the scale. For the unpaced group, immediately after participants had made a rating, a button labelled "done" appeared at the bottom of the screen beneath the scale bar. For this group, the cues and scale bar stayed on the screen until the "done" button was pressed; this immediately revealed the outcome of that trial presented as a message: "A migraine DID occur" or "A migraine DID NOT occur". The outcome alone remained on the screen for 2 s before a

"display next" button appeared at the bottom of the same screen. The next trial appeared only after the "display next" button was pressed.

For the paced group, the screen displaying the food cue stayed for 3 s, during which participants could place and replace a rating arrow. Regardless of whether or not they actually made a rating, the outcome was shown at the end of the 3 s and stayed on the screen for 2 s, after which the next trial began automatically. Otherwise, all other presentation aspects were the same as those in the unpaced condition.

All participants were given four blocks of training trials. As shown in Table 1, the first two blocks of training trials each contained three of P+ and two each of the T+ and N− trials. This was followed by the introduction FG+ and GH− in the third block, so that this contained two each of P+, T+ and N−, and four of FG+ and GH− trials. P+ was then removed and PX− and LM− introduced so that the fourth and last block of training trials contained two each of T+ and N− and four each of FG+, FH−, LM− and PX− trials. All trials in each block occurred in a sequence that was randomized as each participant logged on.

For compound trials, e.g., PX−, on one trial within a block one cue was presented to the left of the other—for example, "bananas and melon"—and on the other this word order was reversed—for example, "melon and bananas". For each participant, 10 food names from the following list were allocated randomly to each individual cue function (P, X, T, N, L, M, F, G, H, and C): bananas, melon, potatoes, rice, beef, chicken, carrots, tomatoes, lettuce, and biscuits.

After participants had completed training, the following message appeared on the screen: "Now that you have observed the pattern of migraines following different foods, it may be possible for you to anticipate which food or foods influence the occurrence of headaches. In the next phase of the simulation, you will be asked to rate the likelihood of a migraine when different foods are consumed. Please make this judgment on the same slider bar as before, but this time you will not be given feedback as to the accuracy of each prediction." After participants read these instructions they began the test phase. This consisted of three randomized blocks, each block containing one of each of the eight types of test trial shown in Table 1. Instead of reversing the left–right sequence of foods on compound trials (e.g., "potatoes and carrots" vs. "carrots and potatoes") within subject as in training, participants were divided further in the testing phase so as to counterbalance cue sequence across subjects. Thus, 16 participants in the paced group and 15 participants in the unpaced group were given the compound sequences, TX and TN, and the remaining were given the reverse—that is, XT and NT. The scale was the same on test trials as it was in training, but remained on the screen until participants had made a rating. Once a rating was made, a "done" button appeared, which when pressed initiated the next test trial. Thus, the test was self-paced for all participants. No feedback was given on any test trial.

Data analysis. In both experiments, the position of the pointer on the analogue scale was converted into units ranging from 0 ("Migraine certain not to occur") to +100 ("Migraine certain to occur"). Mean scores over the three test trials for each cue were used in the analysis of test data. Test compound cue order (e.g., TX vs. XT) was treated as a separate group factor in a preliminary analysis. In neither of the experiments did this additional group factor produce any detectable main effect or interaction, and thus it is not reported. The main test analysis consisted of planned comparisons that excluded the group factor of compound cue order during the test. A statistical significance level of .05 was used throughout all analyses.

Results

As intended, the paced condition reduced the time during training that a participant spent on

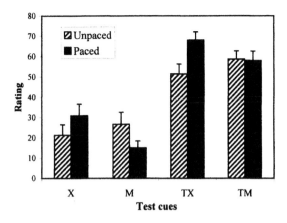

Figure 1. *Experiment 1: Test ratings for critical cues, where X was trained as PX− following training on P+, M was trained in the compound LM−, and T was trained as the single positive transfer stimulus, T+. See Table 1 for details. The paced group was given only 3 s to make a prediction on each trial during training, whereas decision time for the unpaced group was unrestricted.*

making a rating. The mean time per trial in the paced condition was 5.1 s,[1] while in the unpaced condition it was mean 7.4 s, $F(1, 57) > 50$. Many participants in the paced condition failed to make a rating for some of the training trials; on average there were no ratings on 7.2% of trials in this group.

Mean ratings for all test cues are included in Table 1 and those for critical test cues are shown in Figure 1. Planned contrasts between the critical cues X and M for SOC and between TX and TM for inhibitory learning were conducted across the group factor. Thus, there were two important cue by group interactions to indicate that SOC and inhibitory learning were affected by whether or not training had been paced. A higher rating for X than M would indicate SOC, while a lower rating for TX than TM would indicate inhibitory learning, While there were no overall differences between cue X and M or between TX and TM, both $Fs < 1$, both differences interacted with the group factor,

---

[1] The mean time per trial was calculated by dividing the total time for a participant's training session by the number of trials. This average exceeded the nominal time set for the paced condition (5 s) because one self-paced screen at the beginning of the training phase was included in the total training time. This screen was identical in both groups.

Fs (1,57) = 5.29 and 5.80. Test comparisons for SOC, X versus M, and for conditioned inhibition, TX versus TM, were then conducted for each group separately.

In the paced group, X was rated higher than M, $F(1, 29) = 7.26$, but not significantly different from the novel cue C, $F(1, 29) = 2.18$. The reverse pattern was found in the unpaced group, in that X was not different to M, $F < 1$, but was significantly lower than C, $F(1, 28) = 7.89$. As seen in Figure 1, the greater X – M difference following paced training appeared to result from both higher test ratings for X and lower ratings for M in the paced group, although neither of these simple effects was found to be significant. As discussed below, M provided the critical control condition with which to compare X, and the comparisons with C, the novel cue, are more difficult to interpret.

Inhibitory learning was measured in the summation test by comparing TX with TM. In the unpaced group TX tended to be rated lower than TM, but not significantly so, $F(1, 28) = 1.19$. In the paced group, TX was rated significantly higher than TM, a difference consistent with SOC, $F(1, 29) = 12.06$.

Discussion

The main result from this experiment was that a SOC effect was found under paced conditions. That is, restricting participants to making a rating within 3 s during training produced a SOC effect whereby on test cue X was rated higher than cue M. Furthermore, in the present experiment evidence for SOC under paced conditions was also provided by the higher test ratings for TX than for TM. In addition, the critical interaction with group in the present experiment confirmed that SOC is more likely to be detected under paced than under unpaced conditions.

The only possible evidence for inhibitory learning came from the finding of lower ratings by the unpaced group for X than for the novel cue, C. We have previously argued that a novel cue is not an appropriate control for inhibitory learning; it

seems that, because participants have no basis for making any judgement about a cue introduced for the first time on test, they place the pointer around the middle of the scale (Karazinov & Boakes, 2004a), as here (see Table 1). For the same reason C is equally inappropriate as a control cue for SOC; thus the evidence for the latter effect in the paced group—X rated higher than the control cue, M—is not weakened by the failure to find a difference between the ratings for X and C by this group.

The absence of evidence for inhibitory learning in either group contrasts with the results of previous experiments using the same scenario and cues (Karazinov & Boakes, 2004a). However, those experiments used intermixed training and equal numbers of P+ and PX– trials, whereas the cue sequence in this experiment involved the multiphase design in which all P+ trials were presented during the first three quarters of training and all PX– trials were presented in the final quarter. Further, in this experiment, there were only half as many PX– trials as P+ trials. There are a variety of theoretical reasons for believing that the procedure used in the present experiment provides a weak form of training for inhibitory learning (e.g., Mitchell, Livesey, & Lovibond, 2007).

EXPERIMENT 2

There were two aims to this experiment. The first was to attempt to detect both SOC and conditioned inhibition within the same experiment. The second aim was to test whether paced training conditions would facilitate the detection of SOC within a relative cue validity design consisting of intermixed A+ and AB+ trials. Normally such intermixed training leads to reduced excitatory strength for B relative to an overshadowed control stimulus—for example, S, following training on OS+ and no trials with O or S alone (e.g., Aitken, Larkin, & Dickinson, 2000; Chapman, 1991; De Houwer & Beckers, 2003). The question addressed in the present experiment was whether paced training might produce the opposite result—higher ratings for B than for S—which could be attributed to SOC of B resulting from its association with A.

In pursuit of the first aim, and so to facilitate inhibitory learning, eight of each P+ and PX− trials were intermixed. Although there are reasons to think that inhibitory learning can develop with blocked training (e.g., Chapman, 1991), experiments in our laboratory have revealed inhibitory learning more successfully with intermixed training. In pursuit of the second aim intermixed A+, AB+, and OS+ trials were included in training. The complete training design and set of test cues are shown in Table 2.

It may be seen from this table that training also included two fillers, H− and I−. Their purpose was to balance the single positive cues, in that their inclusion meant that there were three positive and three negative single cues, as well as two positive and two negative compound cues. It may be noted that in the previous experiment the training cues were unbalanced. This

allowed the possibility that, for example, learning that a positive outcome was more likely on a single cue than on a compound cue trial may have interfered with learning about the values of particular cues.

Method

Participants

A total of 89 first-year psychology students from the University of Sydney received course credit for taking part in the experiment. According to their time of arrival, participants were allocated to either the paced ($n = 41$) or the unpaced ($n = 48$) condition.

Procedure

The basic procedure was the same as that in the previous experiment, with paced and unpaced training conditions exactly as before. In each of four blocks of training trials each of the trial types listed in Table 2 occurred twice in randomized order—namely, P+, PX−, LM−, T+, N−, A+, AB+, OS+, H−, and I−. The test phase contained the 12 cues listed in Table 2; these included all test cues used in Experiment 1 together with two new control compounds for the summation test, TN and TC, and two stimuli to test for any SOC produced by the relative cue validity training, B and S.

Results

As previously, participants in the paced condition spent less time per trial, mean 5.1 s, than those in the unpaced condition, mean 7.0 s, $F(1, 87) > 100$. Compared to Experiment 1 there were fewer trials without ratings in the paced condition, only 3.0%.

Ratings for all test cues are reported in Table 1, and the critical ratings are also shown in Figure 2. With respect to SOC, the important interaction obtained in Experiment 1 between the X–M difference and group was again found, $F(1, 87) = 4.43$. However, the corresponding interaction for the inhibitory effect, that between the TX

Table 2. *Design and mean test ratings for Experiment 2*

Training cues	Test cues	Ratings Unpaced group	Ratings Paced group
P+	X	11.1	31.7
PX−	M	12.9	20.0
T+	TX	55.0	58.5
N−	TM	59.1	59.8
LM−	TN	57.5	59.8
A+	TC	98.3	68.5
AB+	N	6.6	5.4
OS+	C	41.0	42.4
H−	P	92.4	86.7
I−	T	96.2	89.3
	B	64.0	67.1
	S	66.1	71.5

Note: For training cues, each cue type was presented eight times. Ratings on an ungraduated analogue scale were converted to a scale of 0 ("Migraine certain not to occur") to 100 ("Migraine certain to occur"). Each value corresponds to the test cue listed to its left and represents means over three test trials.

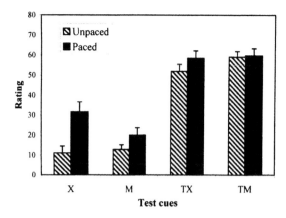

Figure 2. *Experiment 2: Test ratings for critical cues, where X was trained P+ versus PX−, M was trained in the compound LM−, and T was trained as the single positive transfer stimulus, T+. See Table 2 for details. The paced group was given only 3 s to make a prediction on each trial during training, whereas decision time for the unpaced group was unrestricted.*

and TM difference and group, was not found in this experiment, $F(1, 87) = 1.07$.

In analyses of simple effects, the paced group rated X higher than M, $F(1, 40) = 4.58$, but not significantly different from the novel cue C, $F(1, 40) = 2.83$, $p = .10$, while the unpaced group rated both X and M much lower than C, both $Fs(1, 47) > 30$, but no different from each other, $F < 1$. This pattern of results confirms the finding of SOC only with paced training.

With respect to inhibitory learning, planned contrasts for each group separately revealed that the unpaced group gave lower ratings to TX than to TM, $F(1, 47) = 4.20$, but the ratings given to these compounds by the paced group did not differ, $F(1, 40) < 1$. Thus, the experiment achieved its first aim, that of demonstrating that the same basic training could produce both SOC—under paced conditions—and inhibitory learning, as in the unpaced group.

On the other hand, the second aim was not achieved: In neither group did relative cue validity training, A+ and AB+, produce a rating for B that differed from that for the overshadowed control cue, S; for all effects and interactions involving B versus S, $Fs < 1$.

Discussion

The most important result from this experiment was to confirm that the pacing condition made it possible to detect a SOC effect (X rated higher than M) that in this case was produced by conventional conditioned inhibition training, consisting of intermixed P+ and PI− trials. This training produced an overall inhibitory effect (TX rated lower than TM) that appeared to depend on unpaced training. However, the latter conclusion remains tentative because the critical interaction with group was not significant.

One might wonder why the relative cue validity design in this experiment did produce the same SOC effect as did the inhibition design. Theoretically, the second-order learning effect on B in A+, AB+, should have been as large as that on X in P+, PI−. This is because the critical associations, those of the first order association (P+/A+) and the within-compound association (PX/AB), are the same in both designs. A factor that would work against detecting a SOC effect on B is that, because the control for the relative cue validity design, OS+, must also be positively trained, the power to detect the effect is much smaller than when the control is not positively trained, as with the LM− control.

GENERAL DISCUSSION

The main findings from these two experiments were that SOC occurred on cue X following paced training with P+ and PX− cues. Thus, X was rated higher than the control cue M in both experiments. Furthermore, following the blocked training used in Experiment 1, such that all P+ trials preceded PX− trials, the paced group rated TX higher than TM. The latter result was the first time that we have detected a transfer test result in the opposite direction to an inhibitory one. In Experiment 2, but not in Experiment 1, the same training cues given in intermixed sequence resulted in inhibitory learning in that the unpaced group rated TX lower than TM.

What the present study did not quite achieve—although Experiment 2 came close—was a demonstration within the same experiment that both SOC and conditioned inhibition could be obtained depending on variation in some critical parameter. As noted in the Introduction, this aim was inspired by animal learning experiments indicating that brief training on P+ and PX− would result in excitatory conditioning of X—that is, SOC—whereas following more extensive training X became a conditioned inhibitor (Rescorla, 1973; Yin et al., 1994). It is possible that such a result could be obtained in human predictive learning tasks of the present kind, given an appropriate set of conditions. Alternatively, such an outcome might be very difficult to achieve within the present experimental approach because of high variability in the way that human participants perform under these conditions. Thus, some may learn about the inhibitory relationship of X to P much more quickly than others, so that averaging test ratings across participants given the same limited amount of training could mean that inhibitory learning by the quicker participants cancels out any SOC in the slower participants.

The importance of associations between the elements of a compound has been highlighted by analyses of retrospective effects in predictive or causal judgment tasks. In "backward blocking" experiments, for instance, if participants are first trained on AB+, subsequent training on A+ can reduce their ratings of the causal efficacy of B. In explaining such effects in terms of modified Rescorla–Wagner theory (Dickinson & Burke, 1996; Van Hamme & Wasserman, 1994) a critical assumption is that participants need to acquire within-compound associations between A and B. There is good evidence that this assumption is correct (e.g., Dickinson & Burke, 1996). However, this assumption is equally critical for alternative accounts of retrospective effects. One such explanation is in terms of inferential reasoning processes. To explain backward blocking it has been claimed that participants make an explicit logical deduction on test that, if AB and B alone predict exactly the same outcome, then A is not

an effective causal factor. To make this inference participants need to remember that A and B were presented together in compound during training, and there is some evidence that backward blocking occurs to the extent that a participant can explicitly recall that A and B occurred together (De Houwer & Beckers, 2003; Lovibond, Been, Mitchell, Bouton, & Frohardt, 2003; Mitchell, Killedar, & Lovibond, 2005).

What the present evidence for SOC adds to this previous evidence is that associations between cues can directly—and illogically—affect participants' ratings. Thus, while treating X as an inhibitory cue after P+ versus PX− training is consistent with the logical inference approach and can be made consistent with normative contingency models (Karazinov & Boakes, 2004b), SOC is inconsistent with both types of theory. That leaves associative theories and the question of what kind of associative theory is best fitted by the data reported here.

First-generation theories of selective associative learning, such as the Rescorla–Wagner model (Rescorla & Wagner, 1972) or Wagner's (1981) SOP theory, are concerned with associations between successive events and are not easily extended to simultaneous, or within-compound, associations of the kind that are of interest here. These early theories are elemental, in the sense that, when a compound stimulus (e.g., AB) is presented, they assume the elements to be separately encoded and to form separate associative links with subsequent events. This elemental assumption is maintained by more recent theories such as that of McLaren and Mackintosh (2002), in which the development of within-compound associations—links from A to B and from B to A—is of central concern. This provides a ready explanation of SOC. An alternative to an elemental analysis was suggested by Rescorla (1981; see also Rescorla & Durlach, 1981; Rescorla & Freberg, 1978). According to this configural account, SOC occurs as a result of stimulus generalization from an excitatory configural representation to an otherwise neutral element. Thus, in the present case the PX configuration is initially positive, because P alone is consistently reinforced, and inhibitory learning has barely started, and generalization of this excitatory value occurs from PX to X.

However, the detailed model of configural learning first developed by Pearce (1987, 1994) cannot account for SOC. This is because, in contrast to the outline above, PX does not itself gain any excitatory strength as a result of P+ versus PX− training, and thus none can at any stage generalize to X. On the other hand, the recent development of this model to include bidirectional links between input units and configural units can predict SOC early in training, in the way sketched above (Pearce, 2002).

Even if associative learning involving configural units provides the most satisfactory account of SOC in the present study, it does not necessarily follow that it also provides the best account of the inhibitory learning that took place under some conditions. An important finding from the present experiments was that an inhibitory effect on test was found only after intermixed training in which participants could proceed at their own pace. The experiments on conditioned inhibition reported in this issue by Mitchell et al. (2007) led them to conclude that people can only display inhibitory learning if they engage in causal reasoning. It may be noted that their conditions provide ample opportunity for this to take place, in that trials are not paced, and the cognitive load is relatively small, since the number of stimuli involved are far fewer and the number of training trials for each stimulus far greater than in the experiments we have reported here. Furthermore, their scenario includes the use of "herbal remedies" in order, presumably, to evoke participants' beliefs about the preventative function of certain agents in the real world. Even though the present conditions were less likely than theirs to encourage explicit causal reasoning, it is still plausible that such a process produced inhibitory learning under unpaced conditions and that pacing interfered with this process.

The conclusion reached by Mitchell et al. (2007) can be seen as a challenge to search for evidence that, at least under some conditions, people's behaviour is driven by inhibitory associative links in a way that does not involve any form of causal reasoning. If such a process of intuitive inhibitory learning occurred at all in the present experiments, we need to explain why it did not appear under paced conditions. One possibility is that processes occurring before the outcome is known interfere with the acquisition of associations between successive events—for example, learning that X is not followed by the outcome that was expected on the basis of P. It may be possible to test between this and the causal reasoning account, but we have not yet attempted to do so.

As noted by Shanks (2007) in his introduction to this set of articles, "behaviour is sometimes based on rational, cognitive, symbolic thought and sometimes is driven associatively" (p. 297); he then argued that the key question for research on contingency learning is whether "there might be a separate type of thinking (associative) when people make intuitive judgements under conditions of less reflection" (p. 298). The present results indicate that restricting time for reflection represents one condition that encourages the production of purely associative-based judgements.

REFERENCES

Aitken, M. R., Larkin, M. J., & Dickinson, A. (2000). Super-learning of causal judgements. *Quarterly Journal of Experimental Psychology, 53B*, 59−81.

Chapman, G. B. (1991). Trial order affects cue interaction in contingency judgment. *Journal of Experimental Psychology: Learning, Memory and Cognition, 17*, 837−854.

Cheng, P. W. (1997). From covariation to causation: A causal power theory. *Psychological Review, 104*, 367−405.

Cheng, P. W., & Novick, L. R. (1992). Covariation in natural causal induction. *Psychological Review, 99*, 365−382.

Cheng, P. W., Park, P., Yarlas, A. S., & Holyoak, K. J. (1996). A causal power theory of focal sets. In D. R. Shanks, K. J. Holyoak, & D. R. Medin (Eds.), *The psychology of learning and motivation: Vol. 34. Causal learning* (pp. 315−355). San Diego, CA: Academic Press.

De Houwer, J., & Beckers, T. (2003). Secondary task difficulty modulates forward blocking in human contingency learning. *Quarterly Journal of Experimental Psychology, 56B*, 345–357.

Dickinson, A., & Burke, J. (1996). Within-compound associations mediate the retrospective revaluation of causality judgements. *Quarterly Journal of Experimental Psychology, 49B*, 60–80.

Dickinson, A., Shanks, D., & Evenden, J. (1984). Judgement of act–outcome contingency: The role of selective attribution. *Quarterly Journal of Experimental Psychology, 36A*, 29–50.

Holland, P. C., & Rescorla, R. A. (1975). The effects of two ways of de-valuing the unconditioned stimulus after first- and second-order appetitive conditioning. *Journal of Experimental Psychology: Animal Behavior Processes, 1*, 355–363.

Karazinov, D. M. (2005). *Inhibitory learning in human predictive learning.* Unpublished PhD thesis, University of Sydney, New South Wales, Australia.

Karazinov, D. M., & Boakes, R. A. (2004a). Learning about cues that prevent an outcome: Conditioned inhibition and differential inhibition in human predictive learning. *Quarterly Journal of Experimental Psychology, 57B*, 153–178.

Karazinov, D. M., & Boakes, R. A. (2004b). The effectiveness of inhibitors depends on the strength of the positive predictor. *Learning and Behavior, 32*, 348–359.

Leyland, C. M., & Mackintosh, N. J. (1978). Blocking of first- and second-order autoshaping in pigeons. *Animal Learning & Behavior, 6*, 391–394.

Lovibond, P. F. (2003). Causal beliefs and conditioned responses: Retrospective revaluation induced by experience and by instruction. *Journal of Experimental Psychology: Learning, Memory, and Cognition, 29*, 97–106.

Lovibond, P. F., Been, S., Mitchell, C. J., Bouton, M. E., & Frohardt, R. (2003). Forward and backward blocking of causal judgment is enhanced by additivity of effect magnitude. *Memory & Cognition, 31*, 133–142.

McLaren, I. P. L., & Mackintosh, N. J. (2002). Associative learning and elemental representation: II. Generalization and discrimination. *Animal Learning & Behavior, 30*, 177–200.

Mitchell, C. J., Killedar, A., & Lovibond, P. F. (2005). Inference-based retrospective revaluation in human causal judgments requires knowledge of within-compound relationships. *Journal of Experimental Psychology: Animal Behavior Processes, 31*, 418–424.

Mitchell, C. J., Livesey, E., & Lovibond, P. F. (2007). A dissociation between causal judgement and the ease with which a cause is categorized with its effect. *Quarterly Journal of Experimental Psychology, 60*, 400–417.

Mitchell, C. J., & Lovibond, P. F. (2002). Backward and forward blocking in human electrodermal conditioning: Blocking requires an assumption of outcome additivity. *Quarterly Journal of Experimental Psychology, 55B*, 311–329.

Nairne, J. S., & Rescorla, R. A. (1981). Second-order conditioning with diffuse auditory reinforcers in the pigeon. *Learning & Motivation, 12*, 65–91.

Pavlov, I. P. (1927). *Conditioned reflexes,* London: Oxford University Press.

Pearce, J. M. (1987). A model for stimulus generalisation in Pavlovian conditioning. *Psychological Review, 94*, 61–73.

Pearce, J. M. (1994). Similarity and discrimination: A selective review and a connectionist model. *Psychological Review, 101*, 587–607.

Pearce, J. M. (2002). Evaluation and development of a connectionist theory of configural learning. *Animal Learning and Behavior, 30*, 73–95.

Rescorla, R. A. (1969). Pavlovian conditioned inhibition. *Psychological Bulletin, 72*, 77–94.

Rescorla, R. A. (1973). Second order conditioning: Implications for theories of learning. In F. J. McGuigan & D. Lumsden (Eds.), *Contemporary approaches to learning and conditioning* (pp. 127–150). New York: Winston.

Rescorla, R. A. (1981). Simultaneous associations. In P. Harzem & M. Zeiler (Eds.), *Advances in analysis of behavior: Vol. 2. Predictability, correlation and contiguity* (pp. 47–79). Chichester, UK: Wiley.

Rescorla, R. A., & Durlach, P. J. (1981). Within-event learning in Pavlovian conditioning. In N. E. Spear & R. R. Miller (Eds.), *Information processing in animals: Memory mechanisms* (pp. 81–111). Hillsdale, NJ: Lawrence Erlbaum Associates, Inc.

Rescorla, R. A., & Freberg, L. (1978). The extinction of within-flavor associations. *Learning & Motivation, 4*, 411–427.

Rescorla, R. A., & Wagner, A. R. (1972). A theory of Pavlovian conditioning: Variations in the effectiveness of reinforcement and non-reinforcement. In A. H. Black & W. F. Prokasy (Eds.), *Classical conditioning II. Current research and theory* (pp. 64–99). New York: Appleton-Century-Crofts.

Rizely, R. C., & Rescorla, R. A. (1972). Associations in second-order conditioning and sensory preconditioning. *Journal of Comparative & Physiological Psychology, 81*, 1–11.

Shanks, D. R. (1995). *Associative learning theory.* Cambridge, UK: Cambridge University Press.

Shanks, D. R. (2007). Associationism and cognition: Human contingency learning at 25. *Quarterly Journal of Experimental Psychology, 60*, 291–309.

Van Hamme, L. J., & Wasserman, E. A. (1994). Cue competition in causality judgments: The role of non-presentation of compound stimulus elements. *Learning & Motivation, 25*, 127–151.

Wagner, A. R. (1981). SOP: A model of automatic memory processing in animal behavior. In N. E. Spear & R. R. Miller (Eds.), *Information processing in animals: Memory mechanisms* (pp. 5–47). Hillsdale, NJ: Lawrence Erlbaum Associates, Inc.

Ward, W. C., & Jenkins, H. M. (1965). The display of information and the judgment of contingency. *Canadian Journal of Psychology, 19*, 231–241.

Williams, D. A. (1996). A comparative analysis of negative contingency learning in humans and nonhumans. In D. R. Shanks, K. J. Holyoak, & D. R. Medin (Eds.), *The psychology of learning and motivation: Vol. 34. Causal learning* (pp. 89–131). San Diego, CA: Academic Press.

Williams, D. A., & Docking, G. L. (1995). Associative and normative accounts of negative transfer. *Quarterly Journal of Experimental Psychology, 48A*, 976–988.

Yin, H., Barnet, R. C., & Miller, R. R. (1994). Second-order conditioning and Pavlovian conditioned inhibition: Operational similarities and differences. *Journal of Experimental Psychology: Animal Behavior Processes, 20*, 419–428.

THE QUARTERLY JOURNAL OF EXPERIMENTAL PSYCHOLOGY
2007, 60 (3), 461–481

Depressive realism and the effect of intertrial interval on judgements of zero, positive, and negative contingencies

Rachel M. Msetfi

University of Hertfordshire, Hatfield, UK

Robin A. Murphy

University College London, London, UK

Jane Simpson

Institute for Health Research, University of Lancaster, Lancaster, UK

In three experiments we tested how the spacing of trials during acquisition of zero, positive, and negative response–outcome contingencies differentially affected depressed and nondepressed students' judgements. Experiment 1 found that nondepressed participants' judgements of zero contingencies increased with longer intertrial intervals (ITIs) but not simply longer procedure durations. Depressed groups' judgements were not sensitive to either manipulation, producing an effect known as depressive realism only with long ITIs. Experiments 2 and 3 tested predictions of Cheng's (1997) Power PC theory and the Rescorla–Wagner (1972) model, that the increase in context exposure experienced during the ITI might influence judgements most with negative contingencies and least with positive contingencies. Results suggested that depressed people were less sensitive to differences in contingency and contextual exposure. We propose that a context-processing difference between depressed and nondepressed people removes any objective notion of "realism" that was originally employed to explain the depressive realism effect (Alloy & Abramson, 1979).

Learning that behaviour can cause things to occur is a basic requirement to being able to interact adaptively with the environment. In addition to the obvious evidence that people are quite good at learning to control their environments, there is also interesting data that show that people make quite accurate judgements about their degree of control over outcomes (e.g., Wasserman, Chatlosh, & Neunaber, 1983; Wasserman, Elek, Chatlosh, & Baker, 1993). One experimental procedure, used to investigate the psychological mechanisms underlying such learning, involves using discrete trials during which subjects are encouraged to test whether a given response, such as a computer

Correspondence should be addressed to Rachel M. Msetfi, School of Psychology, University of Hertfordshire, Hatfield, Herts. AL10 9AB, UK. E-mail: r.msetfi@herts.ac.uk or Robin A. Murphy, Department of Psychology, Gower Street, University College, London WC1E 6BT, UK. E-mail: robin.murphy@ucl.ac.uk

We thank Esnath Sibanda and Louise Neville for collecting data for Experiment 1. The data from Experiments 2 and 3 formed part of the first author's PhD dissertation.

key press, does or does not cause an outcome, such as a light flash, to occur (e.g., Alloy & Abramson, 1979). The outcome can be programmed by the experimenter to be contingent or noncontingent upon the participant's response. When asked to judge their degree of control over the outcome's occurrence, people generally tend to make judgements that are consistent with the relationship that they are asked to judge (Allan & Jenkins, 1980; Vallée-Tourangeau, Hollingsworth, & Murphy, 1998a; Wasserman et al., 1993).

However, Alloy and Abramson (1979) found that people's mood might alter their perceptions of response–outcome contingencies. They asked nondepressed and depressed students to judge their degree of control over an outcome in two conditions that were both programmed to be non-contingent but differed in the frequency of outcome occurrence. According to Alloy and Abramson, accurate participants should have learnt that there was no relationship between their responses and the outcome in both conditions. They found, however, that when outcomes occurred frequently, nondepressed people seemed to think that they had more control over the outcome occurrence than when it occurred less frequently. Depressed participants, on the other hand, perceived that their behaviour had the same control over the occurrence of the outcome in both conditions. According to Alloy and Abramson the depressed participants did not show an *illusion of control* while the nondepressed did. On the basis of these findings, Alloy and Abramson suggested that depression increased accuracy in the perception of noncontingent relationships. Of course one simple explanation may have been that the nondepressed used the judgement scale in a different way to reflect frequency rather than contingency; however, other more complex explanations were proposed.

One theoretical account of this apparent tendency towards accuracy explains depressive judgements in terms of pessimistic but accurate expectations. In other words, if depressed people, who might expect to have little or no control over their environment, are presented with a situation congruent with these expectations, their judgements will appear to be accurate (e.g., Alloy & Tabachnik, 1984). An alternative interpretation of the depressive realism literature, based on a psychophysical analysis of contingency data, questions whether verbal ratings actually assess sensitivity to the presented contingency (see Allan, Siegel, & Hannah, 2007). However, whether any participant's judgement reflects absolute accuracy assumes that the experimenter is in a privileged position to objectively measure the contingency.

We have suggested that knowing the exact contingency to which a participant is exposed is extremely difficult (see Murphy, Vallée-Tourangeau, Msetfi, & Baker, 2005). For instance, we have found that one particular experimental variable that might not normally be considered by the experimenter to be relevant to participants' judgements—the length of the intertrial interval (ITI)—has a particular influence on judgements (Msetfi, Murphy, Simpson, & Kornbrot, 2005). These findings are described in greater detail below but, briefly, we found that the so-called *illusion of control* with nondepressed is only present in conditions with long intervals between the experimental trials. The theoretical analysis of this effect, which we presented, suggested that the intertrial interval might be being integrated into the perception of contingency. Doing this might radically alter a participant's perception of the programmed contingency. For instance, conditions that are apparently noncontingent from the perspective of the experimenter might be correctly perceived as contingent by the participant. This difference is important for understanding depressive cognition. Indeed the notion of depressive realism (DR) depends upon the assumption that nondepressed people's judgements reflect inaccuracy. In order to illustrate how nondepressed people's apparently optimistic contingency estimates might actually be accurate, the discussion below describes contingency events and shows how the integration of ITIs changes the contingency calculation.

Figure 1 (upper panel) shows how to categorize the four different types of experience that can be used to determine whether any event (in this case the response) and outcome are noncontingent (i.e., independent) or contingent (i.e., related).

	Outcome	
Response	Present	Absent
Present	A	B
Absent	C	D

Positive contingency: ΔP = 0.5

	Light on	Light off	
Button press	20	0	P(O|R) = 1.0
No button press	10	10	P(O|NoR) = .50

ΔP = 1.0 − .50 = 0.5
Power = 0.5/(1 − .5) = 1.0

Zero contingency: ΔP = 0

	Light on	Light off	
Button press	15	5	P(O|R) = .75
No button press	15	5	P(O|NoR) = .75

ΔP = .75 − .75 = 0
Power = 0/(1 − .75) = 0

Negative contingency: ΔP = −0.5

	Light on	Light off	
Button press	10	10	P(O|R) = .50
No button press	20	0	P(O|NoR) = 1.0

ΔP = .50 − 1.0 = −.50
Power = − .5/(1) = − .50

---

40 ITIs included as cell D events

	Light on	Light off	
Button press	20	0	P(O|R) = 1.0
No button press	10	10 + 40	P(O|NoR) = .17

ΔP = 1.0 − .17 = .83
Increase in ΔP = .33
Power = .83/(1 − .17) = 1.0
Increase in Power = 0

	Light on	Light off	
Button press	15	5	P(O|R) = .75
No button press	15	5 + 40	P(O|NoR) = .25

ΔP = .75 − .25 = .50
Increase in ΔP = .50
Power = .50/(1 − .25) = .67
Increase in Power = .67

	Light on	Light off	
Button press	10	10	P(O|R) = .50
No button press	20	0 + 40	P(O|NoR) = 0.33

ΔP = .50 − .33 = .17
Increase in ΔP = .67
Power = .17/(1 − .33) = .25
Increase in Power = .75

Figure 1. *Contingency tables showing (top panel) the four possible combinations of response–outcome information and the generic information from which Δp is calculated, where A, B, C, and D refer to the frequencies of such information.* $\Delta p = A/(A + B) - C/(C + D)$. *The middle panel shows high-density positive, zero, and negative contingencies and the Δp and causal power calculation for each condition. The lower panel shows the effect of adding 40 ITIs, as cell D events, to the Δp and causal power calculations. Note that P(O|R) refers to the conditional probability of the outcome given the presence of the response, and P(O|NoR) refers to the conditional probability of the outcome given the absence of the response.*

The frequency of pairing the response with the outcome (cell A), or the frequency of the response without the outcome (cell B), together define how likely it is that the response will be followed by an outcome. Similarly, the frequency of the outcome by itself (cell C) or the frequency of neither the response nor the outcome (cell D) defines how likely the outcome is to occur in the absence of the response. One frequently used normative measure of the overall relationship, against which to evaluate the accuracy of judgements, is Δp (Allan, 1980). Δp is simply the difference between the probability of the outcome given the response, P(O|R), and the probability of the outcome given no response, P(O|NoR). Δp varies continuously between +1, indicating a perfect positive relationship, through zero, indicating no relationship, to −1, indicating a perfectly negative relationship. A positive value of Δp indicates that the response is related to an increase in the likelihood of the occurrence of the outcome, whereas a negative value of Δp indicates that the presence of the response decreases the likelihood of the outcome occurring.

If judgements are based on a cognitive process that mirrors this relationship, as some have proposed (Cheng, 1997), then one might conclude that judgements were accurate. However, the finding that judgements sometimes deviate from this, or other normative measures, has controversially been used to support the idea that people are not accurate (e.g., Alloy & Abramson, 1979; Dickinson, Shanks, & Evenden, 1984; Smedslund, 1963).

The problem for any claim of an assessment of accuracy is that it assumes that the experimenter can easily identify all the event information that the participant will recruit for their judgement. During a discrete trial training procedure, participants experience trials during which they are encouraged to either perform a response (cells A and B) or withhold responding (cells C and D), thereby providing them with the only relevant data with which to form their judgements. The intertrial intervals in these tasks are simply empty periods during which the participants wait for the next opportunity to learn. However, the intertrial interval, like all experience, could be considered as one of the four relevant event conjunctions that represent the information relevant for judging response–outcome contingency (cell D: See also Baker, Murphy, Vallée-Tourangeau, & Mehta, 2001).

In previous work we showed that the length of the ITI does influence participants' perceptions of contingency (Msetfi et al., 2005; Murphy et al., 2005). Both nondepressed and depressed participants were exposed to the zero-contingency condition, shown in Figure 1, with either short (3-s) or long (15-s) intertrial intervals. Nondepressed people's judgements were significantly more positive in the long than in the short intertrial interval conditions. Moreover, like Alloy and Abramson (1979) this effect was present in high outcome frequency (see Figure 1: $\Delta p = .75 - .75 = 0$) but not low outcome frequency zero contingencies ($\Delta p = .25 - .25 = 0$). This is exactly the result that one might predict if the intertrial intervals were being perceived as evidence—that when participants do not perform the response, no outcome occurs (cell D event). It follows that if ITIs are included in a contingency calculation as cell D

events, then a zero contingency relationship, which might be programmed during the discrete trials by the experimenter, might actually be perceived as a positive contingency by the participant. Figure 1 (middle column, middle panel) shows the traditional calculation of Δp for a 40-trial zero contingency. A 40-trial procedure also includes 40 ITI periods and the impact of including 40 ITIs into the contingency calculation as cell D events is also displayed (middle column, lower panel) and results in an increase in Δp. This increase occurs because in each case extra cell D events only influence one of the two conditional probabilities that describe Δp. They decrease $P(O|NoR)$, while having no impact on the $P(O|R)$, and furthermore this influence should be less dramatic in a low outcome frequency zero contingency. The inclusion of 40 ITIs as cell D events is, of course, purely arbitrary as it is unknown whether one ITI is perceived as more than or less than one cell D event. However, any additional cell D events included in the contingency calculation will have the effect of reducing the $P(O|NoR)$ in the manner described above.

There are at least two possible reasons why nondepressed people's judgements of a zero contingency increased with longer intertrial intervals. The first is related to potential changes to the predictive value of the absence of responding. Lengthening the ITI may increase the perception that, in the absence of any responding, the other experimental cues (the context) fail to elicit the outcome, in spite of the fact that participants have no opportunity to respond during the ITI. The second source of the effect may lie with the difference in the session lengths between short and long ITI conditions. It is possible that the change in judgements reflects greater confidence that might emerge with the longer training following longer ITIs or perhaps some effect due to general habituation to the experimental setting.

EXPERIMENT 1

In the first experiment reported here, to rule out an explanation of the effect based on simple exposure, we manipulated both the ITI length and session length to test which of the two factors results in the increased judgements of zero contingencies. The design involved crossing two levels of ITI length (3 s, 15 s) with two levels of training length (320 s, 800 s), which consequently required varying the number of trials experienced by the four groups. If ITI length is the crucial variable, then both groups of control participants trained with the long ITI should show higher judgements of the zero contingencies, regardless of session length or number of trials. Depressed participants should show no sensitivity to the change in ITI length, and their judgements might be expected to be generally lower than nondepressed participants' judgements.

However, a further variable, which might potentially contribute to the effects we are discussing, is the number of responses that participants perform during the procedure. For example, consider the case of a zero-contingency condition, where the P(O|R) and P(O|NoR) are programmed to be .75. If the participant did not evenly distribute responding, then it is possible that the programmed contingency might drift from the nominal value programmed. In the extreme case, if the participant responded on every trial then they would have no information about withholding responses, and this might lead them to experience a positive contingency with the P(O|R) > P(O|NoR) and consequently higher judgements. Indeed, Matute (1996) showed how higher rates of responding were linked to higher judgements, although this tendency was observed only in conditions where participants were not explicitly instructed to sample response and no-response trials equally. Given that such fluctuations in P(R) could produce long ITI depressive realism effects, in the present experiments we report the P(R) in order to examine this possibility.

Method

Participants

University students received course credit for their participation and were assigned to the nondepressed ($n = 36$) and depressed groups ($n = 39$) on the basis of their scores on the Beck Depression Inventory (BDI: Beck, Ward, Mendelson, Mock, & Erbaugh, 1961). In all three experiments reported here, scores of 8 or below indicated no depression, and scores of 9 or above indicated mild depression. The depressed group produced significantly higher BDI scores ($M = 14.10$, $SE = 0.79$) than did the nondepressed group ($M = 3.78$, $SE = 0.41$), $t(56.342) = 11.578$, $p < .001$, two-tailed, equal variances not assumed. Of the nondepressed participants, 19 were female, and 17 were male. Of the depressed participants, 25 were female, and 14 were male. The distribution of males and females did not differ across the nondepressed and depressed groups, $\chi^2(1) = 0.990$, $p = .320$. Participants were pseudorandomly assigned to the four experimental conditions, and the resulting sample sizes are shown in Table 1.

Design

In this experiment, we used a 2 (ITI length: short, 3 s; long, 15 s) × 2 (overall procedure time: short, 320 s; long, 800 s) × 2 (mood: nondepressed, depressed) fully factorial between-subjects design. Unlike our previous experiments in which all treatments received the same number (40) of trials, in this experiment the number of trials was a function of the combination of ITI length and procedure time. The short ITI length and short procedure time group received 40 trials as before, but the short ITI length group with the long procedure received 100 trials. In the two

Table 1. *Count of nondepressed and depressed participants in each experimental condition*

ITI length[a]	Overall procedure time[a]	Nondepressed	Depressed
3	320	10	8
15	800	9	9
3	800	7	10
15	320	10	12

Note: ITI = intertrial interval.
[a]In seconds.

long ITI treatments, the number of trials was 16 and 40 for the short and long procedure times, respectively. A computerized version of the contingency judgement task used by Alloy and Abramson (1979) was used to obtain judgements of control (for full details, see Msetfi et al., 2005). The task was a high-density zero-contingency condition (shown in Figure 1), where the P(light|response) was .75, and the P(light|no response) was also .75. This contingency was chosen as it is the one in which both Alloy and Abramson and Msetfi et al. found reliable differences between the depressed and control groups. The total numbers of trials, cell frequencies, and Δp for each experimental condition are shown in Table 1. Participants judged their control over light onset on a scale that varied from 0 to 100, where 0 = *no control* and 100 = *total control*. Intermediate values represented varying degrees of partial control.

Apparatus
The presentation of experimental events was programmed using REALbasic (Version 3) software.

Procedure
Participants were briefed verbally and in writing as to the nature of the task requirements and then completed the BDI. Task instructions, displayed on the computer screen, explained how participants were to judge how much control their pressing of a button had over a light switching on and informed them about the necessity of pressing the button on some trials but not on others on an approximately equal number of occasions (see Appendix A). At the beginning of the session, a light bulb graphic in its "off state" appeared on the screen. Each trial was constructed so that there was a 3-s opportunity for the participant to press the button using the space bar on the computer keyboard. This period was signalled by an on-screen message saying, "You may press the button now!" This was followed by a 2-s period, on both response and no response trials, where the light bulb graphic either switched to the "on state" or remained in the "off state". Each trial was separated by an ITI period (3 s or 15 s) where the

light bulb graphic in its "off state" remained on the screen. The probability of the light switching on both after a response and after no response was .75. Judgements of control were made after all experimental trials were completed. Participants were then debriefed.

Results and discussion

Judgements of perceived control over light onset in the high-density zero-contingency condition with short and long ITIs and short and long procedure times are shown in Figure 2. The data suggest that, whereas the nondepressed groups' judgements increased with the longer ITI, this effect was not influenced by the overall procedure time. Depressed participants' judgements, in contrast, were not influenced by either factor.

The data were analysed using a fully factorial analysis of variance, with ITI length (3 s, 15 s), overall procedure time (320 s, 800 s), and mood (nondepressed, depressed) as between-subjects

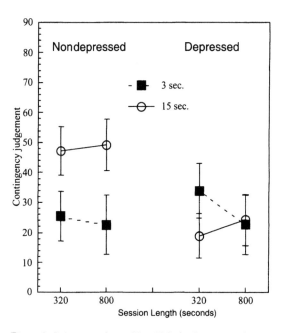

Figure 2. *Judgements of control in a high-density zero-contingency condition as a function of intertrial interval length, overall procedure time, and mood from Experiment 1. Error bars correspond to the standard error of the mean.*

factors. The alpha level was set at .05 unless stated otherwise. The two-way interaction between ITI length and mood was significant, $F(1, 67) = 6.53$, $p = .01$, $MSE = 669.15$, $\eta^2 = .09$. None of the other main effects or interactions reached the level of significance (all $ps > .15$, all $\eta^2 < .03$). A simple effects analysis of the two-way interaction showed that the nondepressed groups' judgements were higher in the long ITI conditions than in the short ITI conditions, $F(1, 67) = 7.72$, $p = .01$, $MSE = 669.15$, $\eta^2 = .09$. However, the depressed groups' judgements were not influenced by ITI length ($F < 1$).

Response rates. The rate of responding for each participant was converted to a probability of response and was analysed using the same procedure as that described above. The mean probability of response for each experimental condition is shown in Table 2.

The analysis showed that the probability of responding was generally higher for nondepressed participants ($M = .595$, $SE = .014$) than for depressed participants ($M = .543$, $SE = .017$), $F(1, 67) = 5.06$, $p = .028$, $MSE = .008$, $\eta^2 = .07$. Participants also made more responses when the overall procedure time was short ($M = .602$, $SE = .014$) than when it was long ($M = .529$, $SE = .016$), $F(1, 67) = 11.776$, $p = .001$, $MSE = .008$, $\eta^2 = .15$. None of the other main effects or interactions were reliable (all $ps > .545$, all $\eta^2 < .006$).

Table 2. *Mean probability of response in each of the conditions in Experiment 1*

		Mood	
ITI length[a]	Overall procedure time[a]	Nondepressed	Depressed
3	320	.613 (.022)	.588 (.034)
3	800	.544 (.023)	.500 (.034)
15	320	.644 (.028)	.568 (.027)
15	800	.561 (.026)	.517 (.035)

Note: ITI = intertrial interval. Standard errors of the mean are shown in parentheses.
[a]In seconds.

Taken together, these findings suggest that the increased judgements observed with longer ITIs are not a function of the increased session length. It is also quite interesting that when ITI length was constant but trials were manipulated (in order to increase procedure time), there was no effect of the number of trials. Previous studies have reported trial effects on contingency judgements (Dickinson et al., 1984; Shanks, 1985), although these effects have been observed using a continuous monitoring procedure (see Baker, Berbrier, & Vallée-Tourangeau, 1989, for a more detailed discussion of why these effects may have occurred).

Even though both mood and overall procedure time were shown to influence the P(R), the observed differences were not large enough to produce fluctuations in the programmed contingency. Moreover, ITI length alone, or in interaction with mood, did not produce differences in the P(R). This result then, is consistent with the conclusion that with long ITIs, nondepressed participants perceive a stronger relation between responding and the occurrence of the outcome.

EXPERIMENT 2

So far we have only studied the effect of ITIs on putative zero contingency learning. The reason for this is that previous studies had suggested that nonzero contingencies do not elicit differences between depressed and nondepressed participants (Alloy, Abramson, & Kossman, 1985; Lennox, Bedell, Abramson, Raps, & Foley, 1990; Vasquez, 1987). Alloy and Abramson suggested that nonzero contingencies might match the expectations that drive judgements in nondepressed participants, whereas zero contingencies do not. This is because, in zero-contingency conditions, nondepressed people's judgements reflect an optimistic bias because they are more likely to expect to have control over outcomes than they actually do (Ackermann & DeRubeis, 1991; Alloy & Abramson, 1979; Alloy & Tabachnik, 1984). In contrast depressed people have unbiased expectations regardless of contingency. Consistent with this prediction there is no evidence, so far, that depressive realism effects occur in nonzero-contingency conditions. However, the possible role of the ITI that we have described can also inform the issue of whether nonzero contingencies might produce mood differences. Positive contingencies are in fact predicted to be less susceptible to ITI effects than are zero contingencies. Furthermore the ITI analysis suggests that the effects might be as strong or stronger with negative contingencies.

According to our analysis, ITIs influence the overall contingency because, if conceptualized as extra cell D events, they reduce the probability of the outcome in the absence of the response, $P(O|NoR)$. However, the effect is predicted to be determined by the specific level of contingency. Consider the high-density zero contingency displayed in Figure 1. If 40 ITIs are included as extra cell D events, the $P(O|NoR)$ decreases from .75 to .25, with a corresponding increase in Δp from 0 to .5. However, in a positive-contingency condition (Figure 1, left column), where the $P(O/R)$ is 1.0, and the $P(O|NoR)$ is .5, the $P(O|NoR)$ decreases from .5 to .17, with the potential increase in Δp being from .5 to .83. Therefore, with the same change in cell D, the increase to the overall relationship is smaller for positive contingencies. In contrast, a negative-contingency condition, where the Δp is −.5 (Figure 1, right column) the change in contingency is greatest, with the contingency going from −.5 to .17. Therefore, changes to $P(O|NoR)$ might be expected to influence negative contingencies more than zero and zero more than positive contingencies. Therefore, what have hitherto been referred to as depressive realism effects, but in our terms the tendency for nondepressed participants to produce judgements that varied from the normative expectations of the experimenter, might be more readily observable in negative and zero contingencies than in positive-contingency conditions. This might explain previous failures to find them in positive contingencies. It is worth noting that this general pattern of changes requires choosing contingencies that are matched on overall number of trials.

The prediction stated above is shared by most theories of contingency learning although for different reasons. The Power PC model (Cheng, 1997), for example, assumes that judgements are based on the intuitive notion of causal power. Generative causal power can be calculated by dividing ΔP by the denominator: $1 - P(O|NoR)$ or in the case of preventative power simply by $P(O|NoR)$. Therefore any reduction in the $P(O|NoR)$, because of the inclusion of extra ITI or D cell events, would result in an increase in both the numerator and the denominator of the equation, as well as the resulting causal power. As in the analysis presented above, the ITI is likely to have less effect on causal power in conditions where the Δp is already positive (see Figure 1).

The associative Rescorla–Wagner model (RWM: Rescorla & Wagner, 1972) makes similar predictions to Δp although for different reasons. In associative language, two associations, the response–outcome association and the context–outcome association, compete for associative strength. The strength of the response–outcome association increases to the extent that the context–outcome association decreases or extinguishes. One interpretation of the increased judgements found with extra intertrial interval experience is that the ITI serves to extinguish the association between the contextual cues and the outcome. However, the difference between the two ITI conditions (short and long) for positive contingencies is predicted to be smaller than that for zero contingencies. Like the Δp and Power PC models, this ITI effect would be predicted to be less apparent in positive contingencies. The aim of the next two experiments was to extend the ITI analysis to conditions with nonzero levels of contingency.

We made two changes to the previous procedure. One involved an attempt to measure the contextual learning that might be taking place during this task, and the other involved shortening the length of the ITI in the short ITI conditions. Previous studies of human contextual learning (e.g., Vallée-Tourangeau, Murphy, Drew, & Baker, 1998b) and animal contextual conditioning

(Murphy & Baker, 2004), which have measured contextual learning using a discrete constantly present cue to represent the context, have found evidence of the reciprocal learning between discrete cues and contextual cues. Furthermore, there is direct evidence that increasing the intervals between trials improves learning about the target stimulus (or response) relative to massing trials, in both animals (Gibbon, Baldock, Locurto, Gold, & Terrace, 1977; Holland, 2000) and humans (Mercier & Parr, 1996). The following experiment included a constantly present cue, and we asked participants to judge the constant cues. However, in order not to contaminate the target cue ratings, context judgements were always taken following judgements of the target.

In order to maximize the difference between the short and long ITI conditions the length of the short ITI in these experiments was reduced from 3 to 0.5 seconds. A shorter ITI should be expected to decrease contextual extinction and therefore the context's impact on judgements, which might then be predicted to strengthen the contrast between the short and long ITI conditions.

Method

Participants

A total of 96 university students were recruited for this experiment using a mass screening procedure and were paid £5 for their participation. They were required to fill in the BDI before being invited to participate in the experiment. On arrival, participants filled in the BDI again and were assigned to the depressed and nondepressed groups as described previously with the constraint that there should be equal numbers of males and females in each group. Experimental conditions ($n = 12$) were matched on age and years of education, $F(1, 88) = 2.91$, $p = .09$, $MSE = 34.97$, and $F(1, 88) = 0.51$, $p = .48$, $MSE = 3.44$, respectively. As expected, depressed groups had significantly higher BDI scores ($M = 16.94$, $SE = 1.05$) than nondepressed groups ($M = 3.27$, $SE = 0.38$), $F(1, 88) = 150.99$, $p < .001$, $MSE = 29.69$.

Design

The experiment utilized a 2 (contingency: zero, positive) × 2 (length of intertrial interval: short, long) × 2 (mood: nondepressed, depressed) × 2 (sex: female, male) fully factorial between-subjects design. Participants were exposed to either a high-density zero (.75/.75) or positive (1.0/.5) contingency condition. The ITI was either short (0.5 s) or long (15 s), and participants were either depressed or nondepressed. Participants made judgements about their own control over the outcome when making the response. They also made similar judgements about a constantly present context cue, an on-screen button that remained in the "on" position throughout the experimental task.

Data analysis. The data were analysed using a multivariate analysis of variance (MANOVA) with ITI length (short, long), contingency (zero, positive), mood (nondepressed, depressed), and sex (female, male) as between-subjects factors with judgements of the response and the context treated as two dependent variables. The MANOVA analysis allows one to determine whether the four factors influence ratings of the response cue and the context cue in the same manner and whether judgements of zero and positive contingencies differ. As sex had no reliable effects on judgements this factor was excluded from further analyses. Probability of response data was also analysed using a univariate analysis of variance (ANOVA) including the same factors as those described above.

Procedure

The procedure was the same as that for Experiment 1 except that there was a variation in task instructions in order to accommodate the introduction of the new context button. Participants were asked to imagine a scenario in which they were scientists testing a piece of experimental apparatus (see Appendix B). Participants were shown a picture of the apparatus, which comprised a small box containing a visible light bulb. Mounted on the apparatus were two buttons— "A" and "B". Button B (the constantly present context) was stuck in the "on" position and could not be pressed. Button A was the only button that participants could press, using the space bar on the keyboard, to assess the extent of their control over light onset. Participants were informed that they would make two judgements, the first about their own control over light onset when pressing Button A and the second about Button B's control over light onset. There was a 3-s button-pressing opportunity signalled by an on-screen message, "You may press the button now!" This was followed by a 2-s period when the light either switched on or remained off. Each trial was separated by an intertrial interval that was 0.5 s long in the short conditions and 15 s long in the long conditions. After completing the 40 experimental trials, participants made their judgements.

Results and discussion

Judgements were made about control over light onset in zero- and positive-contingency conditions with short and long ITIs and are shown in Figure 3. Response judgements appeared to be influenced by contingency and ITI length, whereas context judgements were not.

These observations were examined using an MANOVA. There were no reliable main effects or interactions involving the context judgements. Overall the level of contingency influenced

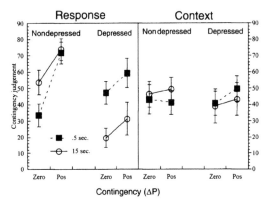

Figure 3. Mean judgements of control for the response and the context in zero and positive contingencies with short and long intertrial intervals as a function of mood from Experiment 2. Error bars represent the standard error of the mean.

response judgements, with positive contingencies judged to be higher than zero contingencies, $F(1, 88) = 14.70$, $p < .001$, $\eta^2 = .14$, $MSE = 689.16$. The ITI length by mood interaction was significant, $F(1, 88) = 13.13$, $p < .001$, $\eta^2 = .13$, $MSE = 689.16$, as was the main effect of mood, $F(1, 88) = 12.35$, $p = .001$, $\eta^2 = .12$, $MSE = 689.16$. None of the other effects or interactions involving response judgements reached the level of significance. Although the three-way interaction between contingency, mood, and ITI length was not reliable, it was necessary to conduct further comparisons involving the contingency factor in order to assess hypotheses about ITI effects being dependent on levels of contingency. Therefore, seven further comparisons were then carried out on the response data with the alpha level adjusted to a conservative value of .007 using the Bonferroni procedure.

There was no evidence that nondepressed people's judgements increased as a function of ITI length in the positive-contingency condition, $F < 1$. Although depressed people's judgements of the same condition appeared to be lower in the long ITI condition, this difference was not significant at the adjusted alpha level, $F(1, 88) = 6.74$, $p = .01$, $\eta^2 = .01$, $MSE = 689.16$.

Depressive realism effects are usually evidenced by nondepressed people's judgements being higher than depressed people's judgements. This was not evident in short-ITI conditions, as both mood groups made similar judgements when the contingency was zero, $F(1, 88) = 1.63$, $p = .21$, $\eta^2 = .003$, $MSE = 689.16$, and when it was positive, $F(1, 88) = 1.36$, $p = .25$, $\eta^2 = .003$, $MSE = 689.16$. However, in contrast, when the ITI was long nondepressed people's judgements were higher than depressed people's judgements at both zero, $F(1, 88) = 10.11$, $p = .002$, $\eta^2 = .02$, $MSE = 689.16$, and positive levels of contingency, $F(1, 88) = 15.66$, $p = .0002$, $\eta^2 = .03$, $MSE = 689.16$. This result replicates previous findings involving long ITIs and depressive realism in zero contingencies and extends them to positive contingencies. It is worth noting that the basic difference between long and short ITI conditions for the nondepressed approached the unadjusted level of significance, $F(1, 88) = 3.51, p < .06, \eta^2 = .001, MSE = 689.16$. It is also worth noting that an effect size calculated for this comparison using the standardized difference between the means (Hedges's g) was 0.79, which is generally considered to be a large effect size. Given this and that we have found this result several times, there is some confidence in accepting this result.

Response rates. The likelihood of participants eliciting a response for all experimental conditions is shown in Table 3.

An analysis of these scores showed that the only factor to affect the P(R) was contingency, with zero contingencies generally producing a higher probability of response ($M = .550, SE = .015$) than positive contingencies ($M = .496, SE = .011$), $F(1, 88) = 8.37, p = .005, \eta^2 = .00, MSE = .008$. None of the other main effects or interactions were reliable (all $ps > .11$, all $\eta^2 < .03$).

The results of the present experiment provide support for the hypothesis that ITI effects would be less evident in positive-contingency conditions, although there was no evidence that the context cue elicited differential judgements. Consistent with predictions of the PPC model, the specific positive-contingency condition used in this experiment produced no evidence of increases in nondepressed people's judgements with long ITI conditions. The data did suggest, however, that depressive realism effects were present in long ITI conditions at both zero and positive levels of contingency. It is also worth pointing out that the depressed people's judgements actually

Table 3. *Probability of response for each of the conditions in Experiment 2*

Contingency	ITI length	Mood	
		Nondepressed	*Depressed*
Zero	Short	.529 (.015)	.585 (.046)
	Long	.527 (.028)	.558 (.021)
Positive	Short	.508 (.007)	.494 (.021)
	Long	.500 (.009)	.483 (.037)

Note: ITI = intertrial interval. Standard errors of the mean are shown in parentheses.

seemed to decrease with longer ITIs. A nonreliable trend for this difference was also reported by Msetfi et al. (2005). This result suggests that depression may be consistent with a decrease in judgements with long ITIs. This finding and its implications are discussed further in the General Discussion.

EXPERIMENT 3

The results of Experiment 2 were consistent with the RWM and Power PC model predictions for a weaker effect in positive contingencies. No reliable difference was found for the nondepressed group between long and short ITI conditions. Of course this inference requires acceptance of the null hypothesis, although in the same experiment the ITI effect was found with zero contingencies. Recall, however, that both models predict that ITI effects should be evident in negative contingencies. We test for evidence of the ITI effect with a negative-contingency condition in Experiment 3. Some previous depressive realism studies have examined judgements of negative contingencies and found no mood differences (Alloy & Abramson, 1979; Kapci & Cramer, 1999; Lennox et al., 1990). However, these studies all used unidirectional 0 to 100 scales. That is, both positive and negative relationships were to be translated to a positive scale. This type of scale includes both the negative ("I prevent the outcome.") and positive ("I produce the outcome.") aspects in the "to what extent do I control the occurrence of the outcome" judgements. So nonzero judgements would indicate some degree of control whether positive or negative. The use of this scale mitigated against finding mood contingency interactions. The following experiment used a bidirectional scale in order to allow negative judgements.

Method

Participants

A total of 48 university students were recruited for this experiment using the same mass screening procedure as that described in the previous experiment and were paid £5 for their participation. Depressed participants scored significantly higher ($M = 16.50$, $SE = 1.12$) on the BDI than did their nondepressed counterparts ($M = 4.13$, $SE = 0.61$), $F(1, 45) = 94.74$, $p < .001$. Experimental conditions ($n = 12$) were also matched on a range of demographic variables, including sex, age, years of education, and National Adult Reading Test scores (all $Fs < 1.6$). However, nondepressed participants had higher digit span scores ($M = 7.21$, $SE = 0.25$) than did depressed participants ($M = 6.52$, $SE = 0.22$), $F(1, 45) = 4.32$, $p < .05$.

Design

The experiment was a fully factorial 2 (mood: depressed, nondepressed) × 2 (ITI length: short, 0.5 s, long, 15 s) × 2 (sex: male, female) fully factorial between-subjects design. The same judgement task as that used in Experiment 2 was employed in the present experiment. In this task, the contingency between the response (pressing Button A) and the outcome (light onset) was programmed to be negative. The P(O|R) was .5, and the P(O|NoR) was 1.0, and therefore the programmed Δp in all conditions was a high outcome density, moderately negative contingency (See Figure 1, right column). The contingency judgements reported in the previous experiments were all made using a unidirectional, 0 to 100 judgement scale (where 0 represented "no control", and 100 indicated "total control"). A bidirectional scale, ranging from −100 (total preventative control) through 0 (no control) to +100 (total causative control), was used in this experiment. The change in judgement scale also required a change in the instructions to introduce the idea that pressing the button might prevent light onset from occurring.

Data analysis. The data were analysed using a similar procedure as that described in the previous experiment. None of the main effects or interactions involving sex approached the level of significance (all $ps > .2$, all $\eta^2 < .08$), so this factor was removed from the model. It might be

considered desirable to enter any nonmatched variable into the analysis as a covariate, although see Miller and Chapman (2001) for an opposing view. However, 1 participant did not complete the digit span test, and including digit span as a covariate would have entailed excluding this participant's data from the analysis. All analyses were conducted both including and excluding the covariate. Digit span had no significant effects on judgements ($F < 1$), and excluding the covariate made no difference to the subsequently reported effects. In order to preserve the equal numbers of participants in each experimental group ($n = 12$), digit span was not included in the reported data analysis.

Procedure

The instructions only differed from those used in Experiment 2 in that they included reference to the possibility that the response could actually prevent the occurrence of the outcome (see Appendix C).

Results and discussion

The judgements of response and context from Experiment 3 are shown in Figure 4. It seems that, as with Experiment 2, the experimental manipulation did not influence judgements of the context cue but appeared to have a strong interactive effect on the response judgements.

The data were analysed using an MANOVA, where mood (depressed, nondepressed) and ITI length (short, long) were between-subjects factors, and judgements of the response and the discrete context were the two dependent variables. There were no reliable main effects or interactions involving the context cue ($Fs < 1$).

However, for the response cue, the interaction between mood and ITI length suggested that the mood groups responded differently to the ITI manipulation, $F(1, 44) = 10.45$, $p = .002$, $\eta^2 = .19$, $MSE = 1,088.47$. None of the main effects reached the level of significance ($Fs < 1$). Further comparisons showed that, as expected, nondepressed participants' judgements increased

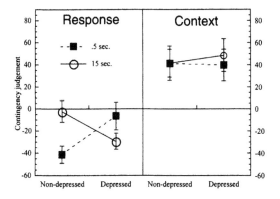

Figure 4. *Judgements of the response and the discrete context's control over the outcome in a high-density negative-contingency condition, as a function of mood and intertrial interval length from Experiment 3. Error bars represent the standard error of the mean.*

Table 4. *Probability of response for all conditions in Experiment 3*

ITI length	Mood	
	Nondepressed	Depressed
Short	.535 (.014)	.554 (.014)
Long	.540 (.016)	.525 (.010)

Note: ITI = intertrial interval. Standard errors of the mean are shown in parentheses.

significantly from very negative in short-ITI conditions to a level close to zero in long-ITI conditions, $F(1, 44) = 8.24$, $p = .006$, $\eta^2 = .11$, $MSE = 1,088.47$. Depressed people's judgements were significantly more negative in long-ITI conditions than were nondepressed people's judgements, $F(1, 44) = 4.00$, $p = .05$, $\eta^2 = .05$, $MSE = 1,088.47$. This showed that although depressed people's judgements did not change as a function of ITI length, $F(1, 44) = 2.89$, $p = .10$, $\eta^2 = .03$, $MSE = 1,088.47$, they were unexpectedly higher than nondepressed people's judgements in short-ITI conditions, $F(1, 44) = 6.62$, $p = .014$, $\eta^2 = .09$, $MSE = 1,088.47$.

Response rates. The probabilities of response for each experimental condition are shown in Table 4. The analysis showed that none of the main effects or interactions approached the level of significance (all $ps > .22$, all $\eta^2 < .03$).

GENERAL DISCUSSION

In three experiments, the relationship between mood, ITI length, and the strength of contingency judgements was examined. The findings support

the idea that nondepressed peoples' judgements are influenced by ITI in a manner consistent with contingency theory, but that depressed people's judgements are not. The implications of these findings for models of contingency learning and for depressive realism are discussed in turn.

Contingency learning

The results of our previous work on depressive realism (Msetfi et al., 2005; Murphy et al., 2005) suggested that longer periods of intertrial interval during learning increase contingency estimates of high-density zero contingencies but did not exclude the possibility that this effect was due to the increase in overall procedure time that accompanies the longer ITI conditions. However, Experiment 1 showed that judgements increased with longer ITIs specifically but did not increase with longer procedure times.

The results of all three experiments also support the general prediction that the ITI effects found with nondepressed participants depended upon the specific contingency tested rather than the distinction between zero and nonzero contingencies made by Alloy and Abramson (1979). As further evidence, the order of effect sizes is consistent with the idea that the effect might be strongest with the negative contingencies we tested and gradually weaker with the zero and positive contingencies. Effect sizes (ES) for each relevant comparison, with nondepressed participants, were calculated using Hedges's *g* (Hedges, 1982), an unbiased estimator of Cohen's *d* (Cohen, 1977), which is scale independent.[1] The ITI effect produced a large ES in negative-contingency conditions (Experiment 3: $g = 1.22$), a medium to large effect in zero contingencies (Experiment 1: $g = 0.84$; Experiment 2: $g = 0.79$) and no perceptible effect when the contingency was positive (Experiment 2: $g = 0.09$).

One associative model that has been applied to human contingency learning, the Rescorla–Wagner model, also predicts this ordinal pattern when ITIs are included as nonreinforced context experience. It should be noted that this prediction was based on the particular set of contingencies that we tested and is partially determined by the exact set of cell frequencies. Figure 5 shows that for any contingency, the increase in Δp, due to increased frequency of cell D events, is positively correlated with the frequency of outcomes. It was for this reason that we argued previously that the inclusion of ITIs into contingency judgements might be also responsible for outcome density effects and showed that outcome density effects were only present in long-ITI conditions (Experiment 2: Msetfi et al., 2005). However, if outcome frequency is held constant, whether low, medium, or high, the ordinal pattern of ITI effects should hold. However, it is unlikely that low outcome frequency conditions would produce perceptible ITI effects in any contingency given that the maximum difference in Δp is predicted to be small.

We also sought to examine whether judgements of a constantly present cue, intended to represent the context, would be influenced by the change in the ITI. During long ITI periods in the absence of the outcome, the context might be predicted to extinguish (i.e., lose association with the outcome). However, contextual learning, as measured by judgements of the button that was always on, was not influenced by any of the experimental manipulations, including contingency and ITI length. This could be taken to indicate that

ITI effects do not occur due to context extinction as some associative models suggest (e.g., RWM). Alternatively, a more cautious conclusion given other evidence that judgements of a constantly present cue do change as a function of contingency (Vallée-Tourangeau et al., 1998b), might be that the constantly present cue, used in these experiments, was ineffective. The context button may have simply been disregarded. Alternatively, the context judgements may have been contaminated by the target judgements. The lack of counterbalancing during the collection of judgements leaves this a possibility.

The Power PC model of causal judgements (Cheng, 1997) also predicts the pattern of ITI effects that we have observed, if longer ITIs increase the frequency of cell D events, as seems to be the case. Figure 1 shows how extra cell D events differentially influence power in negative, zero, and positive contingencies. Although ITIs might be predicted to influence causal power to a greater extent in negative than in positive contingencies, no effect was predicted in the specific positive-contingency condition that we tested, where the $P(O|R)$ was 1.0, and the $P(O|NoR)$ was .5. This is because generative causal power is: $\Delta p / [1 - P(O|NoR)]$, which is: $.5/ (1 - .5) = 1$. In this condition, Δp is also calculated by subtracting the $P(O|NoR)$ from 1.0, which is: $1 - .5 = .5$. Therefore the numerator and the denominator of the generative power would always be identical, $(1 - .5)/(1 - .5) = 1$, no matter how the $P(O|NoR)$ changes. Therefore the pattern of ITI effects observed here are entirely consistent with the Power PC model.

Depressive realism

Depressed people have previously been considered to be more "realistic" in their judgements of

---

[1] Effect sizes like Cohen's *d* and Hedges's *g* are based on the standardized difference between the sample means. (Hedges's *g* is preferred because it uses a pooled within-sample estimate of the population standard deviation, rather than simply the control group standard deviation.) One advantage of this method is that the effect size is expressed in standard deviation units, is easily interpretable, and is subject to the effect size conventions given by Cohen (small ≅ 0.2; medium ≅ 0.5; large ≅ 0.8). Like all effect sizes, the size of Hedges's *g* is not determined by the scale of the dependent variable and is useful as a tool for comparing effects across experiments, including those with different sample sizes.

Positive contingency / no ITI			Positive contingency / long ITI			Increase in Δp
20	0	$P(O|R) = 1.0$	20	0	$P(O|R) = 1.0$	
10	10	$P(O|NoR) = .5$	10	50	$P(O|NoR) = .17$	0.33
$f(O) = 30$		$\Delta p = .5$	$f(O) = 30$		$\Delta p = .83$	
15	5	$P(O|R) = .75$	15	5	$P(O|R) = .75$	
5	15	$P(O|NoR) = .25$	5	55	$P(O|NoR) = .10$	.15
$f(O) = 20$		$\Delta p = .5$	$f(O) = 20$		$\Delta p = .65$	
10	10	$P(O|R) = .50$	10	10	$P(O|R) = .50$	
0	20	$P(O|NoR) = 0$	0	60	$P(O|NoR) = 0$	0.0
$f(O) = 10$		$\Delta p = .5$	$f(O) = 10$		$\Delta p = .5$	
Zero contingency / no ITI			**Zero contingency / long ITI**			
15	5	$P(O|R) = .75$	15	5	$P(O|R) = .75$	
15	5	$P(O|NoR) = .75$	15	45	$P(O|NoR) = .25$	0.50
$f(O) = 30$		$\Delta p = 0$	$f(O) = 30$		$\Delta p = .5$	
10	10	$P(O|R) = .5$	10	10	$P(O|R) = .50$	
10	10	$P(O|NoR) = .5$	10	50	$P(O|NoR) = .17$	0.33
$f(O) = 20$		$\Delta p = 0$	$f(O) = 20$		$\Delta p = .33$	
5	15	$P(O|R) = .25$	5	15	$P(O|R) = .25$	
5	15	$P(O|NoR) = .25$	5	55	$P(O|NoR) = .1$	0.15
$f(O) = 10$		$\Delta p = 0$	$f(O) = 10$		$\Delta p = .15$	
Negative contingency / no ITI			**Negative contingency / long ITI**			
10	10	$P(O|R) = .5$	10	10	$P(O|R) = .5$	
20	0	$P(O|NoR) = 1.0$	20	40	$P(O|NoR) = .33$	0.67
$f(O) = 30$		$\Delta p = -.5$	$f(O) = 30$		$\Delta p = .17$	
5	15	$P(O|R) = .25$	5	15	$P(O|R) = .25$	
15	5	$P(O|NoR) = .75$	15	45	$P(O|NoR) = .25$	0.50
$f(O) = 20$		$\Delta p = -.5$	$f(O) = 20$		$\Delta p = 0$	
0	20	$P(O|R) = 0$	0	20	$P(O|R) = 0$	
10	10	$P(O|NoR) = .5$	10	50	$P(O|NoR) = .17$	0.33
$f(O) = 10$		$\Delta p = -.5$	$f(O) = 10$		$\Delta p = -.17$	

Figure 5. *Contingency tables showing how changes in Δp, occurring when intertrial intervals are integrated into the contingency calculation as cell D events, are dependent upon contingency and the frequency of outcome occurrence $f(O)$. The left panels show traditional Δp calculation, and the right panels show the same calculation with 40 extra cell D events included in each condition.*

contingency (Alloy & Abramson, 1979). Furthermore depressive realism effects were only thought to occur in zero contingencies (Alloy et al., 1985; Lennox et al., 1990; Vasquez, 1987), due to depressed people's negative but accurate expectations. We found that depressed people made lower judgements than did nondepressed people in all contingencies tested, but only when ITIs were long. This did not seem to be indicative of a general tendency towards accuracy on the part of depressed people. Irrespective of ITI length, there was little difference between depressed people's judgements of zero and positive contingencies.

We have also suggested that if nondepressed people include long periods of context exposure occurring during the ITI into their judgements, then perhaps depressed people process these time periods differently and maybe do not include ITIs in their judgements. The current results support the softer claim since there is some evidence that ITI length does influence depressed people's judgements. We previously found that when a short ITI was of a relatively standard 3-s duration, and the long ITI was of a 15-s duration, there was no evidence of an ITI effect (e.g., Msetfi et al., 2005, Exp. 1; Experiment 1 here). However, when the short ITI was of a .5-s duration, as in Experiments 2 and 3 reported here, there was some evidence of a reduction on judgements with longer ITIs (see Figure 3). In fact, in the negative contingency ($\Delta P = -.5$), depressed people's judgements with the short .5-s ITI were high and close to zero. This is more consistent with the suggestion that depressed people process ITIs differently, but it would not be true to say that their judgements are not influenced by ITI length. In fact the pattern of findings seems to suggest that the effect of the ITI in depressed people is exactly in opposition to the same effect in nondepressed people. Longer intertrial intervals increase judgements of zero and negative contingencies in nondepressed people but have the opposite effect in depressed people.

The study of zero and positive contingencies has always been seen as particularly relevant for depression. In this study we also tested for depressive realism effects in negative contingencies, which might also have some particular relevance to depression, because these are conditions in which actions reduce the likelihood of an outcome. The statement, "When I am around, nothing good ever happens", is a statement typical of a depressed person and an instance in which a person believes that their behaviour or presence reduces the likelihood of outcomes. This type of statement implies that depressed people often feel, to some degree, responsible for the nonoccurrence of positive outcomes. However, the latter situation is essentially a perceived negative contingency. Along these lines, in the negative contingency experiment reported here, the ability to control light onset, in the fictional situation of needing to use experimental equipment, might have been seen as a desirable state of affairs or a positive outcome. When there was information available that might have disconfirmed the presence of a preventative relationship (the long ITI or cell D), depressed people were strongly convinced that they were preventing the outcome from occurring. In the field of clinical psychology, this type of negativity is often taken as evidence for the existence of negative depressive schema postulated by cognitive theories of depression (e.g., Beck, 1967). Such schema are negative fundamental beliefs about the self, including themes of helplessness and inefficacy, and bias the selection, coding, storage, and retrieval of incoming information (Clark, Beck, & Alford, 1999). However, the present results suggest that a depressive tendency to underestimate the frequency of events that essentially disconfirm the presence of a preventative relationship between response and outcome (or confirm the presence of a positive relationship) could explain continued depressive negativity in some situations without recourse to schema-based theory (e.g., Beck, 1967), as is traditionally the case.

In summary, this research has illustrated the difficulty in drawing conclusions about the relative accuracy of contingency judgements on the basis of procedures involving normative measures such as Δp. Nondepressed people's judgements change systematically with ITI length in a manner consistent with these time periods being included into the contingency calculation as cell D events. Given that their judgements could be considered to be more consistent with causal power calculated using the "overall Δp" as opposed to the "within trial" programmed Δp, nondepressed people were accurate. However, there was no evidence that the depressed were more accurate in their judgements, as there was little evidence of the ability to discriminate between two different levels of contingency. Thus perhaps depressive realism effects might be more accurately described as mood effects on learning.

REFERENCES

Ackermann, R., & DeRubeis, R. J. (1991). Is depressive realism real? *Clinical Psychology Review*, *11*, 565–584.

Allan, L. G. (1980). A note on measurement of contingency between two binary variables in judgment tasks. *Bulletin of the Psychonomic Society*, *15*, 147–149.

Allan, L. G., & Jenkins, H. M. (1980). The judgment of contingency and the nature of the response alternatives. *Canadian Journal of Psychology*, *34*, 1–11.

Allan, L. G., Siegel, S., & Hannah, S. (2007). The sad truth about depressive realism. *Quarterly Journal of Experimental Psychology*, *60*, 482–495.

Alloy, L. B., & Abramson, L. Y. (1979). Judgement of contingency in depressed and non-depressed students: Sadder but wiser? *Journal of Experimental Psychology: General*, *108*, 441–485.

Alloy, L. B., Abramson, L. Y., & Kossman, D. A. (1985). The judgement of predictability in depressed and nondepressed college students. In F. R. Brush & J. B. Overmier (Eds.), *Affect, conditioning and cognition: Essays on the determinants of behaviour* (pp. 229–246). Hillsdale, NJ: Lawrence Erlbaum Associates, Inc.

Alloy, L. B., & Tabachnik, N. (1984). Assessment of covariation by humans and animals: The joint influence of prior expectations and current situational information. *Psychological Review*, *91*, 112–149.

Baker, A. G., Berbrier, M. W., & Vallée-Tourangeau, F. (1989). Judgements of a 2 × 2 contingency table: Sequential processing and the learning curve. *Quarterly Journal of Experimental Psychology*, *41B*, 65–97.

Baker, A. G., Murphy, R. A., Vallée-Tourangeau, F., & Mehta, R. (2001). Contingency learning and causal reasoning. In R. R. Mowrer & S. B. Klein (Eds.), *Handbook of contemporary learning theories.* (pp. 255–306). Mahwah, NJ: Lawrence Erlbaum Associates, Inc.

Beck, A. T. (1967). *Depression: Clinical, experimental and theoretical aspects.* London: Staples Press.

Beck, A. T., Ward, C. H., Mendelson, M., Mock, J., & Erbaugh, J. (1961). An inventory for measuring depression. *Archives of General Psychiatry*, *4*, 561–571.

Cheng, P. W. (1997). From covariation to causation: A causal power theory. *Psychological Review*, *104*, 367–405.

Clark, D. A., Beck, A. T., & Alford, B. A. (1999). *Scientific foundations of cognitive theory and therapy of depression.* New York: John Wiley and Sons, Inc.

Cohen, J. D. (1977). *Statistical power analysis for the behavioral sciences.* New York: Academic Press.

Dickinson, A., Shanks, D., & Evenden, J. (1984). Judgment of act–outcome contingency: The role of selective attribution. *Quarterly Journal of Experimental Psychology*, *36B*, 29–50.

Gibbon, J., Baldock, M. D., Locurto, C. M., Gold, L., & Terrace, H. S. (1977). Trial and intertrial durations in autoshaping. *Journal of Experimental Psychology: Animal Behavior Processes*, *3*, 264–284.

Hedges, L. V. (1982). Estimation of effect size from a series of independent experiments. *Psychological Bulletin*, *92*, 490–499.

Holland, P. C. (2000). Trial and intertrial durations in appetitive conditioning in rats. *Animal Learning and Behavior*, *28*, 121–135.

Kapci, E. G., & Cramer, D. (1999). Judgement of control revisited: Are the depressed realistic or pessimistic? *Counselling Psychology Quarterly*, *12*, 95–105.

Lennox, S. S., Bedell, J. R., Abramson, L. Y., Raps, C., & Foley, F. W. (1990). Judgement of contingency: A replication with hospitalized depressed, schizophrenic and normal samples. *Journal of Social Behavior and Personality*, *5*, 189–204.

Matute, H. (1996). Illusion of control: Detecting response-outcome independence in analytic but not in naturalistic conditions. *Psychological Science*, *7*, 289–293.

Mercier, P., & Parr, W. (1996). Inter-trial interval, stimulus duration and number of trials in contingency judgments. *British Journal of Psychology*, *87*, 549–566.

Miller, G. A., & Chapman, J. P. (2001). Misunderstanding analysis of covariance. *Journal of Abnormal Psychology*, *110*, 40–48.

Msetfi, R. M., Murphy, R. A., Simpson, J., & Kornbrot, D. E. (2005). Depressive realism and outcome density bias in contingency judgements: The effect of context and the inter-trial interval. *Journal of Experimental Psychology: General, 134,* 10–22.

Murphy, R. A., & Baker, A. G. (2004). A role for CS–US contingency in Pavlovian conditioning. *Journal of Experimental Psychology: Animal Behavior Processes, 30,* 229–239.

Murphy, R. A., Vallée-Tourangeau, F., Msetfi, R. M., & Baker, A. G. (2005). Signal-outcome contingency, contiguity and the depressive realism effect. In A. Wills (Ed.), *New directions in associative learning.* Mahwah, NJ: Lawrence Erlbaum Associates.

Rescorla, R., & Wagner, A. (1972). A theory of Pavlovian conditioning: Variations in the effectiveness of reinforcement and non-reinforcement. In A. Black & W. Prokasy (Eds.), *Classical conditioning II: Theory and research.* New York: Appleton Century Crofts.

Shanks, D. (1985). Continuous monitoring of human contingency judgment across trials. *Memory & Cognition, 13,* 158–167.

Smedslund, J. (1963). The concept of correlation in adults. *Scandinavian Journal of Psychology, 4,* 165–173.

Vallée-Tourangeau, F., Hollingsworth, L., & Murphy, R. A. (1998a). "Attentional bias" in correlation judgments? Smedslund (1963) revisited. *Scandinavian Journal of Psychology, 39,* 221–233.

Vallée-Tourangeau, F., Murphy, R. A., Drew, S., & Baker, A. G. (1998b). Judging the importance of constant and variable candidate causes: A test of the power PC theory. *Quarterly Journal of Experimental Psychology, 51B,* 65–84.

Vasquez, C. (1987). Judgement of contingency: Cognitive biases in depressed and nondepressed subjects. *Journal of Personality and Social Psychology, 52,* 419–431.

Wasserman, E. A., Chatlosh, D. L., & Neunaber, D. J. (1983). Perception of causal relations in humans: Factors affecting judgments of response-outcome contingencies under free-operant procedures. *Learning and Motivation, 14,* 406–432.

Wasserman, E. A., Elek, S. M., Chatlosh, D. L., & Baker, A. G. (1993). Rating causal relations: Role of probability in judgments of response-outcome contingency. *Journal of Experimental Psychology: Learning, Memory, and Cognition, 19,* 174–188.

APPENDIX A

Instructions and question wording for the contingency tasks used in Experiment 1

Screen 1

Imagine the following scenario.

You are a scientist and you are setting up the apparatus for your latest experiment. The apparatus includes a light bulb wired up to a light switch button and has its own power supply.

It is very important for your experiment that you the scientist feel that you can control when the light is switched on or remains off. You are working on a tight budget and had to use an old power supply provided by another researcher. You are slightly worried that the power supply you've had to use may not be suitable for this purpose.

Therefore you want to test the apparatus to assess how much control you have over the light switching on.

Screen 2

At the beginning of the test you will see a light bulb on the screen. There will be a short delay and then the button will appear on the screen too. While the button is on the screen you will be able to press it and see whether the light switches on or remains off.

You can press the light button using the space bar on the computer keyboard. If the light switches on, it will stay on for 2 seconds before switching off.

The button will then disappear from the screen and will re-appear again when you can press the button again. In the test there will be many opportunities to press the button and see what happens.

Screen 3

In order to judge how much control your button pressing has over whether the light comes on, you need to know what happens when you press the button. IT IS ALSO VERY IMPORTANT that you know what happens when you do not press the button.

So, on about half of the button pressing opportunities, you should sit back and see what happens when you don't press the button.

Screen 4

(Graphic shows light bulb) If you press the button below, you will see an example of the light coming on. When you have done that, press the carry on button to proceed.

Screen 5

At the end of the test, you will be asked to make a judgement about how much control your pressing the button had over whether the light came on.

"Total control" means that the light switching on is completely determined by your choice of response—either pressing or not pressing the button.

"No control" means that you have found that your button pressing has no influence at all on whether the light is switched on or not. In other words the light switching on has nothing to do with what you did or didn't do.

"Partial control" means that your pressing or not pressing the button, does influence the light switching on, but not completely. In other words, whether you press or don't press the button matters to some extent, but not totally.

Judgement screen

We would now like you to make a judgement about how much control your pressing the button had over whether the light came on. We will ask you to make this judgement by moving the slider.

If you consider that your button press has total control over the light coming on, you would move the slider to the "total control" end.

If you consider that your button press has absolutely no control over light coming on, you would move the slider to the "no control" end.

It may be that you consider that your button pressing has only partial control over the light coming on, then you would move the slider's position accordingly. Putting it nearer to the "total control" end means MORE control—while putting it nearer to the "no control" end means LESS control.

APPENDIX B

Instructions and question wording used for the contingency task used in Experiment 2

Screen 1

Please imagine the following scenario.

You are a scientist and you are investigating some old equipment in the store cupboard in the lab. You find a piece of apparatus called a PERCEPTOMETER. It resembles a large box with a light bulb attached to it. The box has 2 switches on it—"button A" and "button B" which you assume controls the light switching on, but you are not sure exactly how it works.

You think that the PERCEPTOMETER might be useful for your latest experiment. However because of the nature of your experiment, you need to be sure that you can control when the light switches on quite precisely. If the PERCEPTOMETER is slightly unreliable, it will ruin your experiment!

Click here to see a picture of the PERCEPTOMETER.

Screen 2

Therefore you must test the PERCEPTOMETER to decide, "How much CONTROL DO YOU HAVE over the light switching on." It is possible that you may not have TOTAL control or ZERO control over the light switching on, but some intermediate level of control—slightly more or slightly less.

There is one problem however. "Button B" is ALWAYS stuck in the "ON" position. So you can only test how much control you have over the light switching on, by pressing "Button A".

Test your control over the light switching on by pressing "Button A".

In order to do the test you must press "Button A" lots of times to see what happens. You must also see what happens when you DON'T press "Button A". This is because if the light switches on lots of times when you don't press "Button A", you have less control over the light switching on. At the end of the test, you will be asked to make a judgement about how much control your pressing of "Button A" had over the light switching on.

How much control does "Button B"—not you—have over the light switching on.

Remember that "Button B" will be always stuck in the "ON" position. It might be that "Button B" has more, less or the same control, over the light switching on, as you do! Therefore when you have done the test, you will not only be asked about how much control you have over the light switching on, you will also be asked, "How much control does "Button B" have over the light switching on".

Screen 3

When the test starts, you will see a picture of a light bulb and 2 buttons—button A and button B. When a button is pressed, its onscreen picture is shaded with a darker colour. You will see that Button B is permanently in the "on" position.

You are only allowed to test button A during specific button pressing opportunities. When you are allowed to press button A, a message will appear on the screen saying, "You can press button A now!" This message will appear on the screen for 3 seconds during which time you can press button A once, by pressing the "space-bar" on the keyboard. Once you have pressed button A, it will be shaded dark, to show that you have pressed it. At the end of the 3 second interval, the light will either switch on for 2 seconds or remain off. You will then have to wait for a short period of time for the next button opportunity to test button A.

Screen 4

IMPORTANT INFORMATION:

In order to gauge how much control YOUR pressing of "Button A" has over the light switching on, it is very IMPORTANT, that on some button pressing opportunities you press "Button A". However, it is also important that on approximately half the possible occasions, you DO NOT press "Button A". This is so that you can see what happens when you do not press "Button A".

Therefore, on about half of the button pressing opportunities, DO NOT press "Button A".

Screen 5

At the end of the test, you will be asked to make a judgement—using a slider like this—about how much control YOUR PRESSING "Button A" had over whether the light came on.

(PICTURE OF SLIDER LABELLED NO CONTROL—PARTIAL CONTROL—TOTAL CONTROL—divided into units of 1 from 0 to 100)

"Total control" means that the light switching on is completely determined by your choice of response—either pressing or not pressing "Button A".

"No control" means that you have found that your pressing of "Button A" pressing has no influence at all on whether the light is switched on or not. In other words the light switching on has nothing to do with what you did or didn't do.

Partial control means that your pressing or not pressing "Button A", does influence the light switching on, but not completely. In other words, whether you press or don't press "Button A" matters to some extent, but not totally.

You will also be asked to make a similar judgement about how much control "Button B"—not you—has over the light switching on.

If you are ready, please tell the experimenter.

Button A Judgement Screen

We would now like you to make a judgement about how much control YOUR pressing of "Button A" had over whether the light came on. We will ask you to make this judgement by moving the slider.

If you consider that your button press has total control over the light coming on, you would move the slider to the "total control" end.

If you consider that your button press has absolutely no control over the light coming on, you would move the slider to the "no control" end.

It may be that you consider that your button pressing has only partial control over the light coming on, then you would move the slider's position accordingly. Putting it nearer to the "total control" end means MORE control—while putting it nearer to the "no control" end means LESS control.

Button B Judgement Screen

Remember, "Button B" was always on during the test.

"Button B" might have more, less or the same control over the light switching on, than your pressing of "Button A". How much control do you think that "Button B" had over the light coming on?

Give your judgement on the slider below.

APPENDIX C

Changes to the instructions in Experiment 3

Screen 5

At the end of the test, you will be asked to make a judgement—using a slider like this—about how much control your pressing of "Button A" had over whether the light came on or not.

"Total causal control" means that your pressing of "Button A" caused the light to switch on.

"No control" means that you have found that your pressing of "Button A" pressing has no influence at all on whether the light switched on or not.

"Total preventive control" means that your pressing of "Button A", seems to prevent the light from switching on.

Or you could move the slider to somewhere in between, because you might think that your pressing of "button A" causes the light to switch on to some degree, but not totally; or that your pressing of "button A" prevents the light from switching on, but not totally.

You will also be asked to make a judgement about how much control "Button B" alone—not you—had over the light switching on. If you are ready, please tell the experimenter.

NB: The questions asked in Experiment 3 were similar to those shown in Appendix C but used the bidirectional rating scale.

THE QUARTERLY JOURNAL OF EXPERIMENTAL PSYCHOLOGY
2007, 60 (3), 482–495

The sad truth about depressive realism

Lorraine G. Allan, Shepard Siegel, and Samuel Hannah

McMaster University, Hamilton, Ontario, Canada

In one form of a contingency judgement task individuals must judge the relationship between an action and an outcome. There are reports that depressed individuals are more accurate than are non-depressed individuals in this task. In particular, nondepressed individuals are influenced by manipulations that affect the salience of the outcome, especially outcome probability. They overestimate a contingency if the probability of an outcome is high—the "outcome-density effect". In contrast, depressed individuals display little or no outcome-density effect. This apparent knack for depressives not to be misled by outcome density in their contingency judgements has been termed "depressive realism", and the absence of an outcome-density effect has led to the characterization of depressives as "sadder but wiser". We present a critical summary of the depressive realism literature and provide a novel interpretation of the phenomenon. We suggest that depressive realism may be understood from a psychophysical analysis of contingency judgements.

Alloy and Abramson (1979) reported an unexpected and intriguing result that attracted the attention of many researchers and is discussed in current textbooks (e.g., Myers & Spencer, 2004; Nolen-Hoeksema, 2001). Alloy and Abramson asked depressed and nondepressed college students to rate the degree of control that their responses had over the occurrence of an environmental event. They used the discrete-trial, active (operant) version of the contingency judgement task. In this task, each trial is clearly marked, and the participant has the option of responding (e.g., pressing a button) or not responding (e.g., not pressing a button). At the termination of the response period, an outcome occurs (e.g., the illumination of a light) or does not occur (in this example, the light does not illuminate). At the end of a block of trials, the participant is asked to rate their control over the outcome. The 2×2 matrix relating responding to outcomes is shown in Table 1. We represent an active response as R, an inactive response as $\sim$R, the occurrence of an outcome as O, and the nonoccurrence of an outcome as $\sim$O. The letters in the cells (a, b, c, d) represent the joint frequency of occurrence of the four response–outcome combinations. The measure of the contingency between the response and the outcome is ΔP—the difference between the conditional probability of an outcome given that a response has occurred and the conditional probability of an outcome given that a response has not occurred (Allan, 1980):

$$\Delta P = P(O|R) - P(O|\sim R) = \frac{a}{a+b} - \frac{c}{c+d}. \quad 1$$

Correspondence should be addressed to Lorraine G. Allan or Shepard Siegel, Department of Psychology, Neuroscience, and Behaviour, McMaster University, Hamilton ON, L8S 4K1, Canada. E-mail: allan@mcmaster.ca or siegel@mcmaster.ca

The preparation of this paper was supported by research grants from the Natural Sciences and Engineering Research Council to L.G.A. and S.S. and by a grant from the United States National Institute on Drug Abuse to S.S.

DOI:10.1080/17470210601002686

Table 1. *The 2 × 2 matrix for the response–outcome pairings in the discrete-trial, active contingency task*

	O	~O
R	a	b
~R	c	d

Note: The letters in the cells (a, b, c, d) represent the joint frequency of occurrence of the four response–outcome combinations in a block of trials.

It has been known for some time (see Allan, 1993) that, for a given ΔP value, participants typically report that their responses have greater control over the outcome as the probability of an outcome, P(O), increases:

$$P(O) = \frac{a+c}{a+b+c+d}. \qquad 2$$

This phenomenon of reported increased control between R and O as P(O) increases has been termed the "outcome-density effect" (see Allan, 1993) and has also been referred to as an "illusion of control" (see Alloy & Abramson, 1979). Alloy and Abramson concluded that such an effect is seen in nondepressed but not depressed individuals. That is, rather than displaying the illusion apparent in nondepressives, depressed college students did not inflate their judgements of control when P(O) increased. Such resistance by depressives to concluding that the contingency between a response and outcome is increased when just the outcome density is increased has been referred to as "depressive realism" (e.g., Alloy & Abramson, 1988). As an example, consider the situation where ΔP = 0, and P(O) is varied. Nondepressive ratings of the control of responding over the occurrence of the outcome increased with P(O), an illusion of control since the actual contingency did not change. In contrast, depressive ratings were not influenced by P(O), depressive realism. As the title of their article indicates, Alloy and Abramson (1979) concluded that depressed college students were "sadder but wiser" than nondepressed college students.

Other variables in addition to outcome density have been reported to result in an illusion of control in nondepressives and depressive realism in depressives. While this mood effect has been replicated by other investigators, nonreplications have also been reported. One purpose of the present paper is to provide a critical summary of mood effects in contingency studies in order to assess the reliability of the phenomenon and to delineate the conditions under which it occurs (for a brief earlier summary, see Dobson & Franche, 1989). Recently, there has been a renewed interest in the outcome-density effect, and two novel theoretical accounts have been proposed (Allan, Siegel, & Tangen, 2005; Msetfi, Murphy, & Simpson, 2007; Msetfi, Murphy, Simpson, & Kornbrot, 2005). A second purpose of this paper is discuss the applicability of these accounts to understanding depressive realism.

EMPIRICAL RESEARCH

Almost all the research concerned with depressive realism in contingency judgement tasks[1] has used college students who are divided into two mood groups, "depressed" and "nondepressed", on the basis of their scores on a number of depression inventories such as the Beck Depression Inventory (BDI: Beck, 1967) and the Multiple Affect Adjective Checklist (MAACL: Zuckerman & Lubin, 1965). Both male and female students participated in most experiments. While males and females did not always differ, when they did, differences due to mood were generally greater for females then for males.

---

[1] Many of the papers concerned with contingency judgements and depressive realism cite unpublished experiments. In our review, we only include published work.

Table 2. *A summary of the design of the four experiments reported by Alloy and Abramson (1979)*

Experiment	ΔP	P(O)	O valence
1	± .25	.675	
	± .50	.500	
	± .75	.375	
2	0	.25	
	0	.75	
3	0	.5	win
	0	.5	lose
4	± .5	.5	win
	± .5	.5	lose

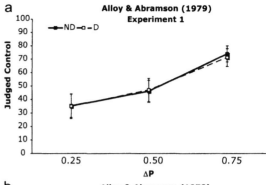

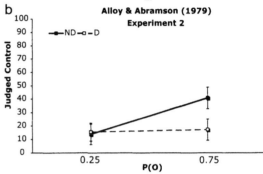

Figure 1. *The data are replotted from the Tables in Alloy and Abramson (1979). Figure 1a shows judged control in Experiment 1 as a function of ΔP for each mood group (ND = nondepressed, D = depressed). Figure 1b shows judged control in Experiment 2 as a function of P(O) for each mood group (ND = nondepressed, D = depressed).*

Alloy and Abramson (1979)

The referent report by Alloy and Abramson (1979) describes a series of four experiments. The designs of these experiments are summarized in Table 2. On each of 40 trials, participants could either press a button (R) or not (~R), and then a green light was illuminated (O) or not (~O). At the end of the 40 trials, the participant rated, on a 100-point scale, the degree of control that their responses exerted over the illumination of the light, where 0 indicated no control, and 100 indicated complete control. One purpose of these experiments was to evaluate the predictions made by the learned helplessness theory of depression (Seligman, 1975). According to this theory, depressed people have generalized expectancies of independence between their responses and outcomes—the depressive is characterized as one who believes that he or she is ineffective and powerless to control outcomes in the world.

A deduction from learned helplessness theory is that depressed individuals should underestimate the degree of contingency between their responses and environmental outcomes (Abramson & Alloy, 1980; Alloy & Seligman, 1979), and Experiment 1 in Alloy and Abramson (1979) evaluated this prediction. The size of the contingency (ΔP = .25, .50, and .75) and the sign of the contingency (positive ΔP and negative ΔP) were varied. The pairs of conditional probabilities—that is, P(O|R) and

P(O|~R), see Equation 1—for the three positive ΔP values were .75 and .50, .75 and .25, and .75 and .00, and the pairs for the three negative ΔP values were .50 and .75, .25 and .75, and .00 and .75. There was no effect of sign[2] on ratings, and the ratings, collapsed over sign, are plotted as a function of ΔP in Figure 1a. Ratings of control increased with ΔP, and there was no difference between depressed and nondepressed participants. The absence of a difference between the ratings of the two mood groups is inconsistent with the predictions of learned helplessness theory—depressives should have underestimated the degree of contingency between response and outcome, but did not.

---

[2] It should be noted that although there were negative contingencies, the rating scale ranged from 0 to 100.

According to Alloy and Abramson (1979), learned helplessness theory also regards nondepressives as having a generalized expectation of control, which should interfere with the detection of noncontingencies.[3] "Just as depressives' generalized expectation of response–outcome independence interferes with their ability to perceive that outcomes are now dependent on responses, nondepressives' generalized expectation that outcomes are dependent on responses should interfere with their ability to perceive that outcomes are independent of responses" (p. 457). Thus, nondepressives should show an illusion of control, and depressives should not when events are noncontingent. In Experiment 2 in Alloy and Abramson (1979), the relationship between responding and the outcome was noncontingent (i.e., $\Delta P = 0$) and P(O) was varied (.25 and .75). The ratings are plotted as a function of P(O) in Figure 1b. It is clear that P(O) interacted with mood state. When the outcome was infrequent, P(O) = .25, ratings were close to zero for both mood groups. Nondepressive ratings increased when P(O) = .75, whereas depressive ratings were unaffected by P(O). Thus, nondepressives showed an illusion of control—judged control increased with P(O)—whereas depressives displayed depressive realism—judged control was unaffected by P(O). Alloy and Abramson argued that the results of their Experiment 2, while showing a difference between depressives and nondepressives, were inconsistent with learned helplessness theory, which predicts that the two mood groups should differ when P(O) = .25 as well as when P(O) = .75. That is, the theory predicts a mood effect, whereas the data revealed a Mood × Density interaction.

In their remaining two experiments, Alloy and Abramson (1979) evaluated the effects of outcome valence, rather than probability, on control ratings in depressive and nondepressive participants. That is, an outcome was made either desirable or undesirable (rather than frequent or infrequent). In

Experiment 3, both ΔP and P(O) were constant, $\Delta P = 0$ and P(O) = .5, and the valence of light onset was manipulated. For the "win" condition, the participant gained $0.25 on each trial on which the light turned on. For the "lose" condition, the participant began the block of trials with $5.00 and lost $0.25 on each trial on which the light did not turn on. There was no contingency between responding and payoff; that is, these payoffs occurred regardless of whether or not the participant responded. As with P(O), outcome valence influenced nondepressive ratings but not depressive ratings. In the lose condition, ratings were low for both mood groups. Nondepressive ratings increased in the win condition, whereas depressive ratings did not. Thus, depressive realism was demonstrated with an "outcome valence effect", as well as with an outcome-density effect.

Experiment 4 also varied the valence of the outcome. In contrast with Experiment 3 (in which $\Delta P = 0$), however, ΔP was set at either +.5 or −.5. When $\Delta P = +.5$, the conditional probabilities were .75 and .25. When $\Delta P = -.5$, the conditional probabilities were .25 and .75. For the win condition, the participant gained $0.10 on each trial on which the light turned on. For the lose condition, the participant began the block of trials with $4.00 and lost $0.30 on each trial on which the light did not turn on. As in Experiment 3, outcome valence influenced nondepressive ratings but not depressive ratings. In the win condition, the two mood groups did not differ, and ratings were at about the middle of the scale (i.e., 50). Nondepressive ratings decreased in the lose condition, whereas depressive ratings did not.

In addition to asking their participants to rate the degree of control of responding on the outcome, in all their experiments Alloy and Abramson (1979) required their participants (a) to estimate the overall percentage of light onset—that is, P(O), (b) to estimate the

---

[3] Alloy and Abramson (1979) do note that not all researchers agree with their interpretation of learned helpless theory (see p. 457).

percentage of light onset when they pressed—that is, $P(O|R)$, and (c) to estimate the percentage of light onset when they did not press—that is, $P(O|{\sim}R)$. In general, depressives and nondepressives were similarly accurate in their estimates of these probabilities, and the two mood groups did not differ significantly. It appears that both groups had the appropriate data with which to make an accurate judgement of control. Alloy and Abramson concluded that the locus of nondepressive errors "is in their *organization* of the incoming response–outcome data and not in the perception of the data themselves" (p. 474).

In summary, the Alloy and Abramson (1979) data indicate that depressed college students are quite accurate in judging how much control they exert over the outcome, whereas nondepressed college students succumb to illusions about their control over the outcome. Specifically, nondepressives overestimated the control that their responses had over the outcome when noncontingent outcomes were frequent (Experiment 2) or desired (Experiment 3) and underestimated the control when contingent outcomes were undesired (Experiment 4).

Replications: Successes and failures

Some investigators have reported depressive realism findings similar to that reported by Alloy and Abramson (1979), but others have reported an inability to obtain the phenomenon.

Replications
In their Experiment 1, Alloy and Abramson (1979) demonstrated that depressives and nondepressives did not differ in their ratings of control when $\Delta P \neq 0$ (i.e., when the relationship was contingent, $\pm$ .25, $\pm$ .50, and $\pm$ .75). This result has been replicated a number of times. Lennox, Bedell, Abramson, Raps, and Foley (1990) conducted a similar experiment but with four patient groups: major depressive disorder, schizophrenia with depression, schizophrenia without depression, and nonpsychiatric medical/surgical. They included four of the ΔP conditions used by Alloy and Abramson ($\pm$ .25 and $\pm$ .75). As in

Alloy and Abramson, ratings of control increased with ΔP, and there were no differences among the four groups (although, in contrast with Alloy & Abramson, Lennox et al. did find that the sign of the contingency mattered, with higher ratings for positive contingencies than for negative contingencies). Vázquez (1987) noted that ΔP and $P(O)$ were confounded in Experiment 1 in Alloy and Abramson (1979) because as ΔP increased, $P(O)$ decreased (see Table 2; this was also the case for Lennox et al., 1990). In Vázquez's Experiment 1, there were two values of ΔP (.25 and .75), generated by the conditional probability pairs of .50 and .25, and .75 and .00. Thus for both contingencies, $P(O) = .375$. The results were similar to those reported by Alloy and Abramson—ratings of control increased with ΔP, and there was no difference between depressed and nondepressed participants. Kapçi and Cramer (1999) also varied contingency ($\Delta P = .5$ and 1) and sign (positive and negative). The pairs of conditional probabilities for the two positive ΔP values were .75 and .25 and 1.00 and .00. The pairs for the two negative ΔP values were .25 and.75 and .00 and 1.00. Thus for all contingencies, $P(O) = .5$. Again, ratings increased with ΔP, and there was no difference between mood groups. As in Lennox et al., but in contrast to Alloy and Abramson, the ratings tended to be higher for positive contingencies than for negative contingencies.

In their Experiment 2 (see Table 2), Alloy and Abramson (1979) demonstrated that, with $\Delta P = 0$, when $P(O)$ is high (.75), but not when it is low (.25), nondepressives rated their control higher than did depressives (see Figure 1b). That is, nondepressives, but not depressives, displayed an outcome-density effect. Vázquez (1987) and Presson and Benassi (2003) have provided independent replications of Alloy and Abramson's (1979) Experiment 2. Experiment 2 in Vázquez was similar to Experiment 2 in Alloy and Abramson (1979), and the significant interaction between mood and $P(O)$ was obtained—nondepressive ratings increased with $P(O)$, and depressive ratings did not change. Vázquez's participants were also college students but at a Spanish university, thus extending the generality of the Alloy and Abramson results. In Presson and Benassi, $\Delta P = 0$ and $P(O) = .75$. Consistent with the findings of Alloy and Abramson and of Vázquez, depressive judgements of control were lower than nondepressive judgements.

Nonreplications

In contrast with the above reports, others have reported inabilities to replicate the difference in control judgements between the two mood states when $\Delta P = 0$. Bryson, Doan, and Pasquali (1984) reported that neither mood group showed an illusion of control—ratings were constant with increases in $P(O)$—whereas Kapçi and Cramer (1999) reported that both mood groups showed an illusion of control—ratings increased with increases in $P(O)$. Dobson and Pusch (1995) used clinical populations rather than college students. There were three patient groups: clinically depressed (currently receiving treatment), previously depressed (no longer receiving treatment), and never depressed. In the Dobson and Pusch study, $\Delta P = 0$ and $P(O) = .75$. The three groups did not differ in their ratings. Although Dobson and Pusch did not vary $P(O)$, they used the level of $P(O)$ at which Alloy and Abramson (1979) found a difference between mood groups.

Summary

When the relationship between responding and the appearance of the outcome is noncontingent (i.e., $\Delta P = 0$), there have been both replications and nonreplications of the findings reported by Alloy and Abramson (1979). In some studies nondepressives show an illusion of control, and depressives do not, but in other studies the two mood groups do not differ. There appears to be consistency among all the studies that the two mood groups do not differ when the relationship is contingent (i.e., $\Delta P \neq 0$). Alloy and

Abramson commented on this absence of a mood difference in their Experiment 1:

Although manipulations of reinforcement frequency affected judgements of control adversely in the noncontingent case, such manipulations were not sufficient to produce errors in the contingent case. These results may imply that noncontingency is psychologically more difficult relationship to perceive or understand than contingency. (p. 474)[4]

As was noted earlier, ΔP and $P(O)$ were confounded in their Experiment 1 and also in Lennox et al. (1990). In the other studies where $\Delta P \neq 0$, $P(O)$ was constant. In Vázquez (1987), $P(O) = .375$ for both contingency values, and in Kapçi and Cramer (1999), $P(O) = .5$ for both contingency values. Given that Alloy and Abramson found an interaction between mood and $P(O)$ when $\Delta P = 0$, it is surprising that investigators have not manipulated $P(O)$ when $\Delta P \neq 0$ and moreover that they have evaluated only low values of $P(O)$—that is, $\leq .5$. On the basis of the available $\Delta P = 0$ data, one would not expect a difference between mood groups with low values of $P(O)$.

In their Experiments 3 and 4, Alloy and Abramson (1979) reported that manipulations of outcome valence (in addition to outcome probability) can be used to demonstrate depressive realism. Subsequent research, inspired by these findings, have additionally evaluated the effects of outcome valence manipulations on mood effects in contingency judgements.

Mood effects and judgements of contingency[5]

Induced mood

The Alloy and Abramson (1979) experiments do not provide information about the causal direction of the correlation between depression and accuracy in judging contingencies. It could be that the depressive mood state causes people to assess contingencies accurately. If so, people should judge

---

[4] Alloy and Abramson (1979) used "reinforcement" interchangeably with "outcome".

[5] Alloy, Abramson, and collaborators published a series of papers in the 1980s. In our review we have included only papers directly concerned with mood effects on judgements of contingency. We have not included papers where the main focus was on learned helplessness theory (e.g., Abramson, Alloy, & Rosoff, 1981; Alloy & Abramson, 1982).

contingencies accurately when they are depressed but not when they are not depressed. Alternatively, those who judge accurately may be more prone to depression than those who misjudge. That is, those who are realistic about their impact on environmental events would be at high risk for depression. Alloy, Abramson, and Viscusi (1981) investigated whether the results reported by Alloy and Abramson would be seen when the mood states were transient. Depressed and elated mood states were induced in naturally nondepressed and depressed female students, respectively. Depressed mood was induced by having participants read self-referent depressing sentences such as: "I have had too many bad things happen in my life" and "I want to go to sleep and never wake up". Elated mood was induced by having participants read self-referent elative sentences such as "Things will be better and better today" and "God, I feel great". Other depressed and nondepressed participants were not induced or read neutral statements, such as "Utah is the Beehive State". The impact of mood induction was assessed on the win noncontingent task used in Experiment 3 in Alloy and Abramson (see Table 2). With no induction or with neutral induction, nondepressed participants gave higher ratings of control than did depressed participants, replicating the results of Alloy and Abramson. Depressives who were given elation induction gave higher ratings of control than did nondepressives who were given depression induction. Thus, depressives made temporarily elated showed illusions of control normally observed in nondepressives, whereas nondepressives made temporarily depressed showed depressive realism normally observed in depressives.

Self and others

Martin, Abramson, and Alloy (1984) compared the relationship between depression and susceptibility to the illusion of control for oneself and for others. Depressed and nondepressed college students rated how much control they themselves had or how much control a male or female confederate had in the win noncontingent task used in Experiment 3 in Alloy and Abramson (see Table 2). In the confederate condition, the participant watched a confederate perform the task, whereas in the self condition, the participant performed the task alone. In the confederate condition, sex of the participant was crossed with sex of the confederate. Self-ratings replicated Experiment 3 in Alloy and Abramson—nondepressives showed an illusion of control, depressives showed depressive realism, and there was no difference between males and females. Others-ratings, however, were a complex interaction of participant mood, participant sex, and confederate sex. Martin et al. concluded that "an adequate understanding of depressive and nondepressive cognition requires an interpersonal as well as an intrapsychic perspective" (pp. 134–135). Depressive realism and nondepressive illusions in judging control may be specific to the self.

Benassi and Mahler (1985) were interested in determining the influence of the presence of an observer on the mood effects reported by Alloy and Abramson (1979). They compared ratings under two conditions: Either the participant completed the task alone or an observer was present. They found that mood interacted with observer present or absent. For example in their Experiment 1, there was no contingency between responding and outcome ($\Delta P = 0$), and the outcome was frequent, $P(O) = .75$. In the participant-alone condition, Benassi and Mahler replicated the basic finding of depressive realism—nondepressive ratings were higher than depressive ratings. However, in the observer-present condition, it was the depressives who had the higher ratings. In Experiment 2, only the observer-present condition was used, and $P(O)$ was varied (.25 and .75). Benassi and Mahler found an interaction between $P(O)$ and mood. When outcome density was high—that is, $P(O) = .75$, depressive ratings were higher than nondepressive ratings, replicating the results of their Experiment 1. At the low outcome density, $P(O) = .25$, the two mood groups did not differ. In Experiments 1 and 2, the observer was present throughout the experiment. In Experiment 3, the observer was present during the 40 response–outcome trials, but not during the ratings. Again, depressive ratings were higher than nondepressive ratings. Thus, the presence of an observer reverses the effects reported by Alloy and Abramson (1979)—depressed college students show an illusion of control relative to nondepressed college students.

Vázquez (1987) was also interested in self versus others in his Experiments 3 and 4. He used sentences (negative or positive) as outcomes and varied the referent in these sentences (self or other). Examples of the four sentence types are: "My problems are unsolvable" (negative self-referent), "My problems are, in general, not unsolvable" (positive self-referent), "Problems of human beings [aggressivity, selfishness, etc.] will never be solved" (negative other-referent), and "Problems of human beings [aggressivity, selfishness, etc.] will be solved at last" (positive other-referent). In Experiment 3 $\Delta P = .25$ (.50 and .25), and in Experiment 4 $\Delta P = 0$ (.75 and .75). Across the two experiments, control judgements were a complex interaction of ΔP, valence, and referent. Overall, nondepressives were more influenced by valence then were depressives. However, when $\Delta P = 0$, depressives showed higher judgements of control than do nondepressives when the outcomes were negative self-referent sentences. Also, outcome valence did not affect the judgements of either mood group when the sentences were other-referent.

Active versus passive

Almost all reported contingency studies concerned with depressive realism have used the discrete-trial, active task described earlier. In a book chapter, Alloy, Abramson, and Kossman (1985) briefly describe three studies that used the passive (Pavlovian) contingency task.[6] In the passive task, a cue is either presented or is not presented, and then the outcome either occurs or does not occur. At the end of a block of trials, the participant is asked to rate the strength of the relationship between the cue and the outcome (in contrast with the active task, in which judgements are about response–outcome relationships). In Experiment 1 in Alloy et al., the cue was a red light (presented or not presented), and the outcome was a green light (presented or not presented). At the end of a 40-trial sequence, the participant was asked "to judge the degree of contingency or predictability (on a 0 to 100 scale) that existed between red light onset and green light onset" (p. 236). There were two values of ΔP (.25 and .75). The pairs of conditional probabilities for the two ΔP values were .75 and .50, and .75 and 00. As in Experiment 1 of Alloy and Abramson (1979), ratings increased with ΔP and the two mood groups did not differ. Experiment 2 was modelled on Experiment 3 in Alloy and Abramson (see Table 2): $\Delta P = 0$, $P(O) = .5$, and the win–lose conditions were used to manipulate outcome valence. Alloy et al. concluded that "there were no differences between depressed and nondepressed subjects' judgements of predictability, and both groups judged relatively accurately that the red light provided little prediction of the green light" (p. 237). In Experiment 3, $\Delta P = 0$ and $P(O) = .75$. For half the participants, the task was active (as in Alloy & Abramson, 1979) and for half the participants the task was passive. Alloy et al. concluded that "whereas nondepressed subjects as a group were more likely than depressed subjects as a group to exhibit an illusion of personal control when the experimental outcome was noncontingent but frequent, nondepressives were no more likely than depressives to exhibit an illusion of prediction about this same outcome" (p. 240). Mood state does not appear to differentially affect predictive judgements.

In summary, in contrast with the findings of Alloy and Abramson (1979) with the active form of the contingency task, Alloy et al. (1985) reported no evidence of depressive realism with the passive form of the task. However, these Alloy et al. data were presented briefly in a chapter and have not subsequently been presented in a more comprehensive form in a journal article (L. B. Alloy, personal communication, April 18, 2005).

---

[6] The three studies reported in this chapter have not been published in a journal article. The description in the chapter is brief, and neither standard errors nor statistical analyses are reported.

Intertrial interval

Msetfi et al. (2005; Msetfi et al., 2007) evaluated the effect of the duration of the intertrial interval (ITI) on the illusion of control. Msetfi et al. (2005) noted that in the Alloy and Abramson (1979) experiments mean ITI duration was 14 s. On the basis of their review of contingency experiments that varied P(O) in active tasks, Msetfi et al. (2005) concluded that an illusion of control is usually seen when the ITI is long and is rarely seen when the ITI is short. Msetfi et al. (2005; Msetfi et al., 2007) reported the results of experiments in which ITI was varied (e.g., 3 s and 15 s). They concluded that when the ITI was short, P(O) did not affect ratings, and this was the case for both depressives and nondepressives—that is, neither mood group showed an illusion of control. At the long ITI, P(O) affected nondepressive ratings but not depressive ratings—that is, nondepressives displayed an illusion of control, and depressives displayed depressive realism. Thus, it appears that mood state interacts not only with P(O) but also with ITI. Nondepressives overestimate their control when the outcome is frequent, and the ITI is long, whereas these variables do not influence depressive judgements.

Summary

Depressive realism is a fragile phenomenon. Nonreplications have been reported. The necessary conditions are difficult to organize into a coherent whole. The complex interactions that have appeared (e.g., under some conditions nondepressives appear to be realistic, and depressives show an illusion of control) are disconcerting.

THEORETICAL ACCOUNTS OF DEPRESSIVE REALISM

The Alloy and Abramson (1979) findings attracted the attention of researchers because they were inconsistent with predictions of the prominent theories of depression that were popular at that time, such as learned helplessness (e.g., Seligman, 1975). To reiterate, according to learned helplessness theory, depressed people have generalized expectancies of independence between their responses and outcomes that should interfere with the detection of contingencies, and nondepressed people have generalized expectations of control that should interfere with the detection of noncontingencies. Alloy and Abramson concluded that their data were inconsistent with learned helplessness theory. It should be noted that their conclusion, though widely accepted by researchers interested in contingency judgements, did generate debate (Alloy & Abramson, 1981; Schwartz, 1981a, 1981b).

As an alternative to learned helplessness theory, Alloy and Abramson (1979) suggested that motivational factors may account for the difference between depressed and nondepressed students' judgements of control in their experiments. According to their motivational account, the mood effects reflect a difference in self-esteem between the two groups. Alloy and Abramson suggested that nondepressives have a higher level of self-esteem than do depressives and engage in behaviour to protect their self-esteem. In particular, nondepressives distort reality in an optimistic fashion. Nondepressives, because they are motivated to maintain or enhance their self-esteem, overestimate their degree of control over desirable outcomes and underestimate their degree of control over undesirable outcomes. Depressives, on the other hand, do not make such errors because they do not have a specific motivation to preserve self-esteem. In a later paper, Alloy and Abramson (1988) concluded:

...one point appears clear: Depressed individuals may be suffering from the absence or breakdown of normal optimistic biases and distortions. Maladaptive symptoms of depression, such as low self-esteem, social skills deficits...may be consequences, in part, of the absence of healthy personal illusions. (p. 257)

In recent years there has been renewed interest in theorizing about differences in contingency judgements of depressed and nondepressed individuals. This interest stems from research on the outcome-density effect. Recently, two novel theoretical accounts have been proposed for the outcome-density effect (Allan et al., 2005; Msetfi et al., 2007; Msetfi et al., 2005), and these accounts provide opportunities for a new look at depressive realism.

ITI hypothesis

We noted earlier that Msetfi et al. (2005; Msetfi et al., 2007) concluded that ITI duration influenced control judgements. Specifically, with a short ITI, P(O) did not affect ratings, and this was the case for both depressives and nondepressives—an outcome-density effect was not seen in either mood group. With a long ITI, P(O) affected nondepressive ratings but not depressive ratings—an outcome-density effect was seen in nondepressive ratings but not in depressive ratings (i.e., depressive realism was observed). To account for their results, Msetfi et al. (2005; Msetfi et al., 2007) suggested that the ITI could be conceptualized as equivalent to cell d of the 2 × 2 matrix depicted in Figure 1—that is, $\sim$R$\sim$O. Thus, the ITI hypothesis predicts an interaction between ITI duration and P(O)—the outcome-density effect should increase with ITI duration.

Msetfi et al. (2005) explained how their ITI integration hypothesis is compatible with both computational models (e.g., Cheng, 1997) and associative models (e.g., Dickinson, Shanks, & Evenden, 1984) of contingency judgements. Computational models specify that judgements are determined by ΔP—and in some versions, ΔP normalized by P(O$|\sim$R). Integration of ITI into cell d would effectively decrease P(O$|\sim$R) and thereby increase ΔP. Since inflation of cell d would be an increasing function of ITI duration, effective ΔP would also increase with ITI. Moreover, the higher the value of P(O), the higher the spurious value of ΔP. Within the framework of an associative model, ITI is conceptualized as the context. Integration of ITI into cell d would weaken the context's association with the outcome, thereby allowing the response to gain more associative strength.

To account for the absence of an ITI effect in their depressed participants, Msetfi et al. (2005; Msetfi et al., 2007) suggested that depressed mood is accompanied by reduced contextual processing—specifically depressives do not integrate the ITI into cell d. They concluded that depressive realism effects occur because depressed people do not use all the available evidence to arrive at their judgements rather than because they are being realistic.

Msetfi et al. (2005) did acknowledge that their ITI account of the outcome-density effect is incomplete. There are many studies that show an outcome-density effect in the passive task when the ITI is short (e.g., Allan & Jenkins, 1983, Exp. 3; Allan et al., 2005; Vallée-Tourangeau, Murphy, Drew, & Baker, 1998). Msetfi et al. concluded that the ITI hypothesis is, so far, restricted to the active contingent task.

Response criterion hypothesis

One phenomenon that triggered interest in depressive realism in the contingency judgement literature was the finding that depressed individuals seemed immune to the outcome-density effect—their judgements of the contingency between responding and outcome were not unrealistically inflated as the outcome density increased. Elsewhere (Allan et al., 2005) we have argued that it is useful to consider an individual's judgement of the magnitude of a contingent relationship as consisting of two components. It is as if the participant asks himself or herself two questions on each trial: (a) "What do I perceive the likelihood of the outcome to be on this trial?", and (b) "Given that likelihood, how should I respond?" These two components of the decision process, of course, correspond to the two variables of classic signal detection theory: perception (d') and response criterion (C), respectively (see Wickens, 2002). Variables that change decision-making behaviour (e.g., outcome density) may be due to their effect on either of these two variables.

As indicated earlier, depressive realism is a fragile phenomenon. There is ample evidence in the psychophysical literature that response criterion effects (in contrast with perceptual effects) are notoriously variable, across individuals and experiments (e.g., Allan, 1968, 2002). The fragility of depressive realism is consistent with its location in the decision process (rather than in the perception process).

In contingency judgement tasks, participants typically rate the relationship between a response (or a cue) and the outcome. These ratings are made after some number of trials (often at the end of a block of trials). Allan et al. (2005) showed that this rating response does not always provide information about the participant's perception of the contingency. Allan et al. used the passive contingency task: On each trial, the cue was either presented or not presented, and then the outcome either occurred or did not occur. In their experiment, Allan et al. varied both ΔP and $P(O)$. Their data showed a strong outcome-density effect in the ratings of the relationship between the cue and the outcome at the end of a block of trials, for both contingent and noncontingent matrices. In addition to ratings at the end of a block of trials, Allan et al. asked their participants to make a prediction response on each trial. Specifically, the cue was presented or was not presented, the participant predicted whether the outcome would or would not occur, and then the outcome either occurred or did not occur. They applied a psychophysical analysis to the trial prediction data that allowed them to examine sensitivity to the contingency independently of any biases in decision processes. They were able to show that as $P(O)$ increased, the participant's criterion for predicting the outcome also changed. The participant became more biased towards predicting that the outcome would occur. This criterion shift was present both on cue-present and on cue-absent trials indicating that the participant's sensitivity to the contingency remained unchanged across different values of $P(O)$. Allan et al. concluded that the ratings were a reflection of the response criterion and were not an accurate measure of the participant's sensitivity to the contingency.

On the basis of a response criterion interpretation of depressive realism, depressives and nondepressives differ not in their perception of contingency, but rather in their willingness to predict that the outcome will occur. There are data that show criterion differences between depressives and nondepressives in a variety of quite diverse tasks, such as short-term memory, gustatory sensitivity, flicker fusion, and judgement of line length (for summaries, see Miller & Lewis, 1977; Herskovic, Kietzman, & Sutton, 1986; Pizzagalli, Jahn, & O'Shea, 2005; Potts, Bennett, Kennedy, & Vaccarino, 1997, respectively). In essence, depressives seem to be "nay-sayers". A number of studies using a psychophysical framework (e.g., Herskovic et al., 1986; Miller & Lewis, 1977; Pizzagalli et al., 2005; Potts et al., 1997) have shown that depressives do not differ from normal controls with regard to sensitivity on these tasks. Rather depressives adopt a more conservative criterion for saying "yes" than do normal controls.

Such criterion differences between mood groups might lead one to expect mood differences in the probability of responding, $P(R)$, in the active contingency task. Matute (1996), for example, varied $P(R)$ through instructions. The task was to determine whether an aversive outcome could be terminated by pressing a button. The actual relationship between button pressing and the outcome was noncontingent. One group of participants (analytic) was instructed "to behave scientifically in order to find out how much control over the outcome was possible"; another group of participants (naturalistic) was instructed "to obtain the outcome" (p. 289). At the end of a block of trials, participants in both groups were asked to rate the degree of control they thought they had over termination of the aversive outcome on a scale that ranged from -100 to $+100$. Matute found a correlation between control ratings and $P(R)$. For the analytic group, $P(R)$ was close to .5, and ratings were around zero. For the naturalistic group, $P(R)$ was close to 1.0, and ratings were around 60. Matute discussed the implication of her results for studies that have found mood effects in contingency judgements. She suggested that nondepressives would be more likely to respond than depressives, and that the illusion of control sometimes observed in nondepressive ratings might reflect this response bias in responding (see also Skinner, 1985). Available data do not permit a strong test of Matute's hypothesis since most of studies concerned with depressive realism and contingency judgements have not reported P(R). However, the few studies that did report P(R) (e.g., Benassi & Mahler, 1985; Dobson & Pusch, 1995; Msefti et al., 2007) do not provide support for Matute's (1996) prediction in that there was not a difference in P(R) between the mood groups.

While Matute (1996) expected mood differences in the relationship between P(R) and ratings, the response criterion hypothesis expects mood differences in the relationship between prediction responses (whether explicitly required by the experimenter or implicitly made by the participant) and ratings. Unfortunately, since prediction responses have not been explicitly required in the active task, the response criterion analysis cannot be applied retrospectively to existing data. The active task could readily be modified to incorporate trial prediction responses. On each trial, after the participant did or did not respond, he or she would then predict whether the outcome would or would not occur. According to the response criterion hypothesis, the participant would be biased towards predicting that the outcome would occur as P(O) increased. If depressive realism is a criterion effect, then the bias should be greater for nondepressives than for depressives.

It is unclear in the writings of Alloy, Abramson, and their colleagues whether they placed the locus of the difference in the judgements of depressives and nondepressives in the perception of the contingency, or in the response criterion. On the one hand, they talk about an "illusion of control", and illusions are usually considered to be perceptual. On the other hand, they talk about "biases" and suggest that both depressed and nondepressed are susceptible to biases, but in opposite directions, "with nondepressives distorting environmental information optimistically and depressives distorting it pessimistically" (Alloy & Abramson, 1988, p. 255). Response biases refer to the criterion applied in deciding whether or not to answer "yes" or "no", given the perceptual information that currently is available. We suggest that understanding depressive realism requires some precision in distinguishing these two processes. When depressed people do not succumb to the outcome density effect it is not because they are particularly "realistic", but rather because they are particularly reluctant to say "yes". The nature of the outcome density manipulation in the contingency judgement task is such that this bias of depressives is experienced, by the experimenter, as an illusion of accuracy.

Summary

For the ITI hypothesis, mood differences are attributed to differential processing of the ITI— "...a context processing difference between depressed and nondepressed people removes any objective notion of 'realism' that was originally employed to explain the depressive realism effect" (Msefti et al., 2007). For the response criterion hypothesis, mood differences are attributed to differential propensities for predicting outcomes. Thus, the two accounts are conceptually similar—depressives and nondepressives do not differ in their ability to detect the degree of control that their responding has over outcomes.

CONCLUSIONS

Since it was first described in 1979, the phenomenon of depressive realism has been subjected to extensive empirical and theoretical scrutiny. There are reports of both successes and failures to replicate Alloy and Abramson's (1979) report. The literature does not readily fall into a coherent picture.

We have concluded that, in general, the outcome-density effect is better understood as a change in C than a change in d'. That is, increasing the outcome density does not affect the participant's perception of the relationship between behaviour (or cue) and outcome. Rather, for any particular contingency, increasing the probability of an outcome increases the tendency for the participant to say "yes, the outcome will occur" (and to respond in ways appropriate to the imminent arrival of the outcome).

It might be said that, when the outcome density is increased, the typical participant displays irrational optimism. When outcome density increases, they increase their bias towards predicting an outcome. Depressed individuals are not optimistic individuals. Compared to nondepressed individuals, depressives are "nay-sayers". They must be very confident that something will occur before they accede to responding in a manner that indicates that the event will, indeed, occur. It is clear that the poorer performance of depressed individuals than nondepressed individuals on tasks involving short-term memory, gustatory sensitivity, flicker fusion, and line length discrimination is located in their decision process, not their perception process. Similarly, we suggest that the differences in depressive and nondepressive responding to outcome density is a manifestation of the depressed individual's relative (compared to the nondepressed individual) pessimism. It is not much of a leap to suggest that manipulations of outcome valence, like outcome density, differentially affect the decision processes of nondepressed and depressed individuals. Since depressive realism resides in decision processes, rather than perception processes, we would expect the phenomenon to be fragile and subject to participants' perceived evaluation of the various consequences of making a correct and incorrect judgement of whether or not an outcome will occur. Minor procedural differences may substantially affect such judgements.

In summary, compared to nondepressed individuals, depressives are "nay-sayers". Depressives may be sadder but they are not wiser; rather, so-called "depressive realism" results from the bias of depressives to say "no".

REFERENCES

Abramson, L. Y., & Alloy, L. B. (1980). Judgment of contingency: Errors and their implications. In A. Baum & J. Singer (Eds.), *Advances in environmental psychology* (Vol. 2, pp. 111–130). Hillsdale, NJ: Lawrence Erlbaum Associates, Inc.

Abramson, L. Y., Alloy, L. B., & Rosoff, R. (1981). Depression and the generation of complex hypotheses in the judgment of contingency. *Behavioral Research and Therapy, 19*, 35–45.

Allan, L. G. (1968). Visual position discrimination: A model relating temporal and spatial factors. *Perception & Psychophysics, 4*, 267–278.

Allan, L. G. (1980). A note on measurement of contingency between two binary variables in judgment tasks. *Bulletin of the Psychonomic Society, 15*, 147–149.

Allan, L. G. (1993). Human contingency judgments: Rule-based or associative? *Psychological Bulletin, 114*, 435–448.

Allan, L. G. (2002). The location and interpretation of the bisection point. *Quarterly Journal of Experimental Psychology, 55B*, 43–60.

Allan, L. G., & Jenkins, H. M. (1983). The effects of representations of binary variables on judgment of influence. *Learning and Motivation, 14*, 381–405.

Allan, L. G., Siegel, S., & Tangen, J. M. (2005). A signal detection analysis of contingency data. *Learning & Behavior, 33*, 250–263.

Alloy, L. B., & Abramson, L. Y. (1979). Judgment of contingency in depressed and nondepressed students: Sadder but wiser? *Journal of Experimental Psychology: General, 108*, 41–485.

Alloy, L. B., & Abramson, L. Y. (1981). Depression, nondepression, and cognitive illusions: Reply to Schwartz. *Journal of Experimental Psychology: General, 110*, 436–447.

Alloy, L. B., & Abramson, L. Y. (1982). Learned helplessness, depression, and the illusion of control. *Journal of Personality and Social Psychology, 42*, 1114–1126.

Alloy, L. B., & Abramson, L. Y. (1988). Depressive realism: Four theoretical perspectives. In L. B. Alloy (Ed.), *Cognitive processes in depression* (pp. 223–265). New York: Guilford Press.

Alloy, L. B., Abramson, L. Y., & Kossman, D. (1985). The judgment of predictability in depressed and nondepressed college students. In J. B. Overmier & F. R. Brush (Eds.), *Affect, conditioning, cognition: Essays on the determinants of behavior* (pp. 230–246). Hillsdale, NJ: Lawrence Erlbaum Associates, Inc.

Alloy, L. B., Abramson, L. Y., & Viscusi, D. (1981). Induced mood and this illusion of control. *Journal of Personality and Social Psychology, 41*, 1129–1140.

Alloy, L. B., & Seligman, M. E. P. (1979). On the cognitive component of learned helplessness and depression. In G. H. Bower (Ed.), *The psychology of learning and motivation* (Vol. 13, pp. 219–276). New York: Academic Press.

Beck, A. T. (1967). *Depression: Clinical, experimental, and theoretical aspects* (2nd ed.). New York: Harper-Row.

Benassi, V. A., & Mahler, H. I. M. (1985). Contingency judgments by depressed college students: Sadder but not always wiser. *Journal of Personality and Social Psychology, 49,* 1323–1329.

Bryson, S. E., Doan, B. D., & Pasquali, P. (1984). Sadder but wiser: A failure to demonstrate that mood influences judgements of control. *Canadian Journal of Behavioural Science, 16,* 107–119.

Cheng, P. W. (1997). From covariation to causation: A causal power theory. *Psychological Review, 104,* 367–405.

Dickinson, A., Shanks, D., & Evenden, J. (1984). Judgement of act-outcome contingency: The role of selective attribution. *Quarterly Journal of Experimental Psychology, 36A,* 29–50.

Dobson, K., & Franche, R.-L. (1989). A conceptual and empirical review of the depressive realism hypothesis. *Canadian Journal of Behavioural Science, 21,* 419–433.

Dobson, K. S., & Pusch, D. (1995). A test of the depressive realism hypothesis in clinically depressed subjects. *Cognitive Therapy and Research, 19,* 179–194.

Herskovic, J. E., Kietzman, M., & Sutton, S. (1986). Visual flicker in depression: Response criteria, confidence ratings, and response times. *Psychological Medicine, 16,* 187–197.

Kapçi, E. G., & Cramer, D. (1999). Judgement of control revisited: Are the depressed realistic or pessimistic? *Counselling Psychology Quarterly, 12,* 95–105.

Lennox, S. S., Bedell, J. R., Abramson, L. Y., Raps, C., & Foley, F. W. (1990). Judgment of contingency: A replication with hospitalized depressed, schizophrenic and normal samples. *Journal of Social Behavior and Personality, 5,* 189–204.

Martin, D. J., Abramson, L. Y., & Alloy, L. B. (1984). Illusion of control for self and others in depressed and nondepressed college students. *Journal of Personality and Social Psychology, 46,* 125–136.

Matute, H. (1996). Illusion of control: Detecting response-outcome independence in analytic but not in naturalistic conditions. *Psychological Science, 7,* 289–293.

Miller, E., & Lewis, P. (1977). Recognition memory in elderly patients with depression and dementia: A signal detection analysis. *Journal of Abnormal Psychology, 86,* 84–86.

Msetfi, R. M., Murphy, R. A., & Simpson, J. (2007). Depressive realism and the effect of intertrial interval on judgements of zero, positive and negative contingencies. *The Quarterly Journal of Experimental Psychology, 60,* 461–481.

Msetfi, R. M., Murphy, R. A., Simpson, J., & Kornbrot, D. E. (2005). Depressive realism and outcome density bias in contingency judgements: The effect of the context and inter-trial interval. *Journal of Experimental Psychology: General, 134,* 10–22.

Myers, D. G., & Spencer, S. J. (2004). *Social psychology* (2nd ed.). Toronto, Canada: McGraw-Hill.

Nolen-Hoeksema, S. (2001). *Abnormal psychology* (2nd ed.). New York: McGraw-Hill.

Pizzagalli, D. A., Jahn, A. L., & O'Shea, J. P. (2005). Toward an objective characterization of an anhedonic phenotype: A signal-detection approach. *Biological Psychiatry, 57,* 319–327.

Potts, A. J., Bennett, P. J., Kennedy, S. H., & Vaccarino, F. J. (1997). Depressive symptoms and alterations in sucrose taste perception: Cognitive bias or a true change in sensitivity? *Canadian Journal of Psychology, 51,* 57–60.

Presson, P. K., & Benassi, V. A. (2003). Are depressive symptoms positively or negatively associated with the illusion of control? *Social Behavior & Personality, 31,* 483–495.

Schwartz, B. (1981a). Does helplessness cause depression, or do only depressed people become helpless? Comment on Alloy and Abramson. *Journal of Experimental Psychology: General, 110,* 429–435.

Schwartz, B. (1981b). Helplessness, illusions, and depression: Final comment. *Journal of Experimental Psychology: General, 110,* 448–449.

Seligman, M. E. P. (1975). *Helplessness: On depression, development, and death.* San Francisco: Freeman.

Skinner, E. A. (1985). Action, control judgments, and the structure of control experience. *Psychological Review, 92,* 39–58.

Vallée-Tourangeau, F., Murphy, R. A., Drew, S., & Baker, A. G. (1998). Judging the importance of constant and variable candidate causes: A test of the power PC theory. *Quarterly Journal of Experimental Psychology, 51A,* 65–84.

Vázquez, C. (1987). Judgment of contingency: Cognitive biases in depressed and nondepressed subjects. *Journal of Personality and Social Psychology, 52,* 419–431.

Wickens, T. D. (2002). *Elementary signal detection theory.* New York: Oxford University Press.

Zuckerman, M., & Lubin, B. (1965). *Manual for the Multiple Affect Adjective Check List.* San Diego, CA: Educational and Industrial Testing Service.

SUBJECT INDEX

For Product Safety Concerns and Information please contact our EU
representative GPSR@taylorandfrancis.com Taylor & Francis Verlag GmbH,
Kaufingerstraße 24, 80331 München, Germany

Batch number: 08151941

Printed by Printforce, the Netherlands